S0-BEZ-600

SAN FRANCISCO ACCESS®

Richard Saul Wurman

*Sponsored by **Pacific Bell Directory***
*publisher of the **SMART** Yellow Pages*

ACCESSPRESS Ltd., 59 Wooster St., NYC, NY 10012-4349

SAN FRANCISCO STREET MAP

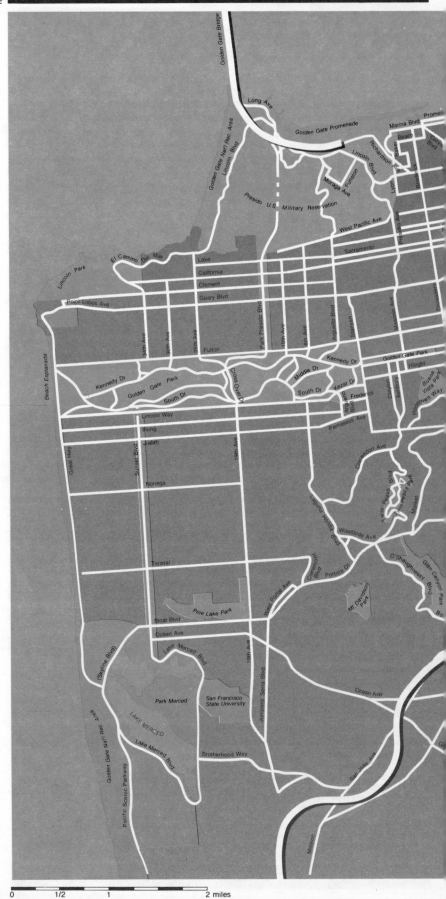

Golden Gate Bridge

Long Ave

Golden Gate Promenade

Marina Blvd   Promen

Beach

Embarc
Blvd

Golden Gate Nat'l Rec. Area

Lincoln Blvd

Richardson Ave

Lincoln Blvd

Baker

Lyon

Roderick

Moraga Ave   Funston

Presidio U.S. Military Reservation

West Pacific Ave

Presidio Blvd

Sacramento

El Camino Del Mar

Lake

California

Clement

Geary Blvd

Lincoln Park

Point Lobos Ave

Park Presidio Blvd

Arguello Blvd

Stanyan

Masonic Ave

14th Ave

20th Ave

25th Ave

Fulton

12th Ave

8th Ave

Haight

Beach Esplanade

Kennedy Dr

Golden Gate Park

South Dr

Cross Over Dr

Kennedy Dr

Golden Gate Park

Middle Dr

South Dr

Kezar Dr

Clayton

Ashbury

Buena
Vista Park

Roosevelt Way

Great Hwy

Sunset Blvd

Lincoln Way

Irving

Judah

19th Ave

Arguello
Blvd

Frederick

Parnassus Ave

Clarendon Ave

Noriega

Market

Twin Peaks Blvd

Twin Peaks Blvd

Laguna Honda Blvd

Woodside Ave

Taraval

Clarmont
Blvd

Portola Dr

O'Shaughnessy

Glen Canyon Park

Blvd

Bo

Pine Lake Park

West Portal Ave

Mt Davidson
Park

Sloat Blvd

Ocean Ave

Lake Merced Blvd

19th Ave

Junipero Serra Blvd

Ocean Ave

(Skyline Blvd)

Park Merced

San Francisco
State University

LAKE MERCED

Lake Merced Blvd

Golden Gate Nat'l Rec. Area

Pacific Scenic Parkway

Hwy 35

Brotherhood Way

San Jose Ave

Mission

| 0 | 1/2 | 1 | 2 miles |

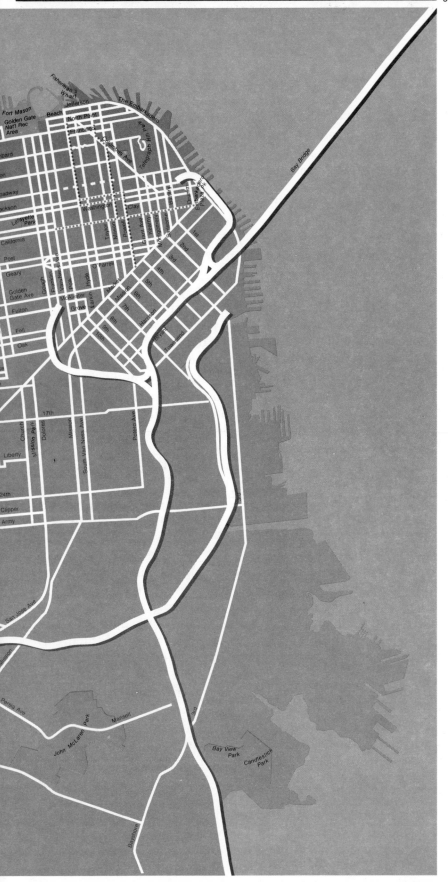

Fisherman's Wharf
Jefferson
Beach
The Embarcadero
North Point
Francisco
Fort Mason
Golden Gate Nat'l Rec Area
Columbus Ave
Bay Bridge
Telegraph Hill
Lombard
Green
Broadway
Jackson
Lafayette Park
Washington
Clay
Embarcadero Plaza SK
Embarcadero
Front
California
Battery
Sansome
Montgomery
Kearny
Grant Ave
Stockton
Powell
Mason
Taylor
Jones
Leavenworth
Hyde
Larkin
Polk
Van Ness Ave
Franklin
Gough
1st
2nd
3rd
4th
5th
6th
Post
Geary
O'Farrell
Market
Mission
Howard
Folsom
Harrison
Bryant
Brannan
Townsend
Golden Gate Ave
McAllister
Grove
Fulton
7th
8th
9th
10th
Fell
Oak
17th
Church
Dolores
Mission
South Van Ness Ave
Potrero Ave
Liberty
24th
Clipper
Army
San Jose Ave
Junipero
Peralta Ave
John McLaren Park
Mansell
3rd
Bay View Park
Candlestick Park
Bayshore

Since **Pacific Heights** emerged from the sand dunes of the past century, San Franciscans have *gone for broke* to live here—the most exclusive neighborhood of them all.

Along with the **Marina**, **Cow Hollow**, **Presidio** and **Jordan Park**, all bordering each other, the area holds more college graduates, professionals and families earning upper middle and higher incomes than any other city district. There are more mansions per city block as well. The fine collection of Victorian houses on **Union Street** has been transformed into a shopper's dream, with more than 300 shops, bars, boutiques and restaurants located behind the gingerbread trim. There are handsome examples of the work of architects **Bernard Maybeck, Willis Polk, Ernest Coxhead** and **William Knowles** on the streets feeding into **Broadway.** One of the oldest houses is at **2727 Pierce Street,** dating back to 1865. The city's most photographed group of small Victorians is along the south side of **Alta Plaza Park.** A drive out Broadway to the **Presidio Gate** will give you a capsule glimpse into the privileged lives of years past. Private ownership of such enormous buildings was destined to die out, and many of the more impressive mansions now house schools, consulates and religious orders, or have been converted into apartments and flats.

Pacific Heights wasn't always the posh purlieu that it is today. Little more than a century ago, it was called **Cow Hollow,** in reference to the 30 dairy farms that were established here in 1861. A tiny lagoon, **Laguna Pequena,** or Washerman's Lagoon, was used as a communal wash basin for the city's laundry. In the late 1800s, tanneries, slaughterhouses and sausage factories moved to the area because of the dairies and fresh water from the lake and springs. But pollution from open sewage, industry and the cows forced the city to banish livestock from the area forever and to fill in the putrid lagoon with sand from the dunes on Lombard Street.

It wasn't until the building of a cable car line through the district in 1878 that Pacific Heights started to become an enclave of San Francisco's *nouveau riche.* They moved into huge gray Victorians, monuments to the bonanza era, and attempted to outdo the wooden castles on Nob Hill with Gothic arches, Cornithian pillars, Norman turrets, Byzantine domes, mansard roofs and enough stained glass to outfit several cathedrals. Their houses lined **Van Ness Avenue**, which was five feet wider than Market Street and considered the Champs Elysees of San Francisco. But the magnificence on Van Ness was short lived. The earthquake reduced the exquisite homes to shambles and the fire department then dynamited the street for a firebreak. The area never fully recovered. Eastern Pacific Heights, like Russian and Nob Hills, was rebuilt with luxury apartment houses, though a substantial number of the original Victorians still remain.

After the fire, San Francisco wanted to show the world that it was the city that refused to die. It proceeded to stage one of the most spectacular fairs of all time—the **Panama-Pacific International Exhibition** of 1915. The excuse was the opening of the Panama Canal, and the exhibition was the springboard for a city-wide open house that drew more than 18 million visitors. On the bay north of Cow Hollow, 600 acres of marshland were filled in, a sea wall running parallel to the shore line was built and sand was pumped up from the ocean bottom to serve as fill. The dredging produced enough deep water to build the San Francisco Yacht Harbor, the present site of the **St. Francis Yacht Club,** and enough land to create the **Marina** district. One of the Exhibition's buildings, the monumental **Palace of Fine Arts,** still stands and was recently strengthened and restored. Designed by Bernard Maybeck in 1915, it is now home to the **Exploratorium,** a participatory science museum.

Today the Marina reflects the Mediterranean revival architecture popular in the 1920s, with mostly low, pastel, single family dwellings or large, well-maintained flats lining the curving streets. First-class shopping facilities can be found on nearby **Lombard** and **Chestnut Streets. Marina Green,** which borders the harbor, is often full of kite flyers, badminton players, sunbathers, joggers and yachtsmen. Nearby **Fort Mason,** originally planned by the Spanish as a gun battery in 1797 for the protection of La Yerba Buena anchorage, now holds art museums, the **Magic Theater**, the **Oceanic Society**, coffee houses, an excellent vegetarian restaurant (**Green's**), special exhibitions and dozens of classes and workshops which are free or close to it.

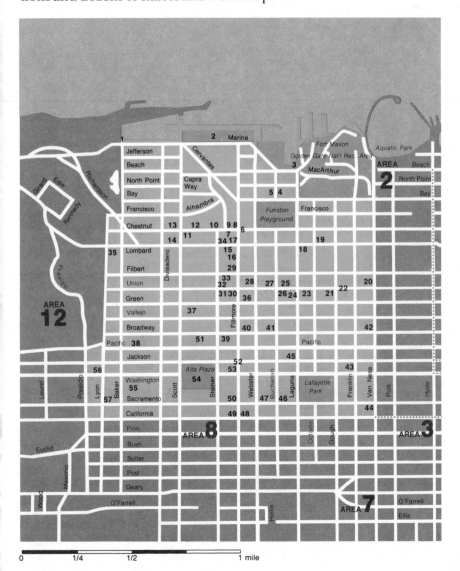

0   1/4   1/2   1 mile

1 **San Francisco Yacht Club.** A Spanish-style building overlooking the bay and Marine Yacht harbor. Badly damaged by a fire on Christmas day in 1976, it has been completely remodelled by **Marquis Associates.** *Private. Marina Blvd. at Baker St.*

2 **Marina Green.** Area residents jog, bike, skate and sun-worship along this green swathe of park that runs from Yacht Harbor to Fort Mason. A glorious place to drink in the magnificent scenic beauty surrounding the bay.

3 **Fort Mason.** (1850s) Dating from the mid-1800s, when it served as a command post for the army that tamed the West, parts of this proud reserve were added by WPA workers in the 1930s. Today the area is part of the **Golden Gate National Recreational Area** (GGNRA) and houses theaters, workshops, restaurants and art galleries. Of particular interest are the **Mexican Museum,** the **Museum of Modern Art Rental Gallery,** the **Museo Italo Americano,** the **S.S. Jeremiah O'Brien,** and the **World Print Gallery,** as well as many special trade shows and exhibitions. *Fort Mason at Marina Blvd. and Laguna. 441-5705*

Within Fort Mason are:

S.S. Jeremiah O'Brien. This is the last Liberty ship still afloat. One weekend each month, the ship's steam engine is in operation (check with Fort Mason's main office for dates). *Admission free. Open Tu-F 9AM-3PM. Pier 3, Fort Mason. Marina Blvd. and Laguna St. 441-5705*

San Francisco Museum of Modern Art Rental Gallery. An arm of the San Francisco Museum of Modern Art which focuses on showing works of lesser known, *emerging* Bay Area artists. It features frequently changing exhibitions and art work is offered for sale and/or rent. *Open Tu-Sa 11:30AM-5:30PM. Fort Mason, Building A. 441-4777*

World Print Council. Each year, this international, non-profit organization devoted to the graphic arts sponsors 10 exhibitions of printmakers from around the world. As a valuable resource for graphic artists and their supporters, it also offers conferences and lectures. Use of the slide library is available to members. *Open W-Su 12-5PM, Th 12-PM. Fort Mason, Building D. 441-0404*

Young Performer's Theater. The theater produces childrens' classics, adaptations and new works with children working alongside professional adult actors. The theater school offers classes year round for children pre-school age and up. Parties are held after Saturday and Sunday shows. Perfect for birthday celebrations. *For Mason, Building C, Third Floor. 346-5550*

The variable **weather** of San Francisco is often more noticeable in Pacific Heights, with the fog funneling through the Golden Gate and flowing around the shore line and hills. At any time of year, you can climb up a gray hillside to the sound of fog horns—reminiscent of Dashiell Hammett — and stare down onto a sun drenched view of the other side.

The Magic Theater. Small (99 seats), young (founded in 1967) and underfunded, the Magic is nonetheless on the cutting edge of American theater. Part of its reputation and success comes from a long association with Pulitzer Prize winning playwright **Sam Shepard,** who has premiered his latest work here for the last decade. But the Magic's success isn't solely dependent on Shepard. The theater also presents a fine season of innovative dramatic works by both new and established playwrights. For true theater lovers, the Magic will be, well, magical. Subscriptions available. Fort Mason, Building D. Ticket information: 441-8822

Greens. ★ ★ ★ ★ $$/$$$ San Francisco's premier vegetarian restaurant—and perhaps the nation's—run by the dedicated disciples of Zen Buddhism. It's so jammed for dinner that you have to reserve two months in advance. The opening of Greens in 1979 made vegetarianism stylish, and it's easy to see why. You won't find any ordinary vegetables-stirred-in-a-wok here; only outstanding culinary creations so tasty and so interesting that you'll forget you're not eating meat. The soups, homemade breads and salads can't be matched. The black bean chile, herb-flavored potatoes baked in parchment and Green Gulch salad with lettuces, Sonoma goat cheese, pecans and oranges are pure heaven. As an added bonus, you'll have a beautiful view of the Bay and the Golden Gate Bridge and can use bathrooms which belong in an architectural guidebook. *American. Open Tu-Sa 11:30AM-2:15PM, 6-9PM, Su brunch 10AM-2PM. Building A, Fort Mason. 771-6222*

4 **San Francisco Gas Light Company Building.** (1880s) This fine brick building that originally held storage tanks for the San Francisco Gas Light Company has now been converted into offices. Notice the corner turret and consistent brick and stone detailing throughout. *3600 Buchanan at North Point.*

5 **Mulherns.** ★ $$ This saloon and eating place serves generous drinks and such specialties as omelettes, exceptional fish dishes, calamari or chicken salad and fantastic desserts. The atmosphere is low key and comfortable. Across the street from the PG&E building and an easy walk from Fort Mason. *Reservations suggested. Open M-F 11:30AM-3PM, 5:30-11PM; Sa 11:30AM-1PM, 5:30-11PM; Su 10AM-4PM, 5-10PM; bar open until 2AM M-Sa. 346-5549*

6 Chestnut Street. A neighborhood shopping district for Marina residents, the street is characterized by ordinary groceries, drugstores, beauty shops, small restaurants and bars and now a few trendy shops and cafes as well.

7 House of Magic. An old-fashioned magic and joke store. Spot the rubber chicken hanging in the window. *Open Tu-Sa 10AM-5PM. 2025 Chestnut St. 929-1670*

8 La Pergola. ★ $$ Northern Italian specialties here include *vitello all'agro di limone* (veal with lemon), *fettuccine Alfredo* and *veal Picante*. This cozy, small restaurant's trellised ceiling gives you a vineyard feeling, and the ample wine list furthers the mood. *Reservations suggested. Open M-Sa 5-10:30PM. 2060 Chestnut St. 563-4500*

9 Kichihei. $$ Try this refreshing change from the usual precious atmosphere of Marina restaurants. The iron pot stews are excellent, but some of the other dishes less so. *Japanese. Open daily for dinner. Closed W. 2084 Chestnut St. 929-1670*

10 Lucca Delicatessen. One of the city's many fabulous Italian delis, it sells cheese, cold cuts, fresh pasta and salads and imported canned goods. *Open M-F 9AM-6:30PM, Sa 8AM-6:30PM, Su 8AM-6PM. 2120 Chestnut St. 921-7873*

11 The Caravansary. A gourmet deli, store and restaurant under one roof. *Open M-Th & Sa 10AM-6PM, F 10AM-7PM, Su 10AM-5PM. 2263 Chestnut St. Restaurant and store 921-3466; deli 921-0534*

12 E'Angelo. ★ ★ $$ Really fine pasta in a bustling Marina setting. It's informal, family-run and very good. But stick to the excellent pastas and avoid the meat dishes. *Italian. Open Tu-Su 5-11PM. 2234 Chestnut St. 567-6164*

13 Bechelli's Coffee Shop. Try their pies, to eat in or take out. *Open M-F 7AM-4PM for breakfast and lunch, Sa & Su brunch 9AM-3PM. 2346 Chestnut St. 346-1801*

14 Scott's Seafood Grill. ★ $$/$$$ People are almost always jammed out the door of this restaurant, which has one of the most interesting bar scenes in the Bay Area. The seafood, however, is very much a mixed bag. Ask what's fresh and have it prepared simply, without any sauces. *American. Open daily. 2400 Lombard St. 563-8988*

15 Le Montmartre. Dance club with top 40, old rock and Brazilian music. *Open Tu-Sa 9PM-2AM. 2125 Lombard St. 563-4618*

16 Soiree. Although the dance floor is not large, this cozy bar is a happy choice for visiting with friends or dancing up a storm. There is a DJ for jazz and Top 40. The ambience is warm and elegant, with decor in tones of peach and much use of natural woods. *Open daily 2PM-2AM. 3231 Fillmore St. 567-4004*

17 Rolands. Bay Area jazz club with salsa on Sundays. Dancing. *Open daily 9PM-1:30AM. 3309 Fillmore St. 921-7774*

18 Ronayne's. ★ $$ A nice alternative to the very crowded **Scott's** just down the street. Like Scott's, there's a large bar and a long fish menu, but here the wait is much shorter and the fish often better. Try their excellent New England clam chowder and tender, greaseless fried calamari in a basket. *American. Open daily 5:30-10:30PM. 1799 Lombard St. 922-5060*

18 Rodin. ★ ★ ★ $$/$$$ This new addition to the Marina achieves the perfect marriage of classic and *nouvelle* cuisine. The theme is underlined in the softly lit dining room, with beige walls lined with dramatic photos of Rodin sculptures. All of the dishes are exquisite, visually and gastronomically. Start with the calamari entwined salmon or the fillet of white Alaskan salmon in dill sauce with sweet scallop mousse, and don't leave without trying the incomparable Grand Marnier souffle dessert. It's well worth the price. *Open M-Sa 6-11PM. 1779 Lombard St. 563-9566*

19 Marina Inn. *Moderate.* An attractive 40-room inn in the Early American theme, ideally located for family sight-seeing, with Fort Mason, Fisherman's Wharf, the Exploratorium and Union Street all nearby. Continental breakfast included. *3110 Octavia St. 928-1000*

20 Off Union Saloon. Club with acoustic, light rock, blues, pop and country music. *W-Sa 9-11PM, Su 7PM-1AM. 2513 Van Ness Av. 928-1661*

21 Octagon House. (1861) Home of the **National Society of Colonial Dames,** this beautifully preserved house is now a museum. Built on the strength of the once popular belief that eight-sided houses were lucky, it has been moved across the street from its original location and the lower floor plan has been changed, but the upper floor displays the original layout with square bedrooms on the major axes and bathrooms and service areas in the remaining triangular spaces. *Admission charge. Open first Su of each month and 2nd and 4th Th, 12-3PM. Closed Jan. 2645 Gough St. at Union. 441-7512*

Restaurants/Nightlife red
Hotels blue
Shops/Galleries purple
Parks/Outdoor spaces green
Museums/Architecture/Narrative black

I love San Francisco because for me it is full of memories. San Francisco itself is art, above all literary art, and I recall to mind, with profound respect, the great writers that were born here or came to write here: Jack London, Mark Twain, Ambroise Bierce and George Sterling. Every block is a short story, every hill a novel. Every home is a poem, every dweller within immortal. That is the whole truth. **William Saroyan,** American writer (1908-1981)

Van Ness

The Coffee Merchant
travel You and Leisure
jewelry The Precious Past
The Great Frame Up

The Chair Store
Pacific Heights Motel

Franklin

doctor Access Health Care
Gold Treasury Jewelry Designs
clothing Says Who?
Thomas Brass Beds
Italian/French bakery Corsagna
Union Street Graphics
children's shop The Effalump

Mud Pie *children's clothing*

Gough

Union Dooz Salon
old silver, militaria William B. Meyer
House of Music Service
cosmetics L'Herbier
Convergence Gallery
gemologists St. Eligius
silver Argentum
Aurum Gallery
European linens O'Plume
plants Art In Plants
manicures Best Nails
Kundus Gallery
ethnic art gallery Images of the North
Oriental art A Touch of Asia
women's clothing Basics

UNION STREET

La Paz Ristorante
Dilelio Antique Jewelry
Opulence *jewelry*
Futons
Made in USA *American handcrafts*
The Greenhouse *plants*
Glenda Queen Goldsmith
Enchanted Crystal
Union Street Furniture
Sugars *restaurant*
Margaritaville *restaurant*
Ricciani *women's clothing*

Octavia

Fox Photo
Art Deco Store
Chinese shop Sanuku
women's clothing Kolonaki
Union Street Optical
cafe What's Cooking?
Quintessence Jewelry
restaurant Mai's Vietnamese
men's clothing Moda In
Italian paper goods Oggetti
restaurant The Courtyard
imports Far Corners
Z Clothing
Flying Colors Sweat Co.
Sauers Antiques
fine Asian art Fumiki's
photocopy Copy Mat

Futur Ancien *Japanese designs*
David Clay *jewelry*
L'Escargot *restaurant*
Hilda of Iceland *clothing*
Laura Ashley *clothing*
Corinth Gallery
UFO Gift Card Shop
JBM Gallery
Thomas Watson Antiques
Pietro's *restaurant*
Your Nails *manicures*
Z Gallerie
Jason Adam Antiques
Pasand *restaurant/jazz club*
Harbor View Restaurant
The Mole Hole *home decorating*
Captain's Scribe *stationery*

Laguna

Wells Fargo Bank
Bepples Pie Shop
bar/restaurant Perry's
women's clothing Via Nova
antiques Art Deco Paris 1925
clothing Bebe
hairdresser Chez Peter
silks & quilts Fabulous Things Ltd.
Deli
women's clothing Janice Lee

UNION STREET

The Bus Stop *bar*
Seven Seas Ltd. *folk art, jewelry, etc.*
La Petite Boulangerie *bakery*
Joji Restaurant
Anne *women's clothing*
Beaux & Belles Bridal
Cole Wheatman Interior Designs
Dreamy Angels *women's boutique*
Staloni's Italian Gelato
Pat Ronik Designs *clothing*
Body Options *dancewear, swimsuits*
Union Gent Haircutters
Benetton *clothing*
Blue Light Cafe
Earthly Goods *jewelry*
Bank of America

Buchanan

Italian restaurant Prego
restaurant Coffe Cantata
men's Italian clothing Milano Vice
restaurant supplier Kaspian Sea Gourmet

Centurion For Her *clothing*
Shaw Shoes
Spartacus Hofbrau *restaurant*
Remi Nightclub

restaurant **Entrecote**
Lilliput Shoe and Leather
food service consultant **Cini Little**
bathroom accessories **Bubbles**
Clark and Wade Framing
hair design **Wing Hair**
Solar Light Books
Haagen-Dazs Ice Cream
Mrs. Fields Cookies
perfume **The Body Shop**
shoes **Kenneth Cole**
Musicland

Farnoosh women's clothing
Jalapenos restaurant
Ocularium eye glasses
Jest Jewels
Metro Theater
Hibernia Bank

Webster

boutique **N.Y. West**
boutique **Mayfair**
Metro Shoes
men's clothing **Orpheus**
Zaki Tailor
restaurant **La Cucina**
Hansa Gifts and Jewelry
Van Galen Upholstery
Chandler's Stationery
Ted Singer Flowers
Japanese clothing **Ehrke**
Union Street Papery
Thriftway Market
La Nouvelle Patisserie
7 Eleven
Michaelis Liquors

UNION STREET

Enzo Valente shoe store
Fashion Source clothing
Black Sheep Needleworks
Isi Flowers
Lorenzini men's clothing
Michael Morgan Gallery
Philippe Salvet boutique
Union Street Cafe
Old/New Estates Jewelry
Three Bags Full women's sweaters
Carnevale men's & women's clothing

Fillmore

Merrill's Drug Center
copies **Carbon Alternative**
photo gallery **Thackrey & Robertson**
flowers **Bed of Roses**
Hollywood Video
Soft Lenses To Go
hairdresser **Chelsea China**
Bridal Galleria
Italian bakery **Il Fornaio**

Leather Mode boutique
Images hairdresser
Gilbert's Men's Clothing
Doidge's Kitchen restaurant
Le Petit Chalet restaurant
Union Street Inn hotel
Masquerade vintage clothing
Victoria's Secret women's lingerie
Red Coach Dry Cleaning
Robert Henri Travel
Kelly 1 Hairstyling
Marina Submarine sandwich shop

Steiner

22 **Union Street.** In the 19th century, this district was known as *Cow Hollow* because it was used as grazing and pasture land for the city's dairy cows. Since the 1950s, the six-block stretch of the street from Gough to Steiner has undergone a dramatic metamorphosis, from sleepy neighborhood to chic shopping and swinging nightlife mecca. Its streets are lined with cleverly remodeled Victorian houses transformed from stables and mews into boutiques, art galleries and cafes. A treasure of a street frequented by local residents and visitors, it is crowded on Saturdays and parking can be difficult. (There is a parking garage at Buchanan and Union and buses run frequently.) Shops offer their elegant goods in an informal, bustling environment. Several men's stores sell imported Italian clothing: **Settepiu, Orpheus** and **Lorenzini.** Imported clothing for men and women can be found at **Benetton** and **Filian's.** Fine women's boutiques include **Options, Farnoosh Fashions, Three Bags Full** (sweaters), **Laura Ashley, Victoria's Secret, Environment** and **Liz's.** The delis, bakeries and gourmet

shops are enticing: **Court of Two Sisters** (fancy pastries), **Il Fornaio** (Italian bakery, fresh pizza, focaccia, panettone, pasta), **Crane and Kelley** (wines and cheeses), **Sonoma Vineyards** (wine tasting) and **Haagen-Dazs** (pristine ice cream). **Quintessence Gemstones and Jewelry,** known as *San Francisco's gem store,* has a large selection of exotic gems. **Oggetti Fine Florentine Papers** imports paper from Florence, hand-decorated the way it was done in the 17th century. **Heffalump** carries unusual and creative children's books and toys. The **Aurum Gallery** has handmade jewelry made by 50 local artists. The two identical houses at **1980 Union Street,** separated by a common wall, were built by a father for his two newlywed daughters.

23 **Pasand.** Live jazz music daily from 8:30PM-1AM and afternoon jazz F-Su from 4:30-8:30PM. *1875 Union St. 927-4498*

24 **Bed and Breakfast Inn.** *Moderate to Expensive.* Located on a quiet mews in the Union Street area, this was the forerunner of the bed-and-breakfast epidemic in the city. Its aim to be a *country inn in town* has been heartily accomplished, evidenced by the need to reserve rooms well in advance. This inn is romantic in atmosphere and has excellent service. There is even a library and garden for guests. *4 Charlton Ct. 921-9784*

25 Perry's. ★ $$ It's boy meets girl at this popular Union Street watering hole, with a bar that is always jammed. But, surprise, the restaurant in back—once your name is called from the long waiting list—is very good. The typically American menu has everything from fried chicken to hamburgers. *American. Open daily 9AM-midnight, bar until 2AM. 1944 Union St. 922-9022*

26 Blue Light Cafe. ★ $$ Boz Skaggs' cafe features Tex-Mex cuisine—ribs, chicken and *fajitas*. The modern interior is crowded with customers, and the drinks are still better than the food. *Open daily 11:30AM-1:30AM. 1979 Union St. 922-5510*

27 Prego. ★ $$ Trendy but informal Italian restaurants are the rage in San Francisco, and Prego's is one of the pace-setters. It's beautifully decorated and you'll enjoy looking at the wood-burning pizza oven, but stay away from the pizza and order the delicious pastas and salads. Lots of light *nouvelle*-style Italian dishes. *Italian. Open daily 11:30AM-midnight. 2000 Union St. 563-3305*

28 Yoshida-Ya. ★ $$ *Yakitori* is a whole different form of Japanese food, featuring all sorts of combinations of fish, meat and vegetables put on skewers and charcoal-grilled at your table. Here you can get things like mushrooms stuffed with ground chicken and asparagus wrapped in sliced pork. A relaxed, pleasant, beautifully decorated restaurant. *Japanese. Open daily 5:30-10:30PM. 2909 Webster St. 346-3431*

29 Balboa Cafe. ★ $$ What used to be a hamburger place in the back room of a bar has been turned into an inspired yet inexpensive adventure in American cooking. Only the freshest ingredients are used and the food has a light French touch. It's usually jammed. *Open daily 11AM-11PM, bar until 2Am. 3199 Fillmore St. 921-3944*

30 Doidge's. ★ ★ $$ One of the best brunches in San Francisco, particulary in summer, when you can get fresh fruit on your French toast. The omelettes, Eggs Benedict and other egg dishes are also perfectly cooked. Be sure to call ahead for weekend reservations. *American. Open daily 8AM-3PM. 2217 Union St. 921-2149*

31 Union Street Inn. *Expensive.* The elegance of a 19th centry Edwardian home combined with the personal welcome and attention found only in the finest European pension. This five-room inn has a small but exquisite garden where breakfast, tea and coffee are served, plus a parlor well stocked with books and magazines for researching your local adventures. The carriage house on the far side of the garden has been converted into a special suite with a Jacuzzi bath. Other rooms have private vanities but share baths. *2229 Union St. 346-0424*

Restaurants/Nightlife red
Hotels blue

32 Il Fornaio. ★ $ An Italian bakery that you have to see to believe. It's beautifully decorated and jammed with breads, pizzas and pastries that will make you want to order one of everything. Not all the food tastes as good as it looks, but the croissants, pizzas and some of the breads are superb. *Italian. Open Tu-Sa 8AM-7PM, Su 8AM-5PM. 2298 Union St. 563-3400*

33 Gelato Classico. ★ ★ $ Incredibly rich Italian ice cream that many San Franciscans swear is the best in the city. In fact it's so rich that you get only one scoop, but it's hard to eat more. Try their knockout espresso flavor. *Open M-Th & Su 12-11PM, F & Sa until midnight. 2211 Filbert St. 929-8666*

34 Village Pizzeria. $ Pizza by the slice. *Open M-Th, Sa & Su 11AM-11PM, F 11AM-12AM. 3348 Steiner. 931-2470*

35 Liverpool Lil's. ★ $ The pub-like atmosphere and good, reasonably priced food bring the locals back again and again. Liverpool Lil's is relaxing and cozy, serving a hearty specialty for the hungry ones—*Manchester Wellington,* ground-round wrapped in ham and a flaky crust. This is a great place for a late after the movies or theater supper, as it serves until midnight (hard to find in San Francisco). *Open M-F 11:30AM-1AM, Sa & Su 10AM-1AM. 2942 Lyon St. 921-6664*

36 Sherman House. *Deluxe.* Built in 1876 by **Leander Sherman,** founder and owner of Sherman Clay Music Company. Chiefly Italianate in style, although heavily influenced by the Second Empire style of French architecture, Sherman House is considered one of the most handsome and well preserved examples of its style and period. The house was awarded historical landmark status in 1972. Owner **Manouchehr Mobedshani,** with the aid of designer **Billy Gaylord,** restored the building with lavish care and reopened it in 1984 as a luxury hotel. Each of the 15 rooms and suites is unique, individually furnished in French Second Empire, Biedermeier or English Jacobean motifs. The carriage house, tucked away in lush formal gardens and cobblestone walkways, contains three bright and airy suites, one of which opens onto its own private garden with gazebo. Another suite has its own roofdeck. All rooms have wood-burning fireplaces and views of the Golden Gate Bridge and Bay, modern amenities such as wet bars, wall safes, TV and stereo systems and phone, mini-TV and whirlpool bath in the black granite bathrooms. The large west wing consists of a three-story music and reception room with a grand piano and a ceiling enlivened by an ornate leaded glass skylight. This room has hosted such greats as Caruso, Tetrazzini, Victor Herbert and Lillian Russell. Now, only a family of finches serenades you from their small chateau—a large cage created especially for them, inspired by Chateau Chenonceaus in the Loire. A double staircase from the music room leads up to a comfortable parlor where cocktails are served in the evening. Downstairs, Swiss chef **Paul Grutter** does his utmost to create special menus for guests in classic French and *nouvelle* styles. The caring service and attention to minute detail make Sherman House popular with celebrities like Shirley MacLaine, Ted Kennedy and Bill Cosby. Services offered include secretarial, translation of documents, tailoring, shoe repair, personalized shopping and arranging special tours and events. There is 24 hour room service, valet parking and chauffered travel in vintage automobiles. *2160 Green St. 563-3600*

37 **Casebolt House.** (1865-66) Noteworthy Italianate-style house; one of the oldest in Pacific Heights. *Private residence. 2727 Pierce St. between Green and Vallejo.*

38 **El Drisco Hotel.** *Moderate.* A San Francisco landmark, the hotel has hosted many a celebrity, including the then General Eisenhower, because of its discreet ambience and unique location (the only hotel for decades in Pacific Heights). Not elegant, but comfortable, with spectacular views. *2901 Pacific Av. 346-2880*

Within the hotel is:

El Drisco Restaurant. ★★ $$ Diners are promised a romantic evening with lavish flower arrangements and candles in candelabras and chandeliers. A harpist plays soothing background music. Chef **Robert Karns** plans a new menu each night; it's somewhat limited but is designed to please a variety of palates. The service is superb and the wine list features an above average choice of French and California vintages. *Open daily for breakfast 7:30-11AM, Su brunch 9:30AM-1:30PM; dinner W-M 6:30-9PM. 346-2880*

39 **Apartment Towers.** (1920s) This part of Pacific Heights has many splendid towers in many different styles. Most have elaborate marble-faced entrance lobbies complete with doormen. The penthouses create interesting silhouettes along the skyline. *Broadway at Steiner and Fillmore. Also Washington and Steiner.*

40 **Flood Mansion.** (1916) Convent of the Sacred Heart. The former Flood mansion, a Spanish Renaissance-style building by **Bliss and Faville.** *Private residence. 2222 Broadway.*

41 **Apartment Building, 2000 Broadway.** (1973, Backen, Arrigoni and Ross) A modern version of the great apartment towers that were built along Broadway during the 1920s. *Private residence. 2000 Broadway at Buchanan.*

42 **Golden Turtle.** ★★★ $$ The well-established *haute* Vietnamese Golden Turtle just off Clement Street has opened a lovely and more commodious restaurant on Van Ness Avenue. The dining room walls are lined with exotic carved wood murals, and every dish prepared by owner/chef **Kim Quy Tran** exudes freshness. The seafood smells fresh from the sea and the sauces are light but intense. All dishes are garnished with Chinese parsley, mint, basil, cucumbers, raw carrots right from their garden. Don't miss the Imperial rolls, lemon grass beef or fresh crab in ginger and garlic sauce. *Open Tu-Su 11:30AM-3PM, 5-11PM. 2211 Van Ness Av. 441-4419*

43 **Haas-Lilenthal House.** (1886) One of the most grandiose *stick-style* houses in the city, it is a great Romantic pile of forms with elaborate wooden gables and a splendid Queen Anne-style circular corner tower. Inside, it has a series of finely preserved Victorian rooms complete with authentic period furniture. *Open to the public W & Su 12:30-4:30PM. 2007 Franklin St. between Jackson and Washington. 441-3004*

44 **Hard Rock Cafe.** ★ $/$$ This lively, trendy spot serves classic American fare—ribs, burgers and fries and a selection of rich, old-fashioned desserts—at reasonable prices. The real attraction is to see and be seen by the boisterous young crowd. The decor features cars smashing through walls and a 50s diner motif. Waitresses dressed like carhops scurry around, while ear-splitting rock blasts out at the diners. This is a cousin of the Hard Rocks in London, Los Angeles, Chicago, Dallas and New York. The public can now buy a piece of the Rock—on the New York Stock Exchange. *Open M-Th 11:30AM-11:30PM, F & Sa 11:30AM-midnight, Su 12-11:30PM. 1699 Van Ness Av. 885-1699*

45 **California Historical Society (Whittier Mansion).** (1895-96) This red-brown sandstone mansion was built for **William Whittier,** a prosperous paint manufacturer. In addition to its period furnishings, the house contains a noteworthy collection of fine 19th century California art. The **California Historical Society's** library is located at the corner of Laguna and Pacific, it contains nearly 25,000 volumes on California history, and rare books, photographs and periodicals. *Tours available. Admission charge. Open W, Sa, Su 1:30-3PM. 2090 Jackson St. 567-1848. Libary open to the public W-Sa 1-5PM. 567-1848.)*

Shops/Galleries purple
Parks/Outdoor spaces green
Museums/Architecture/Narrative black

46 **Mansion Hotel.** *Moderate to Expensive.* Built by Utah Senator **Richard C. Chambers** in 1887, the twin-towered Queen Anne is a museum of eccentric Victorian memorabilia that includes tapestries, art, clothing, toys and curios. Each guestroom honors a celebrated San Franciscan. The garden displays the largest collection of **Benjamino Bufano** statues in the world. Rates include breakfast, Magic Concerts, sauna. Elegant dining room overlooks gardens. *Garage spaces available. 2220 Sacramento St. 929-9444*

47 **Hermitage House.** *Moderate.* A gracious 17 room Greek Revival home built for **Charles Slack** by architect **William Blaisdell.** It has 17 fireplaces and hand-carved redwood throughout. The present owner converted it into an inn in 1978. The larger rooms have fireplaces and most have private baths. Breakfast served. *2224 Sacramento St. 921-5515*

48 **De Paula Restaurant.** ★ $$ Authentic Brazilian cuisine served in a green, candlelit room and amidst a jungle of plants and gorgeous native feather costumes adorning the walls. The restaurant features such exotic dishes as scallops in coconut wine sauce, prawns with coconut milk, tomatoes, red palm oil and herbs and the traditional black bean and pork stew. Sensual Brazilian music accompanies this visually beautiful feast. *Open M-Th 11:30AM-2:30PM, 5-11PM; F 11:30-2:30PM, 5PM-12AM; Sa 5PM-12AM. 2114 Fillmore St. 346-9888*

49 **Vivande.** ★ ★ $$/$$$ Italian chef **Carlo Middione's** trendy and popular delicatessen and restaurant has rescued a neighborhood that a few years back had no decent place to eat. Marvelous pastas and desserts if you choose the restaurant; the best selection of Italian cheeses in the city to go in the deli. You'll enjoy just browsing around this Sicilian equivalent of the increasingly popular French charcuterie. *Open M-F 11AM-7PM, Sa 11AM-6PM, Su 11AM-5PM. 2125 Fillmore St. 346-4430*

50 **The Hillcrest.** ★ $$ American cuisine at its best—the unpretenious menu has regional accents and offers a great variety of dishes with a fresh approach. Don't miss the homemade soup (Louisiana corn chowder, Italian artichoke, and five onion), hearty hamburgers, hot sausage and corned beef and mesquite grilled fish with a dazzling choice of sauces. The restaurant is part of the developing Fillmore scene, which is giving lively competition to the older Union Street. The beige dining room is relaxing, with interesting watercolors and soft lighting. A cozy bar in the corner gives the feeling of being in a private home and offers an extensive selection of California wines. The dessert menu has tortes, tarts, cakes and pies with choices changing daily. Appetizers and desserts are served until 2AM for after-theater patrons. *Open M-F 11:30AM-2:30PM, 5PM-1AM, Sa & Su 10:30AM-11PM. 2201 Fillmore St. 563-8400*

51 **Pacific Heights Victorians.** Some of the finest Victorian mansions grace the tree-lined streets that run along the crest of the hill, offering spectacular views north across the Bay and Golden Gate Bridge. **Broadway 1700 to 2900 Blocks**—houses in Italianate, Stick Georgian, Queen Anne and Dutch Colonial styles. **Vallejo Street 1600 to 2900 Blocks**—Queen Anne houses. Mansions on **Divisadero** and **Jackson Streets** and **Clay Street** at **Steiner.**

52 **Fillmore Street.** Rarely has such a butterfly emerged from such an unpromising cocoon. Until recently. Fillmore was synonomous with deteriorating real estate, danger after dark, and definitely a never-never for anyone touring for fun (with the possible exception of a visit to a jazz club here and there). Today, Fillmore is a spruced-up, slightly shorter version of Union Street, with unusual boutiques, trendy restaurants and a rapidly expanding nightlife. Also, there are some of the best thrift shops in the city, all benefitting education and cultural causes, and they have some real finds. The street is fun and walkable.

Highlights include:

Heartland. Beautiful handcrafts made in the USA. A great selection of quilts, handmade baskets and pottery—handcarved and hand-painted *objects d'art. Open M-F 11AM-6:30PM, Sa 11AM-5PM, Su 12-5PM. 1801A Fillmore St. 931-7622*

Maruya. $ Take out sushi. *Open M-Sa 10:30AM-6PM. 1904 Fillmore St. 921-2929*

Rory's. $ Homemade ice cream in a turquoise and pink neon parlor. Specializes in *twist-ins*—swirls of nuts, chocolate and other treats spun into the ice cream—and delicious homemade waffle cones. *Open Su-Th 11:30AM-11PM, F-Sa 11:30AM-midnight. 2015 Fillmore St. 346-3692*

Mi Burrito. $ Small, pleasant cafe with reasonably priced Mexican fare. *Open daily 11AM-9PM. 1946 Fillmore. 563-3509*

Chestnut Cafe. $ Country feel with dark wood walls and tables. Homestyle sandwiches, soups and salads with an organic touch, as well as great energy drinks. *Open M-F 8AM-5:30PM, Sa 9AM-5PM. 2016 Fillmore St. 922-6510*

Trio Cafe. $ Light, airy room with stand up bar. European sandwiches, pizza and omelettes, and espresso, beer and wine. A pleasant place to read the morning paper. *Open Tu-Sa 8AM-6PM, Su 10AM-4PM. 1830 Fillmore St. 563-2248*

Leon's Cajun and Bar-B-Q. ★ $ Cajun creole-style ribs, links and chicken barbequed over a variety of fruit woods, mesquite and charcoal in Leon McHenry's brick oven. Served with chili, spaghetti or beans. *Open M-Sa 11AM-10PM, Su 1-9PM. 1911 Fillmore St. 922-2436*

Patisserie Delanghe. $ Fine French pastry —exquisite tartes, cakes and petits fours.

Fotomat
magazines **Visuals**
UPS, message service, etc. **Mail Boxes Etc.**
Pacific Heights Cleaners

FILLMORE STREET

Mayflower Market grocery store
Huestons Appliance Service
San Francisco Boot & Shoe Repair
Maureen's hairdresser
Pacific Heights Pharmacy
Bridge of Beauty visionary art & jewelry
Star Time Shop watch & jewelry repair
GJ Mureta's Antiques
Yountville children's clothing
Hedy's Salon
Eugene Anthony Interior Design
Zoe fine apparel

Washington

animal Adoption, vet. **Pets Unlimited**
Pioneer Public Accountant
clothing and lingerie **Mansfield's**
restaurant **Alta Plaza**
Alta Plaza Bar

Belmont Florist
In-Shape aerobics studio
Barry for Pets
Kaleidoscope Travel
Broemmel Pharmacy

Clay

women's clothing **Khyber Crossing**
Clay Theater
Browser Books
men's & women's clothing **Jim-Elle**
Japanese cuisine **Ten Ichi**
JJ's Piano Bar
SF Symphony Thrift Store **Repeat Perfomance**
Mad Hatter Tea and Chesire Cheese
Worden's Fine Framing
cafe **The Hillcrest Bar & Cafe**

La Posada Mexican restaurant
Seconds to Go Sacred Heart thrift shop
The Cafe restaurant
The Way We Wore vintage clothing
Next to New Shop Jr. League of SF thrift shop
Rainbow Records
Body Options dancewear
La Mediterranee restaurant
Kyo's Flowers
D&M Liquors

Sacramento

coffee shop **Sugar's Broiler**
meat/poultry **American Market**
housewares **Fillamento**
men's clothing **The Producer**
take out, catering, cafe **Vivande**
desserts **Sweet Inspiration**
women's clothing **CP Shades**
desserts **Cocolat**
Pacific Heights Health Food Market
accessories **Algebra**
Pacific Heights Haircutting
Le Comfort Bath Shop
pizza deli **Uncle Vito's**

FILLMORE STREET

Time Savings
Designer Frame & Picture Co.
The Beauty Store beauty supplies
39 Minute Photo Finishing
Kozo women's clothing
Da Paula Restaurant
Wells Fargo Bank

California

Rolling Pin Donuts
The Elite Cafe
paint/wallpaper **Color Scheme**
M10 Women's Clothing
Optometrist **Dr. Hedani**
Bay Area Furniture
antiques **GW Smith Galleries**
ice cream **Rory's**
pet shop **Exotic Birds**
Pacific Heights Bar & Grill

Bi-Rite Liquors
Wash Palace laundry
Nail Gallery & Hair Too
Travel Place Travel Agents
Goodwill thrift store
Opportunity Shop thrift store
Harry's Bar
Chestnut Cafe natural foods
The Brown Bag office supplies

Pine

liquor **Kim's Market**
Illustrious Lighting
Japanese food **Osome**
Brentwood Cleaners

Mi Burrito Mexican food
Radio Shack
Fillmore Hardware
Miracle Baths hot tubs

Bush

Olympic Gas Station
American Academy of Opthalmology
Hair Boutique & Nails
American handcrafts **Heartland**
property mngt. **Keynote Properties**

FILLMORE STREET

Delanghe Patisserie Francaise
Fleurtations flowers
Trio Cafe
Hoy's Sportswear
Photomotion film devt.
Eggcentricity eggshaped gifts
Voila clothes
Cottontail and Me children's clothing
Doris women's clothes

Sutter

Open M-F 7AM-6PM, Sa 8AM-6PM, Su 8AM-2PM. Corner of Fillmore and Bush Sts. 923-0711

Harry's Bar. $ Dark mahogany wood room with brass, white tiled floor and grand piano. *Bar open M-Sa 4-11PM, Su 4-10PM; dinner M-Sa 5-11PM, Su 5-10PM. 2020 Fillmore St. 921-1000*

The Cafe. $ Like being in a charming garden house, the Cafe offers a wide selection of wholesome food with generous portions and low prices. Good hamburgers, pasta and a delicious variety of salads. *Open M-F 11:30AM-5PM, Sa 3:30-5PM. 2244 Fillmore St. 346-9211*

D & M Liquors. Incredible selection of California wines. Their specialty is champagne and they feature 170 to 190 different varieties. *Open daily 10AM-10PM. Corner of Fillmore and Sacramento Sts. 346-1325*

Yountville. Elegant clothing for children. *Open M-Sa 10AM-6PM. 2416 Fillmore St. 922-5050*

Tokyo Fish Market. In place for generations, this market showcases almost every type of fish available. Fun to look, even if you're not about to cook. *1908 Fillmore St. 931-4561*

53 **Pauli's Cafe.** ★$$ Almost always crowded, and often a boisterous line of waiting customers spills out onto the sidewalk. The space is extraordinarily bright and sunny, with two walls of windows facing out onto the street, making it the perfect setting for breakfast or lunch. Breakfasts feature standard American cuisine with a twist—such scrumptious dishes as Grand Marnier French toast and Eggs Florentine, blueberry pancakes with old-fashioned maple syrup are a few of the offerings. It's all worth standing in line for. The ambience is warm and the service is excellent. *Open M-F 11AM-2:30PM, 6:30-11PM; Sa brunch 9:30AM-2:30PM, dinner 6-10:30PM; Su brunch 9:30AM-2:30PM, dinner 6-10PM. 2500 Washington St. 921-5258*

54 **Alta Plaza Park.** One of a series of urban parks laid out when Pacific Heights was first developed. Set on the top of the hill with magnificent terraces stepping down to Clay Street, the park offers superb views across the Western Addition to St. Mary's Cathedral and the Civic Center. Around it are an interesting mixture of mansions, apartment towers and false front Italiante row houses. *Between Jackson and Clay Sts. and Scott and Steiner Sts.*

55 **William Sawyer Gallery.** Contemporary painting and sculpture featuring West Coast artists. Look for a yellow house with no sign. *Open Tu-Sa 11AM-6PM. 3045 Clay St. 921-1600*

56 **Swedenborg Church.** (1884, A. Page Brown) **Bernard Maybeck** and **A.C. Sweinfurth**, who were in Brown's office, worked on the designs, as can be seen by the beautiful craftsman-style detailing. The church is adjacent to a fine walled garden which is raised up above the surrounding street and contains trees, flowers and shrubs from every continent on earth. Inside the church is a large fireplace opposite the sanctuary, stained glass windows by **Bruce Porter** and furniture by **Gustav Stickley.** *2107 Lyon St. at Washington.*

57 **Sacramento Street.** A mixture of auto garages, movie theaters, ice cream parlors, gift and antiques shops, boutiques and a store that is open only two months each year to present an incredible selection of Christmas ornaments. This is a less overwhelming, less touristy version of Union Street.

Courtesy Dan Soloman

57 **Sacramento-Lyon Condominiums.** (1980, Dan Soloman and Associates) A modern infill housing scheme designed by the city's best contemporary architectural firm. Notice how the traditional bay windows, stepped hillside profiles and standard 25-foot side frontages have been maintained. Clad in shingles with a nice landscaped courtyard inside. *Private residence. Sacramento and Lyon Sts.*

If you were an ex-president, foreign dignitary or movie star visiting San Francisco, you would no doubt be welcomed to the Golden Gate City with as much glitz as necessary to maintain that gilded reputation. Part of the special welcome would be a very special host: **Cyril Magnin,** aka *Mr. San Francisco.*

Magnin's 80 year love affair with his hometown has created in him the personification of this city loved for its eccentricities. His life and vigorous personality seem to come from a script written for a tuxedoed Fred Astaire. But Magnin's role is real and one he created himself: curator of the city's culture, keeper of the city's keys, sugar daddy to the fine arts and head cheerleader for his greatest passion, the City of San Francisco.

Magnin, more than anyone, sets the style and pace of San Francisco's dinner party set with a Gatsby-an relish for the high c's: haute couture and haute cuisine. After a full day at the office, he begins his real life's work, politicking for and loyally attending the city's fine and performing arts events.

Two generations ago, his grandmother created the San Francisco-based **I. Magnin** chain of fine clothiers. After World War II, Cyril branched off to create the **Joseph Magnin** stores.

Meter maids in the Financial District, the Marina and the Civic Center write tickets an average of every 3 minutes.

North Beach

North Beach guards its reputation against the incredible odds of encroaching neon, skin shows and drag queens of nearby Broadway, as well as the skyrocketing real estate prices that threaten the stability of the long-time ethnic mix. But somehow, the old ingredients of the melting pot neighborhood survive, along with certain remnants of the life that made this area the birthplace of the Beat Generation. North Beach was named after a long-ago beach that extended between **Telegraph Hill** and **Russian Hill** that has long since turned to landfill. Although North Beach is synomomous with *Little Italy,* Italians were not the first nor the last to arrive. Chilean prostitutes came first, attracted by the gold rush, only to be chased out by the Irish, who were eventually replaced by Latin Americans. On a site first occupied by a Russian Serbian Greek Orthodox Church, the Washington Square Theater presented Enrico Caruso in concert. Later this theater became the Palace, playing Chinese movies. Supplemented by small colonies of Basques, young working people and Bohemians, the Chinese began crossing Broadway from Chinatown in the 60s. Today the North Beach population is one-third Chinese.

The area is a mosaic of aromatic coffee houses and shops that sell sausages, cheeses, wines, bagels and delectable Italian pastries. The oldest restaurant in the area, **Fior D'Italia,** has been feeding the neighborhood since 1886. For a glimpse into the mysterious sourdough process, pause at **Boudin Bakery's** picture window on Jefferson Street. Don't miss **Victoria Pastry Company's** St. Honore cake or **Stella's** Sacri Pantina, or Saturday at **Caffe Trieste** where opera singers present their favorite arias. At **Tosca's** there are opera records on the juke box, and the sounds of jazz, New Wave, reggae, blues and rock confuse the ear as you walk down Grant Avenue. When you're ready to rest, relax on a park bench in **Washington Square** and listen to the gossip exchange in Chinese and Italian swirl around you while old men practice Tai Chi and kids hang out on the grass—the perfect place to sample the tempo of the neighborhood. The blocks around **Jackson Square**, on the site of the notorious Barbary Coast, are lined with restored 19th century buildings. Don't miss the outstanding group in the 700 block of **Montgomery Street.**

Telegraph Hill

Bordering North Beach is **Telegraph Hill** with its quaint cottages and vine-covered lanes, flowering gardens and stunning views. It is thought by some to be the most sought after address in the city. Artists and writers once lived here, but now it's mostly lawyers and businessmen. The *Hill,* as residents call it, looked quite different in the days of the Gold Rush. Although the height of the hill is the same (284 feet), the east slope was smooth and round and covered with grazing goats. The barren, jagged cliff you see today was created by sailors digging out ballast for their empty ship holds back when water lapped at the hill's base. The hill went through several names, but when the Morse Code Signal Station was set up in 1853, the name Telegraph Hill stuck. Although most of North Beach burned in the post-earthquake fire of 1906, the Italians managed to save a number of the old wooden cottages on the hill with a bucket brigade, using their barrels of homemade red wine. Many of these tiny shacks, built by early fishermen, are now selling for hundreds of thousands of dollars. Crowning the Hill is **Coit Tower,** named for Lillie Hitchcock Coit. You can take the elevator to the top to see the spectacular view.

Fisherman's Wharf, also bordering North Beach, is still the city's most popular tourist attraction, and it's one area that really must be explored on foot—driving here is impossible. Del Monte's old peach canning plant, nearby, is still called the **Cannery,** but is now filled with shops and restaurants, as is **Ghiradelli Square,** of chocolate factory fame.

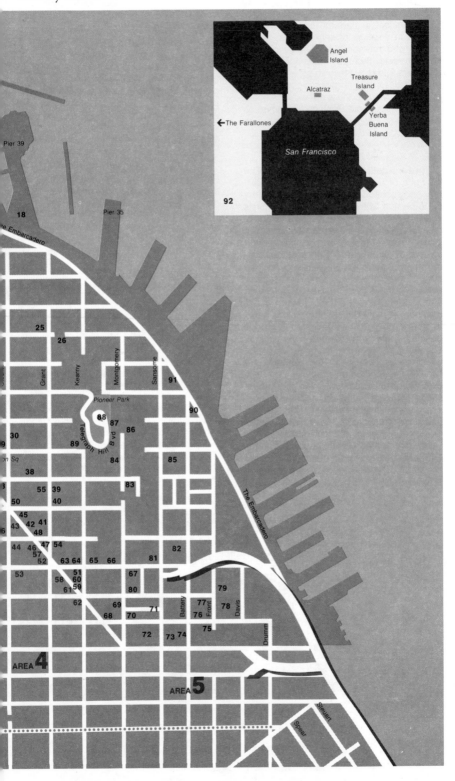

1 Aquatic Park. This terraced park sits adjacent to Ghirardelli Square and overlooking the Bay. Historic ships managed by the Maritime Museum are docked at nearby piers. There is swimming and fishing off Muni Pier, a small beach for jogging and wading and plenty of grass for picnicking. Lifeguard on duty in summer. *556-0560*

2 National Maritime Museum. Part of the Golden Gate National Recreation Area. San Francisco's maritime history is documented in displays of ship models, photographs and memorabilia. The fascinating ship models include passenger liners, freighters and U.S. Navy ships and a model of the *Preussen*, the largest sail-powered ship ever built. Upstairs there are exhibits about shipping in the Gold Rush days. *Admission free. Tours by Rangers are available daily. The library is open to the public during the week. Open daily 10AM-5PM. Aquatic Park, foot of Polk St. 556-8177*

3 Ghirardelli Square. (1860s-1916) The site of a woolen mill during the Civil War and subsequently the chocolate factory of **Domenico Ghirardelli,** this was the city's first factory converted into a substantial commercial complex and it is the most attractive as well. The extensive renovation was done in 1962-67 by **Wurster, Bernardi and Emmons** and **Lawrence Halprin and Associates.** The Square's location is superb, blessed with views of the Bay, Angel Island and Alcatraz, and the hills of Marin in the distance. At night the buildings, clock tower and the large sign are illuminated by strings of lights, making the Square look magical. The **Mermaid Fountain** in the central plaza, designed by local artist **Ruth Asawa,** is a nice resting and meeting place. There is usually free entertainment going on—puppet shows, singers, jugglers and musicians. There are dozens of speciality shops selling fashions, art objects, toys, kites, gifts, jewelry, furnishings and food. **McDermott's** sells contemporary design household items. **Originals by Nature** offers minerals, fossils and gems. **The Hammock Way** has a good selection of hammocks and swings. **Light**

Opera carries unusual handpainted Russian lacquer boxes and art glass. **The San Francisco Ship Model Gallery** sells ship models and shows some amazingly intricate ones. **Pearl of Orient** has reputedly the largest stock of pearls in the Bay Area. The **Information Booth** in the plaza provides a detailed guide to the shops and restaurants and sells Ghirardelli chocolate bars too. *900 North Point (across from Aquatic Park). Information: 775-5500*

Within Ghirardelli Square is:

Lanzone and Son. ★ ★ $$ It's a San Francisco institution and jammed with tourists, but the food is as carefully prepared as at a small neighborhood restaurant. Delicious pastas, particularly the *guanciali al funghi* (raviolis filled with ricotta cheese and topped with mushrooms) and the *agnolotti.* There may be a wait despite reservations, and the service can be impersonal. *Italian. Open Tu-F noon-11PM, Sa-Su 4PM-midnight. 771-2880*

Paprikas Fono. ★ ★ $$ If you think that restaurants in tourist areas have indifferent food, make an exception and try this one. The Hungarian menu is authentic and excellent, and the true paprika comes on virtually every dish as well as in a shaker on each table. The *gulyas* soup with fried bread, the seafood soup with rock cod, clams and crawfish, the tender chunks of veal paprikas and the sweet cheese *palacsintas* for dessert all make for memorable eating. Portions are generous and the service is accommodating. *Hungarian. Open M-Th & Su 11:30AM-10:30PM, F & Sa 11:30AM-11PM. Summer hours: Su-Th 11AM-11PM; F & Sa 11AM-11:30PM. Ghirardelli Sq. 441-1223*

Maxwell's Plum. ★ $$/$$$ This big, gaudy showplace at Ghirardelli Square was redecorated at a cost of a mere $7 million. They should have put some of that money into improving the food, although the simple American dishes are decent and fairly priced. Stay away from anything French. A la carte menu. They serve an impressive Sunday brunch. *Open daily 11:30AM-4PM, 5:30-10:45PM. Su brunch. 441-4140*

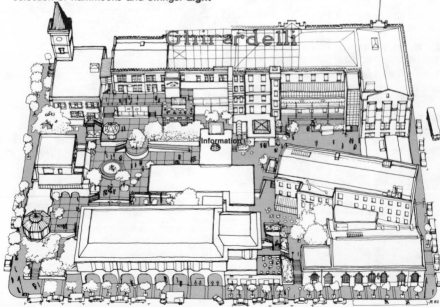

Mandarin. ★ $$$ A beautiful environment with a view of the Bay, as well as exceptional Chinese cuisine. The smoked tea duck is excellent, as is their newest specialty, Baker's Chicken, which you must order 24 hours in advance. The pot stickers are also of the highest quality. Service is quiet and efficient. *Chinese. Open daily 12-11PM. Ghirardelli Sq. 475-5438*

Gaylord India Restaurant. ★★ $$/$$$ Gaylord's is part of a chain of northern Indian restaurants, with branches in New York, Chicago, London and New Delhi, as well as at the Embarcadero Center in San Francisco. What sets this one apart is the glittering view of the Bay that you can enjoy along with their excellent *tandoori* dishes. The tandoori fish and chicken tikka are top selections. If you are feeling more adventurous, try one of their special feasts, like the huge vegetarian meal, with everything from samosas to saffron rice with vegetables. *Open daily 11:30AM-2PM, 5-10:45PM; Su brunch noon-2:45PM. Ghirardelli Sq. 771-8822*

Fanning's Bookstore. A welcome relief to the over-generalized offerings of bookstore chains, privately owned Fanning's offers a specialized selection of works by Northern California writers. A sort of *Mom and Pop* version of a bookstore, the Fannings have personally selected a respectable assortment of publications including every book still in print by Steinbeck, London, Twain and Hammet, whose portraits are featured on the store's sign, as well as in a mural on the back wall. *Open Su-F 10AM-7PM, Sa 10AM-9PM. Ghirardelli Sq., Mustard Bldg., 2nd floor. 775-2067*

San Francisco Craft and Folk Museum. The museum has a variety of folk art exhibits that change every 2 months, such as displays from the Hopi Indians, Japanese textiles and Haitian voodoo flags. *Open W-Su 12-5PM. Ghirardelli Sq. 775-0990*

Chocolate Manufactory. An old-fashioned ice cream parlor and candy store. It's worth standing in line for a scrumptious hot fudge sundae or perhaps even a 5-pound slab of chocolate, supposedly the world's largest chocolate bar. Take a look at the display in the back of some original chocolate-making machinery, once used in the old factory here. *Open daily 10AM-6PM. Ghirardelli Sq. 775-5500*

Chocolate, from the cacao tree, is grown in tropical areas near the Equator. Mexican and Central American Indians grew cacao beans long before the arrival of Columbus in America. The bean was involved in traditions and legends of their cultures. Cortez brought cacao beans home to Spain in 1508 and from there to other parts of Europe.

The beans are blended for color and flavor and processed into a chocolate liquor, from which all chocolate products are derived. Ironically the name of the bean comes from Mayan words meaning *sour water*. A misspelling by English importers probably resulted in the beans being called cocoa.

4 **Chez Michel.** ★ $$$/$$$$ Quite good, actually, although it's not as famous as many of San Francisco's French restaurants. A beautiful, stylish room and *modern-classic* food prepared surprisingly well. *French. Open for dinner only Tu-Su 6PM-12AM. 804 North Point. 771-6077*

5 **Buena Vista Cafe.** $$ Always jammed, this is the place where Irish Coffee got started, and it's still their specialty. There's food too, but do a snack tour of nearby Ghirardelli Square instead, stopping here for the Irish Coffee as the finale. *American. Open daily 11AM-9:30PM. 2765 Hyde St. 474-5044*

6 **The Cannery.** Originally the **Del Monte Fruit Company's** peach canning plant, constructed in 1909. It was remodeled in 1968 by **Joseph Esherick and Associates** following the success of Ghirardelli Square. The 3-story complex contains shops, restaurants and a movie theater. Its sunken courtyard, scattered with snack bars and tree-shaded benches, was formerly a railroad siding and platform and now hosts mimes, music and the like. The Cannery looks in on itself, rather than outward toward the scenic surroundings. This may account for its more subdued atmosphere, in contrast to Ghirardelli. Treasures from the estate of newspaper tycoon **William Randolph Hearst** have been installed in some of the facilities: **Cannery Casuals** on the 3rd floor has a 13th century wood mosaic ceiling. *2801 Leavenworth at Jefferson St.*

7 **Maritime Historic Park.** First and foremost, San Francisco is a seaport. That's why the first settlers came here, and that's why the city has endured. So no visit to the Bay Area would be complete without an historic maritime tour along the waterfront. San Francisco has made a tremendous effort to preserve the rich flavor of its romantic sailing ship days, and now has one of the foremost maritime displays anywhere.

Five vessels are docked at the Maritime Park; the 3 that are open to the public hold artifacts, photograph collections and displays that will help bring this exciting past alive. The **Hyde Street Pier**, docking area of the 5-ship museum, is itself an old ferry slip where Golden Gate ferries once left for Sausalito and Berkeley. *The vessels are open daily May-Sept. 10AM-6PM; Oct-Apr. 10AM-5PM.*

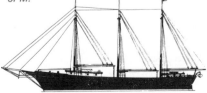

C.A. Thayer. Built in 1895, this 3-masted schooner was the Pacific Coast's last commercial sailing ship. She had been used to transport lumber, had served in 2 wars and was most recently used by the fishing industry. *Hyde St. Pier.*

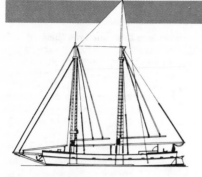

Alma. Tied to the C.A. Thayer but not open for public tours, this is still a fun ship to study from afar. The bay scow schooner, or hay scow, represents the wide-bottom sail boats—once numbering 600—that used to traverse the Bay several times a day carrying cargo to and fro. *Hyde St. Pier.*

Eureka. This was the last of the side-wheel powered ferries to operate in the U.S. Built in 1890, it hauled freight and passengers for the San Francisco and Northern Pacific Railroads. *Hyde St. Pier.*

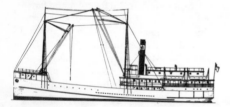

Wapama. This wooden hulled schooner used steam power to haul lumber and passengers up the Pacific Coast to Alaska. Steam schooners like this replaced the sailing schooners like the **C.A. Thayer**. *Hyde St. Pier.*

Hercules. Laying beside the **Eureka**, the **Hercules** is still under restoration and is not yet open to the public. Built in 1907, the ocean-going tug worked north and south from the Bay, hauling cargo, crippled ships, barges and even materials for the Panama Canal. *Hyde St. Pier.*

Balclutha. A favorite city landmark, this is a classic square rigged, 3-masted sailing ship. Built in Scotland in 1883, she sailed the Cape Horn route for many years bringing European goods to the West Coast and taking California grains back home. After the turn of the century, she served as a lumber ship, a salmon cannery in Alaskan waters, and finally as a carnival ship and Hollywood movie prop. Today she is a part of the Maritime Museum and houses exhibits and artifacts. *Open daily 9AM-10PM. Admission charge, children under 12 free. Pier 43, Powell St. at the Embarcadero. 982-1886*

8 **Cannery Wine Cellars.** An exceptional liquor market with an astounding selection of California wines, imported beer, Armagnacs and an extensive assortment of single-malt scotches. *Open daily 10AM-6PM. The Cannery. 673-0400*

9 **The Anchorage.** This huge shopping center is downstream and downmarket from Ghirardelli Square and the Cannery. *Located between Leavenworth, Beach, Jones and Jefferson Sts. Open daily 10AM-6PM; summer 10AM-9PM. 775-6000*

10 **Fisherman's Wharf.** The Wharf was the center of the city's commercial fishing fleet. During the crab season, pots boil, and there are fishing boats to see and fish restaurants to sample, mixed in with the junk food vendors, shops, museums and motels. There are old sailing ships, like the lovely **Balclutha,** to explore, as well as the paddle wheeler **Eureka,** tied up at the Hyde Street Pier with other historic ships that are all part of the **Maritime State Historic Monument.** Although the fishing boats are motorized now, parts of the wharf seem unchanged from the days in the 1880s when it was lined with Italian feluccas and known as Italy Harbor.

11 **Pampanito Submarine.** A World War II original, docked at the pier and open for viewing. *Admission charge. Open Su-Th 9AM-6PM; F, Sa 9AM-9PM. Fisherman's Wharf. 929-0202*

12 **Guinness Museum of World Records.** See the smallest book, the largest guitar and other wonders. In the **Participating Gallery,** you get a chance to experience these marvels by trying to break the record for the loudest snore, or mount an 8-foot, 11-inch ladder to feel like the world's tallest man. *Admission charge. Open Su-Th 10AM-10PM, F-Sa 10AM-midnight. 235 Jefferson. 771-9890*

13 **Ripley's** *Believe It or Not!* **Museum.** Two thousand oddities collected by cartoonist **Robert L. Ripley.** *Admission charge. Open Su-Th 9AM-11PM, F-Sa 9AM-midnight. From June 15-September 15, open daily 9AM-midnight. 175 Jefferson (at Fisherman's Wharf). 771-6188*

14 **Boudin Sourdough French Bread Bakery.** Frenchman **Isadore Boudin** opened the city's first bakery on Grand Avenue in 1849 and became one of the first to bake sourdough bread. Now there are 6 Boudin Bakeries in San Francisco, including this one on the Wharf. You can catch a glimpse of the long and mysterious sourdough process through the window on Jefferson Street. Boudin also sells pizza bread, *panettone,* croissants and submarine sandwiches. *Open M-F 8AM-6:30PM, Sa & Su 8:30AM-6:30PM. 156 Jefferson St. 928-1849*

Several **ferry boats** can be seen along the Embarcadero. The **Klamath** has been restored and is the office of Walter Landor & Associates, an industrial design firm. The old ferry is visible from the Pier 5 gate or from Pier 7. **Las Palmas** is still traversing the Bay with her railroad car cargo. She is visible on the Bay during the early morning. **Dolphin P. Rempp** is a retired sailing ship that is a grand dinner setting. Now authentic decor and excellent food make her a favorite along the water. *Pier 42 at Berry St. 777-5771*

15 **Wax Museum.** Nearly 300 life-size wax figures dressed in authentic period costumes are displayed on 4 floors. There is a special **King Tut** floor, as well as a **Hall of Religion, Hall of Famous People, Chamber of Horrors** and **Fairyland.** You can even take a miniature cable car ride through *old* San Francisco. There are also souvenir shops and an amusement arcade. *Admission charge. Extra for special exhibitions. Open Su-Th 9AM-10PM, F-Sa 9AM-midnight. Summer hours: M-Sa 9AM-midnight. 145 Jefferson St., between Mason and Taylor Sts., Fisherman's Wharf. 885-4975*

15 **Enchanted World of San Francisco.** Here, 150 animated characters will guide your miniature 1880s cable car through scenes of the city's past, including the Gold Rush, the growth of the city, the great earthquake and fire and New Year's in Chinatown. *Admission charge. Open Su-Th 11AM-8PM, F-Sa 10AM-11PM. 145 Jefferson St., Fisherman's Wharf. 974-6900*

16 *Sheraton at the Wharf. Deluxe. A handsome complex of redwood, brick and greenery with 525 guest rooms interspersed with courtyards and a tree-lined driveway, within walking distance of all Fisherman's Wharf attractions and a short bus or cab ride to Chinatown, Nob Hill and Union Square. In addition to being close to many exceptional restaurants, there is one within the hotel that should not be missed—the Grand Exhibition which contains over 30 separate dining areas, each decorated differently to illustrate a specific theme. It makes an extra challenge when selecting your table! 2500 Mason St. at Beach. 362-5500. Toll free 800-325-3535*

17 **Commodore Helicopters.** *Open 9:30AM-sunset, depending on weather, year round. Expensive rates. Kids under 10 half price. Look for the yellow helicopters at Pier 43, Fisherman's Wharf. 981-4832*

18 **Pier 39.** A 2-level shopping street constructed along a pier on the north waterfront near Fisherman's Wharf. Opened in 1978, it was transformed from a cargo pier into a fictional image of a turn-of-the-century San Francisco street scene, although it resembles a village on Martha's Vineyard more than the West Coast city. Over 100 shops cater to specific preferences: teddy bears, unicorns, rainbows, hearts, sea shells, and cats, among other things. There are also T-shirt, jewelry and cookie stores, restaurants and fast food stands. (**Dan White**, the man who killed **Mayor George Moscone** and **Supervisor Harvey Milk** and later killed himself, used to run a hot potato stand here.) Other tourist attractions include a high diving act and a Games Palace, a mini-amusement park with bumper cars and a roller coaster. Don't miss **Ready Teddy,** a boutique specializing in *bears!* with over 2,000 from all over the world. (*Open M-Th 10:30AM-7:30PM; F-Su 10:30AM-8:30PM*). *A parking garage, entrance on Powell St., is located across from the Pier on Beach St. Pier 39 information, 981-PIER. The Blue and Gold Fleet's sightseeing bay cruises depart from the Pier. Phone for schedule. 781-7877*

See plan next page...

Sourdough bread is to San Francisco what the baguette is to Paris, the bagel to New York and the scone to London. The famous crusty loaf is made from a *starter* or *sponge*–a mixture of flour and liquid (anything from water or milk to crushed Zinfandel, cabernet sauvignon or Napa gamay grapes)–which is fermented until it is sour. Scientists believe the San Francisco bread gets its *special* flavor from mysterious organisms in the Bay Area air that *infect* the dough and produce the unique sour flavor.

San Francisco's first bakery was opened by **Isadore Boudin** in the mid-1800s (today there are 5 **Boudin** bakeries in San Francisco). Daily home sourdough bread deliveries quickly became as much of a tradition as receiving the morning paper. The bread was often stuck on special spikes outside the front doors.

Today, a new crop of bakeries has joined in the sourdough tradition, each vying for the title of *Best Bay Area Sourdough*. We favor the original, **Boudin,** and the young upstart, **Acme Bread Company,** but taste for yourself:

Acme Bread Company. *1601 San Pablo Av., Berkeley. 524-1327.*

Baker's of Paris. *1605 Haight St., 626-4076.*

Boudin Bakery. *156 Jefferson St., Fisherman's Wharf, 928-1849; The Cannery, 928-7004; Pier 39, 421-2259; 43 Drumm St., 362-3330; Ghirardelli Square, 928-7404; 399 10th Av., 221-1210.*

The Cheese Board. *1512 Shattuck Av., Berkeley. 549-3183.*

Sonoma French Bakery. *468 1st St. E., Sonoma. 707-996-2691.*

Upper Level

A Kitemakers of
San Francisco
Chic's Place
Eagle Cafe
Camera Cabin
Wildflower
Only in San Francisco

B Various & Sundries
Paper Chase
Belt & Buckle Co.
Pocket Herb
& Apothecary Shoppe
On Edge Two
Bags & Stuff
Dennis Barloga Gallery
Lotus

C P.B. Ross & co.
Pure Fantasy
Rainbow Shop
Old Swiss House

D Swiss Louis
Left Hand World Annex

E Coffee Bean
Sandalmakers
From Fruit to Nuts
Binnacle

F Whittler's Mother
Incredible Machine
Josef Robe Company
Following Sea

G The Stevens Flagship
San Francisco
Shirt Emporium
California Collectables

H Northern Lights
Incurable Collector

I 1000 Cranes
Calico Cat
Fashion Express Imports
The Gift Soap Co.
Dreamweaver Imports

J Palace of Gems
Neptune's Palace
Scrimshaw Gallery
The Sweater Gallery

K San Francisco
Music Box Company
Jade Orient
Silk House

L Restaurant Nakamura
Indian Trading Post
Vanelli's
Yet Wah

M Designs in Motion
Poster Prints
Dante's Sea Catch

N Rub-A-Dub-Dub
Parfumerie Boutique
Dynasty Fashion
Wire Art Jewelry
Evergreen
I Found My Heart
in San Francisco

O Buena Vista Winery
Steinhouse
Sweat Shop
Behind the Wheel

P California Western Wear
Athletic Shoe Co.
National Football League
Major League Baseball
Shop

Pier 39

Lower Level

A Nito Burrito
Kabuki Yakitori
City Sandwiches
Bagel Mayven
Pierside
Bayburgers
The Potato Place
Art Fair
Only in San Francisco

B Hot Dog!
Pier Pizzeria
Mama Parmagiana
Louies Chinese Food
It's My Parsley

C Brass International
Chocolate Heaven
Mrs. Field's
Chocolate Chippery

D The Mouse Club
Southern Antique
Tintype Photography
Quilts Ltd.
Desire

E Le Carrousel Patisserie
Baci

F Shell Cellar
St. Angelo's
Ted E. Bear
Eathquake McGoons

G Puppets on the Pier
Oh Fudge of San Francisco
North Beach Leathers
Boudin Sourdough
Zuniga Art

I The Golden Unicorn
Fromex/One Hour Photo
Kitemakers
of San Francisco II

J What's a Churro
S. Claus
The Toy Store
Mad Hatter
Pier 39 Book Shop

K Aunt Fanny's Hot Pretzels
Kitchens Etc.
Get Framed
Tang Art
Mud in your Eye Pottery

L Butterflys Everywhere
Hollywood U.S.A.
Hogs & Kisses
North Point Yacht Club

L San Benito Vineyards
Tasting Center
The Chipyard
Pepe's on the Pier
Nautilus
Teleford's Pipe & Tabacco
Morrows Gourmet
Nut House

M Sassafras Ceramics
Cable Car Hallmark
Classic T-Shirts
Pearl Shop
Poster Prints
Grin & Wear It
The College Shop
Haberdashers
Ballena Bay Pewtersmiths

N Barbary Coast Dolls
The Puzzle People
Jewelry Art Center
Waxworks

O Courtney Bros.
Film Emporium
Left Hand World
Memory Lane
Candy Shoppe
Carefree Casuals
Bells & Chimes
Jewel Tree
Just in Case
The Miniature Shop
Daisy Hill Puppy Farm
San Francisco
Music Box Company
Victorian Shoppe
Palace of Magic

P Funtasia
San Francisco Experience
Swenson's

19 **Cost Plus.** A big warehouse-style import store, with bargains in brass, housewares, furniture, jewelry, Mexican pottery, gourmet groceries, Chinese toys and more. *Open daily M-F 10AM-9PM, Sa 10AM-6PM, Su 11AM-6PM. 2552 Taylor St. at North Point (at the Bay-Taylor cable car turntable). 673-8400.* (Other locations: *In Marin County at 2040 Redwood Hwy., off Hwy. 101 in Larkspur; in Oakland at Jack London Square.*)

20 **Marriott at Fisherman's Wharf.** *Deluxe.* By far the most elegant hotel in the Wharf area, the Marriott effectively blends apricot marble, comfortable leather and an abundance of greenery. There are 256 spacious rooms and suites complete with good-sized writing desks and cable TV. **Wellington's**, the hotel restaurant, specializes in Angus beef and fresh seafood. The entertainment lounge, **Illusions**, features a complimentary buffet and offers dancing M-Sa until 2AM. *1250 Columbus Av. 775-7555, 800-228-9290*

21 **North Point Public Housing.** (1950) A 2-block International Style public housing project by **Ernest Born** and **Henry Gutterson** built out of poured-in-place concrete and recently repainted in post-Modernist pastel colors—a good example of this type of architecture with its horizontal access balconies and front porches. *Bay St. between Taylor and Mason.*

22 **Vandewater Street.** A short, narrow alley between Powell and Mason Streets that contains several architectural firms and some interesting examples of recent housing —notably no. 55, a condominium development by **Daniel Solomon and Associates** (1981). This has a beautifully proportioned facade with a gently curved arch at the top. A palette of pinks and beiges. Next door, no. 33 by **Donald MacDonald and Associates** (1981) is a simpler version, painted white. No. 22 is an apartment block by **Esherick, Homsey, Dodge** and **Davis** (1976).

23 **Il Giglio.** ★ ★ ★ $$ This popular northern Italian restaurant offers the unbeatable combination of good food and moderate prices in a setting with the old-style elegance of a classic Italian restaurant. Veal dishes dominate the menu, and include the rich *Vitello alla Giglio* (veal medallions in a sherry sauce topped with mushrooms and almonds). The *Scampi alla Lorenzo,* perfectly prepared, also deserves recommendation. With its established compentence, Il Giglio is a welcome relief from the recent overabundance of pricey, trendy operations. *Open M-Th 11:30AM-2PM, 5-10PM; F 11:30AM-2PM, 5-10:30PM; Sa 5-10:30PM. 545 Francisco St. 441-1040*

Former resident Jack Kerouac helped put North Beach on the map when he adapted the word *beat* from beatitude to describe those like himself who were *into poetry, jazz, eastern philosophy and wanderlust!*

Restaurants/Nightlife red
Hotels blue
Museums/Architecture/Narrative black

Courtesy Backen, Arrigoni and Ross

25 **210 Francisco Street.** (1985, Backen, Arrigoni and Ross) This 25-foot-wide row house is a modern reinterpretation of the traditional San Francisco type. It has all the essential elements—the curved bay window, the false facade: but it is constructed out of contemporary materials—white porcelain enamel panels, glass blocks and poured-in-place concrete. *Private residence. Francisco at Grant Av.*

26 **Telegraph Terrace.** (1984, Backen, Arrigoni and Ross) An award-winning design for a group of expensive Spanish-style condominiums that climb the steep hillside and look out over mouldings and details that make this scheme fit into its context. *Private residence. Francisco at Grant Av.*

Dungeness crab is the great fish specialty of San Francisco. It is the Bay's third largest commercial catch, with 5.6 million pounds pulled in each year worth more than $9 million. In its own way, it's as delicious and as great a delicacy as Maine lobster. During crab season, from about mid-November through June, you can have it prepared in all sorts of tempting ways: in a spicy tomato sauce *(cioppinos)* in Italian restaurants, in cold salads or steamed in fish restaurants, and in black bean sauce and—perhaps at its best—cooked with ginger and garlic in Chinese restaurants.

27 Charles Campbell Gallery. Primarily contemporary Bay Area art. *Tu-F 11AM-5:30PM, Sa noon-4PM. 647 Chestnut St., 2nd floor. 441-8680*

28 Buca Giovannini. ★★$$/$$$ The name *buca* means *hole* in Italian, and you reach the dining room by descending a stairway to the lower level. Buca Giovanni's offers at least eleven daily specials in addition to its unusually large selection (54) of classic Italian dishes. The pastas are good, but the servings are too small to make a full meal, holding true to the Italian tradition of eating pasta as a first course. Entrees tend to be inconsistent, but the veal with oyster sauce and mushrooms is highly recommended, and portions are generous. *Reservations. Open M-Th 5:30-10:30PM, F & Sa 5:30-11PM. 800 Greenwich St. 776-7766*

29 Mama's. ★$$ What used to be a little restaurant on Washington Square is now an empire, with several branches scattered around the Bay Area. This is the original, and it's still as good as always. Very satisfying brunch offerings, including great omelettes. Also some unusual sandwiches and spectacular desserts for lunch. *American. Open daily for breakfast and lunch 7AM-3PM. 1701 Stockton St., Washington Square. 362-6421. (Other locations: in Macy's. Closed Su. Stockton and O'Farrell St. 391-3790; Nob Hill.) 1177 California St. 928-1004*

30 Maybeck Building. (1908-09) Well preserved office building built around a courtyard with apartments on the upper floors. Formerly the Old Telegraph Hill Neighborhood Association Building. *1736 Stockton St. between Greenwich and Filbert Streets.*

31 Washington Square. Located halfway along Columbus Avenue and bounded by Filbert, Union, Powell and Stockton Streets, Washington Square is the center of the Italian North Beach community. On the north side is the **Church of St. Peter and St. Paul;** on the east, next to the post office, is the **Italian Men's Athletic Club.** Lunch at **Malvina's** on the corner of Stockton and Union is a pleasant way to see life go by.

32 Washington Square Bar and Grill. ★★$$ A North Beach restaurant jammed with natives as well as tourists. Lots of fun. Avoid the pasta; the best dishes here are fish. *Italian. Open M-Sa 11:30AM-3PM, 6-11PM; Su 11:30AM-3PM, 5:30-10:30PM. 1707 Powell St. 982-8123*

33 Fior D'Italia. ★$$/$$$ One of San Francisco's oldest restaurants—more than 100 years old—and it's been run by the same family since the beginning, although in lots of different North Beach locations. There's a feel of the atmosphere of the old San Francisco Italian community and some excellent veal and chicken dishes to boot. *Italian. Open M-Sa 11:30AM-10:30PM, Su 5-10PM. 621 Union St. 986-1886*

34 Amelio's. ★★★$$$ This interesting and popular restaurant features Italian food with a nouvelle cuisine accent. A new chef has moved it upward several notches on the culinary scale. *Italian. Open daily 5:30-10:30PM. 1630 Powell St. 397-4339*

34 Coit Liquors. If you're a wine buff, this store will impress you with its wide selection, including hard-to-find Italian wines. Prices are aften suprisingly reasonable, especially when you shop from the list of frequent *specials. Open daily 9AM-midnight. 585 Columbus Av. 986-4036*

34 Little City Antipasti Bar. ★★$$ An airy, attractive ambience with diverse and delicious antipasti. It's a perfect place for meeting your friends for drinks and a snack before dinner, or we recommend a meal of the antipasti. *Open daily 11:30AM-midnight; bar open until 2AM. 673 Union St. 434-2900*

35 Club Fugazzi. A cabaret-style club featuring Steve Silver's show, **Beach Blanket Babylon.** The show's theme changes every year. Packed into the musical revue's 90 minutes are an endless array of antics and fun. Although Beach Blanket may be lacking in plot, the continuous songs, wild props, towering headpieces and creative production make this one of the city's zaniest and most enjoyable attractions. *Reservations 3 to 4 weeks in advance. No one under 21 admitted except for toned down Su matinee. Box office open M-Sa 10AM-6PM, Su 12-6PM. 678 Green St. 421-4222*

36 Grifone Ristorante. ★★$$/$$$ A family-run establishment serving good northern Italian cuisine. They also offer an excellent Caesar salad made at your table. *Reservations. Open daily 5-11PM. 1609 Powell St. 397-8458*

37 Mara's Donuts and Italian Pastries. Exceptional coffee pastries. One look at their display window is almost irresistible. Mara's is also the perfect alternative to the super-sweet offerings of nearby bakeries. *Open Su-Th 7AM-10PM, F & Sa 7AM-midnight. 503 Columbus Av. 397-9435*

38 Silhouettes. Featuring a 50s rock'n' roll juke box and dancing, Silhouettes' specials include Ladies' Night, Sunday night shooters and Japanese *midori* night. *Open Sa-Th noon-2AM, F 10-2AM. 524 Union St. 398-1952*

39 Cafe Jacqueline. ★★$$ Name your pleasure—chocolate, fresh raspberries or mushrooms—and Cafe Jacqueline will bake it inside a light brown souffle. Filling favorites include Grand Marinier. *Open W-Sa 11AM-2PM, 5:30-11PM. 1454 Grant Av. 981-5565*

40 RAF Centrogriglia. ★★$$$ Located at the former site of the Old Spaghetti Factory, this restaurant offers food that its ill-fated predecessor never imagined. The menu has modern Italian fare, but still includes some of the irreplacable elements of classic cuisine such as hard-to-find Risotto dishes, game stews with polenta and a variety of grilled meats. (The name, after all, means center *grill*.) The antipasti are also worth your indulging. Although service can be inconsistent, the food and unusually attractive setting makes RAF worth the visit. *Reservations. Open M-F 11:30AM-2:30PM, 6-10:30PM; Sa & Su 6-10:30PM. 478 Green St. 362-1999*

41 **La Bodega.** ★ $ On the well-beaten path of Grant Avenue, this restaurant manages to keep a low profile. Its rustic, homey interior, charming hosts, flamenco dancing to live guitar and reasonably priced Paella make this place a favorite. *1337 Grant Av. 433-0439*

41 **Mama Tina's Trattoria.** ★ $$ Tables topped with white linen are arranged in a cozy dining room with Italian pottery and copper cookware decorating the walls. They serve authentic southern Italian cuisine (the chef is from Brindisi, in the boot of Italy), featuring soups, pastas and main entrees on a trattoria-style à la carte menu. Try the *Orecchiette* pasta and veal *scaloppine. Open daily 6-11PM. 1315 Grant Av. 391-4129*

42 **Calzone's.** ★ $$ Delicious pizzas baked in a wood-burning brick oven. Munch on the sauteed shrimp wrapped in radicchio while people watching through the large picture windows. *Open daily 10AM-1AM. 430 Columbus Av. 397-3600*

42 **R. Matteuchi Street Clock.** (1909) Originally in front of a jeweler's shop of the same name. *229 Columbus Av. between Vallejo and Green Sts.*

43 **U.S. Restaurant.** ★ $/$$ Where do the North Beach regulars go when they want a cheap, filling and good Italian dinner? The U.S. is one of their favorites. You'll see everyone from hippies to poets to elderly Italian couples enjoying the huge portions and friendly service. Good roasts and pastas, and nightly specials. *Italian. Open Tu-Sa 6AM-9PM. 431 Columbus Av. 362-6251*

44 **Victoria Pastry Co.** Delicious St. Honore cake *1362 Stockton St. 781-2015*

45 **Stella Pastry.** Try the Sacri Pantina. *446 Columbus Av. 986-2914*

45 **Millefiori Inn.** (A thousand flowers). *Moderate to expensive.* A European-style hostelry far above the commonplace and one of a few interesting places to stay in this area. Great care has gone into the design of each of the 16 rooms—each one follows the common theme of the Inn's name but features a different flower. There are antiques, gleaming brass and fresh flowers everywhere. The sophisticated style and punctilious service is a bit of a surprise in the midst of the down-home clatter of Columbus Avenue, the main artery of Italian North Beach. Continental breakfast is served in a sunny patio adjoining the hotel, which also connects with a cafe owned by the hotelier. Suites available. *444 Columbus Av. 433-9111*

46 **Molinari's.** A landmark deli; a local monument since 1896. *373 Columbus Av. 421-2337*

47 **Caffe Trieste.** The quintessential San Francisco coffee house; unchanged, unchangeable, authentic. *609 Vallejo. 392-6739*

Restaurants/Nightlife red
Hotels blue
Shops/Galleries purple
Parks/Outdoor spaces green
Museums/Architecture/Narrative black

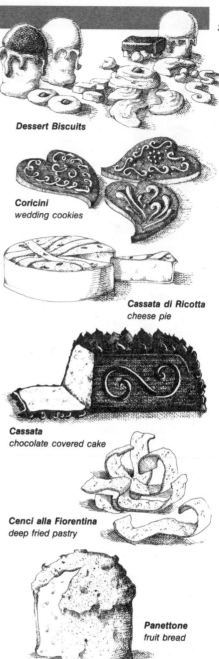

Dessert Biscuits

Coricini
wedding cookies

Cassata di Ricotta
cheese pie

Cassata
chocolate covered cake

Cenci alla Fiorentina
deep fried pastry

Panettone
fruit bread

48 **Caffe Roma.** ★ $/$$ The atmosphere of North Beach is captured in this coffee house, which also serves some excellent pizza. Order a cappucino, prop up a book and spend a couple of hours watching the world go by. *Italian. Open Su-Th 7:30AM-11:15PM, F & Sa 7:30PM-1:15AM. 414 Columbus Av. 391-8584*

49 **Graffeo Coffee Roasting Co.** You can smell the aromatic dark beans being roasted several blocks away. *733 Columbus Av. 986-2420*

50 **North Beach Restaurant.** ★ ★ $$ A popular meeting place for San Francisco's Italian community and everyone else. The appetizers and pasta are a better bet than the meat dishes. *Italian. Open daily 11:30AM-11:30PM. 1512 Stockton St. 392-1587*

50 **Caffe Sport.** ★★ $$ One of the better Italian restaurants in San Francisco. There's a long wait, but you'll love having a beer at the bar and looking at the displays of various trinkets hanging from the walls. The service is friendly and erratic, but the Italian-style seafood dishes are always second to none. All the sauteed dishes that include shellfish or calamari will send you away singing the praises of the chef. Huge portions and lots of garlic. Certainly not an elegant evening, but an enjoyable one. *Italian. Open Tu-Sa noon-2PM and 6:30-11PM. 574 Green St. 981-1251*

51 **Little Joe's.** ★ $/$$ There are lots of tiny, bare-bones Italian restaurants in North Beach that look so pleasant and friendly you desperately want them to be good. Little Joe's is the best of the lot. The cooks stand at the tiny open kitchen and manipulate dozens of frying pans perched over the high flames. Nothing gets overcooked, which is something of a miracle considering how busy the place is. They have genuine specialties like squid cooked in its own ink. *Italian. Open M-Th 11AM 10:30PM, F & Sa 11AM-11PM, Su 2-10PM. 523 Broadway. 433-4343*

52 **Luigi's.** $/$$ One of those low-priced North Beach hangouts where a wonderful mixture of students, dedicated eaters and long-time Italian North Beach residents are served mounds of food. The food may be a little classier elsewhere in North Beach, but you'll enjoy the scene. *Italian. Open W-Su 4-11PM. 353 Columbus Av. 397-1697*

53 **Mon Kiang.** ★ $/$$ A chance to eat a unique kind of Chinese food called *Hakka*, after an area of China near Canton. Their specialties are bean curd and fish dishes, along with salt-baked chicken. If you want some exotic Chinese food the likes of which you've never tasted before, this is the place to come. *Chinese. Open M-W, Fri-Su 11AM-midnight. 683 Broadway. 421-2015*

54 **Basta Pasta.** $/$$ This popular hangout is inexpensive but not particularly memorable. The fresh fish is usually worth ordering and the service friendly. *Italian. Open daily 11:30-2AM. 1268 Grant Av. 434-2248*

55 **North Beach Pizza.** ★$ A cheerful, welcoming atmosphere and a staff that obviously enjoys its work make this above average pizza emporium a happy experience. The variety is impressive, from sausage-garlic-mushroom, vegetarian, clam and garlic to the house special *with all the garbage on it*—and more. Their minestrone is good too. The place gets jammed, but you can always take it out. *Open Su-Th 11AM-1AM, F & Sa 11AM-3AM. 1499 Grant Av. 433-2444*

56 **North Beach Museum.** The history of North Beach, Chinatown and Fisherman's Wharf is presented in old photographs and artifacts. *Admission free. Open M-F 9AM-4PM, Sa 10AM-1PM. Mezzanine of Eureka Federal Savings, 1435 Stockton St. 391-6210*

Museums/Architecture/Narrative black
Restaurants/Nightlife red
Shops/Galleries purple

57 **Cafe Americain.** ★★ $$/$$$ An attractive, spacious dining area with wood accents and a black and white tile floor. Specialties of the house include gourmet pizzas baked in an oak-burning oven, Salmon Terrine and various grilled choice meats. Creative daily specials and select wine by the glass. *Open Su-Th 7-11AM, 11:30AM-2:30PM, 6-10PM; F & Sa 7-11AM, 11:30AM-2:30PM, 6-11PM. 317 Columbus Av. 981-8266*

58 **City Lights Booksellers & Publishers.** More than any other bookstore, this one evokes the atmosphere and accomplishments of literary San Francisco. Owned by poet **Lawrence Ferlinghetti**, the shop's, and North Beach's, heyday was the Beat era of the '50s. Cafe society here was like that of turn-of-the-century Paris, alive with the activity of poetry readings and happenings and gatherings of artists and writers. The store has a marvelous poetry section, featuring many of the writers who immortalized that generation—**Allen Ginsberg, Gregory Corso, Michael McClure, Jack Kerouac** and **Ken Kesey,** to name a few. *Open daily 10AM-midnight. 261 Columbus Av. 362-8193*

59 **Columbus Tower.** A *flatiron* building on the *corner of Columbus, Kearny and Pacific Av.*

Not much more than a memory remains of the **Barbary Coast,** the once notorious neighborhood extending between Montgomery, Pacific, Washington and Kearny Streets. Aptly named for the equally unsavory pirate headquarters in North Africa, it was here that the term *shanghai* originated, describing the all too frequent practice of drugging (often with *Mickey Finns,* another San Francisco invention) and shipping out any hapless seamen who ventured into the local watering holes as a crew member for an undermanned ship. It was a gathering place for *hoodlums*—a word coined in San Francisco during the time it had a worldwide reputation for viciousness. The area was finally shut down after World War I. In the 1950s it was renamed **Jackson Square** by the decorators who renovated the old 3-story buildings, exposing handsome brick walls and otherwise restoring the mid-19th century structures. This resulted in these few blocks becoming the first designated historic site in the city. Currently the buildings house design and textile firms, advertising, antiques and other small businesses.

60 **Greek Taverna.** ★$$ Classic Greek food in a warm setting. Belly dancers and Greek dancing featured nightly. A good place to stop for a lively nightcap. *Open Tu-Sa 5PM-1AM. 256 Columbus Av. 362-7260*

60 **Cho-Cho.** ★$$/$$$ This is one of the original, elegant Japanese restaurants near downtown San Francisco. Its menu may have been interesting years ago, but it's pretty standard today. A very pleasant place to talk, and the food is quite decent, although excelled by other places in Japantown. *Japanese. Open M-Th 11:30AM-2PM, 5-10PM; F 11:30AM-2PM, 5-11PM; Sa 5-11PM. 1020 Kearny St. 397-3066*

61 **Vesuvio's Bar.** If it's atmosphere you're after, this is the place. Vesuvio's is a North Beach landmark, still frequented by artists and poets from the Beat era in addition to more current representatives of the scene. The walls are covered with *objets d'art.* For quieter drinking, go upstairs. *Open daily 6AM-2AM. 255 Columbus Av. 362-3370*

62 **San Francisco Brewing Company.** A happy landing for beer buffs, **Allan Paul's** brewery and saloon is located in what was once San Francisco's Barbary Coast, the busy waterfront of early gold seekers. Now travelers from the nearby Financial District will be rewarded with an offering of 40 types of domestic and imported beers, along with several brewed by the owner on the spot in a gleaming copper kettle. The saloon's interior dates from 1907, with a bar of solid mahogany trimmed in brass and a tile spitoon. **Babyface Nelson** was captured in what is now the ladies' room and **Jack Dempsey** was a bouncer here for a short time. There's a special beer tasting, with light food and lunch, every other Wednesday, and on Wednesday and Thursday evenings, musicians take advantage of the old upright piano in the corner. For those who appreciate beer, the Brewery Company offers the state of the liquid arts. *Kitchen open M-F 11:30AM-2:30PM, 5-9PM; Sa 5-9PM. Bar open M-Th 11:30AM-midnight, F 11:30AM-1:30AM, Sa 3PM-midnight, Su 12PM-midnight. 155 Columbus (at Pacific). 434-3344*

63 **Columbus Avenue Books.** New and used books at discount prices with many used books in good condition and a large travel and guidebook section. *Open M-Th 10:30AM-10PM, F&Sa 10:30AM-midnight. 540 Broadway. 986-3872*

64 **Enrico's.** $$ The great sidewalk cafe of North Beach. A place to have a leisurely drink or espresso and watch all the characters walk by. The food is hit-or-miss except the hamburgers, which are excellent. *Italian. Open daily 11:30AM-3AM. 504 Broadway. 392-6220*

65 **Vanessi's.** ★★$$ If there's one restaurant famous among San Franciscans and tourists alike, this is it. You'll probably have to wait despite reservations, but you'll be happy to people-watch the entire evening. The food quality is spotty: first-rate charcoal-grilled meats and fish, but the quality goes down when you order veal dishes or things with elaborate sauces. No one, however, could criticize their minestrone soup or their creamy zabaglione for dessert. *Italian. Open M-F 11:30AM-11PM, Sa 4:30PM-midnight. 498 Broadway. 421-0890*

66 **Broadway.** Since 1964, when **Carol Doda** first performed her topless act at the **Condor Club**, the brash Broadway strip has been a monument to man's mammary fascination. However, wine, women and Mammon were a part of Broadway's flashy scene long before silicone ballooned Doda's breasts to a perfect 44. Bootleggers thrived on Broadway in the 1930s, and the 1940s saw the street fill with brothels and pool halls. Then in the 1950s, the strip began to clean up its act when the likes of **Lenny Bruce** and **Barbra Streisand** played at **Hungry I**, **Johnny Mathis** sang at **Ann's 448** and folk musicians strummed away at the **On Broadway**. But soon the entertainment boom went bust as high-paying Vegas clubs wooed the big names. By the mid-60s, the lively entertainment scene had turned topless and raunchy. Loud-mouthed barkers lured leering tourists into the 20 topless clubs that featured expensive cover charges, lightly-liquored drinks and  the mammary parade. The strip is still embroiled in controversy. Since 1978, thousands of protestors have annually filled the area, demanding to *take back the night* from the lust-lovers. They say the carnal clubs are part of a crass commercialization of sex that contributes to a society full of raped and battered women. But the protests haven't dimmed the flashing neon. The clubs are still open and thrill-shopping tourists still fill bawdy Broadway.

Also on Broadway:

Finocchio's. For the last 45 years, tourists have been gleefully exclaiming, *only in San Francisco* when they come upon Finocchio's irrepressible drag show. The revue features 10 female impersonators, lots of flashy costumes, ribald humor and some unusual specialty acts. *Cover charge. No drink minimum. 3 shows nightly beginning at 9PM. No one under 21 admitted. 506 Broadway. 982-9388*

66 The Stone. Nightclub with comedy and mostly light rock, jazz and middle-of-the-road music to dance to. *Open daily 8PM-2AM. 412 Broadway. 391-8282*

67 Route 66. ★ ★ $$ Despite the name, this is not a setting for diner food. It offers *eclectic American cuisine, representative of dishes of regional America.* You can't go wrong with the fish dishes. The decor is simple with a great classic juke box. *Open M-Th 11:45AM-3PM, 5-9:45PM; F 11:45AM-3PM, 6-10PM; Sa 6-11:45PM. 373 Broadway. 391-7524*

68 Thomas Brothers Maps (The Map House). An extraordinary selection of maps, from pocket to wall size, as well as globes, atlases and guides. The hanging brass lamps compliment the Victorian premises. *Open M-F 9AM-5PM. 550 Jackson. 981-7520*

69 Ernie's. ★ ★ ★ $$$$ Chef **Bruno Tison's** innovative cooking makes this the best of the very costly San Francisco French restaurants. Skip the standard grilled meat dishes and order the *nouvelle cuisine* specialties. Be sure to try as an appetizer the succulent warm oysters on the half shell. The sweetbreads, in a rich sauce that includes sea urchin roe, put every other sweetbread dish in town to shame. Exceptional squab, too. The atmosphere is formal in a red-plush sort of way, but the service is helpful and not snotty. *French. Open daily 6:30-11PM. 847 Montgomery St. 397-5969*

70 William Stout Architectural Books. One of the few great architectural bookstores in America, it has grown from a handful of books available at Bill's apartment to a collection of over 10,000 volumes of rare books, magazines and portfolios. European and Japanese volumes are available. A wonderful place for the architectural community to meet. Notice the striking lacquered counter. *Open M-Sa 10AM-4PM. 804 Montgomery St. 391-6757*

71 Gold Street. Designated an Historic District in the National Register of Historic Places in Washington, D.C. Be sure to see the **Assay Office**, which was an assay office during the Barbary Coast days. *56 Gold St. 981-4460*

72 Jackson Square District. The distict contains the only group of downtown business buildings to survive the 1906 earthquake and fire, though most date back to the 1850s. It has been designated as the city's first Historic District. Most of the buildings are brick and have been carefully restored and remodeled to become the city's fabric and furniture showroom center. Many of these are open to the trade only. A sign indicating *retail* means open to the public. Architecturally noteworthy buildings include: **470 Jackson**, Solari Building (1852); **432 Jackson**, Yeon Building (1906); **463 Jackson**, Hotaling Annex West (1860); **451 Jackson**, Hotaling Building (1866); **445 Jackson**, Hotaling Annex East (1860); **441 Jackson; 415-31 Jackson; 732 Montgomery; 728-30 Montgomery; 722 Montgomery**, Melvin Belli Building (1851); and **530 Washington**, Burr Building (1859-60).

Some recent warehouse remodelings are also worth studying: **Pacific Avenue at Osgood Place** by **Bull, Field, Volkmann, Stockwell; Musto Plaza**, 350 Pacific Avenue also by **Bull, Field, Volkmann, Stockwell;** and **Sansome and Pacific Building** by Wudtke Architects (1982).

72 Hotaling Street. This one-block-long alley leads from Jackson Street, between Montgomery and Sansome Streets, right into the base of the Transamerica Building on Washington Street. Hotaling has 2 old warehouses that were distilleries in the Barbary Coast days. Like most of the buildings in Jackson Square, they survived the 1906 quake and fire.

72 722 Montgomery. This 3-story brick building is registered as an Historic Landmark. The first meeting of Freemasons in California was held here on October 17, 1849. It now houses the law offices of San Francisco's celebrated lawyer, **Melvin Belli**.

72 Knoll International. The sleek showroom was designed by **Florence Knoll** in conjunction with **Skidmore, Owings and Merrill**. The public may browse, but Knoll sells to the trade only. *Open M-F 9AM-5PM. 732 Montgomery St. 391-3535*

72 Osgood Place. A narrow tree-lined alley between Broadway and Pacific Avenues parallel to Montgomery and Sansome Streets that has been designated an Historic Landmark. Notice the handsome old fire station at the foot of the alley on Pacific Avenue which has been converted into design offices.

72 Pacific Lumber Building. (1982, EPR) An 8-story brick clad office building that is the home for the Pacific Lumber Company. It has a treble-height arcade that cuts through the site on the diagonal. One of the many new brick office buildings in the Jackson Square Historic District. *Sansome at Washington Sts.*

72 Sunar/Hauserman Showroom. (1987, Mark Mack) Mack designed this elegant New Wave showroom for the furniture company. A mixture of traditional and *punk* aesthetics. Notice the galvanized sheet metal vaulting to the colonnade. *Washington at Sansome Sts.*

72 Arch. A beautifully designed architectural supply store where drafting instruments and supplies are imaginatively displayed. Conveniently close to William Stout's Bookstore and within easy reach of the many architect's offices in the neighborhood, it is frequently crowded at lunch hour. *Open M-F 9AM-5:30PM. 420 Jackson St. 433-2724*

73 **U.S. Appraiser's Building.** (1941, Gilbery Stanley Underwood) This U.S. Government building occupies the same block as the **U.S. Custom House** and both represent constrasting attitudes towards Federal architecture. The U.S. Appraiser's Building represents the aesthetics of the WPA era with its stripped down moderne styling. It has recently been reclad by **Kaplan/McLaughlin/Diaz** with precast concrete and a new polished granite base.

74 **U.S. Custom House.** (1906-11, Eames & Young) Older than the U.S. Appraiser's Building on the same block, this Baroque classical building has a massive rusticated base, an elaborate cornice line and a generously proportioned entrance hall. (Room 504 on the fifth floor houses the USGS offices which contain maps for sale of every part of the U.S. including Apollo 11 maps of the Moon.) *Battery St.*

75 **Wine & Cheese Center.** Innovative wine retailer **Dick Allen** offers computerized wine/meal matching, sandwiches and sampling at lunch time. Tastings are held one week out of each month. *205 Jackson St. 956-2518*

76 **Ciao.** ★ ★ $$ A glittering restaurant, as trendy as any in town, with polished brass, mirrors and high-tech plastic. The specialty is the pasta and those with tomato sauces are particularly good. You'll see fresh pasta hanging up to dry on shining racks. Try the antipasto too, a far cry from the usual luncheon meats this dish too often brings. *Italian. Open M-Sa 11AM-midnight, Su 4PM-midnight. 230 Jackson St. 982-9500*

77 **MacArthur Park.** ★ $$ A trendy watering hole with some really excellent barbecue. The meats are cooked in an oak-fueled smoker and come out generous, succulent and tender. The baby back pork ribs and chicken are superb. An excellent California wine list, reasonably priced. *American. Open M-Th 7-10AM, 11:30AM-2:30PM, 5-10:30PM; F 7-10AM, 11:30AM-2:30PM, 5-11PM; Sa 5-11PM; Su 10AM-2:30PM, 4:30-10PM. 607 Front St. 398-5700*

78 **Walton Square/Gateway Commons.** (1980-83; buildings by Fisher, Friedman Architects; office interiors by Robinson Mills and Williams.) Mixed use buildings filling 3 city blocks, each consisting of a complex plan with a central parking garage surrounded by shops and offices on the lower 2 floors and topped by 2 more floors of apartments and townhouses. Clad in brick tile to match the adjoining Jackson Square District, these developments contrast well with the earlier Golden Gateway Redevelopment schemes in their relationship to the street and as a high density/low use alternative to point blocks on a podium. The square fills with office workers at lunchtime and the soft grass hills are ideal places to lie back and watch life go by. *Front and Davis, Jackson and Pacific Sts.*

Restaurants/Nightlife red
Hotels blue
Shops/Galleries purple
Parks/Outdoor spaces green
Museums/Architecture/Narrative black

79 **Square One.** ★ ★ ★ $$$$ Opened by **Joyce Goldstein** from the highly rated **Chez Panisse**, this one is almost always over-booked. The cuisine is innovative with a menu that changes daily. The food has a Mediterranean flavor, and the stews and ragouts always get raves. *American. Open M-Th 11:30AM-2:30PM, 5:30-10:30PM; F & Sa until 11:30PM. 190 Pacific Av. 788-1110*

80 **Pacific Avenue.** Interesting shops include: **Wynne Gilmore,** which has women's fashions, including Gilmore's own designers. (*Open M-F 8AM-4PM, or by appt. 400 Pacific. 421-3291*); **Cornucopia,** a moderately priced breakfast and lunch place, specializing in health food that's good for a quick meal while you're touring this area. (*Open M-F 7:30AM-4:30PM. 408 Pacific. 398-1511*). **LIMN** has architectural and graphic furniture. Its warehouse showroom displays a large choice of furniture for the work space, including desks, lighting and seating. (*Open M-F 9:30AM-5:30PM, Sa 11AM-5:30PM. 457 Pacific. 397-7474*). **Thomas Cara Ltd.** is an old establishment selling all sorts of coffee and espresso machines. They also have kitchen utensils and copperware. (*Open M-F 9:30AM-4:30PM, Sa 11AM-3PM. 517 Pacific. 781-0383*).

81 **Hunan.** ★ ★ $$ Some like it hot, and this is the restaurant that provides it. The warehouse-like restaurant, decorated by a *NO MSG* banner, is a great local favorite, although some question how good the food is under all the finely-chopped chili peppers. *Chinese. Open M-Sa 11:30AM-9:30PM. 924 Sansome St. 956-7727*

82 **Remodeled Warehouses.** Some old warehouses, mostly built in the 1930s, are now being remodeled into offices for architects, graphic artists and most recently for TV companies. Of particular note are *855 Battery St.* for **Channel 5; Westinghouse TV,** remodeled by **Gensler and Associates** (1980-81); *243 Vallejo* by **Marquis Associates;** *222 Vallejo* by **Kaplan/McLaughlin/Diaz Architects** (1978); and *101 Lombard St.* by **HOK** (Hellmuth, Obata and Kassabaum) and completed in 1979. There are fine old brick warehouses on Battery Street between Union and Green Sts, plus the old **Ice House** which is now an office complex. *Sansome and Union Sts.*

83 **Kahn House.** (1939) Similar to his Lovell House in Los Angeles, this **Richard Neutra** building steps down the hill and offers its occupants superb views of the bay. Private residence. *66 Calhoun Terrace.*

84 **1360 Montgomery Street.** A 1937 apartment house in the *moderne* style with exterior murals and a fine glass block facade to the entrance lobby. Featured in the **Humphrey Bogart** movie *The Maltese Falcon. Private residence.*

84 **The Shadows.** ★ ★ $$$ Once a German restaurant with a rustic atmosphere, it has undergone a radical transformation and is now French with an all new look. The main dining room is light and airy, with shades of pink, expanded by mirrored walls which enhance the fabulous view. The contemporary French menu is definitely an improvement from the prior uninspired offerings. You will find some French classics as well as more innovative dishes. Their *fillet de rouget en habit vert* (redfish with julienne of vegetables, wrapped in lettuce leaves and steamed and served in a light wine sauce) deserves honorable mention. The desserts are made on the premises and include homemade ice creams and sorbets. This is definitely the place for a romantic dinner for two. *Reservations. Open daily 5-10PM. 1349 Montgomery St. 982-5536*

85 **Levi Strauss Building.** (1982, HOK) An enormous 3 building development for the Levi Strauss Company, the vast scale has been reduced by stepping back the profiles of the buildings so that they blend into the shape of Telegraph Hill behind. All the buildings are clad in brick tiles that match the adjoining Ice House. Not quite as successful is the integration of the glazed atrium space at the entrance facing the plaza. Landscaping by **Lawrence Halprin.** *Sansome and Battery Sts. at Filbert.*

86 **Filbert Steps.** Leading down the east side of Telegraph Hill, the terrain is so steep that Filbert Street becomes Filbert Steps—a series of precariously perched platforms and walkways with some of the city's oldest and most varied housing. A beautifully landscaped walkway climbs down the hill and gives access to the lanes on either side—Darrell Place, Napier Lane, Alta Street. **228 Filbert Steps,** built in the 1870s, is a fine example of **Carpenter's** Gothic style (private residence)

87 **Julius Castle.** ★ $$$/$$$$ New ownership has revitalized this long-established restaurant. Noteworthy alone for its eccentric architecture and fabulous view of the Bay, it has always been favored by out-of-towners. But now there is an a la carte menu featuring delicious, well-presented French and northern Italian dishes, with particular attention to pastas, seafood and veal. There is an extensive wine list and the service is excellent. Valet parking—a necessity as Telegraph Hill never seems to have parking spaces. *Open M-F 11:30AM-4PM, 5:30-9:30PM; Sa & Su 5:30-9:30PM. 1541 Montgomery St. 362-3042*

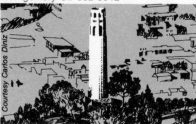

Courtesy Carlos Diniz

88 **Coit Memorial Tower.** (1934, Arthur Brown, Jr.) Located at the top of Telegrah Hill , the tower marks the terminus of where the first West Coast telegraph sent

messages notifying the arrival of ships from the Pacific. Messages were then signaled downtown by a semaphore tower. **Lillie Hitchcock Coit,** who as a girl of 15 had been the mascot of the crack firefighter company Knickerbocker #5, left funds to the city in 1929 to be used to beautify it. Coit Tower was erected as well as a statue in Washington Square dedicated to the volunteer firemen of the 1850s and 60s. Inside are outstanding murals depicting the contemporary labor scene of the 1930s. Take the elevator to the top for a spectacular view of the city and Bay. (Small fee.) *Telegraph Hill Blvd. Access via Stockton and Lombard Sts. No. 39 bus from Washington Sq.*

89 **Telegraph Hill School.** (1981) Contextual series of buildings by **Esherick, Homsey, Dodge and Davis.** *Filbert St.*

FOG CITY DINER

90 **Fog City Diner.** ★ ★ ★ $$/$$$ The look is quintessentially diner, but has an even sleeker image with its polished stainless steel, chrome and neon. However, the menu makes scant reference to traditional diner fare. The cuisine is more reminiscent of the current eclectic California cuisine. There's something for everyone here: Delta catfish with hush puppies, stuffed pasilla peppers grilled with avocado salsa, a gourmet chili made with black beans and sirloin, crab cakes, and on a slightly more prosaic note, you can order a griddled pastrami and jack, or a chili dog. Chef **Steve Pappas** can even offer homemade ketchup, pickles and mustard. Fog City was opened by the same restaurateurs who own the much admired **Mustard Grill** in Napa Valley, and it seems to be sharing the same success. *Reservations well in advance. Open M-Th 11:30AM-2:30PM, 5-10:30PM; F & Sa 5-10:30PM; Su 11:30AM-2:30PM, 5-10:30PM. Open seating only on Su from 2:30-4:30PM and F & Sa 10:30PM-midnight. 1300 Battery St. 982-2000*

91 **Roundhouse Square.** The original concrete-framed engine shed for the San Francisco Belt Railroad has been converted into offices (1985, DMJM). The building's form responds to the radiating train track layout. A few memories of the old rail are still here, including the tracks and a water pump on the Embarcadero side. *Sansome St. at Embarcadero and Lombard Sts.*

ISLANDS

92 **Islands.** The rocky islands in San Francisco Bay are home to a once-notorious prison, naval training stations and wildlife refuges teeming with sea lions and birds. Tours of Alcatraz, Angel and Treasure Island can be arranged, or you can cruise by on one of the many ferries that dock at Fisherman's Wharf.

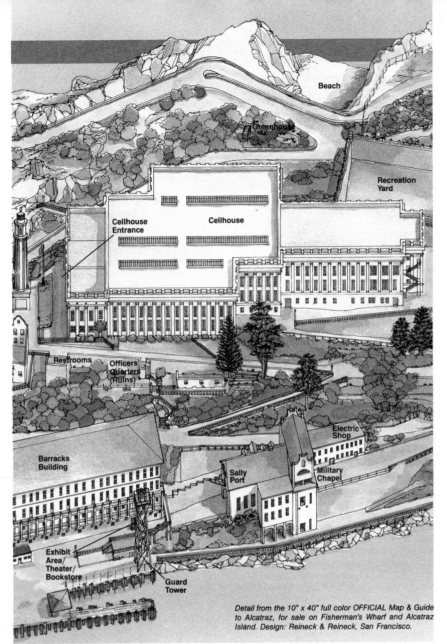

Beach

Greenhouse

Recreation Yard

Cellhouse Entrance

Cellhouse

Restrooms

Officers Quarters (Ruins)

Electric Shop

Barracks Building

Sally Port

Military Chapel

Exhibit Area/ Theater/ Bookstore

Guard Tower

Detail from the 10" x 40" full color OFFICIAL Map & Guide to Alcatraz, for sale on Fisherman's Wharf and Alcatraz Island. Design: Reineck & Reineck, San Francisco.

Alcatraz Island. When **Lt. Juan Manuel de Ayala** discovered the island in 1775, he named it *Isla de los Alcatraces* (Island of the Pelicans) after the colony of pelicans roosting here. The first lighthouse in the Bay was installed here in 1854. The island's strategic and isolated position made it ideal for use as a defensive and disciplinary installation. The first cell block was built by the U.S. Army, and from that time Alacatraz was fated to be a prison facility. During the Civil War (1861-1865), the Island became a military prison; Indians who proved troublesome to white settlers in Arizona were detained here in the 1870s; military prisoners were confined here during the Spanish-American war; after the 1906 fire-quake, prisoners from the crumbled San Francisco jails were temporarily locked up in the island's cells; during World War I conscientious objectors were incarcerated and tortured here. In 1934 it became a Federal maximum security prison for civilians. The fame of *The Rock* spread as it became home to such notorious criminals as **Al Capone, Machine Gun Kelley** and **Robert Stroud,** the **Birdman of Alcatraz,** who spent 40 years in solitary confinement. There is no evidence that any of the many attempted escapes were successful. The prison was closed in 1963. The so-called Indian Occupation from 1964 to 1971 was a peaceful attempt by about 80 American Indians to claim the island for their people. Today Alcatraz is part of the **Golden Gate National Recreation Area** and one-hour guided tours by park rangers are given daily. Dress warmly, as the bay breezes can be chilly. Wear sturdy shoes because the tour covers some rugged and steep paths. The tour takes 2 hours in all, from departure in San Francisco to return. *Admission charge. Reservations. Ferries depart every 45 minutes, 9AM-3PM. Red and White Fleet. Pier 41, at the foot of Powell St. at Fisherman's Wharf. 546-2805*

I was a fool to try it, I'm shot to hell. **Arthur Doc Barker** as he lay dying after he tried to escape from Alcatraz in 1939.

Angel Island. This square mile of rocky land rising to a summit of 781 feet is the largest island in the Bay. It was also the first place **Lt. Juan Manuel de Ayala** anchored in 1775 during the first expedition to sail through the Golden Gate. The island served for many years as a government defense base and detention center. In 1863 it was occupied by the Army and used as a fortification. It then served as a prison camp for American Indians in the 1870s; a Quarantine and Immigration Station in the 1890s; and an internment camp during World War II for Italian and German prisoners of war. It is now a state park and wildlife refuge maintained by the National Park Service and is a fine day's outing for hiking, bike riding or enjoying the island's sandy beaches. Trails meander along rugged slopes on a 5 mile route that encircles the island. There is also a 1 hour narrated tour of the island, plus picnic and barbecue facilities, a snack bar and restrooms. *From July 1-Sept 10 there are elephant train tours in open air coaches that include old fortifications of the East and West Garrisons. Call for schedule, 435-1915. Park open daily 8AM-sunset. Ferries run daily during summer, weekends only during winter. The island is accessible by 2 routes: Harbor Carriers runs ferries from San Francisco. Call for schedule and rates, 546-2805 or 546-2815. The Angel Island State Ferry runs from Tiburon. For information call 435-2131*

Treasure Island. Man-made island created to serve as the site of the 1939 Golden Gate International Exposition. After the awe-inspiring effort to simultaneously construct the 2 largest bridges in the world (Golden Gate and Bay bridges, completed within a few months of each other), it seemed fitting to celebrate by building an artificial 400-acre island for the fair. Later it was to become the San Francisco Airport. Of course it was found to be too small and much too close to the bridge. Instead, the Navy acquired the island as a base, so most of it is off limits, but a trip is worthwhile just for the spectacular view of San Francisco and both bridges. *To reach the island, take the Bay Bridge to the Treasure Island exit or take an AC Transit bus.*

On Treasure Island is:

Treasure Island Navy/Marine/Coast Guard Museum. Located in Building One inside the main gate, the Museum has exhibits on the history of these 3 branches of the military in the Pacific arena. There is an interesting exhibit on the Golden Gate International Exposition of 1939-40 that was held on the island. *Admission free. Open daily 10AM-3:30PM. Closed on legal holidays. Access from the Bay Bridge. 765-6182*

Yerba Buena Island. This island tunnels through the Bay Bridge and connects and anchors the cantilever and suspension sections of the bridge. Known in early days as *Wood Island* to seafarers, it was officially named Yerba Buena (good herb) after wild mint which grew there. For years goats were kept on the island, so it was also called *Goat Island*. Historically, Indians paddled across the water in barges made of bundles of reeds and used the island as a fishing station. Re-

mains of a village and cremation pits have been dug up, along with buried contraband from smugglers, remains of a shipwrecked Spanish galleon, and graves of soldiers, pioneers, and goatherds. Today, the island is a Coast Guard reservation and Naval Training Station. It is connected to Treasure Island by a 900-foot causeway.

The Farallones. This chain of craggy islands is located 32 miles from Point Lobos. In 1872 the islands were incorporated into the City and County of San Francisco. The name *Farallones* derives from the Spanish expression for small, rocky, pointed islands. Inhospitable to man, the islands are closed to the public. Crowds of sea lions surround the precipitous cliffs, which are home to thousands of birds. The islands were declared a bird sanctuary in 1909. There is a Coast Guard station on the South Farallon (the island most visible from San Francisco's shores). A lighthouse and foghorn warn ships to stay away from the treacherous rocks. From the 1850s until 1968, a handful of stoic families lived on the South Farallon. Lighthouse keepers had to climb a steep, zigzag path 320 feet up to the light, sometimes crawling on their hands and knees during the onslaught of a gale or storm. Today the lighthouse is automated. To most San Franciscans, the reality of the Farallones is meteorological, demonstrated by the popular expression here, *On a clear day you can see the Farallones.* They are best seen from Ocean Beach or from Point Reyes in Marin.

Cruises around the Bay

Blue and Gold Fleet. One hour tours of the Bay and the Islands. Refreshments are served on board. *Departures from Pier 39, West Marina. 546-2810*

Gold Coast Cruises leave from *Pier 45, Fisherman's Wharf.* There is a snack bar on board. *Daily departures May 31-October 1. Reasonable rates. 775-9108*

Red and White Fleet. Leaves *Pier 41 at Fisherman's Wharf.* A 2½-hour bay cruise, the *Barbecue Cruise,* includes full service bar, entertainment and dancing, plus a barbecue dinner. *546-2805*

Sailboat Rides

Charter by the hour or day. Sailing and windsurfing lessons are available as well. *Advance reservations advisable. Dock L, east side of Pier 39. 421-8353*

Sailtours Inc. Charter either bareboat or skippered boats. They carry maximum 6 people. *Rent by day or evening. Reserve in advance. Phone or write for rates. Three-hour to week-long cruises are available. K Dock, Pier 39. 986-2590*

Aerial Tour

Golden Gate Air Tours. Aerial views of the San Francisco skyline, Golden Gate Bridge and Alcatraz. *551-6798*

Commodore Helicopters. *Pier 43, Fisherman's Wharf. 332-4482*

Whale Watching

If you visit the Bay Area between January and April, you can arrange a glimpse of the Pacific Ocean's famous **gray whales**. Each winter, the 30-ton giants make a 6,000 mile pilgrimage from their feeding grounds in Bering Straits to their breeding grounds in Baja California. Since becoming protected by the Endangered Species Act of 1973, the California whale population has shot up from 1,800 to 18,000. The following agencies offer whale watching trips:

Blue and Gold Fleet. Expeditions from San Francisco Bay to Point Reyes, in conjunction with the Oceanic Society. Leaves from the West Marina at Pier 39. *441-1106.*

Point Reyes Lighthouse. Rangers at Point Reyes National Seashore, 35 miles northwest of San Francisco, guide you down 300-steps to the lighthouse and help you spot the whales. *663-1092.*

Whale Center of Oakland. 2 ½ hour cruises from Pillar Point at Half Moon Bay and one hour aerial tours lifting off from Oakland International Airport. *654-6621.*

Captain Ron's Pacific Charters. *285-2000.*

Scale comparison of gray whale, African elephant and man courtesy of the Whale Center, Oakland.

Ketchikan Sportfishing. *981-6269.*

Lucky Lady Fishing. *332-4681.*

Ocean Voyages Inc. *332-4681.*

San Francisco Yacht Charters. *459-1450.*

Wacky Jacky Sportfishing. *586-9800.*

They have opened our eyes to the final limits of power, beauty and grace that life can reach. This contribution is to all the peoples of the earth and not only to whalemeat eaters, food processors and fur and tusk hunters. The marine mammals are a shared and universal good, a common heritage of mankind. **Naturalist Victor Scheffer** on saving the whales.

BESTS

William Stout
Architect/Owner
William Stout Architectural Books

City Lights Bookshop. Basement poetry section. A great paperback book resource. *261 Columbus Av., SF. 362-8193*

Moe's Book. Four floors of books. Great art collection. *2476 Telegraph Av., Berkeley. 849-2087*

Military Fortifications, Marin Headlands. A great place to view San Francisco and read.

Mar Vista Cabins, Anchor Bay. A small series of cabins with cooking facilities, reminiscent of the 1950s. *Five miles above Sea Ranch.*

Furniture of the 20th Century. *Market and Van Ness, SF.*

Zuni Cafe. The outdoor restaurant. *1658 Market, SF. 826-6808*

Coit Tower. Murals on first floor depicting old California.

Oakland Museum. Sculpture court.

Ciao Restaurant. Saturday lunch to review the week's books. It's always quiet. *230 Jackson St. 982-9500*

Cindy Pawlcyn
Chef, Fog City Diner

Tommasos Family Pizzeria on Kearny Street. It's one of those wonderful, downstairs kinds of restaurants. There're always a million people lined up out the door.

Tosca Cafe on Columbus Avenue. It's the best bar in the world and by the Italian Opera.

Iacopi Meats on Grand, which is about the best butcher shop in the city, with everything from proscuitto to homemade torta. It has a lot of personality, and the Italian butcher calls everyone *daughter.*

Gourmet Guides on Stockton, which is a bookstore with travel books and antique, new and professional cookbooks.

San Francisco looked like an island, with the white houses, a little like Tunis seen from the sea, with a whiff of the Mediterranean and not at all like a piece of America. But that was an illusion. It was in every sense the place where the West came to an end, the place where the frontier first got tamed. **Lawrence Ferlinghetti,** American poet (b. 1919)

Joyce Goldstein
Chef, Square One Restaurant

Shopping for Italian pottery at **Sue Fisher King**. *3075 Sacramento St.*

Since everything but my ears is covered in a white coat while I'm working, I like earrings, and my favorite place to shop for them is the **Jerusalem Shoppe**. *531 Castro St.*

Browsing for books at the **Writer's Bookstore** *(2848 Webster)*, **Rook's and Becords** *(2222 Polk)*, and **Black Oak Books** *(Berkeley)*.

Espresso and watching people play billiards at **Cafe Italia**. *708 Vallejo* .

Sunday breakfast at the **New York Bagel Shop** on Geary.

Produce at **San Francisco Real Foods**. It's open on Sundays too. *2140 Polk.*

Cooking equipment or household goods at **Whole Earth Access**. *401 Bayshore Blvd.*

Stopping at the corner of **Fillmore** and **Broadway** every morning to look at the Bay in the most beautiful city in the world.

Sunday Chinese tea lunch at **Tong and Fong**. *1045 Sansome.*

Sunday evening sushi at **Kabuto**. *5116 Geary Blvd.*

Browsing for old wines at **Draper and Esquin**. *655 Davis.*

Shopping for flowers at **Paul's**. *2113 Polk St.*

Bruno Tison
Chef, Ernie's

Kabuto. The warmest Japanese welcome in town. The sushi is the freshest and is artistically executed by owner/sushi master Sachio-san. A terrific spot for a late-night sushi run. *5116 Geary Blvd. 752-5652.*

Tommy Toy's. One of the most tastefully decorated dining rooms in San Francisco—a piece of art. The food is authentic Chinese served with the refinement and style of France. My favorite dish is the beef and scallop soup with bamboo shoots served in a coconut shell *encroute* with French puff pastry. The lobster served with rice vermicelli and ginger is another favorite. *655 Montgomery. 397-4888.*

Donatello. The most refined Italian nouvelle cuisine served in an elegant setting. Giancarlo, the manager, will most certainly take care of you in style. *501 Post St. 441-7182.*

Le Central. The closest thing to a French brassiere/bistro serving tasty but hearty regional country cooking. Have their cassoulet on a cold winter day. *453 Bush St. 391-2233.*

Yuet Lee. The decor and ambience have much to be desired, but the food is worth the visit. Try the fresh clams, prawns or any of the seafood. They don't serve alcohol but will allow you to bring in something from their liquor store next door. *1300 Stockton. 982-6020.*

Max's Diner. Fun food in a fun atmosphere. The nostalgic decor captures the all-American spirit of good old-fashioned home cooking. *Third at Folsom. 546-6297.*

Golden Turtle. An unusual facade on Van Ness Avenue, but once you enter, there is warmth and charm. The food is excellent and typically Vietnamese—refreshing and light—and served by a very pleasant staff. My compliments to the owner, who put his heart into his restaurant. The exotic wall murals were also sculpted by the owner. *2211 Van Ness. 441-4419.*

Masa's. The entrance and dining room are unpretentious, but this is one of the finest French restaurants, where the basics of traditional French cuisine are perfectly respected and honored daily. *648 Bush St. 989-7154.*

Mustard's Grill. A bit out of the way of San Francisco, but my favorite California cuisine is at Mustard's in Napa. The California ingredients and French techniques are at their best. Congratulations to a traditional chef for his beautiful and moderate creations. *7399 St. Helena Hwy., Napa. 709-944-2424.*

Yoshida-Ya. The only *yaki tori* bar in San Francisco. The food is grilled on hibachis and served in an authentic setting with folk art and classic Japanese antiques. Dining at the *yaki tori* bar is a pleasant change of pace from the trendy sushi bar craze. *2909 Webster St. 346-3431.*

Caen and Coffee

For more than 25 years, San Francisco columnist **Herb Caen** has been something between court jester, conscience and *camp* counselor to a city where the only fad that never changes is a love of fads. Caen is the *expert* on the city's finest offerings and most titilating gossip; some feel that to be a true San Franciscan, you must need Caen's column to open your eyes as badly as you need that first cup of coffee.

His columns are an upbeat blend of news, gossip, vignettes and thought-provoking dramas, spiced with random schmaltz and an occasional thorn in the side of those in power—proof that if a picture is worth a thousand words, the opposite can also be true. Caen is a wit and a wordsmith, and is one of the most quoted columnists in *Reader's Digest*.

Caen started writing on his high school newspaper before landing a piece in the *Sacramento Union*. He served as a radio columnist for the *Chronicle* before radio and newspaper parted ways. He wrote his first column on San Francisco on 5 July 1938—and was heartily adopted as a native son from then on.

Nob Hill, formerly, and most aptly, 35 christened the *Hill of Golden Promise,* is perhaps the best known of San Francisco's many hills. The name comes from the word *Nabob,* which could have several meanings: rich man, snob or big shot, or, most likely, knoll or rounded hill. The mansions of the rich are gone now, with the notable exception of James Flood's Edwardian brownstone, but they have been replaced with luxury hotels, a world famous cathedral, a Masonic temple, several exclusive clubs and towering apartment houses.

The generally accepted boundaries of Nob Hill are Bush, Larkin, Pacific and Stockton Streets. As you descend the hill, 3-story apartment buildings take over and rents and incomes drop. Nob Hill is still home to more than 9,000 residents.

In 1865, at the site of the **Fairmont Hotel,** Dr. Arthur Hayne cut a trail up the hill through the chaparral with great effort in order to survey the land and build the first home on the hill for his bride. Within a few years, men of means began a mass exodus from Rincon Hill and South Park and followed Hayne's trail. But even the horses found the going difficult. The advent of the **cable car** in 1873 encouraged the uphill flow of money, fueling the unbridled ostentation of the homes of the rich and *nouveau riche.* Ironically, it would all be swept away in one fiery night 30 years later.

The cable car was actually born on the Hill. **Andrew Halladie,** a partner and a gripman for the line, made the historic test run in 1873 from Clay Street up into the fog at Joice Street.

In a sense, Nob Hill is still the *Hill of Palaces.* Fastidious gentlemen still reach their homes or clubs by cable car. The reckless display is gone–the air is more of subdued gentility. But yes, there is still the ambience of power!

Russian Hill next door is a neighborhood of contradiction, at once costly and bohemian. Studded with sleek, highrise apartments and matching doormen, it is also an area favored by the rich and famous. But there are also the working singles, impoverished writers and art students studying at the nearby **Art Institute** who share apartments, cramming 4 or 5 into 2 bedrooms, the only way to afford the high rent.

Within walking distance of downtown, the Financial District and North Beach, Russian Hill is full of picturesque cul-de-sacs, bay views, green, wooded open space and of course that wiggly part of **Lombard Street,** known as the crookedest street in the world. Technically, this Hill extends from Pacific to Bay Streets and from Polk to Mason, but its real heart is contained in the land bordered by Broadway, Chestnut, Larkin and Taylor Streets.

Novelist Herbert Gold calls Russian Hill *a metropolitan village,* and it is indeed the kind of place where customers and shop owners are on a first-name basis, chatting cosily or exchanging recipes.

The first house in the area was built by an Indian fighter named **William Penn Humphries.** Five years later (1857), the Fusier home, one of 2 octagonal houses left in San Francisco, was erected, beginning a tradition that saw some of the most architecturally interesting homes in the city being constructed in this neighborhood.

During the 1890's, the Intellectuals claimed the hill for their own, and people like **Ambrose Bierce, George Sterling, Joaquin Miller, Frank Norris** and **Maynard Dixon** moved in. **Ina Coolbrith,** California's first Poet Laureate, presided over a literary salon visited by **Mark Twain** and **Bret Harte.** The hill is still a favorite dwelling place of writers, well-known and otherwise.

1 Galaxy Theater. (1984, Kaplan/ McLaughlin/Diaz) One of the first movie house complexes to be built in the city in a generation, this building houses 3 theaters. The solid boxes housing each theater meet at a transparent entrance lobby created by a grid of stepping forms. Best seen at dusk when the neon signs glow rainbow colors. *Van Ness Av. at Sutter.*

2 Mayes. ★★$/$$ Opened in 1867, Mayes has been serving its fine seafoods in San Francisco for the past 120 years. The extensive menu offers steaks, chops, poultry and pasta. However, the seafood here remains the real reason for its consistent popularity; the fish entries are first-rate, and Mayes pays special attention to its many oyster dishes. *Open daily 11AM-11PM. 1233 Polk St. 474-7674*

3 Hotel Bedford. *Moderate.* Dating from the 1930s, this 17-story, 144-room inn has been completely transformed. Now there is a stunning lobby, a friendly dining room and intimate bedrooms with the feeling of a private home. It is located 3 blocks from Union Square and close to galleries, theaters and transportation. It is under the same creative management as the Vintage Court, and it is one of the best buys in San Francisco. *761 Post St. 673-6040; 800-227-5642; in CA 800-652-1889*

Within the hotel is:

Cafe Bedford. ★$$ An intimate, California-style bistro with some excellent specialties, including veal and fish dishes and a special warm duck salad. *Open daily 7-10AM, Tu-Sa 6-10PM. 928-8361*

4 Beresford Arms. *Moderate.* One of the finest small hotels in the theater district, with a friendly atmosphere and personal service. There is an unusually attractive lobby for entertaining guests. *701 Post St. 673-2600*

5 York Hotel. *Moderate.* Originally called the Glen Royalle in 1922, this hotel is one of the many small hostelries that has been powdered, painted up and polished, resulting in attractive rooms at moderate prices. It is at a great location, not far from anywhere you would probably want to go. The York also offers trendy features such as chauffeured limousine service. *940 Sutter St. In CA 800-327-3608; outside CA 800-227-3608*

Within the Hotel is:

The Plush Room. $$/$$$ More than aptly named, this unique cabaret features entertainers set in a luxurious, uncrowded space. Note the spectacular stained-glass ceiling. The room books new faces as well as the more familiar. **Eartha Kitt, Carmen McCrae** and **Charles Pierce** are just a few of the singer/entertainers who have appeared here. *Reservations. Admission charge. 2 drink minimum. Minors are not admitted. Shows Th-Sa 8 & 10PM; Tu-W 8PM; Su 7 & 9PM. 940 Sutter St. in Hotel York. 885-6800*

6 Cafe Mozart. ★★$$/$$$ An interesting, tiny little place tucked beneath Nob Hill that offers quite an acceptable alternative to the more expensive French food up the hill. The menu changes, but the food is always well-prepared and reasonably priced. *French. Reservations. Open daily for dinner. 708 Bush St. 391-8480*

7 Stanford Court Hotel. *Deluxe.* America's top executives rank the Stanford Court as their favorite hotel in San Francisco—and it's easy to see why. This sophisticated palace sets the standard of luxury, blending the atmosphere of a beautiful home, unique decor and the services of a European-style hotel. It was built on the site of railroad magnate **Leland Stanford's** mansion, later the location of a 1912 apartment building which in turn was gutted in order to create the hotel within the shell. The only thing remaining from the Stanford days is a 30-foot wall surrounding the property. However, the design borrows something from the original house. The Stanfords had a circular vestibule illuminated from an amber glass dome 3 stories above. A similar effect has been achieved through the lofty stained glass canopy over the hotel's central courtyard and fountain, which visually lead into a lobby, giving the definite feeling of a fine private club. Tea and cocktails are served here. The 402 rooms and suites have individually controlled air-conditioning, marble baths with dressing rooms, color TV well hidden in armoires and heated towel racks. Many have canopied beds. Indoor valet parking. Multilingual staff. *905 California St. 989-3500. In CA (800) 622-0957; outside CA (800) 227-4736*

Within the hotel are:

Cafe Potpourri. ★$$ An elegant place for excellent breakfasts or elaborately concocted French pastries in the afternoon. The Eggs Benedict is done perfectly, and you can always have a bowl of the freshest California fruits. *American. Open daily 6:30AM-2:30PM. 989-3500*

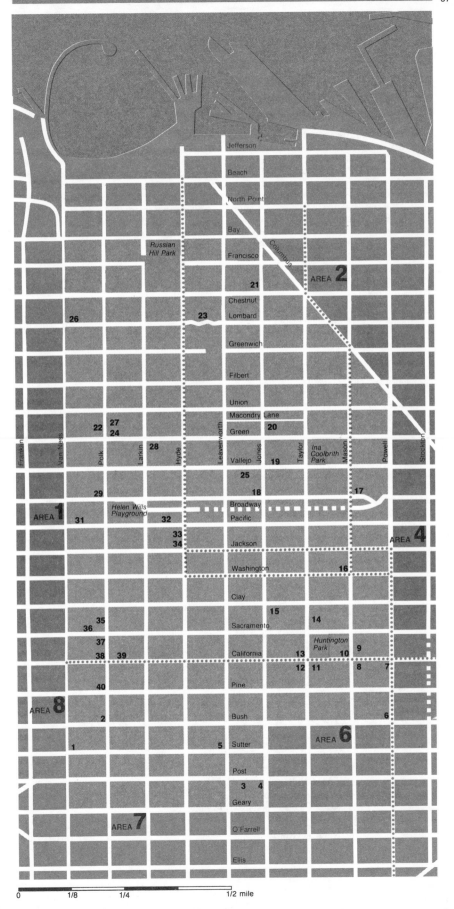

Fournou's Ovens. ★★$$$ An elegant French restaurant with attentive service and some of the best French food you can get in a hotel restaurant. There's an extensive walk-in wine cellar off the dining room. *Open for dinner 5:30-11PM. 989-3500*

8 **Mark Hopkins Hotel.** *Deluxe.* Ever since its opening in 1927, the Mark has been well regarded internationally. It was host to officials attending the first historic meetings during the formation of the U.N. and was a vacation site for Presidents Hoover and Eisenhower and countless other celebrities. In 1939, the **Top of the Mark** opened and became the foremost skyroom cocktail lounge anywhere, with its 360 degree view of the Bay and hills. Designed by **Timothy Pflueger**, it is one of the first examples of the now commonplace hotel feature. Over the years, the famous **Peacock Court** and **Room of the Dons** have been chosen for San Francisco's society weddings, debuts and charity parties. *1 Nob Hill. 392-3434*

Within the hotel is:

Vienna Cafe. $$ A smart, prim and proper hotel pastry shop where you can order breakfast all day and evening. Try the *Danish Ableskivvers*, which are little turnovers stuffed with apples. *Open daily 6:30AM-3PM. 392-3434*

9 **Fairmont Hotel.** *Deluxe.* The Fairmont was built on the property of **James (Bonanza Jim) Fair,** and the foundations of the palace he had planned to build were later incorporated into the hotel. **Hermann Oeirichs**, the husband of one of Senator Fair's daughters, planned and began construction of the hotel, to the consternation of the city fathers who could not understand placing any hotel on Nob Hill so far from the center of the city. New owners took over before the building was complete, hoping to

open it in 1906. Although the Fairmont's frame withstood the earthquake, fire ate up the interior, so work had to begin all over again. When the Senator's daughter offered to take the property back, the disheartened owners jumped at the chance. On 18 April 1907, Mrs. Oeirichs kicked off the opening of the hotel with a magnificent banquet symbolizing the rebirth of the city one year after the earthquake.

Today, with the addition of a 22-story tower, this grand hotel has 600 rooms and suites, 6 restaurants, 6 lounges (including the **Fairmont Crown,** the highest public observation point in the city), 2 orchestras for dancing, international supper club talent and an employment roster that is close to a one-to-one ratio with the number of guests. All the extras you would expect from a world class hotel are here—and then some—all in keeping with the philosophy of providing a real home away from home. *950 Mason. 772-5000*

Within the hotel are:

Fairmont Crown. $$/$$$ The buffet may look great, but it suffers from the perils that lots of hotel restaurants share. Unless you are very hungry and feel like American mixed-bag cuisine, walk down California Street to Chinatown. *American. Open daily. 772-5000*

Squire Room. ★$$$/$$$$ An overly decorated hotel dining room with some good French food and lots of pretentious service. The fish and poultry are particularly good, but the red meats and desserts often disappointing. *French. Open daily. 772-5211*

Masons. ★★$$$ A Pacific restaurant with kimono-clad waitresses and American, Californian and Hawaiian influences in the cooking. This is the sort of restaurant that hotels.

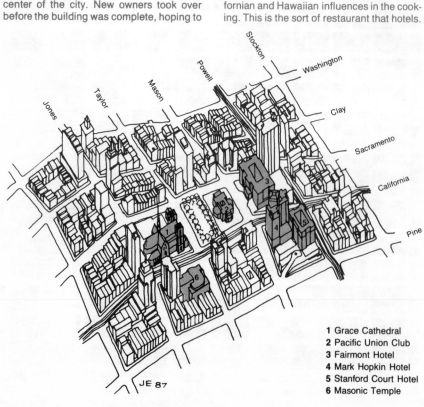

1 Grace Cathedral
2 Pacific Union Club
3 Fairmont Hotel
4 Mark Hopkin Hotel
5 Stanford Court Hotel
6 Masonic Temple

think will appeal to tourists, where the emphasis is on the atmosphere and not on the food. *American. Open daily for dinner. 392-0113*

The Cirque. $$$ Originally opened in 1934, it was one of the first legitimate bars to open in San Francisco after Prohibition. The Cirque was frequented by a colorful crowd, including local writers, artists, politicians and some of San Francisco's elite. The room was designed by society architect **Tim Pflueger** in the art deco style of his time, which perfectly compliments the 9 remarkable circus motif murals that were painted by 3 sister artists **Esther, Helen** and **Margaret Bruton.** The Cirque has been painstakingly restored and is intimate, elegant and comfortable. They offer cocktails, coffee, California wines and champagnes and an unusual-to-find afternoon tea, complete with assorted tea sandwiches, scones and other pastries. *Open M-F 3PM-12:30AM for cocktails; 3-6PM for afternoon tea. 772-5000*

Venetian Room. ★ ★ $$$$ You just may leave your heart in San Francisco after an evening of nostalgic entertainment at the Fairmont's unique supper club which features top-notch headliners. The Venetian Room also offers dining and dancing to a 10-piece orchestra. Regulars include **Tony Bennett,** who first sang about leaving his heart in San Francisco here, **Ella Fitzgerald** and **Sarah Vaughan.** The Room seats 400 to 500 for twice-nightly shows. Its rectangular shape and raised side sections provide an intimate vantage point for almost every table. *Reservations. Admission charge for the show. Jackets for men preferred. Dinner served before the first show only, beginning at 7:30pm. You can skip dinner if you want and arrive at 9PM when the dancing begins. First show 9:30PM. Dancing from 11 to 11:30PM, when the second show begins. 772-5163.*

...it [the Fairmont] is still the grandest tiger in the jungle...   **Margo Patterson Doss**

10 **Pacific Union Club.** (1886) Remodelled by **Willis Polk** in 1908-10 after the quake/fire, this Italianate-Baroque brownstone was originally built for **James C. Flood,** one of the railroad kings. He is reputed to have spent $1,500,000 on the house alone, an enormous sum for its time. Polk added the attic story and the entrance tower, which somewhat mar the original classical lines. *Private. 1000 California at Mason. 775-1234*

11 **Huntington Hotel.** *Expensive to Deluxe.* Small, elegant, impeccably groomed and located on the peak of Nob Hill. It is the kind of place with such a loyal following that advertising is unnecessary, partly due to the permanency of its staff, which does much to preserve the Huntington brand of personal hospitality. No 2 rooms are alike: they all look like they might well belong in a private residence and have a view of either the city or the Bay. Suites are equipped with a complete kitchen or wet bar. In all the furnishings, contemporary or antique, there is the unmistakable look of quality. *1075 California St. 474-5400*

Within the hotel are:

The Big Four. ★ ★ $$ Named in tribute to the 4 railroad magnates of San Francisco, Huntington, Crocker, Hopkins and Stanford, the decor brilliantly evokes the period of the late 1800's at its best, with such touches as etched beveled glass panels and polished woods. The restaurant features a combination of continental and *nouvelle* California cuisine, highlighting seafood and wild game dishes. *Open M-F 7-9:30AM, 11:30AM-3PM, 5:30-11PM; Sa & Su 7-11AM, 11:30AM-3PM, 5:30-11PM. 474-5400*

L'Etoile. ★ $$$$ This plush French restaurant is the place to hobnob with San Francisco's elite. The bar is fine and some of the food is excellent, though other dishes will disappoint you. Quiz your waiter carefully on what is fresh and what is special that day. *French. Open for dinner. Closed Su. 771-1529*

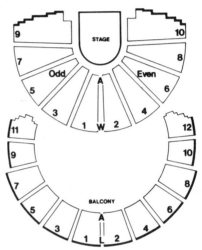

12 **Masonic Temple Auditorium.** Not one of the best spaces in town, the auditorium features orchestras, dance groups and lectures. It is large (3,165 seats), but the sightlines are terrible. *Thrust stage. 1111 California St. 776-4917*

13 **Grace Cathedral.** (1928) Episcopal Church of Lewis P. Hobart. This fine Neo-Gothic cathedral, modelled after Notre-Dame in Paris, took 53 years to build and was finally consecrated in 1965. Notice the beautiful rose window, completed by **Gabriel Loire** in Chartres. There is also a magnificent organ and a not-to-be-missed boys' choir. *1051 Taylor St. 776-6611*

14 **Nob Hill Cafe.** ★ $$/$$$ A delightful little place with just a couple of tables and a lunch counter, but it is beautifully decorated and is really quite elegant in its own way. The food is French and the chef Japanese, a favorite combination these days. Everything that comes out of the kitchen is quite good. *French. Open Tu-Sa 5:30-10PM. 1152 Taylor St. 776-6915*

15 **Le Club.** ★ ★ ★ $$$$ An elegant, expensive French restaurant that takes its food and proper service seriously. It has been outdone in recent years by the food at some of the more interesting, newer French eateries, but you will enjoy it if you want atmosphere—and if you are on an expense account. *French. Open M-Sa 5:30PM-midnight. 1250 Jones St. 771-5400*

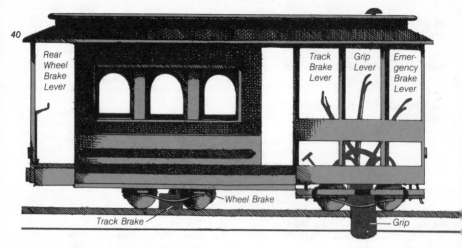

Rear Wheel Brake Lever

Track Brake Lever

Grip Lever

Emergency Brake Lever

Wheel Brake

Track Brake

Grip

CABLE CARS

San Francisco's beloved cable car system made its maiden voyage on 1 August 1873. With its Scottish inventor, **Andrew Hallidie**, at the grip, the car successfully tackled five hilly blocks along Clay Street to Portsmouth Square.

Hallidie, a mine cable designer during the Gold Rush days, was moved to invent the system after witnessing an unfortunate accident on a steep hill: a horsedrawn wagon had faltered and rolled backward, dragging the helpless horses behind. The new system was safer, and it opened up new hillside areas previously thought unusable for home building.

Just before the San Francisco earthquake in 1906, cable cars had reached their peak, with 600 cars traveling a 110 mile route. But the system sustained heavy damage during the quake and fire, and many lines were not rebuilt. Electric trolleys took over some of the lines. The number of cable cars dwindled over the next 50 years. But in 1955, the city voted to preserve and protect the famed hill-climbers and in 1964, they became the U.S.'s first moving National Historic Landmark.

In 1984, and at a cost of more than $60 million, the system emerged after two years of head to toe renovation. Old track and cable vaults were pulled up and replaced. For extra strength, deeper grooved rails and more flexible curves were installed. The track was also realigned or moved to avoid interfering with automobiles, and the pulleys and depression beams that guide each cable were replaced. The historic Washington-Mason car barn was completely renovated and its traditional appearance was preserved. The cars themselves were given a shining coat of maroon, blue and gold paint, as well as new brakes, seats and wheels.

Today there are 3 lines: the **Powell-Mason Line,** the **Powell-Hyde Line,** which is said to offer the most exciting ride, and the **California Line.** There are 37 cars in all, with 26 used at peak times. An average of 13 million passengers travel on the 17 miles of track in a year, which is about 35,616 a day.

Each 6 ton car attaches itself to a cable beneath the street, moving along at a steady 9 m.p.h. by the turning of 14 foot wheels located in barns. A *gripsman* starts and stops the car by mechanically gripping the cable to go forward and by releasing it to stop. The gripsman is able to modify the grip so that the transition is smooth. Tension can be adjusted if necessary to keep the cable from slipping.

Facts and Figures

Cable Car Barn Motors: 4

Horse Power per motor: 510

Sheaves (winder wheels): 8

Cables: 4 (California, Powell, Hyde and Mason)

Terminals: 5

Route Miles: 4.4 (approximate)

Diameter of Cable: 1 5/16 inches

Gauge of Track: 3 feet 6 inches

Maximum Scheduled Cars: 26

Total Cable Length All Lines: 56,600 feet

Total Track Length All Lines: 45,954 feet

Average Cable Life: 110-300 days

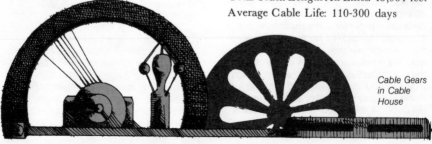

Cable Gears in Cable House

16 **Cable Car Museum.** This is the winding house for the underground cables that control the cars. The building, known as the **Cable Car Barn,** was constructed in 1887, then rebuilt after it was badly damaged in the 1906 quake. When the cable car system was renovated in 1982-84, the barn was reinforced, but the exterior was left alone. The museum now has an underground viewing room where you can watch the cables work. Photographs and memorabilia are also on display, including 3 vintage cable cars and scale models of all the cars ever used. *Admission free. Open daily 10AM-6PM April through October and 10AM-5PM November through March. Washington and Mason Sts. 474-1887*

Gypsy

Lifts **A** *cable into* **B** *grip prior to fully gripping the moving cable*

moving cable

17 **Alfred's.** ★ $$$/$$$$ One of the best steaks in town, served in an old-fashioned steakhouse atmosphere. This is one of the last places left where you get prime beef exclusively. Bring a huge appetite and order the porterhouse rare. If you are really starved, start with their famous antipasto. *American. Open daily 5:30PM-midnight. 886 Broadway. 781-7058*

18 **Allegro Ristorante Italiano.** ★ ★ ★ $/$$ Nestled on Russian Hill, this new restaurant has an intimate dining room painted in shades of mauve, with closely arranged tables in pink. At first glance, the menu doesn't seem that unusual, but how the food is prepared is different. Italian-born owner **Angelo Quaranta** prepares the food himself in authentic, homemade Italian style. Everything is fresh and cooked to order. Specialties include *Bocconcino Allegro,* an appetizer made of roasted bell pepper, grilled eggplant and zucchini and small meatballs; *Penne Arrabiata,* which means *angry pasta,* made of a spicy sauce of olive oil, garlic, tomato and red pepper; *Pollo Al Mattone,* which is a sumptuous marinated half-chicken grilled under a brick. *Scotta Diti (burn your fingers)* is a delicious plate of sliced rack of lamb grilled Romano-style, and *Gamberi Allegro* is prawns cooked in butter and garlic, them arranged on imported Italian raddicchio leaves. Allegro also offers an affordable wine list, with particular attention paid to California Cabernets and Chardonnays. The Italian wine selection is more diverse, but not dominating. *Open daily 5-10PM. 1701 Jones St. 928-4002*

19 **1000 Block of Vallejo Street.** Houses and apartments by **Willis Polk.** One of the city's most attractive residential neighborhoods, it consists of 3 narrow residential streets—Vallejo Street, approached by ramps (designed by Polk) from Jones Street, Russian Hill Place and Florence Street. Polk built 4 Mediterranean-style villas between 1915 and 1916, and another architect, **Charles F. Whittlesey**, did the 3 to the south on Vallejo Street. *Private residences. Vallejo St. at Jones.*

20 **Macondray Lane.** A 2-block pedestrian street on the steep north face of Russian Hill. The condominiums by **Bobbie Sue Hood** successfully fit into the traditional San Francisco bay-windowed residential style. *Between Union and Green Sts. from Leavenworth to Taylor Sts.*

21 **San Francisco Art Institute.** Established in 1871, this is the oldest art school in the West. The Institute has played a central role in the development of contemporary art in the Bay Area. It contains 4 art galleries which are open to the public. Student work is displayed in the **Diego Rivera Gallery.** The **Emmanuel Walter Gallery** and the **Atholl McBean Gallery,** which share a single entrance, show work by professional artists. The **Still Lights Gallery** adjacent to the photography studios has photographic exhibitions. The extension to the Institute (Paffard, Keatings, Clay) is a rare example of *Le Corbusian Beton Brut* style in California. It contains lecture theaters, studios, workshops and exhibition spaces and has been designed with great skill and verve, equal to the Carpeters Art Center in Cambridge, Massachusetts. *Open Tu-Sa 10AM-5PM during the school year. 800 Chestnut St. 771-7020*

22 **Casablanca.** ★ $$ North of the nighttime hubbub on Polk Street, this comfortable, international restaurant offers North African/French-influenced cuisine with some tasty alternatives from farther afield thrown in: Norwegian graviox, American gulf prawns, peppered NY steak. In the Mediterranean mold are the polished hardwood floor, oriental rugs, ceiling fans and Moroccan carvings that surround a small island bar. Pre-theater seating at 6:30PM offers a complete dinner at a la carte prices, as does the late supper, served from 10PM. *Continental. Open M-Sa 6-10:30PM. 2323 Polk St. 441-2244*

Large diameter sheave pulley on a Let-Go curve. Cable Car "lets go" of the cable, coasts around the curve. and "takes up" rope at the other side.

23 **Lombard Street.** Nicknamed the crookedest street in the world, Lombard was designed in the mid-1920's to respond to the extreme steepness of the slope. Faced with brick pavers and carefully landscaped with flowers, shrubs and hedges, it is a fine example of the art of integrating road engineering into the urban fabric. *Lombard between Hyde and Leavenworth Sts.*

24 **Camargue.** ★ ★ $$ *Soothing* is the ambience of this casual, bright and airy restaurant. It's also one of the best buys in town, with a *prix-fixe* dinner, selected from items of the menu of creative French bistro-style cooking. The decor features Country French porcelain animals, blond woods and old copper. The kitchen turns out dishes with mussels, snails, pâtés and sausages, good fresh fish and exceptional hors d'oeuvres. Daily specials may include *minceur* dishes made without butter or cream, roasted chicken with walnut goat cheese and butter sauce, grilled calves liver in horseradish and port wine, and an especially flavorful roast prime rib, boned and grilled. The desserts are exquisite and the wine list is interesting and fairly priced. *Reservations. Open Tu-Th & Su 5:30-10:30PM, F & Sa 5:30-11PM. 2316 Polk St. 776-5577*

Alternative Curves

Twin Peaks. 12 curves in 9,000 feet. Drive up the hill at the intersection of Clarendon Avenue and Twin Peaks Boulevard, then wind down to Portola Drive. The view, 910 feet above sea level, is spectacular.

O'Shaughnessy and Teresita Boulevards. 20 curves in 12,000 feet. Begin at the intersection of Portola Drive and O'Shaughnessy Boulevard, heading southeast. Arrows shaped liked *C's* warn you of the curves. Turn right on Brompton Avenue and again on Joost Avenue. Then turn right on Foerster Street for 2 blocks and again at Teresita Boulevard. The 9-curve block is lined with charming, colorful houses.

Vermont Street. These 6 curves in 400 feet between 20th and 22nd streets in Potrero Hill are even tighter than Lombard's 8, prompting debate over the real *crookedest street in the world.*

Telegraph Hill. 4 curves—and traffic jams—in 2,400 feet leading to Coit Tower.

Courtesy Dan Solomon/Paulette Taggert

25 **Glover Street Duplex.** (1982) One of the **Dan Solomon-Paulette Taggert** team's beautifully designed San Francisco houses, this consists of 2 units interlocked one above the other on its narrow 25-foot lot width. The front facade is an interesting mixture of traditional bay window elements and a classical portico with a severely detailed triangular pediment. The modernist windows and gateway make the design both Rationalist and Contextual. *Private residence.*

26 **The Peacock.** ★ ★ $$/$$$ An elegant Indian restaurant located in a pre-eathquake Victorian mansion. The individual dining rooms are intimate and beautifully appointed. Among the specialties are Tandoori chicken, barbequed prawns and, of course, lamb. Don't miss the frosty Pimm's Cup, which is especially good here. *Open Su-F 11:30AM-2PM, 5:30-10:30PM, Sa 5:30-10:30PM. 2800 Van Ness Av. 928-7001*

27 **Alhambra Twin Theaters.** (1926) A fanciful Moorish movie theater with a romantic Miller and Pflueger silhouette and an elaborate foyer. *Polk between Union and Green Sts. 775-5656*

28 **La Petit Cafe.** ★ $ Stop for a light Sunday breakfast or just a croissant—either way this cafe is a cozy, charming place. Have fresh orange juice and coffee to start your day, or end it. Linger a while over a book from the cafe's bookshelves and a hot cup of cappuccino, or just watch the artsy crowd come and go. *Open M 7:30AM-3PM, Tu-F 7:30AM-10PM, Sa 8:30AM-10PM, Su 8:30AM-3PM. 2164 Larkin. 776-5356*

29 **Pasha.** ★ ★ $$$ A Moroccan restaurant offering some of the best Middle Eastern food around, particularly the hors d'oeuvres *mezza*, which include lovely marinated cold salads. Order the lamb dishes like the shish kebab. *Reservations. Moroccan. Open Tu-Th & Su 6-11PM, Fri & Sa 6PM-12:30AM. 1516 Broadway. 885-4411*

31 **Harris' Restaurant.** ★ $$$ There's no doubt that this steak and prime rib house means business—it prominently displays to passersby on the street a glass refrigerator full of its stock. Harris' was brought to the city by a family that has been in cattle ranching since the last century, and it lives up to its promise to serve top quality prepared-to-order meats. The tasteful decor in its 2 large dining rooms and commodious cocktail lounge is reminiscent of a comfortable, old-money rancher's club. Their restaurant in Central California has been a mecca for beef lovers for years. *American. Open M-F 11:30AM-2PM, 5-11PM; Sa 5-11PM; Su 4-10PM. 2100 Van Ness Av. 673-1888*

32 **Ristorante Milano.** ★ ★ ★ $/$$ A small, stylish restaurant serving delicately prepared Northern Italian dishes at moderate prices. The waiters are polite and knowledgeable; the contemporary decor is an interesting mix of Japanese woodwork and Milanese design in charcoal gray and off-white, resulting in an effect of understated elegance. With plenty of repeat customers and a policy of no reservations, expect a crowd. Once you dine you will know why. *Open Tu-Sa 5:30-10:30PM. 1448 Pacific. 673-2961*

33 **I Fratelli.** ★ ★ $$ An intimate cafe that serves consistently satisfying, fairly priced food. Their pastas are expecially worthwhile. It is usually crowded, so be prepared for a wait. There is, however, a *brother* restaurant down the block at 1896 Hyde St. *Open daily 5-10PM. 1521 Hyde St. 776-8240*

34 **Raw Bar.** ★ ★ $$ This small restaurant is dedicated to exquisitely fresh seafood, and might well be one of the best new versions of such places in San Francisco. The chef specializes in *papillote,* which is seafood cooked in parchment. Raw Bar manages to combine delicious food and exceptional presentation with low prices. If the food alone is not enough, consider the nautical decor, live jazz music and super service. It is on the cable car line, at Hyde and Jackson. *Open daily 11:30AM-3PM, 5-11PM. 1509 Hyde St. 928-9148*

35 **Double Rainbow.** The ice cream is rich and on the chewy side, and some people claim it's the best ice cream in San Francisco. The ultra chocolate certainly is! *1653 Polk St. 775-3220*

36 **Zola.** ★ ★ $$ French country cooking at its best. Zola proves it with an excellent fish stew, fine wines and tantalizing desserts. *French. Open Tu-Su 6-11PM. 1722 Sacramento St. 775-3311*

37 **Szechwan Taste.** ★ $/$$ One of the few places where you can get authentic Szechuan food, and good food at that. Stick with specialties like pork with bean curd and minced squab soup. *Chinese. Open M-Sa 11AM-10PM. 1545 Polk St. 928-1379*

Restaurants/Nightlife red
Hotels blue
Shops/Galleries purple
Parks/Outdoor spaces green
Museums/Architecture/Narrative black

…Nob Hill, the hill of palaces, must certainly be counted the best part of San Francisco. It is there that the millionaires who gathered together, vying with each other in display, look down upon the business wards of the city.

Robert Louis Stevenson

38 **Swan Oyster Depot.** ★ ★ $$ There is nothing but a lunch counter and stools, with no place to even comfortably put your knees. But the cold fish dishes are fantastic and the countermen are the friendliest around. The oysters, clams and salmon are fresh as can be. There is also fish to take out. A favorite fish place among knowledgeable San Franciscans. *American. Lunch only until 5:30PM. Closed Su. 1517 Polk St. 673-1101*

39 **Cordon Bleu.** ★ $ This isn't exactly a place to go for elegant dining, but it is one of the best hole-in-the-wall Vietnamese restaurants. Five-spice chicken, one of the staples of Vietnamese food, is sumptuous here. You can try everything by ordering combination plates. *Vietnamese. Open Tu-Sa 11:30AM-2:30PM, 5-9:45PM; Su 4-9:45pm. 1574 California St. 673-5637*

40 **Polk Street.** Once a neighborhood community, **Polk Gulch,** as it was called, became the focus of the city's gay population. It was transformed into a street of smartly done-up, stylish shops. Now the area appears to be in transition and not as snappy as it was in the '70s. The public spotlight has shifted its glare to the newer gay boulevard, Castro Street. Consequently, Polk Street is more relaxed. **There is a mix of old neighborhood food stores, antique shops and restaurant establishments catering to gays, plus a few more recent specialty shops of no particular distinction.** Health and body shops include **Great Earth Vitamins, The Body Bar, Tanzebar** and the **General Nutrition Store.** For clothes try **Top Sport, Palace Museum, Tibet Shop** and **Leather Forever** and **Roots Natural Footwear** for casual shoes in gorgeous, subtle colors. **Paperback Traffic** and **Waldenbooks** are good book stores and **Gramophone** has records and magazines. **Freed Teller & Freed** is a venerable coffee and tea shop. Polk Street doesn't lack for sweet shops: try **Double Rainbow** for ice cream and **Unknown Jerome's,** with its red neon sign that beams the metaphysical question, *What is a cookie?* **The Flag Store** is heaven for regalia devotees, with flags, flag poles, pennants, emblems and badges.

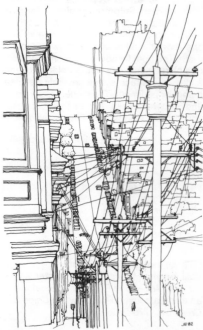

BESTS

Nancy Yow
Concierge, Westin St. Francis

Sipping a cocktail at the **Cliff House** overlooking **Seal Rock.**

Bike riding through **Golden Gate Park.**

Driving down **Highway 1,** the coastal route, to the **Monterey Peninsula.**

Shopping in the **Embarcadero Center.**

Taking a **boat cruise** around the Bay to view the **Golden Gate and Bay Bridges.**

Having breakfast in the cutest little place in Union Square— **Teddy's Cafe.**

Helping a **lost tourist** on the street find their destination.

Strolling through the boutiques in **Sausalito.**

A leisure lunch at the **Caprice Restaurant** in Tiburon.

Leslie Choy
Concierge, Westin St. Francis

What often characterizes San Francisco is the city's continual display of **innovation and tradition.** Whether it be having lunch at the trendy **Fog City Diner** or high tea at the elegant **Compass Rose Room,** San Franciscans and their lifestyles are diverse and exciting!

San Francisco remains a **cable car** and **walking** town. The city is only 7 square miles long, but its rolling hills offer some of the most breathtaking views one can imagine. And where else can one find **Gumps, Tiffany's** and **Cartier** all within a block of each other!

What I really love most about San Francisco is that…thank God…it is not Los Angeles!

Eric Scofield
Chief Concierge, Hotel Californian

The **best view** is in North Beach atop the **Vallejo Street Parking Garage** next to Central Police Station at 766 Vallejo. Take the elevator to the roof and be sure to bring your camera. Best at dusk.

The **best walk** is down the **Filbert Steps to Napier Lane.** Park at Coit Tower and work your way down past the Shadows Restaurant and onto Napier Lane. Continue down to the end of the Steps to the single park bench. Be sure to read the brass plaque mounted on the back of the bench.

The **best swimming** is at any of the **Park and Recreation pools.** They are 100-feet-long, kept at 80 degrees and cost only a dollar per swim.

Mark Belhumeur
Concierge
The Mark Hopkins Intercontinental

The view at night of **San Francisco** from the **Oakland Bay Bridge.**

The view at night of the **Oakland Bay Bridge** from **San Francisco.**

The **Fortune Cookie Factory** on Ross Alley.

The old Chinese men playing mah-jongg at **Portsmouth Square.**

The **Pagoda** of Japantown.

The **cherry blossoms in February.**

The bagels at **The Bagel.**

The **Union Street Victorians.**

Victoria's Secret.

The secret stairway of San Francisco—the **Filbert Steps.**

Union Square flower stands and **Union Square.**

Harry de Wildt
a.k.a. Sir Lunchalot and Columnist
President, Anywhere Travel Corporation

Having been lucky enough to end up here, I have become more chauvinistic than most. People in San Francisco always ask *You do like San Francisco, don't you?* instead of *Do you like San Francisco?* This town is great and here are some of my favorite things. (Hey, this could be a great title for a song?)

Seeing the **Golden Gate Bridge** from underneath, the best spot being at Fort Point in the Presidio.

If you are rich, lunch at **Campton Place Restaurant** at the Campton Place Hotel. If you are poor, look through the windows and use the restrooms. Divine!

The **California Street cable car** that goes from Market Street to Van Ness Avenue, the only one that really goes nowhere and always has space.

Eating a hamburger at the **Balboa Cafe** on Fillmore. The Best. Do not get involved with owner (Slicky). Too time consuming for most people.

Late night champagne at the bar of **L'Etoile** when Peter Mintun plays Cole Porter.

The **Beach Blanket Babylon Show** at the **Club Fugazi,** now in its 12th year. Call Steve Silver, the owner/producer, if you can't get a ticket. Don't use my name.

The **last two blocks on Broadway at the Presidio.** Everybody should live like that! The **Opera House Box Bar** during Opera Season on a Tuesday night, the place to be seen or see. Bring Black Tie.

A table for lunch in the Cabin (only) at **Trader Vic's** against the central wall (only) eating my favorite sea bass, Chinese style. Mike Gutierrez is the guy to talk to for a table. Again, don't use my name.

Any time, any day in San Francisco, when the skies are blue and the views incomparable. Makes one feel super good to be alive and wonder why everybody isn't here.

The **Tosca Cafe** on Columbus Avenue for North Beach ambience. Talk to owner Jeanette Ethredge, which is easy and cheap because she doesn't drink, and do use my name. Guaranteed celebrity viewing, from Barishnikov to Joe Montana.

Lunch in the window of **Le Central** restaurant on Bush Street with some friends of the San Francisco Ballet, several of whom look like they have been made by Faberge (the lucky beasts). Everybody else, eat your hearts out.

The **lobby of the Fairmont Hotel.** Even unshaven, it makes one look glamorous.

Lunch at **Jack's** (are you catching on to where I got the title of Sir Lunchalot?) on Sacramento Street with Dominique as my waiter and their incomparable Sole Meuniere.

The **view of the awesome Pacific from the Sea Cliff** restaurant on a dreary, stormy day, sipping their specialty, Ramos Fizz. After around four, the sun starts shining.

Napa Valley on a weekday, going from winery to winery. Perhaps one should take a driver. I understand that Oakland is also very attractive, but I never got my visa.

Last but not least, in spite of what you read in the foregoing comments, I do not weigh 300 pounds, though I expect to wake up one day a bit like the character in Oscar Wilde's *Dorian Gray,* looking quite similar.

Street Statistics
Oldest: Grant Avenue
Crookedist: Lombard Street
Narrowest: De Forest Way (4 ½ feet)
Widest: Van Ness Avenue (125 feet)
Longest: Mission Street (7.29 miles)
Steepest: Filbert from Leavenworth to Hyde and 22nd Street between Church and Vicksburg (31.5 percent grade)

San Francisco's **Chinatown** is the largest Chinese community on the West Coast—second largest in the United States next to New York City. The tourist area, bound by Stockton, Kearny, Bush and Broadway, holds most of the 80,000 Chinese-Americans living in the Bay Area, but the population extends to North Beach, Russian Hill and beyond to the Sunset and Richmond districts. Because the pulse of the community is still within these perimeters—and because traditions are strong—the suburban Chinese come back on Sundays to shop and dine.

When the first Chinese immigrants arrived, they found a small community huddled around **Portsmouth Square**, still the center of Chinatown today. Once the gold strike was announced, the Cantonese came by the boatload, fleeing from famine and the Opium Wars, until by 1850 there were over 4,000 Chinese men in the area (and only 7 Chinese women). Chinese *coolies*, a term stemming from the word for bitter toil *Ku li*, were tolerated as long as they were performing the work other groups scorned—working the mines, building the transcontinental railroad and later planting the Napa vineyards. But when the work dried up in the 1880's, white San Franciscans shared Rudyard Kipling's view of Chinatown: *A ward of the city of Canton set down in the most eligible business quarter of the City.* A vicious backlash had set in. When hundreds of unemployed whites tried to run them out of town, the Chinese retaliated by organizing *tongs* or associations for protection which soon evolved into warring gangs. They turned to running opium, extortion rings and prostitution, with discipline maintained by squads of hatchetmen. It wasn't until the 1920's that the conflict was banished from Chinatown's streets.

When the big fire totally destroyed the area in 1906, city politicians planned to relocate the Chinese to less valuable property. Instead the industrious Orientals rebuilt with such dispatch that they reclaimed their district before City Hall could act. The new Chinatown was just as crowded as the old. By World War II, an average of 20 persons shared a bath, with an average of 12 to a kitchen. This same area—18 square blocks—is now struggling to absorb the newest wave of immigrants, the ethnic Chinese from Vietnam.

There is so much more to Chinatown than the few commercial streetfront blocks along **Grant Avenue,** marked by the **Chinese Gate** on **Bush Street.** There are the back alleys crammed with herb shops, benevolent societies which promote cultural and civic causes, upper floor residences with balconies, fish hanging on clothes lines, garment-maker sweat shops, the temples and *joss house,* and the action on **Stockton Street,** which has become the true main street of Chinatown since the tourist trade usurped Grant. Here, the food shops are as much of an attraction as the Grant Avenue trinkets. They offer fish swimming in tanks, crawling crabs, live chickens waiting for slaughter, hanging ducks, exotic greens and tempting bakery goods you'll not see elsewhere. It doesn't matter that you can't speak any of the myriad dialects swirling around you; sign language does very well and shopping here can be a remarkable adventure.

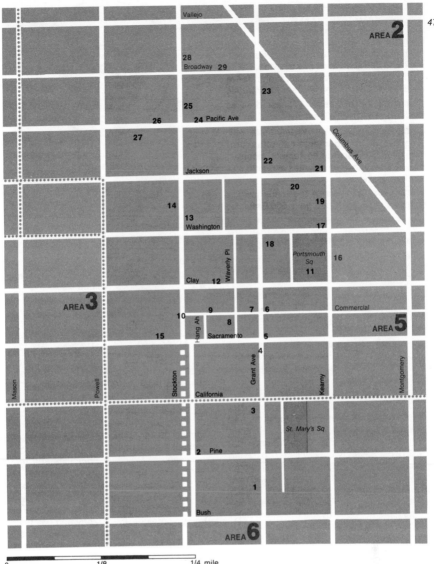

On the map:

Vallejo

AREA **2**

Broadway 28 29

23

25
26 24 Pacific Ave

27

22
Jackson 21

20
14 19
13 17
Washington

18
Portsmouth Sq 16
Clay 12 Waverly Pl 11

AREA **3**

10 9 7 6 Commercial
8 AREA **5**
15 Sacramento 5

Hang Ah

Grant Ave 4

Mason Powell Stockton Kearny Montgomery

California

3
St. Mary's Sq

2 Pine

1

Bush

AREA **6**

0   1/8   1/4 mile

---

1 **Grant Avenue Plaza Hotel.** *Moderate.* A wonderfully convenient, fairly priced hotel bordering the Financial District, Chinatown and Downtown. Color TV, private baths, rollaway beds and family suites available. Seasonal rates. *465 Grant Av. 434-3883*

2 **Old Metropolitan Life Building.** (1909, 1930) Remodeled by **Timothy Pflueger** in 1930 and until recently used by Cogswell College, this white terra cotta-tiled Roman Revival building relates to the grand hotels on the hilltop. *Pine and Stockton Sts.*

3 **Yamato.** ★★$$$ A famous Japanese restaurant specializing in food grilled at your table. Unless you're out for atmosphere, however, you can do better at the little places around Japantown. *Japanese. Open Tu-F 11:45AM-2PM & 5-10PM; Sa & Su 5-10PM. 717 California St. 397-3456*

4 **Grant Avenue.** This is the tourist shopping street of Chinatown. Restaurants and gift stores line the street from the ceremonial gateway at Bush Street to Broadway. The stores are fairly interchangeable; most sell similar gifts and souvenirs. It's fun to stroll along and sample several. Most of the stores are open until 10PM every day, so you can have dinner at one of the many restaurants and then shop. The street is active, crowded and fascinating. Don't try driving down Grant or Stockton in this area. Traffic is congested and slow. Off Grant Avenue, wander among the small, narrow alleys and lanes to really get the feeling of Chinatown. You can easily forget you're in San Francisco and believe for a while it's Singapore, Hong Kong or Shanghai. The nondescript buildings have been brilliantly decorated with balconies and doorways painted green, red, yellow and orange. These little passages hold a hodgepodge of activities: travel services, temples, groceries, laundries, Chinese newspaper and book stores and benevolent associations. The latter are protective organizations, active in the civic and cultural life of the Chinese residents of San Francisco.

Grant Avenue highlights include:

Imperial Fashion. An emporium of clothes and gifts. *564 Grant Av.*

Canton Bazaar. Curios from mainland China. Its ceiling-high shelves are crammed with vases and chinaware. *616 Grant Av.*

Chinese Kite Shop. An incredible assortment of all kinds of kites, including the windsock and fish kites in cotton or nylon. Some would make wonderful decrations for a child's room. Great souvenirs. *711 Grant Av.*

Yum Yum. Specializes in Chinese dresses made to order. *766 Grant Av.*

China Bazaar. A typical variety store with everything from paper lanterns, rattan furniture and lacquerware to temple incense, metal wind-up toys and cable car souvenirs. *832 Grand Av.*

China Gem Co. One of the many jewelry shops for jade, opals and gold. *500 Grant Av.*

5 **Kan's.** ★ $$/$$$ A popular tourist spot for Cantonese food, noted particularly for their Peking duck. But you can do better elsewhere in Chinatown for a much lower tab. *Chinese. Open M-F 12-10PM, Sa 12-11PM. 708 Grant Av. 982-2388*

6 **Eastern Bakery.** Try some of the Chinese cakes such as black bean, lotus and melon or the rice candy. *720 Grant at Commercial St. 392-4497*

7 **Grant Avenue and Commercial Street.** This corner affords a rare unobstructed view east down to the Ferry Building.

8 **Waverly Street.** *Street of Painted Balconies.* Colorful, crowded, noisy and redolent of aromas of exotic foodstuffs and incense. The **Tien Hou Temple,** dedicated to Tien Hou, Queen of the Heavens and Goddess of the Seven Seas, is located on the 4th floor of one of the brightly painted buildings. Flowers, incense and intricately carved statues fill the small sanctuary. Its hours are unpredictable, so your best bet is to take one of the tours arranged by the Chinese Culture Center. But if walking past the temple, you look up and see clouds of incense swirling down from the balcony, you may assume the temple is open. *Usually open Tu-Sa 9:30AM-5:30PM. 125 Waverly St. 4th floor. (No elevator. Stairs only.)*

9 **Hang Ah Tea Room.** ★$ Great for dim sum. There are many such tea rooms in this area. *Open daily 10AM-9PM. Hang Ah St. (off Sacramento, just east of Stockton St.) 982-5686*

10 **Stockton Street.** The street of daily life in Chinatown. No longer exclusively Chinese, other Asian populations have settled and opened businesses here, including Vietnamese, Filipino and Korean. Chinatown residents do their daily shopping in the grocery and butcher shops, bakeries and herb stores along Stockton and its side streets. Herbs and spices are sold here in quaint import-export shops. The street is ornamented with many handsome brick structures from the 1850's intended for plush private residences. **806 Stockton** was the house of **Francis Pioche,** a pioneer financier and *bon vivant* credited with giving San Franciscans an appreciation for fine food. He imported many French chefs and cargoes of vintage wines.

11 **Portsmouth Square. Robert Louis Stevenson** spent many hours writing in this square and his recollections of the area are to be found in *The Wreckers.*

12 **Celadon.** ★ ★ ★ $$/$$$ This award-winning restaurant (cited as one of the 10 best Chinese restaurants in America by *USA Today*) was named in honor of the blue or green porcelain with the distinctive glaze invented by legendary artisans of the Tang Dynasty (618-906AD). The decor in these subtle shades forms a stunning background for the exceptional cuisine. The candlelit dining room is accented by stained glass dividers and original art on the walls. The service by tuxedoed waiters is efficient but unobtrusive. Specialties include minced squab wrapped in lettuce leaves, barbequed quail which is flamed at the table, and a wonderful broiled lobster in ginger sauce . *Reservations highly recommended. Open daily 8AM-3PM, 5:30-11PM. 881 Clay St. 982-1168*

13 **Jade Galore.** Security officers and 2 stone dragons guard the entrance to this jade palace. *1000 Stockton St.*

14 **Old Chinatown Lane.** This narrow, paved street was once called the *Street of Gamblers,* a reference to Chinatown's enigmatic history. **Chingwah Lee Studio** is located here. It contains Mr. Lee's personal collection of Chinese antiquities and treasures. *Open Sa 2-5PM. 9 Old Chinatown Ln.*

15 **Cameron House.** Named after **Donaldina Cameron** for her lifetime of work freeing singsong slave girls. Inside are old carved cornices, calligraphy and paintings. She was called Lo Mo, the mother. *920 Sacramento St.*

Many of San Francisco's **Chinese restaurants** are genuinely authentic, so authentic that speaking English might not do you much good. Don't be intimidated! You can just point to dishes other people are eating that look good, or take your chances with the menu. As a rule of thumb, Cantonese restaurants tend to do seafood much better than anything else. This is natural, since Canton is on the ocean. The sauces are often gloppy with cornstarch, so the lightest seafood dishes are the best things to order. Northern restaurants, by contrast, make good meat dishes sauteed in a wok. But stay away from the beef at an inexpensive Chinese restaurant; beef is simply too costly for them to purchase high-quality meat.

Lots of **Hunanese** restaurants are springing up in San Francisco, and most tend to serve hotly seasoned dishes. If you don't appreciate chili peppers ground into your food, tell them to leave it out. At Hunanese and Szechuanese restaurants (the lines between the 2 blur here), whole fish, poultry, and deep-fried dishes tend to be excellent.

16 **Holiday Inn at Chinatown.** *Expensive.* Located near North Beach, the Financial District, Union Square and the Embarcadero. This unique building is the result of an award-winning design by **Clemmet Chin.** All public rooms are decorated in Chinese themes, and all signs are in Chinese and English. Of interest to families are special rates on food and lodging for children, self-service laundry facilities, Home Box Office TV free of charge, a roof-top swimming pool and a cable car line 3 blocks away. Employees represent 31 languages. Room service until 10PM. Entertainment by Chinese performers. *Five floors of underground parking. 750 Kearny St. 433-6600*

Within the hotel is:

Chinese Cultural Center. A valuable resource and communication center for Chinese culture in the West. There are changing art shows and entertainment programs in its 650-seat theater. The Center also arranges guided tours. *Open Tu-Sa. 10AM-4PM 750 Kearny St., 3rd floor. 986-1822*

17 **Buddha's Universal Church.** A 5-story building built by hand with an exotic variety of polished woods. The church contains mosaic images of Buddha, bronze doors and murals with a *Garden of Symbols* on the roof. *Tours the 2nd and 4th Su of each month. 720 Washington St. 982-6116*

18 **Empress of China.** $$$ One of the fancy, expensive restaurants in Chinatown. You'll like the food, but is it better than other nearby Chinese restaurants that are less than half the price? *Chinese. Open daily 11:30AM-10:30PM, 5-11PM. 838 Grant Av. 434-1345*

18 **Old Chinese Telephone Exchange Building.** Houses a branch of the Bank of Canton and noteworthy for several reasons. The site used to be the home of the *California Star,* the first newspaper in the city and the one used to spread the cry of *Gold!* in 1848, which started the rush. The present building, a 3-tiered pagoda, once housed the operators for Chinatown's telephone system and later the local Pacific Telephone and Telegraph offices. *743 Washington St.*

BESTS

Robert May
Destinations Video, travel programs

Golden Gate Fortune Cookie Factory, at 56 Ross Alley. Great smoky, dim atmosphere with clanking machines spurting batter onto a mechanical merry-go-round of baking cookies. Check it out!

Dim Sum are small tea pastries and an institution that came to San Francisco via Hong Kong. Even today, San Francisco and Hong Kong are the only 2 cities in the world with extensive dim sum eateries. If you have only one Asian meal in San Francisco, this should be it!

Most people eat dim sum for brunch, and the restaurants tend to be open from 9 or 10 in the morning until mid-afternoon. Generally, waitresses come around with carts, and you choose what looks good. Sometimes they won't speak English, but it's worth experimenting. When you're done, they count the number of little plates on the table and draw up the bill based on that.

The most popular dim sum dishes include *cha siu bow* (steamed buns with barbecued pork inside), *har cow* (delicate little dumplings stuffed with shrimp), and egg rolls (you haven't eaten an egg roll until you've tried one at a dim sum place). Don't miss the little custard tarts for dessert—they'll make you think you're in France.

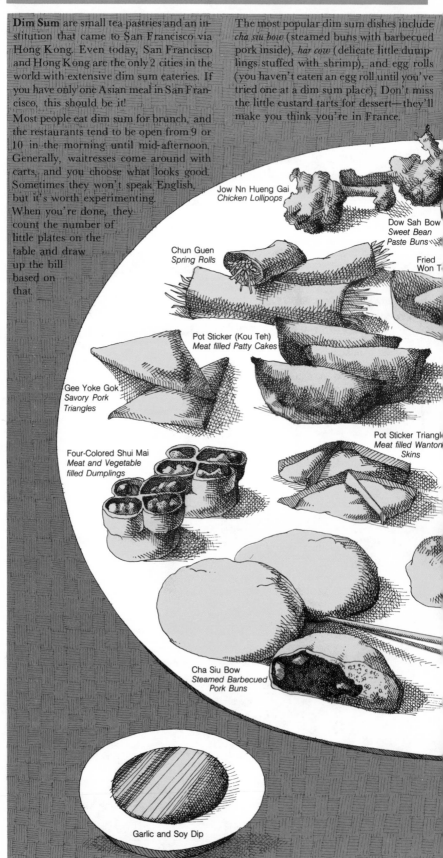

Jow Nn Hueng Gai
Chicken Lollipops

Dow Sah Bow
Sweet Bean Paste Buns

Chun Guen
Spring Rolls

Fried Won T

Pot Sticker (Kou Teh)
Meat filled Patty Cakes

Gee Yoke Gok
Savory Pork Triangles

Pot Sticker Triangle
Meat filled Wanton Skins

Four-Colored Shui Mai
Meat and Vegetable filled Dumplings

Cha Siu Bow
Steamed Barbecued Pork Buns

Garlic and Soy Dip

Sweet and Pungent
Ginger Dip

Gee Cheung Fun
*Steamed Rice
Noodle Rolls*

Siu Mai
*Steamed Meat
Dumplings*

Floweret Shui Mai
Meat Filled Dumplings

Har Cow
*Shrimp
Dumplings*

Jow Ha Gok
Shrimp Turnovers

Char Shui So
Flaky Buns

Fancy Fans
Meat filled Wonton Skins

19 **Hunan.** ★ $$ Some like it hot, and this is the restaurant that provides it. Almost every dish includes lots of finely chopped chili peppers. It is a great local favorite, although some question how good the food is underneath the chili peppers. This is the original Hunan and is much homier than the new one. *Chinese. Open M-F 11:30AM-9:30PM. Reservations. 853 Kearny St. 788-2234*

20 **Great Eastern.** $ Choose from an unusual selection of tasty Szechuan, Mandarin and Cantonese dishes. The lengthy menu offers stuffed crab, Mongolian lamb and crab in black bean sauce. Out-of-the-ordinary food at a reasonable price—an unusual find. *Chinese. Open daily 11AM-3AM. 649 Jackson St. 397-0554*

21 **DPD.** $ One of those little known little places. DPD serves good Shanghai-style foods at great prices. If your budget is tight or you get hungry in the wee hours, this place is a good bet. They also do a super carry-out business. *Open Su-Th 11:30AM-1AM; F & Sa 11:30AM-3AM. 910 Kearny St. 982-0471*

22 **Louie's.** $ Dim sum, one floor up. *Open daily for lunch. 1014 Grant Av. 982-5762*

23 **Chinese Historical Society of America.** Rotating exhibitions of its collection of artifacts, photographs and documents trace the history of the Chinese people in America. Exhibits are captioned in Chinese and English. *Open Tu-Sa 1PM-5PM. 17 Adler Pl. (off Grant Av. a half a block north of Pacific.) 391-1188*

24 **Asia Garden.** ★ ★ $/$$ In a noisy room the size of a football field, you get dim sum as good as you'll find in Hong Kong. Waitresses roll carts up and down the aisles singing over their wares, and you choose what looks appealing. Everything steamed or fried is phenomenal. A trick to beat the wait: go upstairs, where you can share big tables with other people. *Chinese dim sum. Open daily 9AM-3PM. 772 Pacific. 398-5112*

25 **Obrero Hotel.** *Moderate.* For more than 50 years, this was a boarding house for Basque sheepherders visiting the city. Located between Chinatown and North Beach, the Obrero still has the soul of the European-style pension. The 12 rooms available are small and clean, each with a sink; the 4 hall baths are shared. No phones or TV. Breakfast is hearty and included with the room price: ham, eggs, cheeses, rolls, jam and coffee. The large common room is also open for dinner which is served family-style. Easy access to Chinatown, Downtown, Wharf and major bus lines. *1208 Stockton St. 989-3960*

26 **Tung Fong.** ★ ★ ★ $/$$ You'll feel like you're in Hong Kong when you have dim sum in this tiny, plain-Jane sort of place that makes no concessions to Westerners. This is the authentic stuff and perhaps the best **Cantonese** lunch you can have in San Francisco. The little delicacies come around on trays, some steamed, some baked and others deep-fried. You choose what looks good, and at the end of the meal, the waitress counts your plates to determine the bill. *Chinese. Open Su-Tu, Th-Sa 9AM-3PM. Closed W. 808 Pacific St. 362-7115*

27 **Hong Kong Tea House.** ★ ★ $/$$ One of the better Chinatown dim sum restaurants; not quite as good as Tung Fong across the street, but an acceptable alternative and usually quite crowded. They have a particularly adept touch with their deep-fried dishes. *Chinese. Open daily for lunch. 835 Pacific St. 391-6365*

28 **Yuet Lee.** ★ ★ ★ $$ Just imagine a small greenhouse with its huge windows painted in bright green, the inside a nurturing place for good food. The place is packed every night, so be prepared for a wait at prime time—it's worth it. The main specialty is seafood—try the pepper and salt roast prawns in the shell, the sauteed clams with pepper and black bean sauce, or one of the marvelous pan-fried noodle dishes, crisp on the bottom and covered with a choice of meats and vegetables. The place is run by 3 smiling brothers who work with what is called *wok·chi* or wok energy. They don't serve alcohol, so bring your own beer or wine from a nearby grocery. *Reservations. Open M & W-Su 11AM-3AM. Closed Tu. 1300 Stockton St. 982-6020*

29 **Ocean City.** ★ ★ $$ One of 3 *sister* restaurants in the Ocean City empire (the elder sister is in Hong Kong and the other is in Seattle). The San Francisco sister serves excellent Cantonese cuisine to as many as 1,500 diners a day in a spacious 4 story complex. You will find the dim sum—some of the best in the country—on the middle 2 floors, where scores of young women push carts bearing an incredible assortment of dim sum items and pots of tea. With a dim sum chef, a dinner chef, a barbeque chef and 50 assistants, it's no wonder they can back up the extensive menu. Go! *Open daily for dim sum 8AM-3PM, dinner 5-10PM. 640 Broadway. 982-2328*

Chinese New Year celebrations usually fall in February by the astrological calendar, with an elaborate 3-hour parade led by a giant paper dragon. Even toddlers have firecrackers to throw at your feet. The parade is hard to get close to for viewing. The dragon is displayed afterwards in the lobby of 383 Grant Avenue.

Often called the *Wall Street of the West*, the

Financial District

with its **Pacific Coast Stock Exchange**, several corporate headquarters and outstanding examples of commercial architecture, embraces an area bordered by **Folsom, Third, Kearny** and **Clay Streets** and the **Embarcadero.** When thousands of gold hunters were brought to the muddy shores of a shallow indentation known as *Yerba Buena Cove*, they began to grade away the sand dunes along present day **Market Street**, dumping sand into the mud flats of the cove. Before that was completed, they also started to build a sea wall so that ships could unload directly upon the wharves. For its time, this was a stupendous project, taking decades to complete. Meanwhile, the reclamation of the mud flats continued, with some of the city's smaller hills sacrificed to fill the area between the old waterfront and the new wall, until finally, the business and financial district that we know today—everything east of **Montgomery Street**—arose from the sea. Within 5 years of the first news of the gold strike, Montgomery Street was lined with banker's offices. As the gold dust came down from Sacramento, some means of handling it had to be found, and because the first necessities were scales to weigh it in and safes in which to store it, shopkeepers were the first to turn banker.

Paradoxically, though rich in gold, San Francisco was poor in money. A pinch of gold subbed for one dollar and a dollar length of gold wire was divided into 8 parts to serve as smaller coins, which were referred to as *two bits, four bits,* etc. The coins of every nation were pressed into service as well at a rate of exchange based on their size. The Gold Rush boom overreached itself in 1854, ending in *Black Friday's* panic which forced many banks to close. Not until the colossal riches from Nevada silver mines began to flow was San Francisco firmly established as the financial center of the West. The Great Fire in 1906 precipitated the rise of another financial giant, **A.P. Giannini**, a food broker who had retired at age 32 to try out his banking theories with the **Bank of Italy**, founded by Giannini and his stepfather. Before the advancing flames reached his bank, he removed the assets and records and hauled them home in wagons from his warehouse, well camouflaged with heaps of fruits and vegetables. Consequently, the Bank of Italy was the first in the city to reopen. Later, renamed **Bank of America,** it would grow to become the biggest bank in the United States.

Envision that Montgomery Street was at the water's edge or that there was time when Kearny was paved with sticks, stones, bits of tin and old hatch coverings. Today Montgomery Street is both sleek and imposing with walls of stone, glass and marble—and still under construction! It awakens before daybreak when trading begins on the *Big Board* in New York. By 9AM, skyscrapers are filled with hundreds on hundreds of brokers, bankers, insurance executives and clerical workers. By dark its canyons are deserted, except for the cleaning crews and watchmen, and silent, but for the clang of cable cars on **California Street** carrying their cargoes uphill to the lighted apartments and hotels.

1 **Embarcadero Center 1-4.** (1971-82, John Portman and Associates) Known as Rockefeller Center West, these four high-rise slab blocks are staggered so as to allow sunlight to penetrate and to break up the wall-like appearance. At the base of the buildings is a triple level complex of shops, restaurants, sculpture courts, bridges and walkways. The multi-level shopping areas work remarkably well because of the captive audience from the offices above the courts, and the gardens provide a contrast to the surrounding streets. *Battery St. to the Embarcadero between Clay and Sacramento Sts. 772-0585*

Within the Embarcadero Center are:

Just Desserts. This is a favorite bakery and after-the-movie spot. Many varieties of cheesecake and a special chocolate mousse cake are among their enticing desserts. Eat in or take out. *Open M-F 7:30AM-6:30PM, Sa 9AM-5PM. 3 Embarcadero Center, lobby level. 421-1609*

Courtesy John Portman and Associates

Gaylord India Restaurant. ★ ★ $$/$$$ Gaylord's is part of a worldwide chain that started in India decades ago. The style is Northern Indian—subtle seasonings, not fiery hot like some Indian food. The restaurant is superb: beautiful and elegant, with great food. Their specialty is Tandoori dishes, suspended in a clay oven and baked. Tandoori fish is the best of the lot. But try their vegetarian and lamb dishes also. A choice of several kinds of glorious Indian breads: order one of each. Only the soups and icky-sweet desserts are letdowns. *Indian. Open M-Sa 11AM-3PM, 5-10PM; Su 4-10PM. 1 Embarcadero Center. 397-7775*

John Portman and Associates

Hyatt Regency. *Deluxe.* Located in the $300 million Embarcadero Convention Center complex, the hotel has a silhouette that is an unmistakable part of the San Francisco skyline. Its design by **John Portman and Associates** has received national recognition for outstanding and innovative architecture, with an atrium lobby 20 stories high, filled with plants, trees and birds, greenery spilling from the balconies and a 4-story sculpture, *Eclipse,* by **Charles Perry**, soaring from a mirror-like reflecting pool. Various cafes, boutiques and sunken conversation areas are clustered around the sculpture and plaza. The hotel has 5 restaurants: **Hugo's, Mrs. Candy's, Market Plaza, The Other Trellis** and **The Equinox,** a revolving restaurant and lounge on top of the building. The **Regency Club** is Hyatt's special floor for the business traveler who desires luxury combined with the conveniences of home. There are 52 guest rooms personally attended to by a full-time concierge, a bar and game room, lounges and kitchens for guest use. Complimentary continental breakfast, afternoon tea, hors d'oeuvres and drinks are served to guests who request them. A popular feature offered by this hotel is the **Friday Afternoon Tea Dance** to live big band sounds. There is also a new exercise parcourse for guests, accompanied by the 32-page *Spirit of Sports* program prepared for the hotel by *Sports Illustrated. 5 Embarcadero. 788-1234. Toll-free 800-228-9000*

Restaurants/Nightlife red
Hotels blue
Shops/Galleries purple
Parks/Outdoor spaces green
Museums/Architecture/Narrative black

---

2 Federal Reserve Bank. (1983, Skidmore, Owings and Merrill) Carefully scaled to match the adjacent Southern Pacific and Matson buildings, this granite-clad edifice with its large scaled arcade is an important addition to the formal aspects of Market Street. Take in the exhibit on the ground floor. *Market St. between Spear and Main.*

3 Harbour View Village. ★ ★ $$ Crystal chandeliers, etched glass and laquered chairs accent an interior decidedly upscale from many dim sum restaurants. Though more traditional entrees are offered as well, the dim sum selection here is wide and especially good. There's a patio area for those who avail themselves of the outdoor take-out dim sum kiosk. *Chinese. Open M-F 11AM-2:30PM, 5:30-9:30PM; Sa-Su 10:30AM-2:30PM, 5:30-9:30PM. 4 Embarcadero Center. 781-8833*

4 Mangia Mangia. Top 40 dance club with DJ. *Open F & Sa 8:30PM-2AM. 1 Embarcadero Center. 397-8799*

5 Alcoa Building. (1967, Skidmore, Owings and Merrill)) A 25-story high-rise slab block with exposed diagonal steel bracing; it is one of the few buildings that visually demonstrates its ability to withstand the forces of an earthquake. The entrance lobby is 2 floors above the street, and underneath it is a 3-level public parking garage, which unfortunately does nothing for the surrounding streets. Best seen from the park that spreads under the freeway ramp down towards the Embarcadero. *Maritime Plaza between Clay and Washington on Battery St. 434-2000*

6 Punch Line. They sure don't have to turn on any laugh tracks when the jokes start flying here. Part of impresario **Bill Graham's** empire, the club has Graham's characteristic slickness (a panoramic silhouette of the city's skyline behind stage; comfortable cloth-covered tables in front). The club features up-and-coming comedians. *Admission charge. 2 drink minimum per show. Shows Tu-Th 9PM, F & Sa 9-11PM, Su 9PM. Comedy Showcase of 10 to 15 new talents. 444 Battery. 397-7573*

7 Yank Sing. ★ ★ $$ One of the great dim sum houses of San Francisco, only this is in the Financial District and decorated in high-tech—you'll never guess you're in a Chinese restaurant until the food comes. All the dishes are brought around on carts, and virtually everything is delicious. Don't miss the roast duck, steamed pork buns and chicken wrapped in aluminum foil. At the end of the meal, they count your plates and tally up the bill. If you only have one lunch to eat in San Francisco, dim sum should be it. (The other Yank Sing on Broadway in Chinatown isn't nearly as good.) *Chinese. Open M-F 11AM-3PM, Sa & Su 10AM-4PM. 427 Battery St. 362-1640*

8 Washington/Battery Street Building. (1985, Fee and Munson) A narrow office block, only 25-feet-deep, that captures additional space for its tenants by bay windows. The facade facing east towards the freeway off ramp has a large clock. *Washington at Battery Sts.*

9 **Ferry Building.** (1896) Modeled by **Arthur Page Brown** after the Cathedral Tower in Seville, Spain, the Ferry Building tower at the end of Market Street was for many years the tallest building in San Francisco. Today it serves as headquarters of the **San Francisco Port Authority** and the **World Trade Center.** Before the bridges were built, it was the gateway to the city, with ferries disgorging as many as 50 million passengers a year from all over the Bay. Sadly, its facade has been disfigured by the disgraceful Embarcadero Freeway and its fine arcades and internal galleria filled in with undistinguished-looking offices. *Embarcadero and Market Sts.*

10 **Transamerica Pyramid.** (1972, William Pereira and Associates) This building has become a landmark because of its unusual shape and location at the end of Columbus Avenue. It caused great controversy when it was first built and sadly gave credence to the belief that California architecture couldn't be taken seriously. (San Franciscans hastened to add that a Los Angeles firm designed it!) Best seen in the morning when its shadow aligns with the axis of Columbus. *Montgomery between Clay and Washington at Columbus Av. 983-4000*

11 **655 Montgomery Street.** (1984, Kaplan/McLauglin/Diaz) A mixed use tower containing condominiums above offices. Its eroded form acknowledges the diagonal of Columbus Avenue. Clad in two tones of travertine. *655 Montgomery.*

12 **Blue Fox.** $$$$ One of the most famous and most expensive of San Francisco's *gourmet* restaurants, the food is elegantly served but often a disappointment. *Northern Italian/French. Jacket and tie required. Open M-Sa 6-11PM; cocktails 5:30PM. 659 Merchant St. 981-1177*

13 **Jack's.** $$$ This is one of the most famous old-time San Francisco eateries, located in an old house near the Financial District that survived the 1906 earthquake. You feel like you're eating in a dining room unchanged for decades—and you are right. The grilled meats are good, but stay away from the fish. Some of the big names of San Francisco politics and finance appear regularly and get great service along with their favorite tables; you won't be as lucky if you're not known. There's a great collection of 20-year-old gravy-stained ties at the door to loan out if you're not wearing one. *American. Jacket and tie. Open M-F 11:30AM-9:30PM, Sa & Su 5-9:30PM. 615 Sacramento St. 986-9854*

14 **London Wine Bar.** $ An excellent selection of local and exotic wines by the glass awaits you in this cozy, English-style restaurant. Traditional continental food is offered at lunch and dinner, but the wines are the main attraction. *Open M-F 11:30AM-9PM, Sa & Su 12-5PM. 1415 Sansome. 788-4811*

15 **345 California Center.** (1986, Skidmore, Owings and Merrill) This twin towered building houses a luxury hotel (the **Mandarin**) above offices. It has been skillfully inserted into the center of the block and has an arcade linking Sansome, Batttery and California Streets. The 2 towers are connected by glazed bridges and are capped by 2 stainless steel-clad flag poles. The design represents one of the best examples of Modernism and is a stunning addition to the city skyline. *California between Battery and Sansome Sts.*

Within the California Center is:

Mandarin Hotel. *Deluxe.* Stunningly set atop the twin towers of California Center and connected by skybridges is the Mandarin Oriental Hotel Group's first US palace. (Their Oriental Hotel in Bangkok and Mandarin Hotel in Hong Kong are touted as among the world's best.) This small, beautifully finished hotel has 160 select rooms and suites with outstanding views of the city and Bay—those with marble bathtubs looking out picture windows 40 floors high are outrageous. The **Oriental Suite** on the 38th floor is a home-away-from-home in grand luxe style, with a parlor, 2 bedrooms and bathrooms, a pantry and an open-air terrace. The secret at the Mandarin is in the personalized service, with a ratio of one staff member to each guest. Particular attention is paid to visiting business executives with a **Business Center** on the lobby level that is filled with the latest in high-tech office equipment: telex, personal computers, word-processing, photocopying. The skybridge connecting the towers is worth the price of admission. **Silks**, the restaurant on the hotel's second floor, serves breakfast, lunch and dinner. *222 Sansome St. 885-0999*

Monkey Block was the nickname for **Montgomery Block**, a 4-story building standing on the present site of the **Transamerica Pyramid** for 100 years. It was the first office building of any significance in San Francisco and the first fire-proof one. Much of the city's important business was carried on here. When business moved out, an amazing group moved in which included some of the most important names in American literary circles: **Mark Twain,** **Bret Harte, Robert Louis Stevenson, Rudyard Kipling, Jack London, Ambrose Bierce** and **William Randolph Hearst.** All either had office space in the building or regularly hung out at the Bank Exchange, the building's legendary bar. A young doctor named **Sun Yat-sen** plotted the successful overthrow of the Manchu Dynasty and later wrote the Chinese Constitution from a 2nd-floor office here.

1 Mandarin Hotel and California Center, 345 California Street (S.O.M. 1986)
2 Bank of America Headquarters (S.O.M. 1968)
3 J. Harold Dollar Building (George Kelham 1920)
4 Robert Dollar Building (Charles McCall 1919)
5 California First Bank (S.O.M. 1977)
6 Mark Hopkins Hotel (Weeks and Day 1925)
7 Great Western Savings Building (John Carl Warnecke 1968)
8 450 Sutter Street, Dental-Medical Building (Pflueger & Miller 1929)
9 Mills Tower (Willis Polk/Lewis Hobart 1918-31)
10 Standard Oil Building (George Kelham 1922)
11 Sutro TV Tower
12 City Hall

16 **580 California Street.** (1984, Philip Johnson and John Burgee) A pseudo-classical high-rise that is topped by 12 blank-faced statues surrounding the glass mansard roof. Allegedly, they are supposed to represent the Mayor and the 11 members of the Board of Supervisors. Classically, the design is incorrect by subdividing the front facade into an equal number of bays, resulting in a column on axis with the entry. *580 California at Kearny St.*

17 **Bank of America World Headquarters.** (1969, Wurster, Benardi and Emmons Inc., and Skidmore, Owings and Merrill with Pietro Beluschi as design consultant) One of the best high-rise office towers ever built—52 stories clad in dark red carnelian marble, its faceted facade and flush glazing create a changing image depending on season or time of day. At sunset, it can appear like a towering inferno with the reflected sunlight on the windows; at other times it can disappear like a black monolith into the fog. Its asymmetrical profile at the top creates sufficient variety to prevent it from becoming boring. *California and Kearny Sts. 662-3456*

Within the Bank of America Building is:

Carnelian Room. $$$$ High above San Francisco sits this expensive restaurant, providing a beautiful view and less-than-beautiful food. But it's a nice place to watch the sunset and see the fog roll in. *Jacket and tie required. Seasonal American cuisine. Open daily for dinner. 555 California St. 433-7500*

18 **Security Pacific Bank Hall.** (1922, George Kelham) One of the most impressive of the old banking halls in the city. Its giant order granite Ionic columns outside are matched by faux marble columns inside. The spacious volume is appropriate in scale and grandeur to the traditional forms of banking. *Montgomery and California Sts.*

19 **Wells Fargo Bank History Room.** On display in a recently renovated and expanded 4,400 square foot space are artifacts from gold rush days, including old mining equipment, gold nuggets, early banking articles and period photographs documenting Wells Fargo and early state and local history. The star attraction is an authentic 19th century Concord stagecoach that saw service on old California trails. A reference library open to the public re-opens in the Fall of '87. *Admission free. Open M-F 10AM-5PM. Tours can be arranged. 420 Montgomery St. 396-2619*

20 **Bank of California.** (1908, Bliss and Faville) A Corinthian columned temple with a grand main banking hall. *400 California St. at Sansome. 765-0400*

21 **Industrial Indemnity Building.** (1959, Skidmore, Owings and Merrill) Formerly the John Hancock Building, this was contemporary with the Crown Zellerbach Building, also by SOM, but demonstrated more traditional attitudes towards the street and context. It is clad in polished gray granite and has a retail base with a second level walkway above. *255 California at Battery Sts.*

22 **Tadich Grill.** ★ ★ ★ $$ The most famous of those San Francisco fish places that trace their lineage back for

decades, and one of the first to grill fish over charcoal. Skip anything with elaborate sauces and order sand dabs, rex sole, petrale sole, or the splendid calamari steak Bordelaise, and the old-fashioned desserts like baked apples and custard pudding that are better than you've ever had. Unless you eat in mid-afternoon, be prepared for a long wait. *American. Open M-Sa 11:30AM-8:30PM. 240 California St. 391-2373*

23 **353 Sacramento Street.** (1983, Skidmore, Owings and Merrill) A handsomely clad teal and blue metal paneled low-scaled corner office building is a reconstruction of a building that previously occupied this location, which creates a strange juxtapositon of styles and forms. The rotated plan of the tower ignores the grid of the street and street wall. *Sacramento and Battery Sts.*

24 **Schroeder's.** $$ Heavy German food. A popular hang-out for Financial District businessmen. *German. Open M-F 11AM-9PM. 240 Front St. 421-4778*

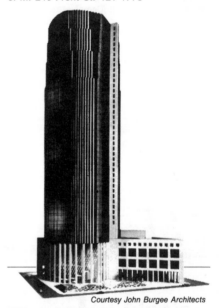

Courtesy John Burgee Architects

25 **101 California Street.** (1983, Philip Johnson and John Burgee) After the Bank of America Tower and the Transamerica Pyramid, this cylindrical building acts as a third major landmark within the Financial District. Its silvery reflective glass looks especially beautiful when seen from the Bay at dusk. Although the entrance lobby is rather ungainly, a sloping glass wall slicing across the 90-foot-high columns makes a dramatic sight. A north-facing plaza on California Street is flanked by 2 mid-rise blocks cut on the diagonal. *California and Davis Sts.*

25 **Restaurant 101.** ★ ★ ★ ★ $$$ Off the open plaza of the glass encased 101 California Street building is this first-rate eaterie combining California and French cuisines. French trained American chef **Fred Halpert's** specialty is fish—poached Dover sole, grilled tuna topped with a puree of mushrooms. The light-filled contemporary dining room with parchment finish walls, rose banquettes and original paintings, flowers, Oriental throw rugs and blonde wood floors makes a cool and sophisticated atmosphere for a special event meal. *Open M-F 11:30AM-2:30PM, 6:15-10PM; Sa 6:15-10PM. 101 California St. (entrance on Front St.). 778-4101*

26 **388 Market Street** (1987, Skidmore, Owings and Merrill) One of SOM's most refined buildings, the mixed-use flat-iron tower contains a luxury hotel above offices. The triangular site is occupied to the property lines, in contrast to the Crown Zellerbach Building 2 blocks away up Market Street by the same firm. The building's form consists of a cylinder attached to a triangle. The hotel at the top has deeply recessed windows, whereas the offices below have flush windows. The building is clad in a dark red polished granite which contrasts with the green window mullions. *Market St. between Pine and Front Sts.*

27 **444 Market Street.** (1981, **Skidmore, Owings** and **Merrill**) A 38-story aluminum panel clad office tower with a sawtooth shape. The building steps back on the 33rd, 34th and 35th floors, opening out onto outdoor gardens that overlook the Bay. Excellently detailed cladding, as one would expect from SOM. *444 Market. 954-3000*

28 **Shell Bulding.** (1929, George Kelham) One of the most beautiful Art Deco towers in the city, it was strongly influenced by Eero Saarinen's entry for the Chicago Tribune Tower competition. Because of its fine proportions, tripartite division of top, shaft and base, distinctive silhouette and contextual relationship to the urban fabric, the Shell Building is now an important source of inspiraton for the next generation of skyscrapers. Clad in glazed terra cotta. *100 Bush St. at Battery and Market.*

29 **Faz.** ★ $$ Another one of super-restaurateur **Fazol Poursohi's** trendy spots (he also owns **Circolo** and **Cafe Latte**). The bywords here are simple, tasty and fresh for a menu that features a range of smoked and grilled foods accompanied by cool and interesting salads and flavorful sauces. The quality is consistently good, the service gracious and the atmosphere sophisticated without being the least bit stuffy. Reservations for lunch are wise, though singles can slip in for a civilized meal at the counter. *American. Open M 11AM-3PM, Tu-Sa 11AM-3PM, 5-9PM. 132 Bush St. 362-4484*

29 **130 Bush Street.** (1910, George Applegarth) Surely one of the narrowest high-rises ever built, at 20-feet-wide and 10-stories high. It has slender Gothic lines and a real top, middle and bottom. *Bush St. between Sansome and Battery Sts.*

30 **Crown Zellerbach Building.** (1959, Hertzka and Knowles, and Skidmore, Owings and Merrill) Following the example

of Lever House in New York, this design represented the current fashion for designing buildings as isolated objects, withdrawn from the surrounding streets by a belt of landscaping, raised up from the sidewalk by the use of pilotis, clad in thin curtain-walling and mosaic tiles on the elevator shaft. How times have changed! It is ironic to think that the suggestion that it might be demolished to make way for a taller building prompted discussion to have the building listed as a landmark in 1981. *Market at Sansome and Battery Sts. 951-5000*

31 **Stevenson Place.** (1986, Kaplan/ McLaughlin/Diaz) One of the first of the new Downtown Plan-generated office towers. The building contrasts with its recent flat-topped International Style neighbors by its distinctive gable roof, vertical shaft and richly detailed granite-clad base. The arcade leads through to a new plaza on Jessie Street with a fountain and seasonal landscaping. The design recalls a pre-modern tradition of tall buildings that respect their context, define the street wall and maintain the continuity of the urban fabric. At night, the top, including the copper-clad roof, is floodlit. *Stevenson St. between 1st and 2nd, Market and Mission Sts.*

32 **Citicorp Building.** (1984, Pereira and Associates) The best aspect of this building is the conversion of the old **Banking Hall** (1910, Albert Pissis) into an atrium space, open to the public during the day. A recently installed cafe, plus the colorful flags, have helped to enliven the space, which previously had a mausoleum-like quality. Pereira's tower, above, is clad in pre-cast concrete. *Sansome at Sutter Sts.*

33 **Hobart Building.** (1914, Willis Polk and Co.) Part high-rise tower, part mid-rise street block. It was for many years one of the tallest structures on Market Street, and is now quite dwarfed by the Wells Fargo Tower next door. *582 Market at Second St.*

Frazzled Financial District office workers are getting stress-relief right at their desks from **Corporate Stressbusters,** an innovative San Francisco company that specializes in stressbuster massages. Owners **Jan Robbins** and **Hilary Bain** take the tools of their trade—a stool, a 3-inch cushion and their hands—to office desks throughout the city and give 15-minute, sit-up *shiatsu* massages that calm and energize overworked nerves. *Shiatsu* means *finger pressure,* and specific points of the body are pressed to release blocked energy and give the body a boost. *Corporate Stressbusters. 985 1/2 14th St. 552-7121*

Restaurants/Nightlife red
Hotels blue
Shops/Galleries purple
Parks/Outdoor spaces green
Museums/Architecture/Narrative black

Courtesy Skidmore, Owings and Merrill

34 **Crocker Bank Tower and Galleria.**
(1982, Skidmore, Owings and Merrill)
Whereas the Bank of America World Headquarters building (1969) represented the
latest ideas towards high-rise towers and
their relationship to the urban fabric, the
Crocker Tower represents current thinking.
It rises sheer from the street without a plaza
and its skin consists of flush 2-tone granite
panels and mirror glazing. The corners are
bevelled, emphasizing the wrap-around
smoothness of the cladding. The glossy/
matte granite and mirror glass create changing patterns at different times of day and
night. The 3-level glass, barrel-vaulted shopping arcade between Post and Sutter Streets
is a welcome asset to the city, with showcase
boutiques and eateries raning from **Mrs.
Field's Cookies** to **Gianni Versace, Ralph
Lauren** and **Marimekko,** and unprecedented
views of the historic Hallidie building. *Kearny
and Post Sts.*

35 **Galleria Park Hotel.** *Expensive.* One of
the small, renovated hotels springing
up around town. The hotel's location is
superb, adjacent to Crocker Center, 2 blocks
to Union Square and the cable cars. Rooms
are equipped with bars and refrigerators, and
some offer the comfort of fireplaces and
whirlpools. Meeting rooms are available, and
there's even a rooftop jogging track. *191 Sutter St. near Kearny. 781-3060; 800-792-9639*
Also at the hotel:

Bentley's. ★★$$ This grand scale oyster
bar and exhibition kitchen features fresh
regional shellfish. The kitchen has the
stainless steel steamers from the famed
oyster bar and restaurant in NY's Grand Cen-
tral Station. Regional recipes and Creole
specialties. *Reservations accepted. Open M-
Th 11:30AM-3PM, 5-9PM; F & Sa until
10:30PM.* 989-6895

36 **Circolo.** ★★★$$$ The third success of
talented restaurateur **Fazol Poursohi**
(**Faz, Cafe Latte**), this one specializes in
homemade pasta (you can see it hanging
from racks by the hearth), smoked salmon
cut thick instead of traditionally thin (you must
try this) and a gourmet pizza baked in a
wood-burning oven that doubles as hearth
in this elegant dining room. As a bonus,
there's a great view of the historic Hallidie

Building across the street. For all the drama
of decor, the atmosphere is cordial and lively and the prices are reasonable. We highly
recommend it. Cocktails and wine by the
glass are offered in the adjoining lounge,
subtitled the **Champagneria.** *Open M-Sa
11AM-10PM. 161 Sutter St. 362-0404*

37 **Hunter-Dulin Building.** (1926, Schultze
and Weaver) With the revival of interest
in pre-Modern architecture, this building has
come to be recognized as one of the finest
in the Financial District. Its tripartite division
of top, shaft and base and rich terra cotta
detailing contrast well with the banality of its
more recent neigbors. French Chateau/
Romanesque style capped by a tile mansard
roof. *111 Sutter St. at Montgomery and Post
Sts.*

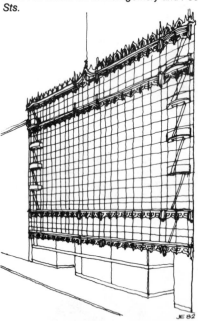

JE 82

38 **Hallidie Building.** (1917, Willis Polk
and Co.) Claiming to be the world's first
curtain wall glass facade, it was built for the
University of California and named after **Andrew Hallidie,** the inventor of the cable car,
who was also a University Regent. The glass
facade is projected a few feet beyond the
floor edge and structure. Decorative railings
integrate the fire escape balconies and stairs
and create a wonderful silhouette at the top.
*130 Sutter St. between Kearny and
Montgomery.*

39 **88 Kearny Street, San Francisco
Federal Savings and Loan.** (1986,
Skidmore, Owings and Merrill) Clad in white
concrete and embellished with blue tiles, this
building has one of the finest new entrance
lobbies and banking halls in the city. The
detailing, materials and lighting evoke an Art
Deco flavor. Notice the reconstruction of the
old facade next door on axis with Maiden
Lane terminating the vista from Union
Square. *44 Kearny at Post Sts.*

Restaurants/Nightlife red
Hotels blue
Shops/Galleries purple
Parks/Outdoor spaces green
Museums/Architecture/Narrative black

San Francisco's Downtown Plan

The 1970s and early 1980s saw unprecedented growth and development within the San Francisco Financial District. The 1968 zoning codes allowed very tall, flat-topped towers to be built and gave development bonuses for such elements as public plazas, off-street car parking and setbacks from the street wall. The result was a series of boxy towers you see on lower Market Street. At the same time, many important listed city landmarks were under threat of demolition. In the late 1970s, public reaction in the form of height control ballot initiatives occurred, and even though none of these passed, they set in motion the process within the City Planning Department that ultimately led to the passage in 1984 of the Downtown Plan. The Downtown Plan is a significant attempt to establish new height, bulk and setback controls for new highrise buildings. Future buildings will have to have sculpted tops, shafts and bases in contrast to the International Style flat-topped towers. In addition, towers will have to respect the street wall instead of being isolated object buildings set in a landscaped plaza. The intention is to repair the damaged urban fabric and for future towers to recall the idiosyncratic forms of some of the towers from the 1920s.

Several buildings demonstrate the intentions of the Plan. These include **Stevenson Place** (1986, Kaplan/ McLaughlin /Diaz), **90 New Montgomery Street** (1986, Gensler and As-

- 1980-present
- 1970-79
- 1960-69
- 1950-59

1	Bank of America World Headquarters
2	Transamerica Pyramid
3	Embarcadero Center
4	Hyatt Regency Hotel
5	Five Fremont Center
6	Stevenson Place
7	Crown Zellerbach
8	Shell Building
10	101 California
11	345 California
12	Alcoa Building
13	333 Bush
14	Crocker Center and Galleria
15	88 Kearny/San Francisco Federal Savings
16	Walton Square
17	Golden Gateway Commons
18	Custom House and Appraisers Building
19	Shaklee Terraces
20	One Market Plaza
21	580 California
22	Ferry Building
23	Hobart Building
24	St. Mary's Square

sociates) and **100 First Street** (1988, Skidmore, Owings and Merrill).

There are other elements of the Plan and associated city policies which will have a significant impact on the city. These include Public Transport First Policy, which prohibits on-site car parking in favor of developers subsidizing public transit; affordable housing policies whereby developers either build or fund the construction of new housing; childcare provisions; open space creation, either on-site or elsewhere; the creation of several new conservation districts; and the landmark listing of many downtown buildings.

40 **Stagecoach Restaurant.** $$ Antiques, leather booths and dark wood walls comprise the old-style San Francisco ambience of this large and well established restaurant. Continuous service from 11AM to 8PM makes it a good late lunch spot downtown, with a broad choice, quality menu and excellent service. Banquet faciltities. *American. Open M-F 11AM-8PM. 44 Montgomery St. 956-4650*

Ways to Eat for Less!

1. U.S. Restaurant. Italian/American (North Beach). *Open Tu-Sa 6:30AM-9PM. 431 Columbus Av. at Stockton. 362-6251*

2. Maykadeh. Persian cuisine (North Beach). *Open Su & Tu-Th 12-10PM, F & Sa 12PM-midnight. 470 Green St. near Grant Av. 362-8286*

3. Pasand Madracuisine. Indian (Marina). *Open daily 11:30AM-10PM. 1875 Union St. 922-4498*

4. John Barleycorn. English-style Pub (Nob Hill). *Open M-F 5PM-2AM, Sa & Su 12PM-2AM. 1450 Larkin St. 771-1620*

5. Grubstake II. American Burgers (Nob Hill). *Open daily 7AM-2:30PM, 3:30PM-10:30PM, 11PM-5AM. 1525 Pine St. near Polk St. 673-8268*

6. Cafe Sinfonia. Italian (Civic Center/Western Edition). *Open Tu-Sa: 11AM-3PM, 5-10PM. 465 Grove St. near Gough St. 431-7899*

7. Prince Neville. Jamaican/West Indian (Western Edition). *Open W-Sa 5-10:30PM, Su 4-9PM. 424 Haight St. near Webster St. 861-9433*

8. Wasabi Sushi. Japanese Sushi Bar (Western Edition). *Open Tu-Su 5-10PM, Sa 11AM-midnight, Su 5-11PM. 1175 Folsom St. 861-2855*

9. Milano Joe's. Italian (South of Market). *Open M-F 11AM-11PM, Sa 11AM-midnight, Su 5-11PM. 1175 Folsom St. 861-2855*

10. La Cumbre. Mexican (Mission). *Open M-Sa 11AM-10PM, Su 12-8PM. 515 Valencia St. 863-8205*

11. El Tazumel. Salvadoran (Mission). *Open daily 10AM-midnight. 3522 20th St. near Mission St. 550-0935*

12. Lady Seikko's. Japanese (Mission). *Open M-F 11:30AM-10PM, Sa 4:30-10PM. 2154 Mission St. near 18th St. 558-8246*

41 **333 Bush Street.** (1986, Skidmore, Owings and Merrill) Another mixed-use tower, with condominiums above offices. A ziggurat top adds a new form to the city skyline. The entrance lobby is curiously proportioned and rather spartan in contrast to the granite clad exterior. *333 Bush St. between Kearny and Montgomery.*

42 **Sam's Grill.** ★ ★ $$/$$$ A San Francisco institution, with its polished wood, private rooms and menu specializing in fish. If you've never eaten here, you've got to try it at least once. The best things are the simple fish dishes, particularly the rex sole and sand dabs. Avoid the fish prepared in elaborate sauces. Also good sweetbreads sauteed in mushrooms. Jammed for lunch, less crowded at dinner if you arrive early. *American. Open M-F 11AM-8:30PM. 374 Bush St. 421-0594*

43 **Mills Building and Mills Tower.** (1892 Burnham and Root; 1907, Willis Polk) A rare example of the Chicago School west of the Rockies, this 10-story building survived the earthquake and suffered only interior fire damage. Notice the fine Richardsonian entrance archway on Montgomery Street, the subtly delineated brick planters and strong cornice and multi-floor frieze. Willis Polk supervised the post-fire reconstruction and also designed the adjacent Mills Tower on Bush St. *220 Montgomery at Bush St. 421-1444*

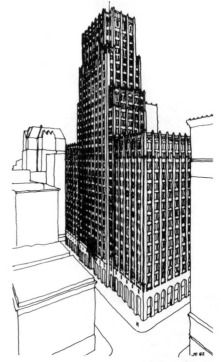

44 **Russ Building.** (1928, George Kelham) A Gothic high-rise modeled after the Chicago Tribune Tower period. Until 1964, it was the tallest building in the city. *235 Montgomery St. between Pine and Bush.*

45 **250 Montgomery Street.** (1986, Heller and Leake) A new office tower clad in glass fiber reinforced concrete and green granite. *250 Montgomery at Pine St.*

46 **Stock Exchange.** (1930, Miller and Pflueger) Architecturally, a strange combination of classical and moderne styles. The Stock Exchange is the heart of the Financial District and is a little brother to those on Wall Street and London. *301 Pine St. at Sansome.*

47 **Royal Globe Insurance Building.** (1909, Howells and Stokes) A fine entrance and base to the building clad in white marble with elaborate sculpture. *201 Sansome St. at Pine.*

Financial District Highrise Walking Tour

Start at the corner of Sutter and Sansome Streets at Market Street and you will see the elegant **Crown Zellerbach Building** at 1 Bush Street by Skidmore, Owings and Merrill (1958). This was the first International Style building in San Francisco and was a prime example of a radically new attitude towards urban design—the tower in the park. On the other side of Bush Street at the corner of Battery and Market is the **Shell Building** by George Kelham (1929), which represents the best of the Moderne Era and has now become a source of inspiration for the next generation of Downtown Plan towers. Just south of Market Street between the two Chevron Towers is **Stevenson Place** by Kaplan/McLaughlin/Diaz (1986), one of the newest Post-Modern towers that recalls the Pre-Modern form of highrise building. Notice the granite clad lobby and arcade.

Proceed up Sansome Street past the **Stock Exchange** at the corner of Sansome and Pine Streets until you reach **345 California Street,** also called **California Center** and the **Mandarin Hotel,** by Skidmore, Owings and Merrill (1986). It is a large midblock mixed-use tower with a shop-lined arcade running through Battery and California Streets.

Further down California Street, you will arrive at the 600-foot-high cylindrical tower of **101 California** by Philip Johnson and John Burgee (1983). Notice the tall atrium entry

lobby. Right next door is **388 Market Street** by Skidmore, Owings and Merrill (1987), a dark red granite clad flatiron building.

Proceeding up Front Street, you will pass the tall gray slabs of the **Embarcadero Center** by John Portman and Associates, with their multi-level shopping levels and pedestrian bridges linking one block to another. Front Street is terminated by the dark, diagonally braced **Alcoa Plaza Building** by Skidmore, Owings and Merrill (1964), one of the few buildings to express its seismic bracing on the outside.

Turn up Washington Street to Montgomery at the foot of Columbus Avenue and you will find the **Transamerica Pyramid** by William Pereira and Associates (1973). This has now become a San Francisco landmark despite its rather ridiculous form.

Continue down Montgomery Street to California Street and you will arrive at the **Bank of America World Headquarters** by Skidmore, Owings and Merrill and Wurster, Bernardi and Emmons with Pietro Belluschi (1959), one of the most imposing highrises in America. Opposite at the corner of Kearny and California Streets is Philip Johnson and John Burgee's (1984) Post-Modern **580 California Center,** topped by 12 statues and a glass-clad mansard roof.

Turn back down Kearny Street to the **Crocker Center** at Post Street by Skidmore, Owings and Merrill (1982), a rather severe granite-faced tower with a glass roofed shopping arcade adjoining it. Opposite is another Skidmore tower, **88 Kearny Street,** the home of the SF Federal Savings and Loan (1986). This has one of the most beautiful new entrance lobbies of recent times.

BESTS

John Gaulding
President and CEO
Pacific Bell Directory

Fog City Diner. *1300 Battery, 982-2000*
Donatellos. *501 Post St., 441-7182*
Fleur de Lys. *777 Sutter St., 673-7779*
Le Piano Zinc. *708 14th St., 431-5266*
Harry's Bar and Grill. *220 Fillmore, 921-1000*
The **Mandarin House** in San Rafael
Driving through **West Marin County**
Driving down the **Waldo** through the **Tunnel**; it's new every time
Dawn at the **Palace of Fine Arts**
Fog clearing at the **Banker's Club**
Lunchtime shopping at the **Hound** at the Embarcadero Center
Walking on **Sutter Street**
Hanging out at **RAB Motors**
A good **Sausalito Flea Market**
A Saturday stroll in **Mill Valley**
Umberto's. *141 Steuart St., 453-8021*

Union Square

is the nearest thing to a crossroads that you will find in the city. The Square itself is filled with chess players, trysting lovers, old men, brown-baggers tanning when the sun is out, soapbox orators of every political and religious persuasion, many beautiful flowers and many, many greedy pigeons. On bordering streets are most of the chic shops that you hear about, and some that you never will. It's all here, from sublime to sleazy, whether you want high fashion clothing or an inexpensive souvenir, jewelry, perfume, art goods, books, household items, antiques, kitchenware, Oriental rugs or art. (For shoppers, there's a convenient parking garage below Union Square.)

Enlivening the area as you shop are the street musicians, some of outstanding calibre. Many, in fact, play professionally in the evening and use their street time for practice and making pocket money. There are street artists as well, with a wide range of talents. Most colorful of all are the curb-side flower stands selling whatever blooms are in season for a bit less than the florists. The flower stands owe their beginning to **Michael de Young,** who in the late 1800s allowed the vendors—usually youngsters of Italian, Belgian, Irish or Armenian descent—to sell their flowers in front of the de Young building and protected them from the police. They were licensed in 1904, and, as with the cable cars, any attempt to suppress the stands has been halted by a sympathetic public. **Maiden Lane** is an elegant alley lined with trees that extends 2 blocks from Stockton Street by Union Square to Kearny Street. It was once known as Morton Street, a kind of bargain basement to the Barbary Coast. Now there are small exclusive shops and several restaurants here. Especially interesting is 140 Maiden Lane, which was designed by **Frank Lloyd Wright** and currently houses the **Circle Gallery.** The pet store at **135 Maiden Lane** has been in business since 1849.

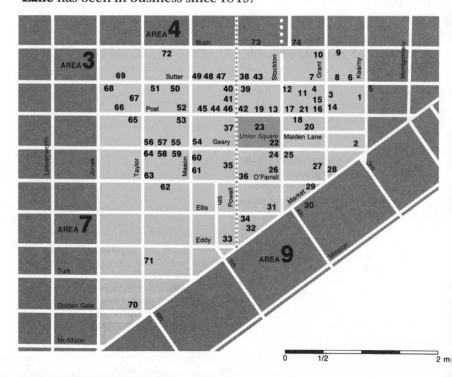

1 Sherman Clay. Founded in 1870 when **Leander S. Sherman** bought out his employer after spending years there repairing music boxes. The store sells pianos and sheet music. *Open M-Sa 9:30AM-5:30PM. 141 Kearny St. 781-6023*

2 Gallery Paule Anglim. This gallery shows work by celebrated contemporary American artists and emerging artists as well. *Open Tu-F 10:30AM-5:30PM, Sa 1-4PM. 14 Geary St. 433-2710*

BANANA★REPUBLIC
TRAVEL & SAFARI CLOTHING Cº·

3 Banana Republic. This unique San Francisco-based specialty chain store offers top quality safari-style clothing in a safari-fantasy atmosphere. Banana Republic has recognized the place of cotton and khaki in the fashion industry and added their touch, with finished seams, double stitching and rugged reinforcements. These fashions, combined with the very best **travel book store** and climate desk, make their 18 chain stores a roaring success. The bookstore gives the traveler a vast assortment of guide books and maps, and the climate desk offers information on climates all over the world and advice on what to wear in each one. *Open M-W 11AM-6:30PM, Th & F 10AM-8PM, Sa 10AM-6:30PM, Su 12-5PM. 224 Grant Av. 788-3087*

4 Portico d'Italia. This elegant leather accessories shop benefits from the personal touches of its owner **Christina D'Amico,** who gained her experience in her family's shipping business in Italy and has brought many of the latest styles in leather goods to the US. The shop is enhanced by many handmade Italian artifacts, such as wrought iron wall hangings, brick floor tiles and travertine marble benches. It shares the same manufacturers who supply Gucci, Bottega Veneta and Fendi, but the prices are less here. There is a nice handbag selection and also mini-leather Kleenex boxes and silk or cotton scarves. They will also special order any request. *Open M-Sa 9:30-5:30PM. 469 Sutter St. 434-2602*

5 Brasserie Chambord. ★$$ A consistently good, fairly priced French restaurant with more zest to its cuisine than most. The service is attentive and the decor attractive. Imaginative specials feature fish, and fine wines are available by the glass. Adjoining is a small dining area called **Crepe Escape** which serves morning coffee, croissants and more modest lunches. *Open M-F 9:30AM-2:30PM; Sa & Su until 1AM. Reservations necessary, especially for lunch. 152 Kearny St. 434-3688*

6 Braunstein Gallery and Quay Gallery. Two galleries share the same space and show art primarily by California ceramists. The Quay Gallery also shows painting and photography. *Open Tu-Sa 11AM-6PM. 254 Sutter St., 2nd floor. Braunstein, 392-5532; Quay, 982-3252*

7 Caravansary. A gourmet shop selling cheese, coffee and cookware. The mezzanine has a nice espresso bar and there's a restaurant on the 2nd floor. *(Other locations: in the Marina at 2263 Chestnut St. 921-3468; and in Berkeley at 2908 College Av. 841-1628.) Coffee section and espresso bar open M & Sa 7:30AM-5:30PM, Tu-F 7:30AM-6PM; deli open M & Sa 10AM-5:30PM, Tu-F 10AM-6PM. 310 Sutter. 362-4641*

8 Jeanne Marc. Unique women's clothes by this local designer, Jeanne Marc, whose signature is strong-patterned quilted jackets. Lately the designs heed current fashion trends. *Open M-Sa 10AM-6PM. 262 Sutter. 362-1121*

9 Le Central. ★$$/$$$ The Mayor of San Francisco or the Speaker of the Assembly might be at a nearby table if you stop by for lunch. The simple brasserie cooking is pulled off well, although there are far more exciting French restaurants nearby. Try their pâtés and desserts. *French. Open M-Sa 11AM-10:30PM. 453 Bush St. 391-2233*

10 Kinokawa. ★★★$$$ A great sushi bar and, as such, a *must* to visit for this most interesting form of traditional Japanese food, which sandwiches raw fish, sticky rice and often vegetables. You can sit at a long counter and watch the sushi-maker at work, his hands moving so fast they're often a blur. The array of available fish is spread out in front of you, and you can point to what you want. Don't miss the grilled sea eel or the sea urchin if you like exotic food. It stays open into the wee hours, and sushi makes a fine late-night snack. *Japanese. Open daily 11:30AM-2:30PM, 5-11PM. 347 Grant Av. 398-8226*

11 Janot's. ★★$$/$$$ The most interesting daily specials in town. The menu features robust provincial food: there are several main course warm salads as well as steak with *pommes frites,* lamb chops with zucchini spaghetti and seafood sausage with buttered cabbage. Two experienced chefs are the owners and the bistro atmosphere feels authentic. The small dining room is cast in the mold of a typical French bistro, with tables and diners crowded closely together. It is often crowded with shoppers at lunch, so reservations are in order. This is not the time to skip dessert. Try the hazel nut Napoleon or orange custard tart. *Open M-Sa 11:30AM-1PM, 2:20-10PM. 44 Campton Pl. 392-5373*

11 Stephen Wirtz Gallery. Spacious skylit gallery of contemporary photography, painting and sculpture. *Open Tu-Sa 11AM-5:30PM. 345 Sutter St., upstairs. 433-6879*

11 Jessica McClintock. Romantic and fanciful garments by San Francisco designer Jessica McClintock are set off perfectly in the exquisite post-modern ambience. *Open M-Sa 10AM-6PM. 353 Sutter. 397-0987*

Restaurants/Nightlife red
Shops/Galleries purple

12 **Campton Place.** *Deluxe.* Opened in the fall of 1983, this small and luxurious hotel a half a block from Union Square is the result of an \$18 million renovation of the Old Drake Wilshire. Although the ambience and decor are stunning, it is the service and extra touches usually found only in Europe's top hotels that the staff likes to emphasize. Professional valets pack and unpack for you, a French laundry and dry cleaning service is available in-house, secretarial assistance is immediate, shoes are shined each night, and each of the 136 rooms contains a working-size desk and fresh flower arrangements. Corner suites are cozy and chic. The staff is young and enthusiastic, mostly alumni from the Stanford Court. *340 Stockton St. 781-5555*

Within the hotel is:

Campton Place Dining Room. ★ ★ ★ ★ \$\$\$\$ The epitome of conservative elegance: quiet, understated and comfortable. Chef **Bradley Ogden** belongs to that new generation of chefs dedicated to presenting familiar dishes in interesting new ways. The result is gourmet American cuisine. The tender roasted loin of lamb seasoned with bacon and mustard greens is excellent, as is the veal, scallops and grilled quail. Finish it off with the best in old-fashioned apple pie. And don't miss the breakfast—it's one of the best in the city. *Reservations requested. Open daily 7-11AM, 11:30AM-3PM, 6-11PM. 781-5155*

12 **Wilkes Bashford.** Beautiful, expensive designer clothes for men and women served up with disarming nonchalance. Music and wine are part of the seduction. The window displays are in a class by themselves: witty and surreal epitomizing the spirit of the place. (**Polo/Ralph Lauren at Wilkes Bashford,** their other store, in the new Crocker Center. Ralph Lauren clothes for men, women and children.) *Open M-Sa 10AM-6PM. 375 Sutter. 986-4380*

12 **Victoria's Secret.** Couture lingerie. *(See their other store at 2245 Union St. 921-5444). Open M-Sa 10AM-6PM. 395 Sutter. 397-0521*

Scene Stealers

An average of 36 films and television series episodes and 50 to 75 commercials are shot in the city each year. Some memorable locations include the **Fairmont Hotel**, which is the prototype for the St. Gregory on *Hotel;* **Spring Mountain Vineyards** in St. Helena, the home of *Falcon Crest*; and the Carrington home on *Dynasty,* which is not in Denver at all but in the **Fioli mansion** in Woodside, 30 miles south of San Francisco. (*Tours by reservation only in advance, Tu-Sa. No tours from 15 Nov to 17 Feb and no children under 12. 364-2880.*)

13 **Bullock & Jones.** A narrow neo-classical facade squeezed between Saks and the Hyatt Hotel. Burberry of London rainwear (for men and women) is sold here, as well as traditional men's clothing. *Open M-Sa 9:30AM-5:30PM. 340 Post St. 392-4243*

Courtesy Carlos Diniz

13 **Hyatt on Union Square.** *Deluxe.* This dramatically designed complex overlooks the palm trees and park of Union Square, and every guest room has a picture postcard city view. The lobby is also worth a walk through, with its unusual floral arrangements that echo the colors in the 3 spectacular giant tapestries with the themes of sun burning off the morning fog and sun setting over the Bay of San Francisco. The hotel is just 4 blocks from the airport terminal *(at Taylor and Ellis Sts.)* and furnishes complimentary limousines to the Financial District. There are several restaurants and bars within the hotel, including the **Plaza Restaurant,** featuring excellent food and stunning decor; **Napper's Two,** a deli-style cafe; **One-Up,** which offers a city view from 40 stories up in excellent surroundings and nouvelle cuisine; and **Reflections,** their spectacular rooftop nightclub. *345 Stockton St. 398-1234*

Within the hotel is:

Regency Club. Like a small hotel within a big one, Hyatt's Regency Club consists of floors set aside for guests who pay a surcharge. These rooms command top service, with a separate lobby on each floor where a concierge checks guests out, arranges theater tickets, etc. An honor bar is kept on each floor and continental breakfast is available. There are also 2 floors of suites served by trained butlers who see to it that bars are stocked, parties arranged and dinner served. Top of the line in service and price, these rooms are luxuriously decorated without the *hotel* look.

Restaurants/Nightlife red
Hotels blue
Shops/Galleries purple
Museums/Architecture/Narrative black

14 **Tom Wing & Sons.** Jewelry and antiquities; jade is a specialty. *Open M-F 9:30AM-5:30PM, Sa 9:30AM-5PM. 190 Post. 391-2500*

14 **228 Grant Avenue.** This nondescript building houses some of the city's most prominent galleries of contemporary art. The John Berggruen Gallery occupies the 2nd and 3rd floors. This prestigious gallery handles some of the most celebrated names in modern American art. In recent years, exhibitions of museum calibre have also been presented here. These have included the works of **Matisse, Picasso** and early California artists. *(Open M-F 9:30AM-5:15PM. 781-4629.)* The **Fuller Goldeen Gallery** occupies the 5th floor. This gallery shows well-known artists, primarily from the Bay Area. *Open M-Sa 9:30AM-5:30PM. 982-6177*

15 **Charlotte Newbegin, Tillman Place Bookshop.** This choice bookstore is owned by the Newbegins, who have been in the book business for years. The original large store facing Union Square is now the home of Qantas Airlines. You come upon this small court rather suddenly, and it's like stepping into the London of Charles Dickens. This cluster of half-timber-fronted shops and the **Temple Bar** restaurant were built in 1906. Mrs. Newbegin sells a rich variety of fine books, mainly hardcover, for adults and children. *Open Tu-F 9AM-5:30PM, Sa 9AM-4:30PM. 8 Tillman Pl., off Grant Av. between Post and Sutter Sts. 392-4668*

16 **Shreve & Co.** Established in 1852, it sells fine jewelry, silver and crystal. *Open M-Sa 9:30AM-5:30PM. Corner Grant Av. and Post. 421-2600*

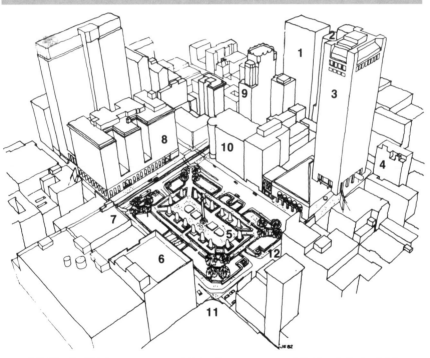

1 Holiday Inn Hotel	**5** Union Square	**9** Sir Francis Drake Hotel
2 450 Sutter	**6** I. Magnin	**10** Sak's Fifth Avenue
3 Hyatt Union Square Hotel	**7** Macy's	**11** Neiman Marcus
4 Campton Place Hotel	**8** St. Francis Hotel	**12** Maiden Lane

BESTS

Holly Stiel
Chief Concierge, Hyatt on Union Square

I grew up in the midwest (Cleveland, Ohio), and 8 times out of 10 when I looked up, the sky was gray or non-descript. When I first came to San Francisco as a child, I was over-whelmed by the **beautiful sky**—and I still am. Even when it's gray here, it's beautiful. Taking the **ferry** on a gray, cloudy day can be just as special as taking it on a cloudless, blue one. I am constantly amazed at the physical beauty of San Francisco. So when you visit San Francisco, look up and I'm sure you'll very rarely be disappointed.

Take the **ferry** and **feed the gulls.** I commute on the **Sausalito Ferry** and I love to bring bread and feed the seagulls as they fly overhead. They fly with such perfection and are so perfectly sculpted. Just stand at the side of the boat, raise your hand with the food in it and they will swoop down on it. Leave plenty of room between you and the food—the gulls are hungry and will bite your fingers if you're not careful.

17 **Gump's (S.G. Gump & Co.).** Founded in 1865 by the 2 Gump brothers, who were German immigrants and former linen merchants. It is world-famous for its jade, represented in every conceivable color in the **Jade Room**. Gump's also sells imports of Oriental treasures, including rugs and silks. Its outstanding stock of contemporary wares includes a **Steuben Glass Room** and silver and china. Traditionally, this is the place where brides-to-be register for fine housewares. Gump's window displays are always special. *Open M-Sa 9:30AM-5:30PM. 250 Post. 982-1616*

18 **Gucci.** Internationally famous Italian leather goods, gifts and apparel. *Open M-Sa 9:30AM-5:30PM. 253 Post. 772-2539*

19 **Jaeger.** Fine woolen sportswear imported from England. *Open M-Sa 9:30AM-5:30PM. 272 Post. 421-3714*

19 **Alfred Dunhill of London.** Famous for its pipes, cigars, humidors and lighters. It also sells leather goods. *Open M-Sa 9:30AM-5:45PM. 290 Post. 781-3368*

20 **Maiden Lane.** This exclusive lane was once know as Morton Street and had a less-than-chic reputation. Until the 1906 fire cleaned out the cribs, prostitutes sat at opened windows and solicited passersby, and there was an average of 2 murders a week. As the street struggled to overcome its past and shops took the place of bordellos, Morton was changed to Maiden in the hopes of sparking a new era—and it has. Today, except for the occasional delivery truck, this is a pedestrian way. On fine days, tables are set out in front of the **Nosheria** for *al fresco* snacking. The discreet, quiet district is lined with exclusive boutiques. Of particular interest is the building housing the **Circle Gallery** at 140 Maiden Lane, designed by **Frank Lloyd Wright.**

20 **Circle Gallery Building.** (1940, Frank Lloyd Wright) This exquisite building contains a spiral ramp leading to the upper floor and was the prototype for Frank Lloyd Wright's Guggenheim Museum in New York City. The exterior is faced with brickwork and has a superbly detailed archway at the opening. *Open M-W & Sa 10AM-6PM, Th & F 10AM-7PM. 140 Maiden Ln. 989-2100*

21 **Brooks Brothers.** Home of the button down shirt, with classic clothes for men and women. *210 Post; entrance on Grant Av. also. 397-4500*

21 **Eddie Bauer.** Fine, traditional store for country and sports clothing; also camping equipment. *220 Post. 986-7600*

22 **San Francisco Ticket Box Office Service.** Tickets to major events; discounts. *Stockton between Geary and Post.*

23 **Union Square.** Since 1850, the Square has been the heart of downtown San Francisco. Its name commemorates a Civil War rally, where demonstrators pledged their loyalty to the Union. This is a 2.6-acre park of flowers, trees, box hedges, benches and criss-crossing paths in the midst of the city's most bustling shopping area. A granite shaft celebrating the victory of **Admiral Dewey's** fleet at Manila Bay during the Spanish-American War rises in the center of the Square. The face of the bronze statue of *Victory* atop the monument was modeled after a well-known San Francisco benefactress, **Mrs. Adolph de Bretteville Spreckels.** The square has a 4-level underground garage. It's a good idea to use it, or another parking facility, as traffic is congested. (It's much faster on foot in this part of town.)

Kearny

Oriental accessories **Orientations**		**Iron Horse Restaurant**
stationary **San Francisco Paper World**		**Gardner Communications** *ad agency*
Sergio Old Prints	MAIDEN LANE	**ERA Electronics**
Richard Thompson Gallery		**Leo A. Daly Architecture**
		Galley in the Alley *hamburgers, etc.*
		Nasheria Expresso Bar
		77 Maiden Lane *office complex*
		Canterbury of New Zealand *clothing*

Grant

clothing **Brooks Brothers**	**Crate & Barrel** *housewares*
old fashioned tea room **The Mayfair Restaurant**	**Alcott & Andrews** *women's clothing*
PBA Travel	**Jos A. Bank Clothiers** *men's clothing*
jewelry **Cartier**	**Robinson's Pets**
fine art **Conacher Gallery**	**Lanz** *women's clothing*
Circle Gallery	**Yosh** *hairdresser*
boutique **Gucci**	**Mocca Charcuterie Restaurant**
gifts, etc. **Orvis**	**Spectacles** *eyeglasses*

Stockton

24 **I. Magnin & Co.** This white marble clad building is the city's finest department store for expensive fashions and accessories. It probably has the poshest ladies' powder room in town: all mirrors, gilt and green marble. There's a small gourmet food store, **Edibles**, with candies and coffee on the lower level. *Open M, Th & F 9:30AM-8PM, Tu, W & Sa 9:30AM-6PM, Su 12-5PM. South side of Union Sq., Geary at Stockton St. 362-2100*

24 **Narsai's at I. Magnin.** ★ $$/$$$ **Narsai David**, the well-known Berkeley restaurateur and caterer, opened this basement take-out charcuterie and small restaurant to give San Franciscans a chance to sample his pâtés, croissants and other delicacies. Pick up things for a picnic at nearby Union Square. Not cheap, but very good. *French. Open M, Th, F 10AM-7PM; Tu, W, Sa 10AM-4:30PM; Su 12-5PM. 362-2100*

25 **Neiman Marcus.** This branch of Texas' swanky department store was designed by **Philip Johnson** and **John Burgee** in 1980-82. The architecturally underwhelming design—both inside and out—has provoked heated debate among San Franciscans. Many opposed the destruction of the **City of Paris**, a popular store occupying the site since 1896. A compromise stipulated that the building should incorporate the enormous glass dome which surmounted the old store. *Open M-W, Sa & Su 10AM-6PM, Th-F 10AM-8PM. Stockton and Geary Sts. 362-3900*

26 **Macy's.** Large and varied selection and price range—from budget to costly. Its *Shop on the Square* contains small mini-boutiques of haute couture fashions. *Open M-F 9:30AM-9PM; Sa 9:30AM-6:30PM; Su 12-5PM. Stockton and O'Farrell Sts. 397-3333*

27 **Fraenkel Gallery.** This gallery shows photography exhibits, exclusively. *Open Tu-Sa 10:30AM-5:30PM. 55 Grant Av. 981-2661*

28 **Wells Fargo Bank Building.** (Clinton Day) A Beaux Arts design with a gently curved facade on Market Street. The building compliments its classical neighbor, the **Security Pacific Bank** by **Bliss and Faville** (1910) across the Street. *744 Market St.*

29 **Phelan Building.** (1908, William Curlett) One of the best flatiron buildings, located at the intersection of the north and south of Market grids. This cream colored terra cotta-clad building may have been a source for more recent flatirons such as the new 388 Market Street. *Market St. at O'Farrell and Grant Av.*

30 **Humbolt Bank Building.** (1906, Meyer and O'Brien Architects) A narrow-fronted tower that was rebuilt after the earthquake. It has recently been restored to its original finery and is capped with a small dome that is floodlit at night. *Market St. at 4th St.*

31 **Les Joulins.** ★ $$/$$$ Pâtés, truffles, baguettes, croissants and beautiful pastries, all to eat here or take out. Next door is a full-fledged restaurant, featuring a spectacular salmon baked in pastry crust, run by the same management. *French. Pastry shop open M-F 7:30AM-8PM, Sa 9AM-6PM. Restaurant open M-F 11:30AM-3PM, Sa 5-10PM. 44 Ellis St. 397-5397*

32 **Emporium-Capwell.** The largest general department store in San Francisco, with everything from gourmet cookware and wine to shoe repair and a post office. *Open M-F 9:30AM-8PM; Sa 9:30AM-6PM; Su 12-6PM. 835 Market St. 764-2222*

33 **Hallidie Plaza.** (1973) As part of the BART/Market Street Renewal Program, the opportunity was taken to create a downtown plaza, and the subway entrance allowed the design by **Mario Ciampi, Lawrence Halprin and Associates** and **John Carl Warnecke and Associates,** to take the form of a terraced amphitheater. *Market at Powell St.*

34 **Union Square Hotel.** *Moderate.* In keeping with the 30s theme (when **Dashielle Hammett** wrote part of his *Thin Man* series here), the hotel has been lovingly redone with Art Deco touches. There are 141 rooms, including 2 penthouses with roof decks. The main building has a foyer on each floor and elegantly furnished oversized rooms with baths. There is also a wing with somewhat smaller rooms and baths. Either way, it's a bargain for this convenient location. Complimentary coffee and croissants each morning. Free parking. *114 Powell St. 434-4560; 800-227-5442*

35 **Villa Florence.** *Moderate.* Yet another one of the great refurbishing jobs going on around town, a $6.5 million facelift for a dreary old building (the Manx) transforming it into a princess of a hotel. (Don't be put off by the grungy block; it's still only a few yards away from Union Square.) The lobby is stunning with wood burning fireplaces, murals of Florentine scenes and fresh flowers everywhere. Guests are served complimentary wine here in the evening. The bedrooms are gracious with high ceilings and country house chintz on comfortable chairs. No room service is provided as one way to keep the room rates below average, but a continental breakfast is served. *225 Powell St. 397-7700; in CA 800-243-5700*

San Francisco has the 13th largest city population and the 15th smallest city area.

35 **Kuleto's.** ★ ★ $$ The name of this restaurant in the **Villa Florence** comes from the architect who designed it, but he doesn't own it—the owners were simply grateful to him for creating such an exciting interior. If you enter through the bar, you'll find a delightful place to unwind— dark paneled woods, marble tile floors and strings of garlic and dried peppers and cheeses and sausages hanging over a giant old-fashioned bar. If you're alone for dinner, go to the rear where you can sit at a counter and watch the chefs in the huge open kitchen as they work. Adjoining is another room with ficus trees illuminated by stained glass windows overhead, tables with white napery and a more formal feeling. The food is Northern Italian with some original pastas, spit-roasted meats and fowl, smoked rabbit and chicken from the grill and an outstanding fish selection that changes daily. The desserts are incredible too. Think deep-dish peach tart with polenta crust or rich chocolate gelato. *Open daily 7-10:30AM, 11AM-11PM. 221 Powell St. 397-7720*

36 **Little Omar's Cafe.** $ Run by the same family that ran the late restaurant **Omar Khayyam's.** This one serves some of the best light lunches in town at bargain prices and does a brisk take-out business with their mouth-watering Middle Eastern foods. They have squeezed in a lot of charm into 5 tables. Beer, wine and cocktails. *Open daily 8:30AM-6PM. 208 Powell St. 781-1010*

37 **Westin St. Francis Hotel.** *Deluxe.* The second oldest hotel in the city. The St. Francis has been a focal point for the social functions and events in San Francisco's history for many years. Royalty, political leaders, literati and theatrical stars have all made it their headquarters. The hotel was built in 1904 by **Charles T. Crocker** and his friends to cope with what they felt were inadequate accommodations for the new class of bonanza kings and their entourages. Much effort was made to initiate new ideas for better service: electric grills that cooked a steak in 5 minutes, perambulators that brought food to the tables, a pneumatic tube which sent service orders to the dining room instantly, and pipes that dumped in ocean water to the Turkish baths. After severe damage in 1906, the reconstructed St. Francis was so successful that an addition brought the room total to 750, making it the biggest hotel on the Pacific Coast. Presently the hotel has 1,200 rooms and a Grand Ballroom that can handle 1,500, plus 7 restaurants. Outdoor glass elevators have been added and they

offer a stunning view of the city. *Union Square. 397-7000*
Within the hotel is:

Hasting's. Conservative clothes catering to businessmen. *393-8912*

Victor's. ★ $$$ Named after the hotel's famous chef, who cooked for 2 decades after the earthquake. The restaurant was transported to the top of the St. Francis tower, where you get a glorious view as you eat. The food is called California cuisine, and the most famous dish is the legendary *Celery Victor. Jackets required. California cuisine. Open M-Sa 6-10:30PM, Su 10AM-2:30PM for brunch, 6-10:30PM. 956-7777*

38 **Holiday Inn at Union Square.** *Expensive.* Actually one block from the Square, the Holiday Inn offers an ideal location as well as fabulous views of the city. The unique **S. Holmes Esq. Public House and Drinking Salon** features a Victorian atmosphere and a 30th-floor view of San Francisco. There are restaurants within the hotel. *480 Sutter St. 398-8900*

39 **Sir Francis Drake Hotel.** *Expensive.* The hotel seeks to preserve some of the flair of its namesake, personified by the doorman in full Yeoman of the Guard attire. The lobby, with its murals, crystal chandeliers, mirrors, sweeping marble staircase with bronze balustrade and vaulted gold-leaf ceiling, reflects the splendor and romance of the 1930s. The hotel is small by the standards of its neighbors (435 rooms and suites) and therefore able to integrate the luxurious advantages of a larger hotel with a more personal approach to hospitality. The special *Junior Suite* for the business traveler has a roomy desk and seating area for interviews or briefings. *Powell and Sutter Sts. 392-7775*

40 **Sears Fine Foods.** ★ $/$$ An old-fashioned coffee shop with great brunches, particularly their Swedish pancakes and creamy sourdough French toast. You get 18 tiny, light and fluffy pancakes per order. The lines are long at peak breakfast hours so come early. *American. Open W-Su 7AM-2:30PM for breakfast and lunch. Closed M, Tu. 439 Powell St. 986-1160*

41 **Chancellor Hotel.** *Moderate.* This fixture on Union Square since 1914 has been completely renovated, leaving the Edwardian exterior intact, solid and well soundproofed and its 140 rooms fresh and contemporary, with 6 new 2 room suites. The Art Deco **Clipper Ship** lounge—a popular meeting place for WWII servicemen—has been carefully restored to serve as a party and meeting room. It still contains the 85-foot photo mural of an aerial view of San Francisco. Rates, always a bargain for those in the know, have not changed much and are definitely moderate for this prime location. The Chancellor treats its guests with personal interest, even sending birthday cards to those who have stayed here. No wonder they are now entertaining the grandchildren of some of their original guests. There's a restaurant on the premises and room service is available. *433 Powell St. 362-2004; 800-428-4784*

Courtesy Carlos Diniz

42 **Saks Fifth Avenue.** Formerly located on Grant Avenue and Maiden Lane , Saks' present home was designed by **Hellmuth, Obata, Kassabaum (HOK).** Its curved glass entrance leads to an interior decorated in sunset colors. Inside, the store has more space, but has lost its exclusive charm. *Open M-W & Sa 10AM-6PM, Th & F 10AM-8PM; Su 12-5PM. 384 Post St. 986-4300*

43 **450 Sutter Street Office Building.** (1930, Timothy Pflueger) This medical/dental office building clad in undulating terra cotta is a good example of Art Deco architecture. Notice the elaborately designed entrance lobby with its pre-Columbian styling. *450 Sutter St. between Stockton and Powell.*

44 **Swaine Adeney.** This store signifies the first and only American branch thus far in the 235 year history of Swaine Adeney Brigg and Sons Ltd. of Piccadilly Street in London. According to **Robert Adeney,** the 7th generation chairman of the company, they chose San Francisco because *there's a certain style in San Francisco not found in other parts of the US,* and when he found the former premises of Howell's prestigious rare bookstore, he knew he had discovered the location *with character and tradition* he had been looking for. In addition to the famous Brigg umbrellas they manufacture, the shop carries handmade whips, riding breeches, Norfolk jackets, suits, shoes, gloves, luggage and other accessories. *Open M-F 9:30AM-6PM, Sa 10AM-6PM. 434 Post. St. 781-4949*

N·Peal

44 **N. Peal Cashmere.** A shop in the historic Burlington Arcade in London has settled into its nest at Swaine Adeney. As a store within a store, N. Peal compliments its conservative *host* shop with its myriad of styles and colors of cashmere. N. Peal is located in the back with no divider except for the track lighting and the sweaters themselves. The shop offers everything from updated classics to glamorous wraps, robes, dresses and tunics. For men, there's an extensive range of sweaters, dressing gowns and one of the largest selections of cashmere socks in the world. *Open M-F 9:30AM-6PM, Sa 10AM-6PM. 434 Post St., within Swaine Adeney. 421-2713*

45 **Theatre on the Square.** This 800-seat house, just a half-block from Union Square, has enlivened San Francisco theater by bringing in quality off-Broadway shows. *450 Post St. 433-9500*

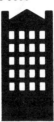

45 **Kensington Park Hotel.** *Expensive.* Just a half block from Union Square, the expensively renovated Elks Lodge now has 81 spacious rooms and 2 elegant antique-filled suites with traditional English furniture, damask fabrics of rose and blue, Chippendale-style armoires and bathrooms in marble and brass. Amenities include terry robes, complimentary breakfast and tea and sherry served among the palms every afternoon in the beautifully restored lobby with a hand-painted Gothic ceiling. The views of the city and Bay are especially good from the upper corner rooms. *450 Post St. 788-6400; 800-553-1900*

46 **Inn at Union Square.** *Expensive.* A small, elegant bed and breakfast with great emphasis on personal touches and superb service. The 27 rooms are individually decorated with Georgian furniture and beautiful fabrics. Each floor of 7 rooms has its own lobby where guests can enjoy breakfast or afternoon tea. This is one place where the concierge and staff have time to attend to your requests—and will even arrange a picnic. *440 Post St. 397-3510*

47 **The Orchard.** *Moderate to Expensive.* A full-service European-style hotel in a gracious building dating back to 1907. The Orchard offers a high standard of personalized service. The 96 elegant rooms are equipped with private baths, color TVs, direct dial telephone service, refrigerated mini-bars and turn-down maid service at night. Room service and special secretarial services are available around the clock. On Mondays through Fridays, a special continental breakfast is served and a complimentary limo ride to the Financial District is available in the morning. Located one block from Union Square. *562 Sutter St. 433-4434; in CA 800-433-4434; in US 800-433-4343*

Restaurants/Nightlife red
Hotels blue
Shops/Galleries purple
Parks/Outdoor spaces green
Museums/Architecture/Narrative black

47 **Pasquale Iannetti, Inc.** An extensive collection of prints by old masters up through the 20th century, including **Goya, Daumier, Picasso, Miro, Klee,** to name a few of the greats. They also have changing exhibitions of graphic art. *Open M-Sa 10AM-6PM. 522 Sutter St. 433-2771*

48 **Cartwright Hotel.** *Moderate.* Another downtown hotel that has been redone and prides itself on personal touches. The lobby incorporates large arched windows, giant plants, Oriental rugs and comfortable seating and reading areas. The rooms are small but attractively appointed in natural wood furniture, old fashioned quilts and prints. Continental breakfast at modest price. *524 Sutter St. 421-2865, 800-227-3844 (US), 800-652-1858 (CA)*

Within the hotel is:

Town and Country Tea Room. $ This charming installation serves savories, sweets and other proper English tea time accompaniments in a provincial atmosphere. *Open daily 7AM-12PM. 421-2865*

49 **Williams-Sonoma.** Gourmet foods and cookware. *Open M-Sa 9:30AM-5:30PM. 576 Sutter. 982-0295*

49 **La Ville du Soleil.** French country housewares. *Open M-Sa 9:30AM-5:30PM. 556 Sutter. 434-0657*

49 **Pierre Deux.** Elegant fabrics and housewares. *Open M-Sa 9:30AM-5:30PM. 532 Sutter. 788-6380*

50 **Beresford.** *Moderate.* A modest European-style hotel centrally located downtown near the theater district. The rooms are small but pristine and comfortable. This hotel has long been considered a *find*—a good value. The **White Horse Inn** off the lobby serves breakfast and lunch and has a cozy bar, which is a replica of an Edinburgh pub. *Family rates. Restaurant open daily for breakfast, lunch and dinner. 635 Sutter St. 673-9900*

51 **Vintners Building.** Home of the *Vintners Club,* a members-only wine connoisseur's club, and *Draper & Esquin,* which specializes in rare California and French selections, but has an excellent general offering. *655 Sutter.*

The **water** you drink in the Bay Area has been on quite a journey, starting in a mountain valley 150 miles away, then moving on through several hundred miles of pipeline, 85 tunnels, several tons of lime, soda and chlorine and the services of more than 800 people.

Courtesy John Portman and Associates

52 **Portman Hotel.** *Deluxe.* The first *small* hotel designed and built by well-known architect **John C. Portman, Jr.,** who has an established reputation for large, dramatic atrium hotels with large open public spaces. The building is clad in brick and precast concrete panels with semi-circular windows in an attempt to relate to the adjacent buildings. Opened in the spring of 1987, the Portman has 21 stories with 348 spacious rooms and 2 penthouse suites. The bathrooms are marble with large dressing areas, built-in cabinetry and telephones. One personal valet is provided for every 7 rooms, and room service is available 24 hours a day. The Portman stresses extra special personal service, such as a private car waiting for you at the airport to drive you into town. Business facilities include 4 conference suites and a boardroom with a private dining facility which provides continuous buffet service for all meetings. Secretarial, translation and audiovisual services are offered and personal computers are available. In addition, there is a solarium, ballroom and a rooftop club with breathtaking views for breakfast, tea or cocktails—a place to bring a client or chat with a friend. The **Portman Grill** in the lobby features an imaginative selection of the best of each season's American cuisine. *500 Post St. 771-8600*

Memorable San Franciscans

Isadora Duncan (1878-1927), dancer.
Robert Frost (1874-1963), poet.
Bret Harte (1836-1902), western writer.
Jack London (1876-1916), writer.
Robert S. McNamara (b. 1916), US Secretary of Defense and president of World Bank.
Levi Strauss (1829-1902), founder of Levi's.
Yehudi Menuhin (b. 1916), violinist.
Linus Pauling (b. 1901), scientist.
Janis Joplin (1943-1970), singer.
Earl *Fatha* **Hines** (1905-1983), jazz pianist.
Bernard Maybeck (1862-1957), architect.
Lana Turner (b. 1920), actress.
Turk Murphy (1915-1987), jazz musician.

53 **Donatello Hotel.** *Deluxe.* One of the lesser known hotels in town, best summed up by *grand luxe.* It is indeed a polished jewel. The lobby is small and uncluttered, with flawless marble floors and a handful of sofas and stunning antique pieces. Everywhere there is a tasteful blend of Italian marble, Murano glass, European antiques and contemporary art. The 140 rooms and 9 suites are designed to make every guest on business feel like the Chairman of the Board. The rooms are larger here than in any other hotel in the city. Especially appealing are the 5th floor rooms, which open onto a private terrace. A complimentary American-style breakfast is served in the **Donatello Restaurant.** The hotel is the creation of **A. Cal Rossi, Jr.,** who masterminded the Stanford Court Hotel, but here, in the absence of a Nob Hill view, the staff compensates with extraordinary service as well as luxury. Highly recommended. *501 Post St. 441-7100. Toll free in California 800-792-9837; in U.S. 800-792-9837*

Within the hotel is:

Donatello. ★ ★ ★ ★ $$$$ If you want excellent (but expensive) Italian food in a dining room pretty enough for the most important of occasions, this is the place! Any of the pasta dishes are superb as a first course. Then you go on to the beautifully prepared fish. The veal here, as in so many San Francisco restaurants, is a notch below everything else. *Italian. Jacket and tie required. Open daily 7-10AM, dinner served from 6PM with last seating at 9:30PM. 441-7182*

54 **Raphael.** *Moderate.* Modeled after the *little* hotels of Europe. The 155 rooms have been refurnished, and the multilingual international staff is available to serve you. A restaurant within the hotel is open 24 hours. *Family plan available. 386 Geary St. 986-2000, 800-821-5343*

54 **One Act Theatre Co.** This is the only theater in the country devoted solely to the development and production of one-act plays. Usually an evening's production consists of 3 to 4 plays presented in the intimacy of a 99-seat house. Recently, the management opened One Act II, a 70-seat space designed to test out new, original works, many by Bay Area playwrights. *430 Mason St. 421-6162*

55 **Hotel Diva.** *Moderate.* The Diva's leather, marble, glass and chrome Euro-tech look may lure the style conscious business traveler, but there are also classic creature comforts like down comforters and VCRs in each of the 110 rooms and suites. Each mini-fridge is stocked with refreshments and original art adorns the walls. Limo service, valet parking, nightly shoe shines and continental breakfast are also provided. Opposite the Curran and Geary Theaters and 2 blocks from Union Square, the Diva's choice location and accommodating staff make it a most rewarding stay. *440 Geary St. 885-0200; 800-553-1900*

56 **Regis Hotel.** *Expensive to Deluxe.* One of the latest arrivals on the local hotel scene, this truly deluxe hostelry was born within the shell of a 1910 hotel and offers 86 rooms and suites at a premium location next door to theaters, restaurants, Union Square shopping and 2 blocks from the airporter terminal. The Regis' objective is to create a soothing private world in each room, providing these luxury accommodations at less then luxury prices. The management is experienced at working with large deluxe hotels and also with the intimacy of a bed and breakfast operation. They bring the best of both worlds to the Regis. The decor features the quiet richness of a mix of French and English antiques—armoires, Louis XVI canopied beds, writing desks, lush fabrics and fireplaces in some of the suites. Special sound proofing takes care of street noise. The silver dome in the center of the lobby frames an unusually beautiful chandelier from Laura Ashley's French chateau. Of definite interest to business travelers are 2 computer age conference rooms and a business center with personal computers, office supplies and secretarial services. The executive board room has a mangificent antique leather-topped table that seats 16. There is also 24 hour room service and concierge and limousine service. *490 Geary. 928-7900; in US 800-345-4443; in CA 800-854-0011*

Within the hotel are:

The Lobby Bar. High tea in the afternoon and an *After the Arts* menu of light refreshments.

Regina's. A full service restaurant serving breakfast and French Creole cuisine at lunch and dinner. In addition, a unique arrangment has been made with the Clift Hotel across the street that permits Regis' guests to sign checks at the Clift's restaurants and bar.

57 **Hotel Savoy.** *Moderate.* Completely renovated, the Savoy is in the heart of the theater district, 3 blocks from Union Square and an easy walk to Chinatown and downtown art galleries. The 83 rooms have private baths and TV. There is no dining room, but room service will bring you breakfast from 7-11AM. A pub adjoining the oak-paneled lobby is open for cocktails and snacks. *580 Geary St. 441-2700; 800-227-4223; in CA 800-622-0553*

San Francisco's per capita income was $21,219 in 1986, making it the most affluent major city in the nation.

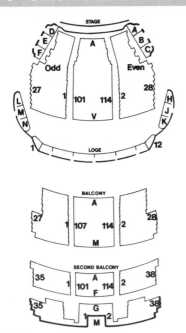

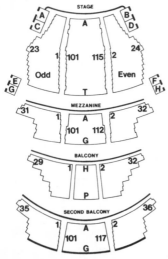

58 **Curran Theatre.** Producers **Carole Shorenstein** and **James M. Nederlander** advertise this 1,768-seat house as the chief pit stop for their *Best of Broadway* series, a misnomer if you're at all familiar with what Broadway really has to offer. But, the live and sometimes lively productions can be worth the hefty price of admission. Avoid the rear balconies unless you're a lip reader— the acoustics are impossible. *445 Geary St. 673-4400*

59 **Geary Theatre.** This 1,300-seat house is home to the renowned **American Conservatory Theatre**. With a $7.7 million annual budget, 34-week season, 53 professional actors on payroll and a 16-year history, A.C.T. is certainly the city's premier repertory company. It is also a play-it-safe company dependent on the conservative tastes of its 20,000 subscribers. But if you too take your theater safe and easy, the A.C.T. will give you a fine evening of entertainment. Note: The old theater's many cramped seats can be torturous unless your legs end at the knees. *415 Geary St. 673-6440*

60 **King George Hotel.** *Moderate.* Billed as *a unique antique in the center of the city*—and in deed it is. Its location is superb—in the theater district within walking distance of many restaurants and the shopping on Union Square. The hotel, built in 1915 for the Panama-Pacific Exposition, is tall and narrow, much like an Amsterdam canal house, and holds 9 floors of 143 rooms, all refurbished, with private baths and in-room safes. Continental breakfast is available daily, as is a lavish English High Tea complete with scones, crumpets and finger sandwiches. The hotel has vacation packages that include whale watching, theater and meals. *334 Mason St. at Geary. 781-5050; in US 800-227-4240; in CA 800-556-4545*

61 **Irchin.** ★ ★ $/$$ A medium-priced Japanese restaurant with top quality sushi. Unlike many, they acknowledge traveling families with a child's plate. *Open M-F 6-10AM, 11:30AM-2PM, 5-10PM; Sa & Su 5-10PM. 330 Mason St. 956-6085*

62 **Hilton Hotel.** *Moderate to Expensive.* Seven somewhat grim floors where motoring guests can register and park near their rooms via an interior ramp. An open garden terrace with heated pool and deck on the 16th floor. The newly completed 46-story tower has a stunning observation room, cocktail lounge and restaurant, **Henry's Room at the Top.** *333 O'Farrell St. 800-445-8667*

63 **Gray Line.** Ride a British double-decker bus on a loop tour from downtown San Francisco to Sausalito and Larkspur Landing, back via Pier 39 and Ghirardelli Square. *Departures every 30 minutes. Tour charge. 420 Taylor St. 869-1515*

64 **Four Seasons Clift Hotel.** *Deluxe.* A San Francisco landmark for more than 65 years, the hotel has held a reputation for just that long for extraordinary service and fine cuisine. It has undergone a multi-million dollar (but discreet) face lift, but it is still the high standards and individualized attention that bring its loyal following back time and time again. Guests select their own profile here. If celebrities wish to come and go so that no one knows they are in town, the hotel protects them. If they want a press conference, the hotel can arrange that too. There are 326 guest rooms furnished in simple elegance, with many suite combinations. The amenities include extraordinary service and a fine afternoon tea served in the lobby. The Clift is located 2 blocks from Union Square, 2 blocks from the airport bus terminal and adjoins the theater district. *Geary at Taylor. 775-4700*

Within the hotel is:

French Room. ★ ★ ★ $$$/$$$$ It's hard to imagine a prettier place to eat, and the award-winning food is highly recommended. Canadian chef **Kelly Mills** make sure its worth the price with a happy balance of new flair and tradition. The Caesar salad here is superb, as is the Norwegian salmon, grilled to order and framed with beautifully arranged vegetables, and the fish and veal. This is also the place to splurge on dessert—the chocolate mousse cake with raspberry sauce is impossible to resist. *Reservations suggested. Open daily 7-11AM, 12-2PM, 6-10:30PM. 775-4700*

Redwood Room. A classic Art Deco room with its original 1933 carved redwood panels and light fixtures of the period, spectacular Gustav Klimt prints and the soft background of an expertly played grand piano, all making this a delightfully soothing place to lunch, cocktail or enjoy an after dinner drink. *Open daily 11AM-2:20PM, 4PM-1AM. 775-4700*

65 **Emperor Norton Inn.** *Moderate.* This inn strives to honor **Joshua Abraham Norton,** one of San Francisco's most memorable and beloved characters, as well as one of the shrewdest and most creative entrepreneurs of the the Gold Rush period. This bed and breakfast of *legendary character* is beautifully furnished in the Victorian motif of the time with oak furnishings, stained glass windows and bathrooms with clawfoot tubs and brass fittings. The inn also features modern comforts such as color TVs, European-style mini-refrigerators and small kitchens. Continental breakfast and wine, coffee, tea and nighttime sweets are included in the rates. The Norton is near Union Square and is a charming alternative to the larger hotels in the area. *Weekly and monthly rates. 615 Post. St. 775-2567*

66 **The Andrew's Hotel.** *Expensive.* In a city rife with the posh and chic, the principal charm of this small hotel lies in its atmosphere of civilized informality. The Andrews eschews fussy details in favor of a residential-style warmth. Well-behaved families would be comfortable here. The complimentary breakfast can be carried back to bed on trays from hallway buffets. *624 Post St. 563-6877; 800-227-4742 in US; in CA 800-622-0557*

66 **Post Street Bar and Cafe.** ★★$$/$$$ Annexed to the Andrews Hotel, this cafe has drawn some deservedly enthusiastic critical attention, hosting a loyal local clientele. A brief but nicely balanced menu changes frequently and features fresh, high quality foods, many from local farms and ranches. The bar also serves a good selection of California wines by the glass. *Open M 11:30AM-2:30, Tu-Sa 11:30AM-2:30PM, 6-10PM. 632 Post St. 928-2080*

67 **Trader Vic's.** ★$$$ This is the flagship of the internationally famous chain of Polynesian-style restaurants. Eat here more for the experience than the food, which can be disappointing. But it has a great bar, with interesting, exotic drinks, and the menu lists lots of satisfying appetizers. A place to dress up and to people-watch. *Polynesian. Jacket and tie required. Open M-F 11:30AM-2:30PM 5PM-midnight; Sa & Su 5PM-midnight. 20 Cosmo Pl. 776-2232*

68 **Fleur de Lys.** ★★★$$$$ This beautiful and expensive French restaurant was catapulted into the front ranks in 1986,

when talented chef **Hubert Keller** moved from **Sutter 500** to take over the kitchen. His light and creative touch has resulted in fine *nouvelle cuisine* that suits the elegant red and gold paisley dining room to a tee. The Norwegian salmon in a light saffon sauce, mussel soup and scallop mousse are just a few of his special dishes. *French. Jacket required. Open M-Sa 6-10PM. 777 Sutter St. 673-7779*

69 **Canterbury Hotel.** *Moderate.* Known as the garden hotel, this is an intimate, reasonably priced downtown hotel in the English manner that sometimes seems more museum than hostelry. The lobby is a melange of old armor, wall hangings, eccentric lamps, statuary and plants. A new addition, the **Whitehall,** has an antique gallery on its first floor. The cocktail area off the lobby re-creates the ambience of the neighborhood pub. All rooms have telephones and private baths; some have refrigerators. The staff is multi-lingual. *750 Sutter St. 474-6464; in CA 800-652-1614; in US 800-227-4788*

Within the hotel is:

Greenhouse Restaurant. The interior fountains, wicker gazebos and plantings, including flowers and palms from the estate of the owner, require 3 full-time gardeners. The Sunday brunch includes 40 different specialties. *Open M-Sa 6:30AM-3:30PM, 5-11PM; Su 9:30AM-2:30PM, 5-11PM. 474-6464*

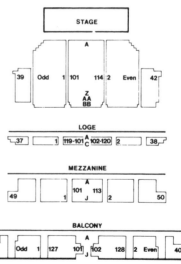

70 **Golden Gate Theatre.** This is one of the latest additions to the Shorenstein Nederlander theater empire. The management put a lot of money into refurbishing the 2,400-seat house and it shows in the gleaming interior. Unfortunately, sightlines in the orchestra remain poor. Try the mezzanine. The theater books popular musical attractions such as *Evita. 25 Taylor St. 775-8800*

71 **Original Joe's.** ★$/$$ A colorful, crowded restaurant with the feel of old San Francisco and absolutely the best hamburgers in town, served with grilled onions on hollowed-out French bread! The wide, hand-cut french fries are tops too. Good for a late-night sandwich. *American. Open daily until 1:30AM. 144 Taylor St. 775-4877*

72 **White Swan Inn.** *Moderate to Expensive.* An exciting and romantic find in this era of bustling hotels with indifferent service. The **Four Sisters Inc.** have managed to turn a 1900 hotel on downtown Bush Street into an English garden inn that epitomizes charm and quiet taste. There are 27 rooms, each with a bath, fireplace and refrigerator, all furnished in handsome antiques and lovely fabrics. There's a stunning common room adjacent to a tiny garden where a bountiful breakfast and high tea including home-baked breads and pastries is served. You can also have sherry and wine before the fireplace and browse through the latest periodicals. Most important of all, the feeling of a real family welcome surrounds every service. *845 Bush St. 775-1755*

72 **Le Petite Auberge.** *Moderate to Expensive.* Just a few doors up Bush Street from the White Swan Inn, you find another offspring of the **Four Sisters.** This one has a French country theme and is a bit less spacious, more understated and slightly less expensive. But if you can get past the vast collection of teddy bears inhabiting the rooms and lobby, you'll find the same kind of warmth and family hospitality that characterize the White Swan. A continental breakfast is served. *863 Bush St. 928-6000*

Four Sisters Inc. is the brainchild of **Roger Post,** the father of 4 daughters, who began in the business by opening his family home in Pacific Grove to tourists once his daughters had grown. He and his family now run 5 inns: **Green Gables Inn** and **Gosby House Inn** of Pacific Grove; the **Cobblestone Inn** of Carmel; and **Le Petite Auberge** and the **White Swan Inn** of San Francisco.

73 **Hotel Vintage Court.** *Expensive.* Known mainly as the home of **Masa's,** this intimate European-style hotel is charming. There is a refrigerator in each of the 106 rooms, complimentary wine waiting for you every afternoon in the cozy lobby, and limousine service to the financial district on weekday mornings. The location is convenient for shopping or gallery hopping. Highly recommended. *650 Bush St. 392-4666*

Within the hotel is:

Masa's. ★ ★ ★ ★ $$$$ When chef and owner **Masa Kobayask** died tragically in 1984, there was much speculation regarding the survival of his superb restaurant. Not to worry. The entire kitchen staff stayed on as well as the maitre 'd who was so important to its day to day smooth operation. If anything, the food got better and better. Chef **Bill Galloway,** who worked under Masa in 2 restaurants, was a creative and thoroughly cabable successor. Galloway left in the spring of 1987 to apprentice himself to chefs in France, and his talented assistant, **Julian Serrano,** has taken over. Among the dishes not to be missed are an appetizer, *coulibiac* of salmon, which is always fresh and perfectly cooked with *duxelles* of wild mushrooms, herbs and puff pastry; New Zealand venison, marinated several days and served with a rich sauce that is magnificent; and the veal dishes and organically grown vegetables, which are all presented with exquisite artistry—they must be seen. The desserts are perfection too. *Reservations required 21 days in advance. Open Tu-Sa 6-9PM. 989-7154*

74 **Hotel Juliana.** *Expensive.* A $5 million renovation by new owners has retained and enhanced the charm of their 85 year old, 107 room hotel perched at a convenient location just between downtown shopping, the Financial District and Nob Hill. The decor is clever and colorful, making the building's modest proportions interesting. Rooms are appointed with comfortable and sophisticated touches. The full range of services include continental breakfast, honor bars, room service and limousine service. *590 Bush St. 392-2540; CA 800-372-8800; US 800-382-8800*

Within the hotel is:

The Palm. ★ ★ $$$ A simple menu and copious proportions have proved the ticket to success for the San Francisco Palm, one of an 11 city chain originating in New York. The Palm's walls are filled with caricatures of celebrity faces, both local and national. The well-prepared steaks, lamb, fish and shellfish are served by a practiced crew of white-coated waiters. The bar is packed by 5:30PM. Reservations are a must. *Open M-F 11:30AM-10:45PM, Sa 5-11PM, Su 5-10PM. 586 Bush St. 981-1222*

BESTS

Marce von Pressentine
Concierge, Donatello

Norman's Spicy Chicken Wings at the **White Horse Restaurant** by the Beresford Hotel on Sutter Street.

View from atop **Nob Hill** at Mason and Sacramento looking out over North Beach, Peter and Paul Catholic Church, the cable cars and sailboats in the Bay—picture perfect!

Vanilla bean ice cream at Gelato on Post Street.

Neil Hoffman
President, California College of Arts and Crafts

Sitting in a restaurant in **Jack London Square** and gazing at the **Beastiary**, a sailboat.

Bradley Ogden
Chef, Campton Place

Star's. A fun place to be, with innovative cuisine for the adventurous palate. An exceptional variety of tastes. *150 Redwood. 861-7827.*

Masa's. Classically French, with superb sauces and very professional service. *648 Bush St. 989-7154.*

Hayes's Street Grill. Large selection, with the freshest seafood available, all grilled correctly. *320 Hayes St. 863-5545.*

Pat O'Shea's Mad Hatter. My only hesitation to mention this place is that it will become more popular than it already is, making it impossible to get in. The menu changes daily, with excellently prepared items and reasonable prices. *Third and Geary. 752-3148.*

Square One. Great crusty Italian bread. Chef Joyce Goldstein has her own style. She offers a wide variety of tastes and creatively assembled dishes. *190 Pacific. 988-1110.*

Fog City Diner. Upscale diner with great appetizers and a wide range of selections. *1300 Battery. 982-2000.*

Fleur de Lys. Modern French cuisine, with wonderful, full-bodied sauces and an emphasis on ingredients and lightness. *777 Sutter St. 673-7779.*

Casa Madrona. French California cuisine in a beautiful location. Chef Steve Simmons is my former sous chef. He is busy developing his own style, using the freshest ingredients in imaginative ways. *801 Bridgeway, Sausalito. 331-5888.*

Butler's. Beautiful open restaurant serving California cuisine, with a constantly changing menu and great combinations of ingredients. *625 Redwood Hwy., Mill Valley. 383-1344.*

Chez Panisse. The freshest and most unusual ingredients available prepared perfectly. *1517 Shattuck Av., Berkeley. 548-5049.*

Bridge Creek. A favorite breakfast place. The atmosphere is informal and pleasant and the food is unpretentious and down to earth. Great ingredients prepared simply and with great care. *1549 Shattuck Av., Berkeley. 458-1774.*

Monterey Market. Fresh produce and unusual ingredients. They consistently offer the very best of what's available. *1582 Hopkins, Berkeley. 525-5600.*

Curds and Whey. Excellent California olive oil from Santa Barbara. *6311 College Av., Oakland. 652-6311.*

Real Foods. Small but high quality selection, from excellent smoked sturgeon to yogurts. Also a wide variety of beans, grains and vinegars. *1023 Stanyon St. 564-2800*

Petrini's. Grocery stores located throughout the Bay Area. Great meats and fresh seafood. A large selection in every department.

William F. Wilkinson
President, Campton Place Hotel

Dinner for 6 at the **Mandarin** in Ghiradelli Square.

Salmon caviar with quail egg sushi at the bar of **Sushi Gen** on 18th Street.

Bar menu at **Stars** on Redwood Alley before or after the theater.

Oysters and Champagne at **Zuni's** sidewalk tables on Market Street, a real treat after previews at **Butterfields** auction house.

Salad composee and pizza with prosciutto outside at **Esprit Cafe** on Illinois Street; just as chic as the clothes.

A picnic from **Openheimer** on Divisadero Street, and Bay sailing around **Angel Island.**

Lunch en route to Napa Valley, standing up at Alice Waters' **Cafe Fanny** in Berkeley.

A weekend in the Napa Valley, with spectacular food at **Domaine Chandon,** intimate lodging, croquet, golf and tennis at **Meadowood Resort.**

Holly Stiel
Chief Concierge, Hyatt on Union Square

If nothing but shoes will do, I run down Sutter Street to **Sacha of London** (210 Sutter). They have *fun* shoes in bright colors, very highly styled. I always find something I want. Warning for Brooks Brothers types: Do not follow my advice for clothes or shoes. For you, I recommend **Alcott & Andrews** on Maiden Lane.

For the non-conservative dresser like myself, you can shop at **Jeanne-Marc** at 262 Sutter. You can find some wonderful things in the back of the store.

Also on Sutter Street is **Jessica McClintock** (353 Sutter). Go downstairs where the merchandise on the wire hangers is reduced substantially.

If I am feeling really extravagant, I will go to **Elizabeth Arden** at 230 Post Street. There are usually excellent sales in the back on the main floor.

If I am feeling like a quick pick me up—a fun sweater or Guess jeans—I will go to the junior department at **Saks Fifth Avenue.** When you shop in junior departments, you will find that you can often get similar merchandise at a lower cost.

There are those days when only a new hat will do, and there is no question where to go—**Hats on Post** on the second floor of 210 Post Street. The hats and the proprietor are both divine.

The **Civic Center** is acclaimed by critics everywhere as one of the great architectural complexes and by far the finest collection of Beaux Arts buildings in America. **Daniel Burnham**, the architect who was invited to design the master plan for San Francisco, had a philosophy in keeping with his grand scheme: *Make no little plans,* he said. *They have no magic to stir men's blood, and probably of themselves will not be realized. Make big plans...* Creative dreaming by several unusual San Franciscans who agreed with Burnham was responsible for the Civic Center. Burnham was the nation's leading city planner of his era and combined a highly developed aesthetic sense with the know how of a skilled politician. He was invited to the city for consultation by millionaire and former mayor **James Phelan,** who with other prominent citizens had become concerned with the man-made ugliness that was blighting the town. Burnham came, accompanied by his young assistant from the West, **Willis Polk,** and was so impressed with the potential of the natural setting that he agreed to return. In 1904 he set up a cottage office on **Twin Peaks** so that he could look down on the terrain as he worked out his recommendations for the future of the city. He was generations ahead of his time in suggesting such things as one-way streets, downtown subways and blocks where backyards would be merged into a common park in the center of the block. He wished to preserve the crest of the hills in a state of nature with access roads that wound to follow the contours of the land rather than the conventional gridiron patterns of the past. He designed a huge park for Twin Peaks where the slopes would be landscaped and a special watercourse would spill the city's water supply down from the heights.

The city fathers were more than impressed. But before any real action could be taken, much of the city, including the old **City Hall**, collapsed in the quake, literally burying his plans. Burnham was not ready to give up. With his enthusiastic supporters (**McLaren, Phelan, Spreckels** and others), a campaign was set in motion to rebuild the city from the ruins.

Political scandal delayed their plans, but Burnham finally returned to salvage part of the project and convinced the supervisors to finance the monumental Civic Center. It was not until after his death that Burnham's recommendations were revived.

The man largely responsible for actually getting the City Hall built was **Sunny Jim Rolph.** Mayor for 2 decades, he considered the Hall his proudest achievement. (Other projects he got off the ground were the **Library, Civic Auditorium**, Hetch Hetchy Aqueduct, the yacht harbor, San Francisco City Airport and the campaign to build the Bay Bridge.)

The architect for City Hall was **Arthur Brown, Jr.,** a designer who had what **Bernard Maybeck** admiringly called *perfect taste.* He attended the Ecole des Beaux Arts in Paris along with a fraternity brother of his, **John Bakewell, Jr.** At school he won more prizes than had ever been received by an American. Upon their return, the 2 young men set up the architectural firm of **Bakewell and Brown.** They soon won a contest for designing the City Hall in Berkeley, which gave them the confidence to compete for the greater prize—the key building in the Civic Center master plan. Feeling they had no chance of winning, they ignored sensible restrictions and produced instead the *ideal* building—a spectacular structure that by today's standards was exorbitant in design and expense. But the time was ripe, and the new team won out over established stars in the field. The victory catapulted Brown to the front ranks of American architects.

By 1936, when the **War Memorial Opera House** and **Veteran's Auditorium** were in place, a unified square of Beaux Arts architecture was created. It was in this Opera House that the charter bringing the United Nations into being was signed.

One of the latest addition to the complex—which breaks completely with this design tradition—is the **Louise M. Davies Symphony Hall,** inaugurated in 1981, and rehearsal space for the **San Francisco Ballet** was added in 1984.

1 **Cathedral Hill Hotel.** *Moderate to Expensive.* Known by an affectionate generation as the **Jack Tar Hotel,** the name change was accompanied by $4,000,000 in renovation. There is convenient free indoor parking for guests and one of San Francisco's few outdoor swimming pools on a landscaped terrace high above the streets. *Van Ness Av. and Geary. 776-8200*

2 **Lombard Hotel.** *Moderate.* A successful small hotel (100 rooms) which works to combine the atmosphere of the '20s with all the '80s conveniences. Total renovation has given the hotel the feel of a fashionable European hostelry with canopied beds, shuttered windows and an open courtyard. The lower lobby has facilities for meetings and private gatherings, and there is a rooftop deck as well. Complimentary services include tea and sherry in the lobby, a Thursday night cocktail party, first run video movies and limo service from the hotel to downtown and the Union Square area. The **Gray Derby** restaurant off the lobby serves breakfast and lunch daily and dinner Thursday through Saturday. *1015 Geary St. 673-5232; in US 800-227-3608; in CA 800-327-3608*

3 **Grosvenor Inn, Civic Center.** *Moderate.* Completely redecorated with 1900s ambience. Children under 16 free when sharing room with parent. *Van Ness Av. and Geary. 673-4711. 800-227-3154*

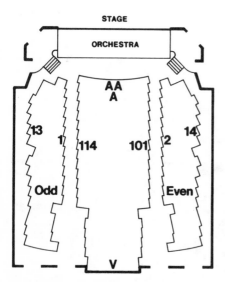

4 **Music Hall Theatre.** This 260-seat house has gone through a lot of changes, from movie house to disco and now to supper club. You'll have a wide range of choices at this snappy cabaret as far as ticket prices go depending on the night you attend and whether you choose the full or light dinner. *Reservations advisable. Seating on a first-come basis. 931 Larkin St. 776-3996*

5 **Great American Music Hall.** A premier music club that attracts the talented many who play the circuit, from pop music to comedy acts. It's a large place with a balcony, but the sights and sounds remain excellent from almost any table. *Dinner served. 859 O'Farrell St. 885-0750*

6 **California Culinary Academy.** This is San Francisco's best known cooking school. The students may change, but the standards of the sitdown dinners are uncompromisingly high. A great bargain, considering the quality, portions and price. *Reservations. Open M-F with seatings for lunch at 12 & 12:30PM (11:45 & 1PM on balcony); dinner 6, 6:45 & 7:30PM. 625 Polk St. 771-3500*

7 **The Phoenix.** *Expensive.* This unique urban inn is an oasis on an acre of ground surrounded by business and government buildings and the arts district. It has a resort-like environment, with a pool, outdoor cafe, garden, massage and other bodywork services on site and an athletic club. The Phoenix Art Gallery, bedrooms and grounds feature original art from Bay Area artists. The hotel also has an arrangement with one of the Civic Center's historic office buildings that allows guests to use office suites. Complimentary breakfast. On-site free parking. *Larkin at Eddy. 776-1380*

8 **Club 181.** This club features progressive European imports, urban soul, funk, live music, cabaret, musical theater and a nightly DJ. Dancing. *Open Th-Sa 10PM-4AM. 181 Eddy. 771-2393*

9 **Squid's Cafe Bar.** ★$/$$ This bright pink new wave eatery serves seafood, sausage, salads and chicken, but specializes in the many splendors of squid. Braised, sauteed, broiled or deep fried, the squid attracts a variety of afficionados. Turning up for the lunch crush are 3-piece-suited City Hall attorneys elbow to elbow with the distinctly unconventional. Fun for a quick meal at the bar or a more extended repast in one of the booths lining the walls. *American/seafood. Open daily 11:30AM-3PM, 5PM-12:30AM. 96 McAllister St. 861-0100*

10 **Hibernia Bank.** (1892, Albert Pissis) Described by **Willis Polk** at the time of construction as *the most beautiful building in the city,* it turns the corner of Jones and McAllister Streets at Market Street with a domed entrance vestibule.

11 **United Nations Plaza.** A memorial to the fact that the U.N. Charter was written and signed in this city in 1949. The fountain changes with the time of day. *U.N. Plaza at Market and Fulton Sts.*

12 **Orpheum.** In bygone days, the Orpheum was an important part of the vaudeville scene. Today, its huge space (2,503 seats) is largely wasted. The management insists on bringing overblown productions full of kitsch and marketed for the polyester set. Even worse, the theater's sightlines are dreadful, with an inadequately raked orchestra. After you leave the theater, don't hang around deserted Market Street too long. It's not the friendliest part of town. *1192 Market St. 473-3800*

13 San Francisco Public Library Entrance Lobby. The lobby was remodeled by **Danial Solomon and Associates** in 1986. Within the exisiting entrance lobby (1916, **George Kelham**) are new classical temples where you check books in and out. The newly remodelled toilets contain the only real granite in the whole building. Elsewhere, what looks like granite is either terra cotta or plaster. *Civic Center Complex. McAllister at Larkin St.*

13 San Francisco History Room & Archives. A combination document and photograph museum and research library. You will enjoy the glass cases of memorabilia, including photos of some of the city's classic buildings which no longer exist and of historic events such as the opening of the Golden Gate Bridge. *Open Tu-Sa 10AM-6PM, W 1-6PM. Third floor of Main Library, Civic Center Complex. 558-3949*

14 Maltese Falcon Tours. Take a 3-hour walking tour through the San Francisco of detective writer **Dashiell Hammett.** *Tours meet Su 12PM in front the the main branch of the San Francisco Public Library at Larkin and McAllister Sts. 564-7021*

15 Abigail Hotel. *Moderate.* Built in 1926 to house members of visiting theater groups, the Abigail greets guests in the lobby with a smiling moose, buffalo and a family of elk peering down from above the desk. The narrow building is 6 stories high and has 62 rooms, reached by an ancient elevator or, if you prefer, a harrowingly steep staircase. The exceptional collection of 18th century hunting prints along the stairs makes the exercise worthwhile. The small rooms are appointed in 18th century style, with huge closets designed to accommodate the oversized luggage and trunks of the stage. Rooms include private baths, phones and TVs. The complimentary breakfast is traditionally English with scones, crumpets and tea, served in the old carriage house adjoining the lobby. *246 McAllister St. 861-9728; in CA 800-553-5575; outside CA 800-243-6510*

Within the hotel is:

Melon's. ★ ★ $$ A combination continental and new American cuisine in a thoroughly Victorian setting, as befits a restaurant at the **Abigail.** One room just off the lobby serves lunch only, while down a few steps is a larger dining area converted from a carriage house. Don't miss the scallops in champagne and ginger sauce, the salmon topped with a necklace of red and white caviar, and such freshly-made desserts as a wonderful English trifle. Live piano music at lunch and dinner. *Reservations requested. Open M 11:30AM-2:30PM; Tu-F 7AM-11PM; Sa & Su 8AM-2PM, 5:30-11PM. 626-5675*

16 Federal Office Building. (1959, Albert F. Roller, Stone/Marraccini/Patterson and John Carl Warnecke) The bland face of federal government, with a Miesian slab block set back from the street and offering a somber contrast to the ornate designs of the Civic Center. *450 Golden Gate Av. between Polk and Larkin Sts.*

17 A Clean Well-Lighted Place for Books... This store in Opera Plaza is clean, well-lighted and full of a good general selection of the latest books. *Open M-Th & Su 10AM-11PM, F & Sa 10AM-midnight. Opera Plaza. 601 Van Ness Av. 441-6670*

17 Max's Opera Cafe. $/$$ Jeans and evening gowns mix in the New York-style deli and bar. Waiters and waitresses sing arias and cabaret tunes nightly from 8PM-midnight. Cordial, informal and an easy stroll from Civic Center symphony and opera spots. *Open M-Th 11:15AM-midnight, F & Sa until 1AM, Su 11:30AM-11PM. Opera Plaza. 601 Van Ness Av. 771-7300*

18 Modesto Lanzone's. ★ ★ $$$ Familiar San Francisco restaurateur **Modesto Lanzone** opened this lovely trattoria a stone's throw away from the city's performing arts hub at the Civic Center. Pre-theater seating is popular and post-performance supper attracts luminaries of the opera, symphony and ballet worlds. The often excellent Italian dishes are served with dignified enthusiasm. Lanzone, often on hand, likes to talk about his restaurant's extraordinary collection of contemporary paintings and sculpture. *Open M-F 11:30AM-midnight, Sa 5PM-midnight. Opera Plaza. 601 Van Ness Av. 928-0400*

19 Stars. ★ ★ ★ ★ $$$$ The tallest and proudest feather in the cap of renowned local chef **Jeremiah Tower** (he used to own **Balboa Cafe** and **Sante Fe Bar and Grill** as well). Stars claims that the food matters most here and offers a large, open, working kitchen in full view. The cuisine has a surprising simplicity and is not dominated by sauces, as is the French style. The produce comes fresh from local gardens or from Tower's ranch in the Napa Valley. Among the specialties are an exceptional pasta salad with crayfish and tiny yellow tomatoes and a Fish Paillard with cilantro and chives. The desserts are also spectacular. *Reservations required. Open daily 11:30AM-2:30PM, 5:30-11PM. Valet parking. 150 Redwood Alley betw. Polk St. and Van Ness Av. 861-7827*

Restaurants/Nightlife red
Hotels blue
Shops/Galleries purple
Parks/Outdoor spaces green
Museums/Architecture/Narrative black

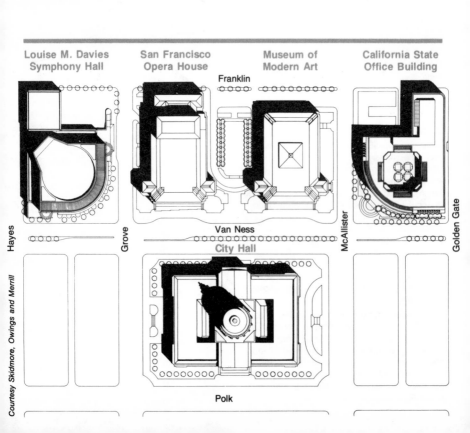

20 **City Hall.** (1915 Bakewell and Brown) The **Civic Center Complex,** one of the great architectural complexes in America, is a result of **Daniel Burham's** plan for San Francisco, conceived in 1905. The focal point is **City Hall**, a magnificent symbol of government with its huge dome, baroque stairs and echoing marble-clad corridors. The dome is modeled after St. Peter's in Rome. The Plaza in front of City Hall is disappointing by comparison and is at its best when used for such civic functions as welcoming the victorious **'49ers** after their Super Bowl victory in 1982.

21 **State Office Building (Edmund G. Brown Building).** (1986, Skidmore, Owings and Merrill) The design compliments

buildings along this stretch of Van Ness Avenue. Clad in white precast concrete, it has a large seal of the State of California above the entry to the courtyard. The courtyard is disappointingly institutional in scale. *Van Ness Av. at McAllister.*

22 **Harry's Bar and American Grill.** ★ ★ $$/$$$ With the Harry's Bars in Venice and Florence as role models, Spectrum Foods has launched Harry's Bar number 3 with no expense spared. The wood in the interior and woodworkers were brought in from Italy. There are 6 rooms with round tables and dark burgundy velvet covered armchairs. The Northern Italian specialties include grilled radicchio, antipasto misto, angel hair

Courtesy Skidmore, Owings and Merrill

Louise M. Davies Symphony Hall

San Francisco Opera House

Museum of Modern Art

California State Office Building

Franklin

Hayes

Grove

Van Ness

McAllister

Golden Gate

City Hall

Polk

braised onions and black risotto blended with baby squid and squid ink. And of course, don't forget Harry's famous hamburgers. *Reservations suggested. Open M-Th 11:30AM-3PM, 5-11PM; F 11:30AM-3PM, 5PM-midnight; Sa 5PM-midnight; Su 5-11PM. 500 Van Ness Av. 864-2779*

22 **Spuntino Ristorante.** ★$ A high-Italian-tech cafeteria with amazing black plastic cutlery. They make good salads and pizzas, and best of all, open early and stay open late. The rest of the fare is average Italian. *Open daily 7AM-midnight. 524 Van Ness Av. 861-7772*

In the 1950s, the *beatniks* (as **Herb Caen** named them), sought asylum in North Beach. These writers, artists, poets and philosophers were in rebellion from society's structures and were seeking refuge from New York's harshness. Their bohemian lifestyle shocked the *silent generation* of the '50s. When **McCarthy's** House Un-American Activities Committee held hearings in City Hall, youthful protestors were washed out of the Rotunda with fire hoses.

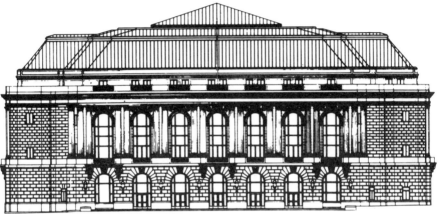

Courtesy San Francisco Museum of Modern Art

23 **San Francisco Museum of Modern Art.** This was California's first museum devoted to 20th century art. Its galleries are located on the 3rd and 4th floors of the **Veterans' Building.** The permanent collection contains works by **Picasso, Matisse, Kandinsky,** the Abstract Expressionists (including large holdings of **Clyfford Still), Albers, Noguchi, Calder** and distinguished California artists. Its changing exhibition program includes traveling shows from museums throughout the world, and it also originates landmark circulating exhibitions. More than a museum, SFMMA functions as a cultural center for contemporary art, poetry readings, dance presentations, films and music recitals. Lectures and panel discussions enliven the changing exhibitions. The museum's active photography department presents frequent exhibitions from its extensive permanent collection and temporary shows of 20th century photography. The **Bookshop,** on the main floor, has the city's best selection of modern art books and catalogues. It also sells posters and cards. There is a small, pleasant, modestly priced cafe on the 4th floor. The **Library** on the 3rd floor is open to the public M-W 1-5PM. Docent tours are given daily at 1:15PM. There is an admission charge to the galleries. (No charge Tuesdays.) You can use the cafe and bookshop without paying admission. *Galleries open Tu, W, F 10AM-6PM; Th 10AM-10PM; Sa-Su 10AM-5PM. Bookshop open Tu-F 10AM-6PM; Sa-Su 11AM-5PM 863-8800. Cafe open Tu-Su 10AM-4PM. Van Ness Av. at McAllister St. 863-8800.* **The Rental Gallery** is located at *Fort Mason, Building A. Open Tu-Sa 11:30AM-5:30PM. 441-4777*

John Lane
Director
San Francisco Museum of Art

Classic European Modernism: **Henri Matisse,** *The Girl with Green Eyes,* 1908; **Georges Braque,** *The Gueridon,* 1935; **Vasily Kandinsky,** *Brownish,* 1931; **Joan Miro,** *Painting,* 1926

Early American Modernism: **Georgia O'Keefe,** *Black Place,* 1944; **Arthur Dove,** *Silver Ball No. 2,* 1930; **Stuart Davis,** *Deuce,* 1954

Latin American Modernism: **Joaquin Torres-Garcia,** *Constructivist Painting No. 8,* 1938; **Frida Kahlo,** *Frieda and Diego Rivera,* 1931; **Diego Rivera,** *The Flower Carrier,* 1935

American Abstract Expressionism and After: **Arshile Gorky,** *Enigmatic Combat,* 1936-37; **Jackson Pollock,** *Guardians of the Secret,* 1943; **Clyfford Still,** (35 works spanning the artist's entire career); **Philip Guston,** *Red Sea; The Swell; Blue Light,* 1975; **Jasper Johns,** *Land's End,* 1963; **Robert Rauschenberg,** *Collection,* 1953-54; **Frank Stella,** *Adelante,* 1964

California and San Francisco Bay Area Artists: **Richard Diebenkorn,** (7 works spanning the artist's career to date); **Elmer Bischoff,** *Orange Sweater,* 1955; **David Park,** *Man in a T-Shirt,* 1958; **Sam Francis,** *Red and Pink,* 1951; **Peter Voulkos,** *Sevillanas,* 1959; **William T. Wiley,** *Ship's Log,* 1969

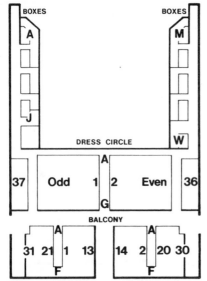

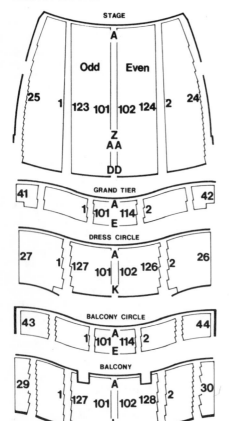

24 **Herbst Auditorium**. Built in 1932, this minor part of the city's Performing Arts Center was refurbished in 1978. Still, it's not one of the city's best entertainment spaces. The orchestra seats are badly raked and the balconies sit too far back. The 915-seat house is best for small theater, dance groups and recitals. The hall is beautifully adorned by the **Brangwyn Murals**, brought from the *Panama-Pacific Exposition* of 1915. *401 Van Ness Av. 431-5400*

25 **Opera House**. Opulent...ornate...splendid. These words all come to mind when you consider this crown jewel to San

Francisco's Performing Arts Center. The 3,525-seat house, which opened 15 October 1932 with a performance of **Puccini's** *La Tosca,* is the home of the city's renowned opera and ballet companies. The opera season begins when the tuxedoed gentlemen and society matrons attend the gala opening in September and runs through December. The ballet fits itself in whenever the plump ladies aren't bursting forth in song. *301 Van Ness Av. 431-1210*

26 **San Francisco Ballet School**. (1984, Beverly Willis) A modest addition to the Civic Center composition, this builidng contains offices and dance studios. A *troupe l'oeil* has been painted on the driveway at the rear. *Franklin and Fulton Sts.*

27 **Inn at the Opera**. *Deluxe.* Only a few steps from the Opera House and Davies Hall is this 48 room hotel built in 1927 to house visiting opera stars. Recently and elegantly restored, the luxuries include queen-sized beds, large bathrooms, wet bars, small refrigerators and microwaves, 24 hour room service, concierge service and convenient parking. The rooms also have some of the most spectacular floral arrangements seen in any hotel. The Inn's staff will attend to both personal and business needs, such as providing meeting rooms and secretarial service, arranging tours and limousine service and getting tickets to the opera, symphony or ballet. *333 Fulton St. 863-8400; 800-325-2708; in CA 800-423-9610*

Within the hotel is:

Act IV Lounge. ★ ★ $$ The fireside seating, plush furnishings you can sink into, oil paintings on the dark polished paneling and soft piano music in the background all add up to a romantic hideaway spot to lunch or dine before or after the theater. The menu is limited but excellent, and they are geared to serve gracefully while meeting the curtain time. *Open daily 7-10AM, 11:30AM-2PM, 5PM-midnight. 863-8400*

28 **Kimball's**. ★ ★ $$/$$$ A successful conversion of an old brick building to an attractive, 2 level, sky-lighted contemporary restaurant and jazz club. Live music is featured most nights, with some of the top jazz names. There are 2 shows on the weekends, at 9:30 and 11PM. The restaurant features continental dishes, such as fried brie, poached sole Florentine, roast duck, New York steak and an oyster bar. It's an easy walk from here to the symphony, opera and ballet. *Reservations suggested. Open Tu-Sa 11AM-2:30PM, 5-8:30PM. Closed Su and M if there is no show. 300 Grove St. 861-5555*

Restaurants/Nightlife red
Hotels blue
Shops/Galleries purple
Parks/Outdoor spaces green
Museums/Architecture/Narrative black

29 **About Music.** A tiny shop that stocks books about music. *Open Tu-Th 11AM-6PM, F-Sa 11AM-8PM. 357 Grove St. 647-3343*

30 **San Francisco Opera Shop.** Across from the Symphony Hall, the shop attests to the city's enthusiasm for opera. Browse among the books, recordings, T-shirts, posters, kids' books and gifts on the performing arts. This civilized establishment also has an espresso bar. Drop in before curtain time for a pair of opera glasses or perhaps some Madame Butterfly-style hair ornaments. *Open Tu-F 11AM-8PM, Sa noon-8PM, Su noon-6PM. 199 Grove St. 565-6414*

31 **Hayes Street Grill.** ★ ★ $$/$$$ Good grilled fish, delicious French fries and excellent sourdough bread. They also have some excellent French-style appetizers and desserts. If you're not in the mood for fish, they'll grill sausages, chicken and steak and offer specials like duck and sweetbreads. Unlike most fish restaurants, you can make reservations. *American. Open M-F 11:30AM-10PM, Sa 6-11PM. 324 Hayes St. 863-5545*

32 **Vorpal Gallery.** Large banners dress the front of this spacious gallery with a varied collection that emphasizes prints. *Open daily 11AM-6PM, Th until 8PM. 393 Grove St. 397-9200*

33 **Symphony Restaurant.** ★ ★ ★ $$ An attractive French restaurant with Thai overtones specializing in seafood and poultry, conveniently near the Opera House, with beautifully prepared food served in a gracious, traditional dining room. Especially interesting are: Spicy Fisherman's Soup, a dish of Thai origin loaded with mussels, calamari, clams, scallops and a sprinkling of mint (you have your choice as to how hot you want it seasoned); the grilled salmon with a delicate curry sauce; grilled freshwater prawns, *beurre blanc*; and the chicken mixed grill with *pommes frites*. Desserts include an exceptional Caramel Custard, fabulous cakes and an old-fashioned, well executed Baked Alaska. Chef-owner **Pommarong Nimearm-On** apologizes that they are closed on Sundays and promises to open specially if you want to have dinner there on Sunday! *Open M-Sa 11:30AM-2PM, 5:30-9PM. 298 Gough St. 861-3388*

34 **Cafe d'Arts.** ★ ★ ★ $$$ Perhaps it should be called *Cafe of Artistry* because, without a doubt, this one is a culinary star! This masterpiece was created by a Dutchman who once owned an art gallery and a Bostonian chef who was formerly a dancer. Evidence of their intense interest in Art is everywhere: in the elegance of the room decor, a soft background for the original art; in the unusual hand-painted Italian place plates; in how the food is arranged, transforming a simple dinner plate into a work of art. The emphasis here is on simple and fresh, with no salt in the cooking, little butter or cream in the sauces, and still the food seems to burst with flavor. It is *haute* cuisine at its best. Many of the entrees are presented on a bed of delicate pasta. The grilled loin of rabbit is served on black pepper pasta and the chicken on a tomato pasta with an incredibly light sauce which includes kernels of corn, tomato and saffron. The desserts take off into the *out of this world* category. The one big negative is that the wine list is unjustifiably expensive. *Open W-Sa 6-10:30PM. 205 Oak St. (Gough) 626-7100*

34 **Teddy Bears.** $$ Owner Victor Davis's pack of 5000 teddy bears were driving him out of his mansion so he has opened a bistro to house over half his collection. Lunch features simple salads, sandwiches and pasta dishes. At dinner there's a limited but good menu which includes Prime Rib and a jazz club lined with his bears called the **Bear's Den** with live musical entertainment 9PM-midnight. *Open daily 11:30AM-2PM, 6-10PM; Sa & Su Champagne Brunch 11:30-3PM. 131 Gough St. 621-6766*

34 **Albion House Inn.** *Moderate.* This bed and breakfast, reminiscent of the best European pensiones, is located in a 1906 building which was once a boarding house for immigrants and later a meeting place for musicians. Just a few blocks from the San Francisco Performing Arts Center and Civic Center, the Albion is a tranquil getaway for vacationers and business travelers. Breakfast is served at a long board table in the high-ceilinged living room, which has a fireplace and French doors. Max the cat keeps the house safe. *135 Gough St. 621-0896*

BESTS

Jeremiah Tower
Owner/Chef Stars Restaurant

Scandalous lunches in the main dining room of the **Clift Hotel**, because everyone except the staff is shocked. *Geary at Taylor. 775-4700.*

Saturday lunches at the **Cafe** at **Chez Panisse**, when Fritz Streiff is maitre d.'*1517 Shattuck Ave., Berkeley. 548-5555.*

Steak with white truffles at **Jack's** on Fillmore (seasonal). *1601 Fillmore. 931-8454.*

Black Oak Books in Berkeley for their combination of old and new books. *1491 Black Oak Ave. 486-0698.*

View from the lookout high above the **Golden Gate Bridge** at the Main side, especially during an October sunset or winter storm, sipping negronis.

Sunday brunch on the deck of someone's house in Belvedere on the water in May.

The **Auberge du Soleil** large suite, Picardie, a summer evening slowly slipping into fog, with caviar, the champagne cooling and a playmate nearby. *Rutherford Hill Rd., Rutherford. 707-963-1211.*

The little **Crystal Palace** in **Golden Gate Park** when orchids are in bloom.

Macy's Easter show when the gigantic azaleas fill up the first level of the store.

Acme Bread Company. *1601 San Pablo Ave., Berkeley. 524-1327.*

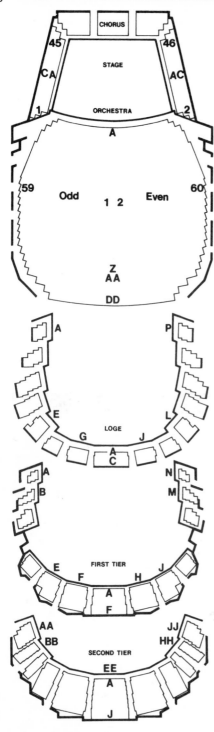

35 **Louise M. Davies Hall.** (1981, Skidmore, Owings and Merrill) Built to the tune of $33,000,000—all but $5,000,000 of it raised privately. It's the home of the **San Francisco Symphony**, whose season runs from October through May. The 3,036-seat house—named after culture maven **Louise M. Davies,** who contributed $5,000,000 towards its construction—opened in September 1980 after more than a decade of squabbling. According to the designers, the Hall is structured to provide guests with an instrument-level view of the stage from any-

where in the house. Also, seating is available behind the orchestra, offering a close-up view of the musicians at work. Besides the Symphony, Davies regularly books other musical and touring groups. *201 Van Ness Av. at Grove St. 431-5400*

36 **Pensione San Francisco.** *Moderate.* An attractive and pristine hotel. Located on the quiet side of Market Street, it has front door access to the city's major transportation facilities. *1668 Market St. 864-1271*

36 **Zuni Cafe.** ★ ★ $$ Did you ever hear of New Mexican food? Well, that's what Zuni is—a combination of the charcoal grilling so popular in the U.S. with the sorts of sauces you find in Mexico. The menu features fish perfectly grilled over mesquite wood. But there's far more than that—there are always some innovative dishes on the frequently changing menu. Also outstanding moderately-priced California wines, many sold by the glass. *American. Open M-Sa 11AM-midnight. 1658 Market St. 552-2522*

37 **Red Desert.** Cacti and succulents in a simulated desert setting, sand and all. Some of the specimens are 10 feet high. *Open M-Sa 10AM-6PM. 1632 Market St. 552-2800*

38 **Bank of America Building.** (1978, Skidmore, Owings and Merrill) A massive white concrete-clad fortress with a short octagonal tower above. The building houses Bank of America's credit card services. *1407 Market St. between 10th and 11th Sts.*

BESTS

Diane Feinstein
Mayor of San Francisco

I'm a native San Franciscan and terribly in love with my city. Selecting a favorite place is consequently very difficult since there are simply miles and miles of pleasures and delights packed into our 49-square-mile area.

However, caveats aside, I always recommend that visitors to San Francisco stroll through **Golden Gate Park,** with its more than 1,000-acres of magnificent trees, plants and greenswards. The park also houses our renowned **Japanese Tea Garden,** a very special park within a park whose ambience is unmistakenly Eastern and a wonderful place to reflect and relax.

Some of San Francisco's finest **museums** are also located within Golden Gate Park—the **Asian Art Museum,** the **de Young Museum,** the **Fine Arts Museum,** the **Academy of Sciences** and **Steinhart Aquarium.** These facilities are tremendous urban resources for education and great places to see some of America's and the world's finest works of art.

Besides Golden Gate Park, I also recommend visiting San Francisco's **Chinatown**—the largest one outside of Asia—where you can eat exquisitely for very low prices and shop for virtually anything.

And don't forget to ride one of San Francisco's **Cable Cars!** The city, with tremendous support from the private sector, has recently rehabilitated this century-old transportation system— and America's only moving national monument—and it remains a great way to see San Francisco's incredibly hilly streets and spectacular views.

I also recommend visiting **Fisherman's Wharf** and sampling our incomparable Dungeness crab, sourdough bread and succulent seafood. Be sure to take a boat ride on **San Francisco Bay** too, one of the world's most beautiful deep-water bodies. You can sail right under the **Golden Gate Bridge**—celebrating its golden anniversary in 1987—as well as the equally impressive **Bay Bridge.** Views of San Francisco from the Bay are breathtaking.

As for restaurants, we have more per capita than any city in America; and they range fully across the world's most exciting cuisines. We have food for literally every palate!

Shopping is also excellent, with **Union Square** in the heart of downtown San Francisco one of the nation's leading retail centers. And that's only the beginning. There's a tremendous volume of top quality goods and services available throughout San Francisco.

My final recommendation is probably the most important one: be sure to meet our citizens. San Francisco is a cultural cornocopia of the world's peoples, most of whom are friendly, helpful and eager to share their insights about life in San Francisco with visitors.

Enjoy your visit to San Francisco and come back as often as you can!

A Brief History of San Francisco

1579—Sir Francis Drake anchors on the northern California coast.

1595—Captain Sebastian Cermeno is shipwrecked north of the Golden Gate, claims the land for Spain and names it Puerto de San Francisco.

1769—Spanish explorers, led by Don Gaspar de Portola, discover San Francisco Bay.

1776—Padre Junipero Serra founds the Mission of St. Francis on the shore of Lake Dolores. Captain Juan Bautista begins building the presidio.

1792—George Vancouver anchors off Yerba Buena Cove, the spot from which San Francisco grew.

1806—California is declared a province of the Republic of Mexico.

1846—The American flag is raised in Portsmouth Square and Yerba Buena becomes San Francisco. Captain John C. Fremont coins the term *Golden Gate.*

1848—The Gold Rush begins.

1854—First lighthouse built on Alcatraz Island.

1864—Young reporter Mark Twain begins writing about life in San Francisco for *Morning Call.*

1869—The transcontinental railroad is completed, providing new trade and travel routes to the West.

1870—Golden Gate Park is begun.

1872—First Japanese ship arrives in San Francisco loaded with tea.

1873—The Cable Car comes to San Francisco.

1876—Electricity lights up San Francisco just in time for author Jack London's birth.

1904—Bank of Italy, to become Bank of America, is created by Italian merchant A.P. Giannini.

1906—Earthquake and fire destroy much of the city.

1915—Panama-Pacific International Exhibition commemorating the opening of the Panama Canal is held in San Francisco. Twenty million people attend.

1927—Opening of San Francisco International Airport.

1934—July 5 was Bloody Thursday, the head-on confrontation between the Industrial Association scabs, the International Longshoremen's Union and the police.

1936—Oakland Bay Bridge is dedicated.

1937—Golden Gate Bridge opens.

1945—United Nations Charter is signed in San Francisco.

1960—Candlestick Park opens.

1963—Alcatraz closes due to old age, while renovated Ghirardelli Square opens.

1968—Summer of Love: hippies, the Free Speech Movement, drugs and the sexual revolution.

1974—BART's first run through the Transbay tube.

1978—Mayor George Moscone and Supervisor Harvey Milk are shot to death in their offices. Diane Feinstein becomes mayor.

1982—The San Francisco 49er's win the Superbowl in Cincinnati, repeating their performance 2 years later.

1986—Downtown Plan limits building in San Francisco.

The **Lower Haight** area, once depressed, is now blossoming with an interesting stretch of new shops and restaurants along **Haight** and **Fillmore** streets. Since this is one of the few areas where housing costs are less than astronomical, young professionals are buying and renovating the old Victorians and transforming the area into a safe and satisfying place to live.

Referred to as *The Fillmore* by residents who loved it, as writer **Charles Dobie** says, *for its supreme grotesqueness,* in early years the area was ignored. Others called it the *Great Sand Waste* for its succession of sand hills from **Van Ness Avenue** to the beach. Fog and wind constantly plagued these hills, but since the first development was for the dead, as the site of a municipal cemetery, it didn't really matter. Meanwhile, as Van Ness Avenue became fashionable, waves of middle class row houses and Victorians spread West to reach the cemetery—and the decision was made to build the new City Hall there. The bodies were exhumed and moved.

The city government was to enjoy their new quarters for only 7 years. The building was destroyed in 1906. But, by and large, earthquake damage in this area was moderate. The district was left with the only functioning streetcar line in the city. Fillmore Street rapidly became a main business artery and for a while the area thrived. A wonderful example of the architecture of this era can be found in a picturesque alley near Bush and Fillmore called **Cottage Row** and at **1801-45 Laguna Street.** In one of the houses, a mansion at Octavia and Bush (presently the site of a hospital), a mysterious black woman was *housekeeper* for **Thomas Bell. Mammy Pleasant**, as she was known, was a former madam, an exceptional cook, and thought to be a formidable sorceress. She seemed to have unusually powerfull connections and was devoted to the Abolitionist cause, giving large sums of money to **John Brown** and others to help escaping slaves. Some say she pushed her employer to his death from the 3rd floor balcony.

Japantown

, nearby and well worth some browsing time, is a surprise oasis—a pristine village within the city located within the approximate boundaries of **Octavia, Fillmore, California** and **Geary Streets.** This is called by its own residents *Nihonmachi,* or **Japantown.** Ever since World War II, when the Japanese Americans returned to find their former homes occupied, the greatest proportion have lived in other neighborhoods. Only 4 percent of San Francisco's Japanese-Americans actually live in Japantown, but most return here regularly for shopping, social and religious activities.

In the gardens along the neat rows of Victorians, you will see exotic shapes in the shrubbery and a stone lantern here or there in the well-tended grounds which have been planned with obvious respect for the tea garden tradition. Notice the curving roof line of the **Konko Mission,** and explore the **Japanese Cultural Trade Center** with its garden, hotel and pagoda. Here also are restaurants, 3 Buddhist churches, a Japanese theater, 2 movie houses showing Japanese language films, massage and hot bath establishments, and many small shops crammed with fascinating merchandise.

1 Rosalie's. ★ ★ ★ $$$ The epitome of whimsical in decor and trendy in cuisine. You might try the Shellfish Pan Roast or the pasta specialty, *Mezzaluna,* stuffed with ricotta cheese. Other specialties are rabbit and pheasant. The menu changes every 5 to 6 weeks. This place is fun and worth seeing if only to fulfill a fantasy about California dining. *Reservations suggested. Open M-F 11:30AM-2:30PM, 5:30-10:30PM; Sa & Su until 11:30PM. 1415 Van Ness Av. 928-7188*

2 St. Mary's Cathedral. (1971, Pietro Belluschi, Pier Luigi Nervi and McSweeney, Ryan and Lee) This modern cathedral consists of 4 hyperbolic paraboloids creating a 190-foot roof over a square plan on a podium. It seats 2,500 people around a central altar and is similar to other modern cathedrals in Liverpool and Brasilia. *Geary Blvd. at Gough St. 567-2020*

3 Majestic Inn. *Expensive.* The Majestic has a long, murky history, being possibly the city's oldest surviving hotel according to an 1888 document. It was untouched by earthquake and fire, and at that time was used as a shelter for the homeless. During the 1930s, actresses **Joan Fontaine** and **Olivia de Havilland** are reputed to have lived here. Today, after a $6 million reconstruction, its 60 rooms (including 9 luxurious suites) are complete with furniture from the French Empire and English manor houses, fine paintings, large, hand-painted four-poster beds and many fireplaces. The antique-filled lobby has been restored far beyond its initial grandeur. *1500 Sutter St. 441-1100*

Within the hotel is:

Cafe Majestic. ★ ★ ★ $$$ Innovative California and contemporary cuisine and some San Francisco turn-of-the-century recipes are served here by award winning chef **Stanley Eichelbaum.** The dining room has high ceilings and tall mirrors and is done in peach and gray with a kind of Victorian reserve and a European-style dining ambience. The adjacent bar has the air of a private gentleman's club with its 19th century mahogany horseshoe bar. The lunchtime platter of 4 kinds of charcuterie with garnish of sweet vegetable relish is good, as is the seasonal veal chop topped with fontina, the scallops with ginger and Grand Marnier, and the chicken breast with Greek olive paste. For dessert, the Linzertorte, Key lime pie and individually baked fruit tarts are delicious. The service is exceptionally caring and the prices are sensible. *Reservations essential on weekends. Open Tu-Su 7:30-10:30AM, 11:30AM-2:30PM, 6-10:30PM. 776-6400*

Restaurants/Nightlife red
Hotels blue
Shops/Galleries purple
Parks/Outdoor spaces green
Museums/Architecture/Narrative black

4 **St. Paul's Lutheran Church.** (1894) More like a cathedral than the one up the street. The front entrance porches were modeled after those at Chartres by **A.J. Kraft.** *994 Eddy St. at Gough St.*

5 **St. Francis Square.** (1961, Marquis and Stoller) The designers created a series of squares and other supervised public spaces. This moderate income cooperative complex is respected nationally. *Geary Blvd. betw. Webster and Laguna Sts.*

5 **YMCA.** (1914, Julia Morgan) Built around an internal top lit courtyard and modeled on an Italian palazzo. *1515 Webster.*

6 **Nihonmachi or the Japan Center.** A 5-acre mercantile complex within 3 square blocks, it opened in 1968 as the commercial and cultural center for San Francisco's more than 11,000 Japanese-American residents. The Center consists of 3 commercial buildings, a **Consulate,** the **Miyako Hotel,** the **Japan Trade Center,** the **Japan Center Theater** and the **Webster Street Bridge of Shops** (an Oriental *Ponte Vecchio*). Designed as a miniature *ginza,* the 2-level shopping area encloses pedestrian malls, Japanese gardens, shops, restaurants, art galleries, tempura bars and teahouses. **Rai Y. Okamoto** designed the Center, which replaced 2 rows of Victorians. *1520 Webster at Geary St.*

Within the Japan Center are:

Kabuki Hot Springs. Japanese-style community baths. Their *shiatsu* (Japanese massage) is the specialty. Phone a day or 2 in advance for an appointment. *Open M-Sa 10AM-10PM. 1750 Geary Blvd. 922-6000*

Fuki-Ya. ★★$$$ This first-rate restaurant in the Japanese Trade Center is divided into 2 parts: the *yakitori bar* for charcoal-grilled meats (and tasty crab croquettes) and the *sushi bar* for raw fish creations. You'll want to jump from one to the other and order one of everything. If you like exotic dishes, order the grilled eel, the sea urchin roe and the broiled salmon skin at the sushi bar. *Japanese. 22 Peace Plaza. 929-0127*

The Miyako. *Expensive.* Located in the Japanese Center complex, this hotel cultivates the distinctive atmosphere of a merging of East and West. The 172-room, 14-story hotel features authentic Japanese suites with futons as well as 14 suites with American beds and built-in saunas. Most rooms have deep, Japanese-style baths; all rooms reflect something of the Japanese traditional interior with *shoji* screens, terraces, shrines, bronze lamps, *tatami* mats and brocade quilts. Drinks in the **Garden Bar** are served by waitresses in colorful kimonos. The hotel is well located for downtown transportation and is surrounded by the Japanese shops, restaurants, tempura houses and sushi bars of the quarter. This is a Westin hotel. *1625 Post St. 922-3200; 800-228-3000*

Kinokuniya Book Store. Books about Japan in English, as well as Japanese publications and records. *Open daily 10AM-7PM. 1581 Webster St., upper level of West Building. 567-7625*

The Peace Pagoda. The focal point of the Center, it rises 100 feet in 5 tiers from the reflecting pool in the middle of the Peace Plaza.

Mifune. $ The Japanese version of fast food, presenting every sort of noodle dish you could think of—and then some. Do you want them cold or hot? In a bowl of steaming soup? With vegetables, fish or beef? You name it, and they probably have it. *Japanese. Open M-Th & Su 11AM-9PM, F & Sa 11AM-9:30PM. 1737 Post St. 922-0337*

Isobune. ★★$$ Sushi boats float by you around an oblong bar which captures the chefs in its center. Choose your favorite traditional sushi and beer in this popular spot. *Japanese. Open daily 11:30AM-10PM. Japan Center, Restaurant Mall. 563-1030*

Restaurant Isuzu. ★★★$/$$ Decorated with restrained elegance and serving creative, exquisitely presented Japanese dishes, this Japanese restaurant has been called one of the best in San Francisco. (Just ask **Raymond Burr,** who is a regular here.) Specialties include Lobster *Koganeyaki,* a type of Thermidor, and *Futomaki* sushi. *Open M, Tu, Th, F 12-2:30PM, 5-10PM; Sa & Su 12-2PM, 5-10PM. Closed W. 1581 Webster St. 922-2290*

Mitoya. $/$$ The chef across the *robata-yaki* (grilled foods) counter passes you finely grilled tidbits on a long wooden paddle. And fine they are—pick morsels of octopus, trout and other treats from an ice bed in front of you. Take off your shoes and stay awhile. *Japanese. Open daily 11:30AM-10PM. Japan Center, West Building. 563-2156*

Sapporo Ya. ★ ★ $/$$ The best Japanese noodle shop in town. The shop displays its busy noodle machine up front—fresh and thick soft noodles. Ignore the Western-style cafe interior; the noodles are the real thing. *Open M-Sa 11AM-midnight. Japan Center. 563-7400*

Shige Nighiguchi Kimonos. A shop for sight-seeing as well as buying, with vintage kimonos. *Open daily 10AM-6PM. 1581 Webster St.*

7 | **Sanppo.** ★ $$ Elegant Japanese food in a setting that's better than most. Try *yosenabe*, a one-pot seafood dish, or barbequed eel *unajyu* steamed in its own iron pot. *Japanese. Open Tu-F 11:45AM-10PM, Sa & Su 3-10PM. 1701 Post St. 346-3486*

7 | **Ino Sushi.** $$/$$$ One of the best of San Francisco's sushi bars, serving only the freshest fish in a modern, blond-wood setting typical of what you'd find in Japan. *Japanese. Open for dinner. Closed Su. 1620 Webster St. 922-3121*

7 | **Akasaka.** ★ $$$ Elegant Japanese dining, particularly if you order the *Chef's Dinner*, which is sent out one beautiful course after another. The food is so beautifully served that you'll wonder whether to eat it or frame it. *Japanese. Open daily 11:30AM-10PM. 723 Buchanan. 921-5360*

8 | **Restored Victorian Row Houses.** These houses were moved from their former sites when the Western Addition was being destroyed in the name of urban renewal. They have been carefully restored and given front gardens in contrast to their previous condition, when they were located on the street front. *Bush St. between Steiner and Gough Sts., south side.*

9 | **Queen Anne Hotel.** *Expensive.* Although this is one of the largest bed and breakfasts in town, no 2 of the 48 rooms or suites are decorated alike. Each has private bath, telephone, TV and king or queen size bed. Ten have fireplaces and all are furnished with English antiques. Of architectural interest are the oak paneling in the hall, the massive Spanish cedar carved staircase and inlaid floors of exceptional quality. The building was originally built by **Senator James Fair,** one of the Comstock silver kings, to house a girls' school. It served in turn as an elite gentlemen's club, a home for young working women and finally a hotel. The hotel prides itself on such personal touches as shoes polished at night, breakfast served in the room, special access and elevator for the handicapped and a parking area for guests with cars. Tea and sherry are served in the drawing room every afternoon. *1590 Sutter St. 441-2828*

10 | **Hank Baum Gallery.** Contemporary California paintings and sculpture. *Open M-F 11AM-5:30PM. 2140 Bush St. 921-7677*

11 | **Elite Cafe.** $$ This New Orleans creole restaurant has taken San Francisco by storm, even though the food has gone downhill since the opening weeks. Good cocktails and baked spicy Creole fish dishes such as blackened redfish and creole-style stuffed eggplant. *American. Open M-Sa 10AM-3PM, 5-11PM; Su 10AM-10PM. 2049 Fillmore St. 346-8668*

12 | **Eichelbaum & Co.** $$ This tiny take-out place (with a few tables), run by the former *San Francisco Examiner* music critic, was an instant success. Where else can you have superb French meals and desserts packed up to eat at home? Light lunches too, tending toward the Italian. The service often drops below expected standards. *Continental. Open Tu-F 8AM-9PM, Sa & Su 8AM-5PM. 2417 California St. 929-9030*

13 | **Mount Zion Hospital Psychiatric Wing** (Originally **Maimonides Health Center**). (1950, Eric Mendelsohn and Michael Gallis) Designed by 2 of the International Style masters, the wing has been significantly altered and its balconies filled in. *Sutter and Divisadero Sts.*

14 | **1111 Oak Street.** (1860) This is one of the oldest houses in San Francisco. Recently restored, it is now used for office space. Nearby buildings from the same era have also been converted for commercial use.

15 | **VIS Club.** Dance club with punk, reggae and blues music. *Open daily 10PM-2AM. 628 Divisadero St. 567-0660*

16 | **601 Steiner Street.** (1891) Queen Anne house with elaborate carving and a fine turret. *Private residence.*

17 | **Amacio Ergina Housing.** (1986, Daniel Solomon and Associates) These 72 dwellings are an example of how to build affordable housing in a way that respects the traditional urban fabric. In contrast to so much recent public housing, the white painted wood-framed scheme holds the street, creates a defensible interior courtyard and includes a mid-block alley. The facades have bay windows, false fronts and walk-up entries at regular intervals. The rear elevations are more informal than the fronts, with external stairs and balconies. *Ellis and Scott Sts.*

18 | **700 Block of Steiner Street.** (1894-95) The six identical houses by the carpenter **Matthew Kavanaugh** have been carefully restored and painted. With the backdrop of the city's Financial District skyline, this row is often featured in tourist photographs of the city. *Private residences.*

19 | **Cafe Sinfonia.** ★ ★ ★ $ A tiny gazebo-like place with good food at incredibly reasonable prices. Chef-owner **Tony Nika** is Albanian, the food is Milanese Italian and the result is a culinary treasure. Pasta Sinfonia is outstanding, as is the Calamari Vinaigrette appetizer and the Eggplant Parmigiano. Scallops Sauté is a generous serving of shellfish with a delectable lemony sherry sauce, punctuated with bits of green onion and tomato. There's no wine list, but one decent wine is available. The service is gracious. Since it is close to the Civic Center, it gets the theater and opera crowd, but reservations are accepted. Beer and wine only. *Open T-Sa 5-10:45PM. 465 Grove. 431-7899*

20 | **Pendragon Bakery.** Serves coffee, espresso, delicious scones and pastries and also light lunches. *Open M-F 7AM-4:30PM, Sa 8:30AM-4PM, Su 8:30AM-3PM. 400 Hayes. 552-7017*

21 **294 Page Street.** (1885, Henry Geilfuss) A beautifully preserved Victorian stick house. *Private residence.*

22 **Prince Neville's.** ★ $/$$ This restaurant serves the unique and truly delicious cuisine of Jamaica. Tropical murals, reggae music and the eager, friendly service help foster the illusion that you are really on the island. The best bets here are the seafood dishes—fresh, spicy and prepared with delicacy and care. Other choices are fried plantains and, for the more adventurous, curried goat. Extensive beer and wine list. *Open daily 5-10PM. 424 Haight St. 861-9433*

22 **Club Noc-Noc.** A very new wave bar featuring black walls, buzzing TV sets and, in the words of one patron, *a clientele so relentlessly hip as to make the South of Market trendies look like geriatric polyesteroids.* For those young, hip and brave enough to handle the crowds and the attitudes, this is a fun place to spend the evening. *557 Haight St. 552-1090*

23 **Thep-Phanom.** ★ $ A small, attractively decorated eatery serving a great combination of bright tastes and striking textures. Particularly good is the *Tomkha Ghi,* or chicken soup with coconut milk and ginger. Other entrees include *Kiew Warm Ghi,* a green curry chicken, and *Sam Kastr,* a firey pork curry. A wonderful bargain. *Open daily 5-10PM. 400 Fillmore St. 431-2526*

24 **Germania Street Houses.** (1984, Donald MacDonald) Two miniscule dwellings each occupying a 20-by-20-foot footprint and proving that it is possible to build affordable housing in San Francisco. It has basic detailing and an almost cartoon-like house form. *Germania St. Steiner.*

25 **Archbishop's Mansion.** *Expensive.* This has to be one of the most spectacular bed and breakfasts in San Francisco. Built for the archbishop in 1904, this quite incredible building has been lovingly restored by its present owners. It features a 3-story open staircase covered by a 16-foot stained glass dome, 18 fireplaces with magnificently carved mantelpieces and Belle Epoque furnishings with Victorian and Louis XIV chandeliers. There are 15 guest rooms in all, each with private bath; 10 rooms have fireplaces and several are suites. An elaborate breakfast is included in the rate. *1000 Fulton St. 563-7872*

9 SOUTH OF MARKET

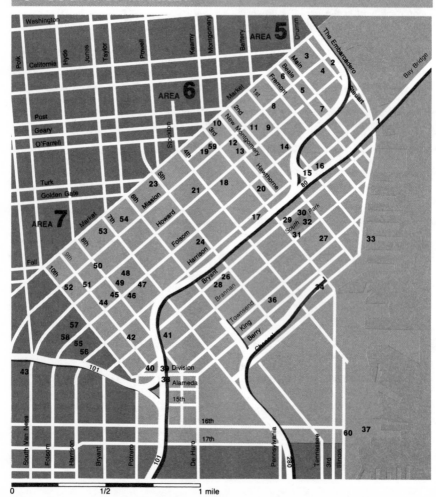

South of Market

as a kind of catch-all for anything and everything that won't fit elsewhere: gay bars, punk rock hangouts, tattoo museums, a wholesale flower market, street people's park, bus terminals, a convention center and warehouses with the district's newest residents—the artists, dancers and musicians who like the low rents they pay for huge spaces they convert to studios and living quarters. **SoMa,** as locals call this industry-turned-artsy area, is also the home of a dynamic new nightlife scene, with comedy, jazz and dance clubs staying open until the sun comes up.

This part of town has always been home to industry situated as it is, close to the Embarcadero and the Bay. Several foundries could be seen here in the 1850s, along with rows of tiny houses, many prefabricated in the East, housing the town's first industrial population. But when it became apparent the climate was the warmest in the Bay Area, **Rincon Hill,** long since blasted away and buried under the approach to the **Bay Bridge,** became the most prestigious address. **Second Street** was filled with small elegant shops. Adjacent **South Park** was a pioneer real estate development promoted by an Englishman who set out to model an exclusive community for 64 families after the plan of terraces in London—stately Georgian houses built around an enclosed park to which only the residents had a gate key. Here, among others, lived cattle king **Henry Miller, Senator Gwin** and **Hall McAllister,** until he lost his mansion in a poker game. But the decline of Rincon Hill set in from the industrialization of the neighborhood before the park was half built. Its residents fled to Nob Hill, leaving their abandoned houses to Japanese immigrants. Rooming houses and machine shops have taken over, but here and there remnants of grandeur can still be seen, especially on **Third Street** between **Bryant** and **Brannan Streets.**

Today, South of Market is almost half industry. But once again the face of the terrain is changing. The construction of the **Moscone Convention Center,** with its satellite restaurants, shops and living accommodations, is beginning to impact the territory. The Center itself, named after the late mayor, can accommodate up to 600 conventioneers with an 880-foot-long Exhibit Hall and 31 meeting rooms. It covers an 11-acre block. The district, sprinkled with artists' lofts and galleries, is reminiscent of New York's SoHo. Commercial pressures are being felt as more newcomers move in and rents are already beginning to climb. The visitor will find a mixture here of old-time establishments and new boutiques. South of Market is also now home of a theater renaissance, with several theaters that present innovative and avant-garde works by contemporary artists—a welcome contrast to the often staid offerings of the downtown theaters.

Because of its geographic orientation, the South of Market area doesn't get as much wind as its neighbors to the north, which contributes to its being the warmest district in San Francisco, with temperatures slightly above the annual average of 62.5 degrees.

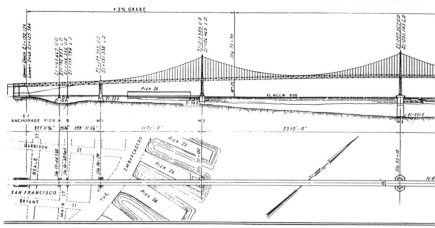

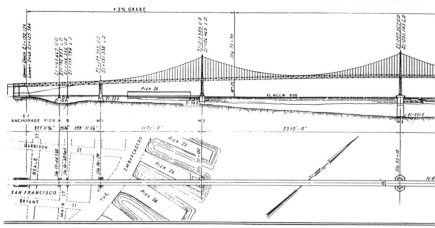

1 **The Bay Bridge.** (1936) **Charles H. Purcell** was chief engineer on this, the longest steel high-level bridge in the world. It is, in fact, 2 bridges separated by a tunnel through Yerba Buena Island. Its construction was the most expensive for a single project ever undertaken. The foundations of one of the piers extend deeper below water than those of any other bridge ever built—242 feet. The pier is bigger than the largest of the Pyramids and required more concrete than the Empire State Building in New York. It took over 3 years to build and is 8¼ miles from approach to approach. (The bridge itself is 4½ miles long.) The San Francisco side consists of a double suspension bridge; the Oakland side is a cantilever bridge. It has 2 levels with 5 lanes in each direction. Originally electric trains and trucks ran on the lower deck and cars on the upper deck, but the tracks were removed in the late 50s when the trains were replaced by buses. The best views are from Yerba Buena Island, or from below on the Embarcadero in San Francisco.

The Bay Bridge celebrated its *golden* anniversary on 12 November 1986 after 50 years of eliminating the isolation between the cities of San Francisco and Oakland. The month-long celebration included a parade of Navy ships, a series of aerial feats by the Blue Angels, a 5 mile run at Chrissy Field, an antique car parade across the bridge and fireworks displays over the Bay. In 1936, **Governor Frank Merriam** cut through the ceremonial chain, officially opening one of the largest, most costly structures ever completed. Today the Bay Bridge is the busiest thoroughfare in the Bay Area. An estimated 2,250,000,000 vehicles have crossed it over the years. Tolls paid by these vehicles have raised enough revenue to pay for other means of public transportation in the Bay Area, including the Bart tube, the San Mateo-Hayward Bridge and most of the Dunbarton Bridge. Established as the workhorse of the bridges on the Bay, it has endeared itself to worker and wanderer. In the words of Purcell, the Bay Bridge is *a tribute to the intelligence of the American working man.* It was and is an extraordinary accomplishment in engineering, construction and design. *Toll westbound.*

Nuts and Bolts

70,000 miles of wire and cable hold up the bridge.

When it's cold, the bridge can shrink as much as 10 feet.

250,000 vehicles cross the bridge on an average day.

More than 400,000 gallons of paint were used to paint the bridge; it is repainted every 7 years.

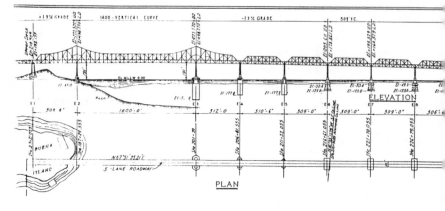

EAST BAY CROSSING

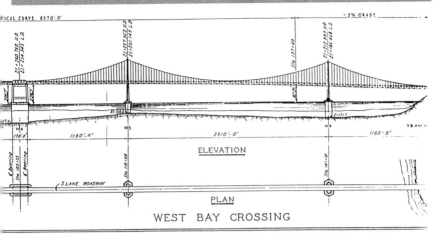

ELEVATION

PLAN

WEST BAY CROSSING

San Francisco Bay is in trouble, reeling from industrial and agricultural waste that is harming the fish and wildlife. The fact that the Bay is shrinking has only worsened the problem: ⅓ of the original 680 square miles of the Bay have been filled in for waterfront projects.

When Spanish army captain **Don Gaspar de Portala** accidentally discovered **Francisco Bay** in 1769, he found an exceedingly rich and diverse natural environment—and the home of the **Ohlone Indians**, a tribe of hunter/gatherers, or *diggers* as the Spanish called them, and the fullness of their tables was great. The Bay was full of shellfish and the miles of marshland teemed with birds, ducks and geese. But now San Francisco Bay faces the possible extinction of several animals. Some native species have left the area already; sea otters, certain fish, fur seals. Occasionally the **peregrine falcon** and **black brant** are seen. **Marsh song sparrows** are greatly reduced in number. The **California clapper rail,** also called a **marsh hen,** is a speckled brownish-grey chicken-like bird with a short white tail. It digs in the mud with its long bill for frogs and clams, and must nest in the tall grass. It tries to keep a low profile and is found almost exclusively in the San Francisco Bay. During high tide, it is visible in San Leandro Bay and Palo Alto. The **California black rail,** also a loner, is a tiny black bird with white spots and a rust-colored neck. In addition to bay marshes, it occasionally goes south or inland to fresh water. The **Brown pelican's** birth rate has dropped off dramatically because of pesticide use. This big billed brown bird uses its pouch to catch and carry fish. You can recognize him by his 6-foot wing span as he swoops down to snag a fish, or characteristically poses, bill and pouch nestling into his chest. The pelican's number is shrinking, but he can be found in the Bay from June to September. The **California tern** is endangered, due mainly to people seeking its plumage; it can be seen in the Bay from April to August or on the islands near Redwood City. This yellow-billed grey and white bird has a black feathered head and a tiny body. The **salt marsh harvest mouse** nests in the Bay shore area or the marshes around Palo Alto, Alviso and San Pablo Bay. Predatory creatures consider this tiny creature a tasty morsel, and this, along with destruction of its natural habitat, has lead to the decline in its numbers.

Courtesy California Department of Transportation

KEY SYSTEM FILL

2 **Umberto's.** ★ ★ ★ $$/$$$ The softly lit archways, pottery and paintings inspire nostalgia for Mediterranean nights. The superb dishes skillfully meld the very best in Southern French and Northern Italian cuisines. Only the freshest ingredients are used. Some of the oustanding seafood and veal dishes are served with unusual, subtle sauces which never overpower the natural flavor. Portions are generous but not heavy. Excellent wine list. Highly recommended. *Reservations suggested. Open M-F 11:30AM-2:30PM, Sa 5:30-11PM. 141 Steuart St. 543-8021*

3 **d'Audiffred Building.** (1889, Hipolyte d'Audiffred) A pre-earthquake brick building, the only one south of Market to survive the fire. Ironically, it burned down in 1981 and is now restored. *Mission at Embarcadero.*

4 **Rincon Center.** (1940, Gilbert Stanley Underwood). The **Rincon Annex Post Office Building,** one of the city's masterpieces and a truly civic piece of design, is being incorporated into a massive mixed-use complex of offices, shops, plazas and apartment towers by **Pereira Associates.** The **Anton Refregier** murals that were in the Annex lobby are the centerpiece of Rincon's 85-foot-high skylighted atrium. The complex is the first to pass muster under the city's Downtown Plan. The post office that used to be here has been moved to 50 First Street. *Mission at Spear St.*

5 **Rockin Robbins.** 50s rock and roll dance club with DJ. *Open M-F 7PM-midnight. 133 Beale St. 543-1961*

6 **Five Fremont Center.** (1984, Skidmore, Owings and Merrill) Its eroded zigzag corners and setbacks at mid-level and penthouse give this 600-foot-high tower a *moderne* look that sets it apart from its International Style neigbors. It is clad in travertine marble with mirror-glass windows. The plaza on the First Street side is surrounded by shops and restaurants, including a chic **McDonald's** and a new wave **Pastabella.** The **World Savings and Loan** branch was designed by **Jennings and Stout** (1984). *Fremont at Mission St.*

7 **Mailways—Trains Are Us.** A great place for train buffs. Model trains for everyone, from beginner to connoisseur. *Open M-F 8AM-4:45PM, Sa 10AM-2PM. Folsom and Main Sts. 982-2523*

8 **Transbay Terminal.** (1939, Timothy Pflueger; Arthur Brown Jr. and John L. Donovan, consulting architects) When the Bay Bridge was opened, this austere, functional building replaced the Ferry Building as the gateway to the city. *Mission and First Sts.*

Restaurants/Nightlife red
Hotels blue
Museums/Architecture/Narrative black

9 **Club DV-8.** This 2-level dance club with an elegant room with a dance floor and bar and a disco downstairs has progressive, industrial sound and classic rock music. DJ. *Open W & Th 9PM-2AM, F & Sa 10PM-4AM. No cover charge on Th with student ID. 55 Natoma. 777-1419*

10 **Sheraton Palace Hotel.** *Deluxe.* This is the oldest grand luxury hotel in the city today. From the time of its opening in 1875, it has been the showplace of the Gold Rush town known for its extravagance. The West had never seen anything like it: 7-stories high, 800 rooms and a dining room 150-feet-long. The original Palace was rebuilt after the 1906 quake and the renowned Garden Court restaurant became a sensation with the elite, with its leaded glass dome roof, 16 ionic marble columns and 20 crystal chandeliers. *639 Market St. 392-8600; 800-325-3535*

Within the hotel is:

Palm Court Garden. ★ ★ $$$ A restaurant that has to be seen—an elegant Victorian dining room with a huge skylight. It's all in the tradition of the grand old hotel dining rooms you encounter in Europe. Famous for Sunday brunch, although the food could be better. *American. Open M-F for breakfast and lunch, Su for brunch and dinner. Sheraton Palace Hotel at Market and New Montgomery Sts. 392-8600*

11 **Triangle Gallery.** This large gallery shows abstract painting and sculpture, primarily by Bay Area artists. *95 Minna at 2nd St. 777-2710*

12 **Yin Place.** ★ $$ Come here for the delicious dim sum lunch, served daily in this attractive restaurant with pale pink walls, hardwood floors and white tablecloths. Other Chinese dishes are also available. *Open daily 11:30AM-3PM. 605 Mission St. 777-2929*

12 **Rialto Building.** (1902-10, Meyer and O'Brien) The building survived the earthquake and was rebuilt after the fire by **Bliss and Faville.** It has an unusual *U-shaped* plan with a light court after the entrance. The cornice has also been rebuilt. Brick and terra cotta facade. *116 New Montgomery at Mission St.*

13 **Pacific Telephone Building.** (1925, Miller and Pflueger; A.A. Cantin Architects) One of the most beautiful skyscrapers in San Francisco, it owes much to **Saari-**

nen's celebrated design for the Chicago Tribune Tower in its profile, detailing and vertical emphasis. Notice the *moderne* entrance lobby with its Chinese decorated ceilings. *130-140 New Montgomery between Mission and Howard Sts.*

14 **J. Canes.** Antiques and collectibles. *Open M-Th 9:30AM-5:30PM, F 9:30-5PM, Sa & Su 10AM-4PM. 530 Folsom. 495-3579*

15 **76 Tower Union Oil Company Building.** (1941, Lewis P. Hobart) A landmark on top of Rincon Hill, its triangular shaped tower is directed toward the approach ramp to the Bay Bridge. It's clad in white porcelain enamel—a material that architects have recently rediscovered. *425 First at Harrison St.*

16 **Sailors' Union of the Pacific Building.** (1950, William S. Merchant) This building symbolizes the power that unions gained after the bitter struggles and bloody strikes of 1934. It contains a fine auditorium, foyer and stairways. In style, it is reminiscent of European constructivist buildings of the 30s. *450 Harrison at First St.*

17 **City Nites.** Dance club with DJ and occasional live music. *Open Th 9PM-2AM, F & Sa 9PM-3AM. 715 Harrison St. 546-7774*

19 **Pacific Gas and Electric Substation.** (1907, Willis Polk) Another of **Polk's** masterpieces; it is in a sad state of disrepair, but is due to be restored as part of the Yerba Buena Redevelopment Project. Located on an alley between Mission and Market Streets, its fine brick and stone facade with its elaborately detailed portal and carefully proportioned windows should make a splendid exhibition hall. *Jessie between 3rd and 4th Sts.*

20 **Max's Diner.** ★ $$ Yet another satellite restaurant bordering the Moscone Convention Center, Max's Diner (of **Max's Opera Cafe** and **Max's 888 Club**) serves up delicious and generous portions of everything you always wanted to eat but never dared to. The decor is modern/vintage at its best—comfy booths, or a long counter for those who prefer to get it quick, and a cocktail lounge with a circular bar and full-time rock 'n roll. Make sure you're hungry because there's lots to eat: hearty deli sandwiches and burgers, baked meat loaf and roast turkey, cheese steak and pan fried pork chops, a full-range of baked goods and a soda fountain. As their logo on the front door reads, *This is a bad place for a diet. Open daily M-Th 11AM-midnight, F 11AM-1AM, Sa 12PM-1AM, Su 12PM-11PM. 311 3rd St. 546-6297*

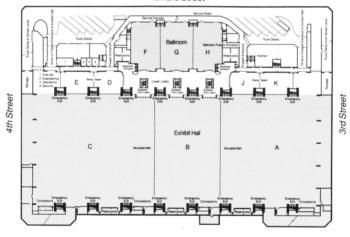

Howard Street

4th Street

3rd Street

Courtesy Moscone Center

18 **Moscone Center.** (1981 Hellmuth, Obata and Kassabaum) Moscone Center, part of the Yerba Buena Development is named after the slain mayor, **George Moscone.** After over a decade of controversy, this vast underground exhibition hall by **HOK** is the first part of a redevelopment program that will ultimately cover many city blocks. It is a structure which combines functional design with architectural grace. The glass-walled lobby frames the City's skyline, while on the lower level sweeping arches support the structure to create one of the largest column-free exhibit halls in the world. Moveable soundproof walls divide the Exhibit Hall into three halls making the space ideal for conventions and trade shows of all sizes.

Moscone Center has been part of the revitalization of South of Market. Proposed additions will double the Center's usable exhibition space and will also be built underground. *Howard St. between 3rd and 4th.*

20 **St. Francis Place Housing.** (1985, Kaplan/McLaughlin/Diaz) A mixture of apartment towers, townhouses above retail shops and offices. The entrance staircase at 3rd and Folsom Streets is organized on the diagonal to relate to the Moscone Center opposite and bring visitors up the 3rd level podium.

21 **Cadillac Bar and Grill.** ★ $$ Traditional Mexican food in an authentic looking place. The Cadillac offers carnitas, fajitas and other favorites. A popular spot to eat and/or drink. *Open M-Th 11:30AM-11PM, F 11:30AM-midnight, Sa 3PM-midnight. 1 Holland Ct. 543-8226*

One of San Francisco's most important industries is **tourism**. Every year, visitors outnumber the resident population by 5 times, with almost a third of these 3 million people coming for conventions.

23 **Old Mint Building Museum.** (1869-74, A.B. Mullett) This brick and stone building in the classical style is one of the few important monuments to survive both the earthquake and fire intact. It symbolizes the Jeffersonian ideals of the young republic. Tours of the building include viewing a million dollars in gold, a million dollar coin collection and restored Victorian rooms. There's also a 30-minute movie, *The Granite Lady*. *No admission charge. Open M-W 10AM-4PM. 5th and Mission Sts. 556-3630*

24 **Milestones.** Dance club with live jazz daily. *Open M-F 3PM-2AM, Sa & Su 6PM-2AM. 376 5th St. 777-9997*

25 **Crown Point Press Gallery.** Known internationally for the high quality and standards of its etchings. It prints and publishes etchings by artists who work here by invitation. Crown Point also stages performances, readings and exhibitions of their printwork in their gallery. They produce books, periodicals and records. *Open Tu-Sa 10AM-5PM, M by appointment, 871 Folsom St. 974-6723*

26 **Antonio's Antiques.** Three floors of 17th, 18th and 19th century French, English and Continental antiques, furnishings and accessories. Fine porcelain, sculpture and Oriental carpets. *Open M-F 8:30-6PM, Sa 10AM-3PM by appt. anytime. 701 Bryant St. 781-1737*

27 **S.F. Fire Department Pumping Station.** (1920, Frederick Meyer) A stripped down classical building that houses pumps for the elaborate water system designed after the 1906 earthquake and fire. It was built to ensure that the city would never again be left without adequate means of fighting a massive fire if the major water mains from outside were ruptured. *698 Second St. at Townsend.*

28 **Santa's Helpers, Woods and Woods Inc.** You can take a 30-minute tour of their stuffed toy factory that covers all steps involved in toy production. Their specialties range from the celebrated *Colonial Teddy* and *B.B. Bear* to unicorns, rabbits and stuffed airplanes. *Call in advance for tours. 444 De Maro St. 626-0781*

29 **Connoisseur Wine Imports.** They feature a great number of French wines and also stock some California and German labels. *Open Tu-F 10AM-6:30PM, Sa 10AM-5PM. 462 Bryant. 433-0825*

30 **South Park Cafe.** ★ $$ This intimate neighborhood spot bordering the park is a straightforward and elegant interpretation of the French cafe experience. The room, washed in gold tones with colorful flowers, has small tables lining the far wall which overlook the park through large windows and French doors. The menu offers a pleasing variety of thoughtfully prepared dishes, which are briskly served by young (mostly French) waiters. A small bar and a few tables provide an area at cocktail hour to sip an aperitif and choose from their long list of *tapas*, Spanish hors d'oeuvres. *Open M-F 8AM-10PM; Sa 6-10PM. 108 South Park (Between 2nd & 3rd Sts., and Bryant & Brannan Sts.) 495-7275*

31 **Jack London's Birthplace.** Marked with a plaque on the **Wells Fargo Bank** at *Brannan and 3rd Sts.*

32 **South Park Studios.** (1985, Toby Levy and Associates) A burnt-out row house that was converted into an architect's studio and dwelling in 1985, with a mixture of traditional and new wave aesthetics. South Park was originally laid out by English developer **George Gordon** in 1856, when this part of San Francisco promised to be a posh residential district. It was modeled on the London squares and originally had Italianate townhouses around the perimeter. It now has an interesting mixture of industrial, residential and studio buildings. *South Park between 2nd and 3rd Sts. and Brannan and Bryant.*

33 **Sailing Ship Restaurant.** ★ $$ Once known as *Ellen,* she carried lumber and spices to the South Seas, Africa and Central and South America at the turn of the century. She transported wounded troops and needed supplies in WWI, then turned coat to smuggle rum between England and the United States during the Prohibition. She was eventually bought by Columbia Studios and was given starring roles in *Hawaii* and *Mutiny on the Bounty*. Then she was retired from her colorful past by owner **Dolphin Rempp** and was transformed into one of San Francisco's most romantic dining spots. The Sailing Ship now sits in an earthquake-proof concrete cradle on Pier 42 south of Fisherman's Wharf. Chef **Doug Achterberg** creates a menu with a wide range of fresh seafoods embellished with fresh cilantro, garlic, ginger and tangy sauces. The menu changes every 2 months. The dining room is simply decorated with long, tan booths that run the length of the room, lit by candle lanterns and accented with brass. The restaurant's windows and deck overlook the harbor view. The nautical theme is more pronounced in the downstairs bar, which lacks the view but has tranquility and a private ambience. A wonderful and unusual spot to relax and enjoy your dining and an expansive view of the Bay without crowding. The ship is also available for private parties and weddings. There's a lot of parking alongside the ship. *Coats required after sundown. Reservations suggested. Open Tu-Sa 6-10PM. Pier 42, the Embarcadero. 777-5771*

34 **China Basin Building.** (1922, Bliss and Faville) If this building were put on end, it would be one of the tallest structures in the city—850 feet high. It is a warehouse/office building located on the edge of the China Basin. In 1973 it was handsomely repainted by **Robinson and Mills** in blue with white

---

Restaurants/Nightlife red
Hotels blue
Shops/Galleries purple
Museums/Architecture/Narrative black

stripes resembling an ocean liner. Visit the restaurant **(Polos)** on the waterfront. Sandwiches, salads and hot meals are served either indoors or on the deck overlooking the harbor. *Berry between 3rd and 4th Sts.*

36 **4th and Townsend Train Depot.** The terminal for the former Southern Pacific Railroad line. This now houses the commuter trains to San Jose, but originally was the starting point for the famous Coast Starlight and Daylight Express trains to Los Angeles. The Old Mission style station (at 3rd and Townsend) was demolished in 1979 for the present utilitarian structure. Best seen at the evening rush hour when the sleek double decker stainless steel trains leave at 10 minute intervals for their journeys down the Peninsula.

37 **Mission Rock Resort.** $ Hidden away on the docks of China Basin is one of the best hamburger spots in San Francisco. An unexpected pleasure: the terrace overlooking the slips and dry docks. A hidden treasure in SF. *Open daily 9AM-3PM. 817 China Basin Rd. 621-5538*

38 **Henry's.** Club with jazz, rock and soul music and dancing. *Open M-Sa 11:30PM-2AM. 2 Showplace Sq. 626-3804*

39 **Galleria and Showplace Square.** Restored brick warehouses that have become the city's furniture showroom center. The Galleria consists of 2 warehouses linked by a modern glass-faced atrium building that is used for exhibitions and conferences. There is a cafeteria on the 2nd floor. *Henry Adams (Kansas St.) at Division near 8th and 9th Sts. 431-2321*

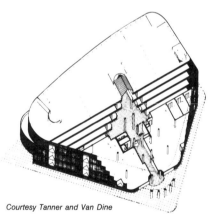

Courtesy Tanner and Van Dine

40 **999 Brannan Street, SF Datamart Center.** (1985, Tanner and VanDine) A 3-story glass-block-clad building that was intended to house showrooms for Silicon Valley computer companies. Arranged around a top lit atrium space, it has car parking on the roof, reached by a long ramp against the adjacent freeway. The building often appears in TV advertisements for people doing healthy things like drinking milk, jogging, etc. *999 Brannan St. at 9th St.*

40 **Gift Center.** (1917, Maurice Couchot; 1984 renovations, Kaplan/McLaughlin/Diaz) Formerly the BMT warehouse, it was renovated in 1984 with the construction of a large atrium space in place of the original

light well. This space, designed in an Art Deco style, is intended for parties and dances and is seen at its best at night when in use. *599 8th Street at Brannan.*

41 **Max's 888 Cafe.** ★$ Within the Art Deco Gift Center, Max's serves wonderful salads, a variety of fish dishes, barbecued burgers and fabulous desserts. Full bar and live piano. The setting is well worth a trip. Lunch and continental breakfast only. *Open M-F 11:30AM-3:30PM. 888 Brannan St. 552-8555*

42 **Paramount Flag Co.** Flags of every size and description. You can special order them too. *Open M-F 9AM-4:30PM. 450 9th St. 626-3188*

43 **San Francisco Herb Company.** Here you can buy herbs in large quantities at wholesale prices. *Open M-F 10AM-4PM. 215 14th St. 861-7174*

44 **Billboard Cafe.** ★ ★ $$ Opened in 1984 by artist/entrepreneur **Mark Rennie** (known around town for his gigantic billboard paintings), the Billboard originally catered to locals, with a 20 percent discount for artists. Rennie saw the restaurant as yet another canvas and attracted media attention when he mounted a large billboard on the top of his own restaurant. At its peak, the dining room was serving 400 meals a day. Although things have calmed down a bit, the Billboard offers good, inexpensive food in a fascinating atmosphere—the crowd is an amazing mixture of punk and establishment types. The menu is modest but varied with an emphasis on fish. *Open M-Th 11AM-11PM, F & S 11AM-midnight, Su Brunch 10:30AM-4PM. Folsom at 9th St. 558-9500*

45 **Augusta's.** ★$ Immense burgers in an environment that may surprise you. The hearty beef, pasta and sandwiches draw a variety of leather-wearers and just plain folk, but be forewarned. Trendy and popular. *Open M-F 11:30AM-3PM. 1256 Folsom (8th St.) 626-4459*

46 **Milano Joe's.** ★ ★ $$ Delicious Italian cuisine in an atmosphere of casual elegance can be had in this spacious one room restaurant, decorated in sleek black and white and accented by exquisite flowers. The varied menu has well prepared dishes and generous portions. The chefs prepare their veal and pasta specialties out in the open—to the delight of customers seated at the bar. Grill items are cooked over mesquite and the varied dessert menu changes daily. *Open M-F 11AM-11PM, Sa 11AM-midnight, Su 5-11PM. 1175 Folsom St. 861-2815*

47 **Rings.** ★ ★ ★ $$$ One of the more elegant spots south of Market, with just the right touch of fresh chic on a good base of homestyle charm. Warm, salmon-colored walls hung with a revolving show of paintings accentuate the focal point of the room, a glass block counter in front of the open kitchen, which provides seating and great entertainment for single customers who enjoy watching the chefs at work. The outdoor patio has a sliding roof to accommodate the fickle San Francisco weather. The menu is imaginative with interesting specials such as an exceptional turkey pot pie. All pasta dishes may be ordered in half portions as appetizers, an idea that deserves its popularity. The wine list is excellent, but the rooms are a bit noisy if you're craving a quiet dining experience. *Open M 11:30AM-3PM; Tu-F 11:30AM-3PM, 5-10PM; Sa 5-10PM. 1131 Folsom St. 621-2111*

47 **Eddie Jacks.** ★★$$ Another recent addition to the Folsom Street line-up. This cozy bistro offers a small but unusual menu of simple dishes served in a dramatic environment. The dark taupe walls and theatrical lighting of the back dining room enhance the rose marble bar and cocktail lounge in the front, warmed by splashy flower arrangements everywhere. The menu features succulent treats such as warm chicken salad with pear and rosemary sauce, an open-faced grilled lamb sandwich with feta cheese and flank steak with lime, cilantro and miso sauce. It's a great place for the cocktail hour, with hors d'oeuvres of sweet potato chips, fried polenta sticks and gorgonzola sauce, and barely grilled marinated tuna. The desserts are fabulous too. *Open M 11:30AM-2:30PM; Tu-F 11:30AM-2:30PM, 6-10PM; Sa 6-10PM. 1151 Folsom St. between 7th and 8th. 626-2388*

48 **Half Shell Seafood Bar and Grill.** ★$$/$$$ On a narrow alley between warehouses and art studios, the Half Shell offers seafood almost exclusively—and any way you want it. The environment is perhaps more suited to daylight dining in the plant-filled patio or at tables in the redwood dining room overlooking the patio. The restaurant has happy hour M-F with complimentary hors d'oeuvres from 5-7PM. *Open M-F 11AM-10PM, Sa 6-10PM. 64 Rausch St. 552-7677*

49 **Modernism.** Gallery features 20th century art, avant garde periodicals and books. *Open Tu-Sa 10AM-5:30PM. 685 Market St. 541-0461. 236 8th St. 552-2286*

50 **Philippine Grocery.** Filipino specialties include salted eggs. *Open daily 10AM-6PM. 8th and Minna Sts.*

51 **Lipps Underground.** Club with performance art, DJs, video, rock, funk, world beat, recent classic, reggae and industrial music. *Open W, Th 10PM-3AM; F, Sa 10PM-5AM. 201 Ninth St. 552-3466*

52 **Woodwind & Brass Workshop.** It buys, sells and repairs woodwind and brass musical instruments. *Open M-F 9AM-6PM, Sa 10AM-4PM. 122 10th at Mission St. 864-2440*

Restaurants/Nightlife red
Hotels blue
Shops/Galleries purple
Parks/Outdoor spaces green
Museums/Architecture/Narrative black

53 **Tattoo Art Museum.** Founded by famous tattoo artist **Lyle Tuttle,** it contains the world's largest memorabilia collection of this unusual art form. Tattooing is performed in the adjacent studio. Visitors, if they like, may watch. *Open M-Sa noon-9PM, Su noon-5PM. 30 7th St. between Market and Mission Sts.*

54 **Post Office and U.S. Court of Appeals Building.** (1903-1905, James Knox Taylor) Baroque stone-clad federal building with a fine marble-faced postal lobby. *7th and Mission Sts.*

55 **Oasis.** Live rock, R&B, new wave and avant garde music. There's an indoor bar, with dancing outdoors on the pool or indoors near the bar. An outside terrace overlooks the dance floor. *Open daily 9AM-2AM. 11th St. and Folsom. 621-8119*

56 **DNA Lounge.** Alternative music, poetry readings, fashion shows, crazy parties. Dancing. Special events of Wednesdays. *Open Tu-Su 10PM-dawn. 375 11th St. 626-1409*

56 **Taxi.** ★★$$ A casual atmosphere planned by a team of owner/chefs from **Balboa Cafe** and the **Santa Fe Bar and Grill** who believe in offering good portions at moderate prices. This American bistro is already attracting an interesting mix of opera and symphony goers, fashion staffers, photographers and advertising types. *Open M-W 11AM-11PM; Th-Sa 11AM-midnight; Su 5-11PM. 374 11th St. 558-8294*

57 **The Warehouse Restaurant.** ★★$$ Located in the newly renovated **Old Jackson Brewery,** the Warehouse opened in 1986 to rave reviews about its unique theme of *industrial cuisine*—good food and plenty of it. The designer **Gary Walker** has created an impressive showcase for the food while retaining the physical beauty of the original building with its exposed brick, galvanized steel bar and fixtures enhanced by theatrical lighting. The kitchen features crisp roasted duck and chicken, pizza and calzone, hearty salads and homemade breads. The spot is a great choice for a late-night stop between clubs—it's within one block of the Oasis, the Stud and DNA Lounge and it's open until 3AM. *333 11th St. 621-5902*

58 **The Stud.** Rock, funk, oldies, new wave and world beat music. *Open daily 5PM-2AM. 1535 Folsom. 863-6623*

Bay to Breakers is a 6.73-mile footrace, first run in 1912 and held the third Sunday in May. The route begins at the foot of Howard Street, threads through downtown, then up the Hayes Street hill, across Golden Gate Park and out to Ocean Beach. What other race gives a costume award? It's not only for serious runners, but for those who want to have a good time. The event is more like a huge block party, and has recently drawn as many as 60,000 participants. If you're in town at the time, why not join the party? *For more information call the San Francisco Examiner, 777-2424*

59 **Hotel Meridien.** *Deluxe.* Built in 1983 by Air France, this elegant hotel with marble and brass, fine art and furnishings from Europe and Asia contains 700 rooms and suites, many with sweeping city views. There are 2 floors of meeting rooms, a multi-lingual staff, concierge, 2 superior restaurants and 24-hour room service. On the club floors, visitors can enjoy breakfast with croissants baked on the premises, or afternoon refreshments in luxurious privacy. The 2 French restaurants periodically send their chefs to France for refresher courses. In a short time, this has become one of the city's best hotels. *50 3rd St. 974-6400; 800-223-9918. In NY 800-442-5517*

PiERRE
AT MERIDIEN

Pierre at Meridien. ★ ★ ★ ★ $$$$ Formal French dining is absolute perfection here, with all the nuances of creative food and service, thanks to the expert direction of chef **Sebastian Urbain.** Specialties include oyster ragout, sweetbread salad and lobster medallions, and the wine list tops 200 entries. The serene atmosphere and attentive service make the Pierre the perfect place for high-level business lunches and quiet dinners. *Open M-F 11:30AM-10:30PM, Sa until 11:30PM. 974-6400*

Restaurant Justin. An Executive Luncheon Express Buffet is featured during the week and a sumptious seafood brunch on Sundays. *Open daily 6:30AM-10PM. 974-6400*

60 **ESPRIT Outlet.** The popular and highly successful Esprit fashion manufacturer has opened a huge clothing outlet which is frequented regularly by the teen set. The ESPRIT Sport division is a little more expensive and offers styles for anyone who is young at heart. *Open M-F 10AM-9PM, Sa 10AM-6PM, Su 11AM-5PM. 16th St. at Illinois St. 957-2500*

60 **Caffe ESPRIT.** ★ $/$$ Adjacent to the ESPRIT Outlet, this cafe is a convenient lunch stop during a shopping break. They offer fresh, organically grown salads, gourmet pizzas and generous sandwiches such as the chicken breast club sandwich, served on a toasted brioche with chive mayonnaise and filled with moist, grilled chicken, bacon and fresh lettuce. You can finish off your meal

with a delicious Double Rainbow ice cream sundae from their soda fountain. *Open daily 10AM-11PM. 16th St. at Illinois St. 777-5558*

San Francisco Murals
North and South of Market

Rincon Center Lobby, 99 Mission St. *History of San Francisco,* **Anton Refregier,** 1947.

Coit Tower, Telegraph Hill. 19 Murals by WPA artists, 1934.

North Beach Housing, 600-650 Franciso. **Jackie Ortez,** 1977; **Kim Sites,** 1981.

San Francisco Art Institute, 800 Chestnut St. **Diego Rivera,** 1931.

Ping Yuen Playground, 795 Pacific Av., **Jim Dong,** 1983

Ping Yuen Housing, 799 Pacific Av. *Ping Yuen Tai Chi Mural.* **Josie Grant,** 1982

Ping Yuen Housing, 895 Pacific Av. *Mural of the Bok Sen (8 Immortals), 3 Wisdoms and the Chinese Zodiac.* **Josie Grant,** 1982

1852 Sutter St. **Jim Dong,** 1982

California League for the Handicapped, 1299 Bush St. *Tactile Mural.* **Cynthia Grace,** 1976

222 Hyde St. **John Wullbrandt** with **John Wherle,** 1983

St. Patrick's Day Care Center, 366 Clementina St. **Johanna Poethig** with **Selma Brown & Claire Josephson,** 1982

South of Market Cultural Center, 934 Brannan St., *Buffalo Sky.* **Fran Valesco,** 1982

New College of California School of Law, 50 Fell St. **Ray Patlan,** 1980-81

Page-Laguna Mini-park, 273 Page St. **Josie Grant,** 1975

BESTS

Cyril Isnard
General Manager, Hotel Meridien

Square One for an authentic Italian dinner and a great choice of wines.

Ciao for, again, excellent Italian food in bright surroundings.

The **Mandarin** for a formal Chinese dinner and a spectacular view.

Brandy Ho's for informal Chinese cuisine without MSG.

La Taqueria La Cumbre, on 16th and Valencia, for the greatest steak burrito.

Kite watching on the **Marina Green** on Sunday afternoons.

Taking out-of-towners to the **Schlock** shop on Upper Grant.

Taking a drive from the **Golden Gate Bridge,** along the coast, to the **Palace of the Legion of Honor.** Great vistas!

Walking through the **boat houses** in **Sausalito.**

The **Mission** is the most self-contained of all neighborhoods—traditionally conscious of a sense of community, a sense of belonging found nowhere else in San Francisco but North Beach. Originally the site of an Indian village, Spanish settlers led by **Captain Jose Moraga** founded the mission in 1776 just 5 days before the signing of the Declaration of Independence. This, the 16th mission in the chain, was dedicated to St. Francis of Assisi, but became better known as **Mission Dolores,** named after a nearby lagoon called Lake of Our Lady of Sorrows. The 4-foot-thick adobe walls have survived the intervening years without serious decay or the necessity for extreme restoration to become the oldest building in San Francisco. As a religious community, the mission was never a success. Time spent wandering through the secluded little cemetery garden next to the mission will evoke the past. In addition to several historical figures, over 5,000 native Costanoan Indians are buried here, most having died from the various diseases the white settlers brought.

Early in the 1800s, this warm, fog-free valley became a rural locale for resort activities. When a private franchise was granted to construct a 40-foot-wide planked toll road from present day 3rd to 16th Streets, gambling houses, saloons, dance halls, pleasure parks and race tracks sprang up to take advantage of the road and mixed with the farm houses and country homes. In the next 30 years, the residents multiplied from 23,000 to 36,000, and besides the Mission adobe, not a trace of the Spanish remained. Victorian row houses were everywhere. Yankees, Germans and Scandinavians moved in, and after the earthquake and fire which raged through North Beach and South of Market, the homeless Italians and Irish moved in. It was then that the residents began cultivating a kind of Spanish revival—palms were planted along **Dolores Street**, the Mission was re-stuccoed, a pseudo-Spanish church was built alongside the old Mission and red tile roofs appeared on public buildings. Latinos began to pour into the area, and this population continues to expand.

Today you find heavy traffic, palms and a few parks here. (In spite of the fact there are more children concentrated here than anywhere else in the city, streets must serve as playgrounds). Residential hotels are refuge for the improverished elderly and the district provides haven for the followers of alternative lifestyles as well. Nearby Castro flamboyantly accommodates gay men, while Valencia Street, much more low key, caters to feminists and lesbians. Many art groups have found new homes here, and blended into the Latino neighborhood are Filipinos, Samoans, Southeast Asians, most of the city's American Indians and remnants of the earlier Irish community.

When industry expanded from the Mission south, the marshlands were bridged to provide additional access and a new 5 mile street car line was added, opening up this area as the city's first suburb. The Spanish had named it Potrero Nuevo or *new grazing ground.*

Potrero Hill is a kind of isolated country town of artists, non-conformists and colonies of immigrants. It's a com-

munity of small and colorful houses with a few contemporary apart-ments here and there that suns itself while the rest of the city shivers—a place where some of the cottages have *banyas* (Russian steambaths) in the backyard. This is not tourist country. The shops are utilitarian, not chic. At the foot of the hill are early 19th century warehouses, including **Showplace Square** which houses one of the West's largest wholesale furnishing centers. The neighborhood re-mains, for the time being, working class and heterogeneous. Rus-sians, Scots and Irish followed the Spanish here over the years. Blacks and Latinos make up about half the population now. And the sum-mer climate and sweeping views have attracted artists and profes-sional people whose lifestyle ranges from high rental to low. But the thriving community gardens at **McKinley Square,** where neighbors work side by side, are proof of the neighborhood's ability to assimilate many different ethnic groups.

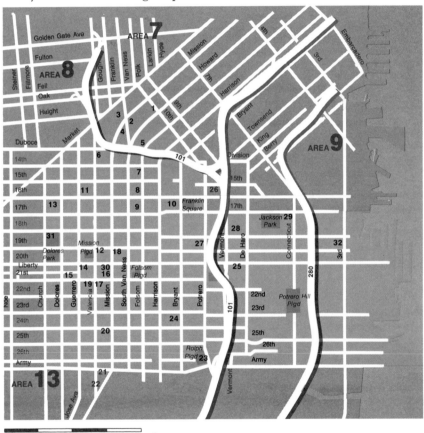

0   1/2   1 mile

1 **Hoyt Byron Sheet Music Service.** This shop has the biggest selection of sheet music in the city. *Open Tu-Sa 9AM-5:30PM. 190 10th St. 431-8055*

2 **Camerawork.** Photo gallery. *70 12th St. 621-1001*

3 **La Mamelle.** This alternative space is active in video production, maintains video archives and publishes a quarterly, *Art Com. Open Tu-Sa noon-5PM. 70 12th St. 431-7524*

4 **ACLU District Offices.** (1981, James Tanner and Peter VanDine) On one of the upper floors of this old concrete frame warehouse, the architects have designed an intriguing post-modern interior on a shoe-string budget. The central focus is the libra-ry/conference room lined with tomes which has an axial entrance complete with *missing* keystone over the doorway. Notice how the rhomboid structural bay plan has been regularized by the addition of 4 fake columns. *1663 Mission St.*

An area of children, adults, and oldsters of every imaginable ethnic and ideological stripe and per-suasion...it is alive, muscular, and rich with human diversity and tenacity. (From a report by neighborhood groups to city planners, 1977)

5 **Hamburger Mary's Organic Grill.** $/$$ This is a place to see a side of San Francisco that will make your eyes bulge out. Gays, men dressed in leather, transvestites and even lots of straights having a terrific time. Good drinks and sandwiches and huge hamburgers. *American. Open daily 10AM-1:15AM. 1582 Folsom St. 626-5767*

6 **Levi Strauss & Co.** The company conducts tours of the cutting and sewing operations of their blue jeans manufacturing plant. *250 Valencia St. 544-7082*

7 **Mission District Murals.** Painted by Mexican-American artists and other residents, the murals are a colorful example of community spirit. The artists have brightened and humanized their urban environment with vivid wall paintings dispersed throughout the neighborhood, between Mission and York Streets, and 14th and Army Streets. They decorate the walls of banks, restaurants, schools, housing projects and community centers. Some of the murals are inside buildings. Sightseers may do a self-guided walk or take a docent tour. *Tours are given the 1st Sa of each month. They start at 10AM at the Mexican Museum's Mission District premises, 1855 Folsom at 15th St. Self-guiding maps are available from the Mexican Museum's exhibition galleries at Fort Mason, Building D. Charge for tour. Phone for information, 441-0404*

8 **Cuba Restaurant.** ★$$ A really authentic rendition of Cuban food. Fish is their specialty, and there are some interesting fish stews, plus exotic dishes like octopus cooked in its own ink. In Latin style, service can sometimes be maddeningly slow. *Cuban. Open daily 12-9:45PM. 2886 16th St. 864-9871*

9 **Oberlin Dance Studio Extension.** (1982, James Tanner and Peter Van-Dine) A nice post-modern extension that complements the original building. Rusticated base, layered facade and seemingly randomly placed windows. *3153 17th St.*

10 **Le Domino.** ★★$$ A well-kept secret among San Francisco diners. Although Le Domino is popular, it still manages to keep out of the dining scene limelight, probably because it doesn't need it. The restaurant offers the desirable combination of good, classic French cuisine in a tastefully decorated, romantic setting, complete with antiques, candlelight and fresh flowers. Dinner opens with a simple butter lettuce salad tossed in vinaigrette. The entree menu includes sirloin steak, lamb, pork, chicken, rabbit and fish dishes all expertly executed. Desserts are also delicious and range from rich chocolate pastries to lighter fruit concoctions such as fresh pears poached in wine or fresh raspberries with creme fraiche. Le Domino is not far from the Opera House and is in the midst of the progressive South of Market theater and nightclub scene. *Reservations suggested Open M-Th 5:30-10PM, F & Sa 5:30-11PM. 2742 175th St. (at Florida). 626-3095*

Restaurants/Nightlife red
Shops/Galleries purple
Museums/Architecture/Narrative black

11 **Firehouse 7.** This dance club has rock, reggae and African music. The live music schedule varies. *Open daily 12PM-2AM. 3160 16th St. 621-1617*

12 **Chatterbox.** A young, artsy crowd frequents this club with rock records, tapes and videos and live music on Fridays and Saturdays from 10PM to 1AM. *Open daily 6PM-2AM. 853 Valencia. 821-1891*

13 **Mission Dolores.** (1782-91) The Mission San Francisco de Assisi, its proper name, is the 6th of the 21 missions founded by Franciscans along the El Camino Real from Mexico to Sonoma. It is also San Francisco's oldest building. The mission has survived 3 major earthquakes and is the only one of the original 21 missions that has not been restored. **Mission Dolores Basilica** (the larger church next to the Mission) was rebuilt in 1918 by and was declared a *basilica* in 1952 by Pope Pius XII. *Open daily May to Sept 9AM-4:30PM, Oct-Apr 9:30AM-4:30PM. Dolores Av. near 16th St., south of Market St.*

14 **El Tazumal.** ★★$/$$ You don't necessarily have to eat tacos, enchiladas and that sort of stuff when you're in the Mission District. Tazumal is Salvadorean, and offers a whole page of specialties from El Salvador that are very unlike the cooking you associate with Mexico. There are 2 great dishes here: the beef tongue and the whole red snapper, which is deep fried and served in a light sauce including onions and tomatoes. Cheap, hearty and satisfying. *Salvadorean. Open Su-Th 10AM-10PM, F-Sa 10AM-11PM. 3522 20th St. 550-1928*

15 **Liberty Street.** The blocks from Castro to Valencia Streets contain some of the best Italianate houses in San Francisco, unspoiled since the last century. Of particular note are *159*, built in 1878, where **Susan B. Anthony,** whose dollar coin we now seem to have forgotten, used to visit her fellow suffragettes. *109* was built in 1870. *Liberty St. between Castro and Valencia, 20th and 21st Sts. (Take J Church Streetcar from downtown).*

The 151 brick circles at major intersections throughout San Francisco mark large underground **cisterns,** each filled with about 75,000 gallons of water for fire emergencies.

16 La Olla. $$ The cafeteria-style food doesn't taste cafeteria, especially the excellent soups and good entrees at reasonable prices. There is also a gallery with Latin crafts and artwork. *Mexican. Open M-Sa 11:30AM-8:30PM. 2417 Mission St. 282-6086*

17 La Rondalla. ★ ★ $/$$ It's nothing to look at, but it's a hugely popular Mexican restaurant whose menu goes far beyond the traditional tacos and enchiladas. You can get interesting grilled pork dishes, goat stew and Mexican egg dishes for a fine late-night snack. If you think goat is tough and chewy, wait until you try it here. *Mexican. Open daily noon-3:30AM. 901 Valencia St. 647-7474*

Movie Makers

San Francisco has always been a filmmaker's dream. If you count the early silent days, when the city was a major filmmaking center, literally hundreds of films have been shot here. Even if you ignore those prehistoric one- and two-reelers, there are still far too many San Francisco-shot features for a manageable list. Second-rate obscurities are in plentiful supply, and there's not much point in enumerating them. What follows is a selective list by Michael Goodwin, first appearing in the *San Francisco Magazine,* of important films shot entirely (or partially) in San Francisco.

Greed (1923). Erich von Stroheim directed, and the (long-lost) original, uncut version ran 9 ½ hours. Universally considered one of the greatest films of all time.

The Barbary Coast (1935). Howard Hawks's brawling, period adventure film, with Edward G. Robinson and Miriam Hopkins.

Dark Passage (1947). Bogart and Bacall star in an atmospheric thriller set in the foggiest Frisco you ever saw.

Out of the Past (1947). Arguably the greatest *film noir* ever made, featuring Robert Mitchum as a cynical, wisecracking detective and Jane Greer as the lethally attractive woman who proves his cynicism inadequate.

I Remember Mama (1948). Sentimental favorite.

Raw Deal (1948). Hard-boiled tale of revenge among the gangsters, directed by cult favorite Anthony Mann.

The Lady from Shanghai (1949). See Orson Welles and Rita Hayworth stroll through Steinhart Aquarium! See the Laughing Fat Lady of Playland-at-the-Beach! This pyrotechnic thriller (arguably Welles' best) was mostly shot in studios, but sharp-eyed viewers will spot several fascinating location sequences.

It Came from Beneath the Sea (1955). Monster destroys the city, courtesy of special effects wizard Ray Harryhousen.

Pal Joey (1957). Cleaned up screen version of Rodgers and Hart's great musical, featuring Frank Sinatra and Kim Novak.

Vertigo (1958). Hitchcock's classic starring James Stewart as an obsessed lover trying to remake Kim Novak into the long-dead Madeleine. Shots at some of the city's finest popular and over-looked locales.

The Lineup (1958). Taut crime thriller, directed by action ace Don Siegel, with Eli Wallach and Robert Keith.

Days of Wine and Roses (1962). Drunks in San Francisco, with Jack Lemon and Lee Remick under Blake Edwards's direction.

Guess Who's Coming to Dinner (1967). Socially conscious interracial comedy directed by (who else?) Stanley Kramer, with Spencer Tracy, Sidney Poitier, and Katharine Hepburn. Katie won an Oscar.

Point Blank (1967). Brilliantly made existential thriller featuring Lee Marvin as a gangster bent on revenge and Angie Dickinson as his faithless wife. John Boorman directs.

Bullitt (1968). Cars go flying in what many consider *the* definitive San Francisco chase sequence. Steve McQueen plays a police detective; Peter Yates directs.

Petulia (1968). Julie Christie, George C. Scott, and Shirley Knight in Richard Lester's sad, moving love story about being alive in the 1960s. Highly regarded by critics and a growing audience.

Psych-out (1968). Early performances by Jack Nicholson and Bruce Dern are highlights of this cult item, set during Summer of Love.

Dirty Harry (1971). Action masterpiece from director Don Siegel stars Clint Eastwood as mean Inspector Callahan. Siegel's brilliant visuals show San Francisco to fine advantage.

Harold and Maude (1972). Swinging septuagenarian (Ruth Gordon) and suicidal youngster (Bud Cort) fall in love in Hal Ashby's popular black comedy.

What's Up Doc? (1972). Peter Bogdanovich's screwball remake of Howard Hawks's *Bringing Up Baby* features Barbra Streisand, Ryan O'Neal, and some of the funniest car chases ever filmed.

Freebie and the Bean (1973). Comic cops-and-robbers with James Caan and Alan Arkin plus flying cars—all directed by Richard Rush.

Magnum Force (1973). Sequel to *Dirty Harry* misses director Siegel, but includes some amusing moments.

The Conversation (1974). Gene Hackman stars in Francis Coppola's masterpiece of paranoia, probably the director's best film.

Invasion of the Body Snatchers (1978). Bay Area film maker Philip Kaufman's stylish remake of Don Siegel's scary original.

18 Bruno's. ★★$$ One of the old, original San Francisco Italian establishments. Steeped in atmosphere. *Italian. Open M-Sa 11-2AM, Su 4PM-midnight. 2389 Mission St. 824-2258*

19 Cendrillon. ★★★$$/$$$ The Mission district, once almost exclusively filled with Latin restaurants and Taquerias, is surprising us with the appearance of a European faction, namely French and Italian. Cendrillon is one of these surprises, and a pleasant one indeed. Great French food is served in a sophisticated yet romantic atmosphere. For an appetizer, try their unusual rendition of Escargots, *Brochettes d'Escargot,* which is 2 skewers of snails alternated with bacon and onions, served with 2 sauces—a light onion cream and a drizzle of garlic butter. Their Soup with Puffed Pastry is fish-based, spiked with shellfish and crowned with puff pastry. The Gigot of Chicken is a boned leg, filled with pistachio nut-studded veal mousse, and then finished with a creamy port sauce. Desserts are also excellent. The Chocolate Charlotte with Rum arrives surrounded by crème anglaise that's enhanced by swirls of blackberry puree. The wine list features French and California wines, and they offer a decent house wine as well. *Open M-Sa 5:30-10:30PM. 1132 Valencia (near 22nd St.) 826-7997*

20 La Traviata. ★★★$$ You don't expect Italian restaurants in the Mission District, particularly one this good. It's a friendly place built around the theme of opera; pictures of opera stars line the walls and opera music plays constantly. Everything is bustling; don't try to get in without reservations. First-rate milk-white veal dishes in a city whose veal can often be tough. One of the best squid dishes around is their calamari sauteed with mushrooms in a tomato and caper sauce. Good cakes for dessert. One of the best in the Mission for the price. *Italian. Open daily 4-10:30PM. Reservations. 2854 Mission St. 282-0500*

21 Cesar's Latin Palace. A club with Latin jazz and salsa, rock, disco between sets and tango on Sundays. *Open Th 8PM-2AM, F & Sa 9PM-6AM, Su 8PM-2AM. 3140 Mission. 648-6611*

22 El Rio. Dance to the beat of Latin, Cuban, Brazilian salsa and African world music. There are live shows on Sundays. *Open daily 12PM-2AM. 3158A Mission. 282-3325*

23 The Farm. A neighborhood community and cultural center occupying 2 old buildings and a barn. Numerous activities include theater productions, art exhibitions, a pre-school, local meeting center and tours for school children of the collection of rabbits, goats, ducks and geese. Its network of activities extends into the community. It operates 3 gardens nearby, including one underneath the freeway at the Army-Potrero interchange. *Open daily 9AM-5PM. Admission free. Call for information on current exhibitions and theater programs. 1499 Potrero Av. 826-4290*

24 China Books and Periodicals. The shop specializes in imported books from China, with some in Chinese and many in English. They also have a good selection of books on history, politics and Third World issues. *Open M-F 10AM-6PM, Sa 9AM-6PM. 2929 24th St. (at Bryant). 282-2994*

25 Vermont Street. Southern San Francisco's own Lombard Street, the second *crookedest street in the world.* The view is nice and the absence of tourists mobs even nicer. *Vermont south of 20th St.*

26 Il Pirata. $/$$ Heaping platters of Italian food served family-style at one of the few good restaurants on Potrero Hill. A good value. *Italian. Open Tu-Sa 11:30AM-3PM, 5:30-11PM. 2007 16th St. 626-1845*

27 300 Pennsylvania Street. (1868) Situated midway up Potrero Hill, this was one of a series of mansions built as the city grew south of Market. *Private residence.*

28 San Francisco Barbeque. ★$ There are few restaurants that can consistently produce a good meal time and time again without comprising the basic quality. San Francisco Barbeque, despite its limited menu and simple presentation always comes through with good, honest food. The Thai-style BBQ dishes are addictive. The chicken and pork ribs are the most popular, cooked to lean succulence and flavored with a medium-hot, sweet-sour Thai sauce. The fish is also a treat here. Try the BBQ Squid Salad as an appetizer. The noodle dishes are a delicious alternative for light meat eaters. Service is friendly and efficient, and although the tables are closely arranged, you still feel comfortable. Wine and beer only. *Open Tu-Sa 11AM-2PM, 4:30-9:30PM; Su 3-9PM. 1328 18th St. 431-8956*

29 Asimakopoulos. ★★★$/$$ A contemporary version of a Greek restaurant in both atmosphere and cuisine. The dining room is set up cafe-style with small wooden tables and a long wood counter with cushioned stools for single dining. The look is clean, sunny and uncluttered, and the food is flavorful but not fussy. The combination *Souvlakia,* skewered lamb, chicken and pork that has been marinated and grilled, is well prepared and satisfying. The classic *Spanakopetakia,* filo pastry-wrapped herbed spinach, is light and flaky. Asimakopoulos also has a reasonably priced wine list, and the service is pleasant and efficient. *No reservations. Open M-F 11:30AM-10PM, Sa 5-10PM. 288 Connecticut St. (at 18th St.). 552-8789*

Restaurants/Nightlife red
Hotels blue
Shops/Galleries purple
Parks/Outdoor spaces green
Museums/Architecture/Narrative black

30 **Old Uncle Gaylord's.** 30-minute tours of the ice cream parlor, freezer room and small museum of old-fashioned ice cream apparatus, plus enough time to sample some great ice cream. Call in advance. *2435 Mission St. 648-2166*

31 **Dolores Park.** A quiet green space in the middle of the Mission District, enjoy a panoramic view of the city. Noteworthy neighborhood architecture. *18th, 20th, Church and Dolores Sts.*

Moshi Moshi

32 **Moshi Moshi.** ★ ★ $ Good Japanese food at prices that are more than fair. The decor is simple—almost spare—with bleached wood tables and chairs and pale green walls. The back porch has been turned into a dining area for an outdoorsy feel. If you're hungry, start with an order of *gyoza*— a generous helping of stuffed pasta, Japanese style. The menu offers all the classic favorites: chicken and steak *teriyaki* (served quite rare, as it should be), shrimp *tempura* and *yakitori*. For dinner there are more seafood dishes, and although they feature sushi, better can be found in Japantown. But the overall quality and value received here is difficult to top. Beer and wine only. *Open M-Th 11:30AM-3PM, 5-9:30PM; F 11:30AM-3PM, 5-10PM; Sa 5-10PM. 292 3rd St. 861-8285*

BESTS

Mel Ziegler
President, Banana Republic

Sunrise from Coit Tower. A mystical, exotic experience. Climb Telegraph Hill before dawn, descend by the Filbert Street steps and return to North Beach for cappucino at **Cafe Puccini** on Columbus.

South of Market District. Fresh, burgeoning scene with restaurants, clubs, galleries. Try **Billboard Cafe** for lunch (299 9th St.).

Jogging from Marina Green to Aquatic Park. If you are really adventurous, cool off with a quick swim in the icy bay, or at least watch the geriatric swimmers who live to be 100 because they do.

La Petit Cafe. (Larkin at Vallejo). Genuine, neighborhood coffeehouse for Russian Hill creative types.

Olivetti Restaurant. (5655 College Avenue, Oakland). Innovative rustic cuisine from Italy, Spain and France. Could be the next Chez Panisse. Interesting East Bay neighborhood, easily accessible by BART.

The San Francisco Style. It is all about quality of life, tolerance and appreciation of the authentic (vs. the ersatz). See if you can spot it in your exhanges with people, in your rambles about town.

San Francisco Real Food Company. (2140 Polk Street). Now this is what a supermarket ought to be. Think of it as a *Safer-way.*

The neighborhoods. Walk 24th Street one end to the other for a samplet. There are many San Franciscos.

City Lights Bookstore. (261 Columbus Avenue). Browse with the ghosts of Beatniks.

Banana Republic Outlet Store. (175 Buxome Street). Best kept secret in town. Saturdays only.

Anchor: America's Best Beer

It's San Francisco's own version of a Dickens tale: Young heir of the Maytag washing machine concern, **Fritz,** a carefree college student, stops into his local beerhall and discovers Anchor Steam Beer, a rich amber brew. Fritz is delighted and becomes an instant aficionado, but with graduation his thoughts turn to family business and away from beerhalls. Meanwhile, on the other side of town, **Lawrence Steese** is struggling to keep the old Anchor Brewery alive. Having survived prohibition, inflation and America's changing taste in beer, by 1965 bankruptcy looms for Anchor and it looks like the brewmeister has filled his last keg. Of course, this is where our hero, Fritz Maytag, steps in and saves the company, a red-letter event for connoisseurs of American beer. To many, Anchor Steam Beer is America's first brew. They argue that it is one of the few *real* beers left, a simple blend of water, malted barley, hops and yeast. Anchor uses no additives, preservatives, fillers or colorings. Fritz Maytag's successful revival of Anchor Steam Beer is due to his combined respect for traditional brewing methods, plus his willingness to innovate. Visitors to the brewery will notice an anachronistic air, with fine old German-made copper brewing vessels working in conjunction with newly designed bottling production lines. Today the company is still tiny, but its reputation is tremendous, and volume and success have grown steadily each year.

A Rand McNally study claims San Francisco is the best place to live in the state, but the fastest growing cities are south of Bakersfield.

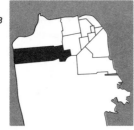

Golden Gate Park & Haight-Ashbury

at the exact geographic center of San Francisco is a district of extremes. Rather than one big look-and-think-alike neighborhood, this one is a complex of subcultures. It includes **Golden Gate Park, Buena Vista Hill, Ashbury Heights, Edgewood** and the **University of California Medical Center** on **Parnassus Heights,** as well as the celebrated **Haight-Ashbury.** There are villas and ghetto flats, new developments and baroque mansions, and what is probably the oldest house in San Francisco, shipped around the Horn in sections as a gift for a homesick bride.

All this was once part of a 4,000-acre land grant to a man named **Noe,** a mayor in the early 1800s. The area was developed somewhat later than the Western Addition so the houses have the more rococo character of the 90s. And by then it was everything a proper Victorian neighborhood should be, with over 1,000 Victorian houses (many still standing), the beginnings of Golden Gate Park and a landscaped strip for promenading called the **Panhandle** which looked something like Boston's Commonwealth Avenue, except for the difference in the architecture of the homes that lined it.

Other streets nearby honor the men who worked to make the Park possible: **Cole, Clayton, Schrader, Stanyan** and **Ashbury.** The neighborhood's decline began in 1917 with the Twin Peaks tunnel serving to encourage people to move out toward the Sunset, and it continued through the 50s. The big houses were divided into flats and then divided again. Then there was the *Happening*—the blossoming of the Flower Children and the Hippie Movement. Haight Street

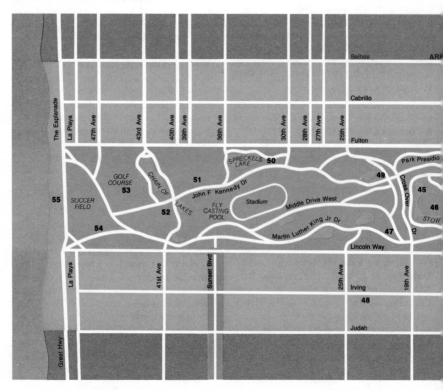

was once known as the main promenade of the Flower Children. It soon fell into a state of decay—a place only the city street-wise could walk comfortably. But the city-wide gentrification trend soon reached the Haight and transformed the once bleak and dangerous area into a shopping mecca. From Masonic Street to Stanyan, Haight Street is lined with interesting shops, nightclubs and restaurants. The yuppies and the new wavers rub shoulders with the remnants of the 60's, resulting in a bustle of eclectic eccentrics who make Haight a must for people watchers.

1 **Victoriana Inn.** *Moderate/expensive.* This Queen Anne style mansion once known as **Clunie House** was built in 1897, Queen Elizabeth's Jubilee Year, and is now a registered landmark. All rooms are furnished with antiques and large beds with down comforters and pillows. Several of the rooms still have the original fireplaces, with turn-of-the-century handmade tiles. Fresh flowers are everywhere, and stunning old photographs provide a glimpse into the 19th century. Homemade baked goods are served for breakfast in the oak-paneled dining room; sherry is served in the evening in the library. The top floor has a suite in the Belvedere tower. *301 Lyon St. 931-1830*

2 **Park Hill Condominiums.** (1986, Kaplan, McLaughlin, Diaz) A conversion of the former St. Joseph's Hospital building into residences. The former chapel has been converted into a recreation center and the whole scheme has been repainted in warm pastel shades. *344 Buena Vista Av. East.*

3 **329 Divisadero.** (1850) This is the oldest house in San Francisco, hidden away in the middle of the block. It has been moved twice and a glimpse of it can be caught on Oak Street at Divisadero. *Private residence.*

4 **Buena Vista Park.** The park affords a wonderful view of the **Coast Range** mountains as far as **Mt. Tamalpais** to the north, **Mt. Hamilton** to the south and **Mt. Diablo** to the east.

The Panhandle and Golden Gate Park has beautiful **bicycling** trails. Take the 7 ½-mile route from the Panhandle through the park out to Lake Merced. If you need to rent a bike, there are many shops circling the park.

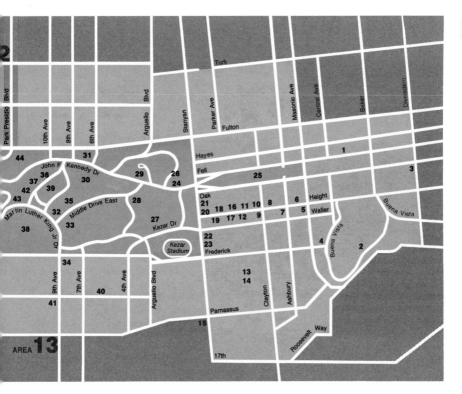

AREA **13**

4 **Spreckels Mansion.** *Expensive.* Situated on a hill next to Buena Vista Park is this mansion, originally built in 1887. Celebrated guests have included **Ambrose Bierce** and **Jack London.** The mansion is romantic, private and conveniently located for strolls in the park or shopping. Each room has a stunning view, a comfortable sitting area and a private bath. Large suites are available too. Good public transportation and plenty of parking. *737 Buena Vista West. 861-3008*

5 **Hunan's on Haight.** $ Tastier than most Chinese food, the dishes here are tangy, spicy or downright ignitable. The modern interior is accented by fresh, exotic flowers placed around the tables. *Open M-F 12-10:30PM, Sa & Su 12-11PM. 1419 Haight St. 621-0580*

6 **Sugartit.** Exquisite vintage clothing and Art Deco objects. *Open M-Sa 11AM-6PM. 1474 Haight St. 552-7027*

7 **Aardvark's Odd Ark.** A reasonable vintage clothing store where you can sometimes obtain a real find, especially in men's clothing. *1510 Haight St. 621-0141*

8 **Artery.** This shop sells primitive art, such as African and Oriental masks, tapestries and jewelry. *Open M-Sa 10:30AM-6:30PM. 1510 Haight St. 621-2872*

9 **Bakers of Paris.** The genuine stuff, just like in France. Thin, crusty baguettes, croissants, a Normandy loaf made with milk. *Open daily 7AM-7PM. 1605 Haight St. 626-4076*

9 **The Grand Victorian.** ★ ★ $$/$$$ This airy, elegant restaurant features black-tied waiters, crisp linen and delicious continental food at suprisingly reasonable prices. The early dinner special from 5:30 to 7:30PM is a bargain, as are the weekend brunches. *Open M-F 5:30-11PM; Sa & Su 10AM-3PM, 5:30PM-midnight. 1607 Haight St. 861-4346*

10 **Heaven's Cake.** $ Sinful baked goods and excellent coffee. The decor is sparse and contemporary, with splashes of red neon and large picture windows for watching the colorful parade of neighborhood types. *Open daily 7AM-midnight. 1654 Haight St. 626-2862*

The San Francisco Earthquake: 1906

California is constantly straining as the land along either side of the St. Andreas Fault slides in opposite directions. Occasionally rock spurs along the fault interlock, and pressure builds up until the spurs are crushed. The result is a tremendous release of pressure called an earthquake. But few of these quakes are actually felt and only one every 30 years causes great damage by releasing as much power as 200 million tons of TNT or 10,000 times that of the bomb dropped on Hiroshima. It was April 18, 1906, just before sunrise when 2 major tremors jolted San Franciscans out of bed. The quake lasted only a minute, shaking buildings, rupturing pipelines and starting fires. But this was the largest and most destructive earthquake in American history. It was estimated at 8.3 on the Richter scale. (In this logorhythmic thermometer for earth's inner tension, each whole number is 10 times greater than the preceeding one. In other words, an 8.6 quake isn't twice as strong as a 4.3, but 10,000 times as strong.) After the morning quake, the city burned out of control for 3 days, and it was the fire that caused the greatest damage. Water mains had broken, communications thrown into chaos, and the fire chief killed, all adding to the city's delay in bringing the fire under control. The citizens of San Francisco reacted heroically. Telegraph Hill's Italian residents used their wine stocks to douse fires and save the district, while in other areas whole blocks of lovely Victorian homes were sacrificed—dynamited to create firebreaks. Finally the wind changed and the fire was brought under control. Four-and-a-half square miles lay in smoldering rubble, with 674 people dead or missing and 28,000 buildings destroyed. In 490 ravaged city blocks, 300,000 people had been left homeless, and they gathered around campfires in Golden Gate Park. Help poured in from every state and many foreign nations while residents waited patiently for gas and water lines to be repaired. Within 3 years, like the phoenix rising out of the ashes that is today the city's emblem, San Francisco had replaced the majority of her structural losses. From this catastrophe, major earthquake safety codes were pioneered, and laws now set strict guidelines for all California buildings.

One city landmark that survived the 1906 quake was **Jack's** restaurant, located at 615 Sacramento. The restaurant celebrated its centenniel several years ago and is still going strong, with much of its charm being its stability. The old building, once a bordello, clings to the trappings of a private gentlemen's club that it had when political boss Abe Ruef or actor John Barrymore ate here. Atmosphere and food are both recommended.

11 **Spellbound Vintage Clothing.** Vintage clothing stores abound here, and this is one of the best—and priciest. Don't expect thrift store bargains, but what you can expect are mint condition men's and women's fashions from the 20s, 30s and 40s. *1670 Haight St. 863-4930*

12 **The Red Victorian Hotel.** *Moderate.* The only surviving hotel (circa 1904) on Haight Street, it was purchased in 1977 by **Sami Sunchild**, a painter of *Visual Poetry.* Originally a resort hotel, then a care home and in the 60s a meeting spot for hippies with a Chinese grocery downstairs, the building was in a vastly deteriorated state after years of changing roles. The present owner strives to preserve the unique history and character of the building in the form of an Art Gallery, Human Relationships Center and Bed and Breakfast. She designed the corridor gallery and meditation room before the 14 guest rooms were fancifully decorated with rainbow colors, old photos, lace curtains and appropriately named. Rooms are attractive and clean and the atmosphere is welcoming. Bathroom facilities shared. Continental breakfast. Easy access to major bus lines and very close to Golden Gate Park. There is a movie house downstairs that shows old classics. *1665 Haight St. 864-1978*

12 **Forma.** This unusual store houses an odd combination of hi-tech furniture, wind-up toys and new wave art objects. Don't miss **VendArt**, a 50s vending machine which dispenses works by local artists for only a quarter. *1715 Haight St. 751-0545*

13 **The Other Cafe.** Now here's a bit of genuine San Francisco, far from the tourist crowds. This watering hole presents a good mix of the local comedy circuit almost every night of the week. The relaxed atmosphere gets even looser on *Open Mike Nights, M-Tu. Cover on those nights. 100 Carl St. 681-0748*

14 **Ironwood Cafe.** ★ $/$$ American cuisine with a small but inspired menu. Specialties change daily. There are also superb homemade American-style desserts. The decor is simple, with warm kerosene lamps on each table. *Open M-Sa 11:30AM-2:30PM, 5:30-10PM. 901 Cole St. 664-0224*

15 **Gelato.** Incredibly rich Italian ice cream that has its own contingency of natives to swear it's the best in the city. So rich you get only a tiny scoop, but it's hard to eat more. Interesting flavors, including a knockout espresso ice cream. *Open M-Th &*

Sa 11AM-11PM, F & Sa 11AM-midnight. 201 Parnassus St. 566-9696

16 **I Beam.** Dance club with rock and new wave music. There's live music on Mondays and a DJ during the rest of the week. *Open daily 9PM-2AM. No cover with student ID on W and Th. 1748 Haight St. 668-6006*

17 **Full Moon Saloon.** Dance club with live rock, R&B, blues and videos. *Open daily 9AM-2PM. 1725 Haight St. 668-6190*

18 **Holos Gallery.** This gallery boasts the largest selection of holograms in Northern California. Holograms are 3-dimensional photographs created with laser beams. Holographic products are also for sale. *Open Tu-Sa noon-6PM. 1792 Haight St. 668-4656*

19 **Cha Cha Cha.** ★ ★ ★ $$/$$$ Although they serve a number of delightful dinner specialities, most people come for the *tapas,* which are Spanish appetizers such as calamari in cream sauce, grilled shrimp and medallions of chicken with mustard, served with excellent Sangria. The food here reflects Spanish, Cajun and Caribbean influences. The bright, new wave decor, friendly service and reasonable prices make this restaurant one of Haight Streets best bets. *Open M-Th 11AM-3PM, 5-11PM; F & Sa 11AM-3PM, 5-11:30PM; Su 11AM-3PM, 5-10PM. 1805 Haight St. 386-5758*

19 **Nightbreak.** Local and out-of-town bands play at this club. Modern, contemporary rock and new wave music. There is also a DJ. *Open daily 9AM-2AM. 1821 Haight St. 221-9008*

19 **Mountain Avenue Cyclery.** Bicycle rentals. *Open M-Sa 9:30AM-5:30PM, Su 10AM-4PM. 1865 Haight and 756 Stanyon. 387-3155*

20 **Rockin' Robbins.** Dancing to 50s and 60s rock. DJ. *Open daily 12PM-2AM. 1840 Haight St. 221-1960*

21 **California Scooter.** Moped rentals for a zippy, economical tour of the area. *640 Stanyon St. 751-4100*

22 **Stanyan Park Hotel.** *Moderate/expensive.* The Stanyan opened in 1983 after extensive renovation and has become another stylish establishment near Golden Gate Park. The buildings exhibit the designers' elegant style of transition from Queen Anne to Beaux Arts Classicism. The hotel has 30 rooms and 6 suites that blend the old-fashioned with the modern: queen size beds, plush reading chairs, wood writing desks, TVs and phones. Many of the rooms have fireplaces and bay windows overlooking the park. *750 Stanyan St. 751-1000*

23 **Avenue Cyclery.** *Rentals. Open Tu-Su 9:30AM-5:30PM. 756 Stanyan. 387-3155*

23 **Stanyan Cyclery.** Rentals. *Open M-Sa 9AM-5:30PM, Su 10AM-4PM. 672 Stanyan. 221-7211*

Restaurants/Nightlife red
Hotels blue
Shops/Galleries purple
Parks/Outdoor spaces green
Museums/Architecture/Narrative black

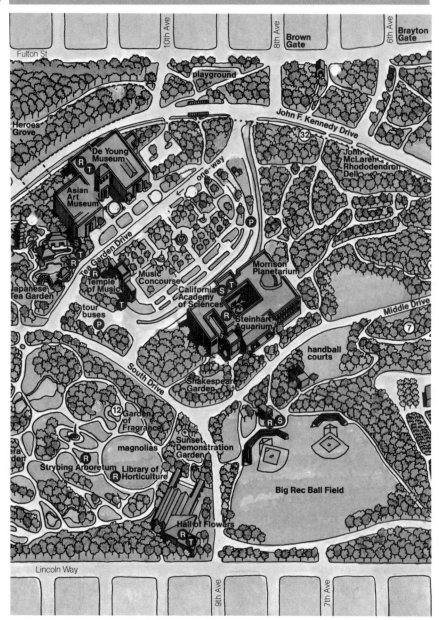

Detail from 10" x 34" full color Map & Guide to Golden Gate Park, for sale at McLaren Lodge and all concessions in Golden Gate Park. Design: Reineck & Reineck, San Francisco.

24 **Golden Gate Park.** This is truly one of the wonders of the world. From a desolate, windy wasteland of shifting sand hills, man created this lush, verdant parkland. Three miles long and half-a-mile wide, from Stanyan Street to the Pacific Ocean, it covers over 1,000 acres. Before the park's creation, Sunday drivers who wanted to spend the day at the beach and the fashionable Cliff House had to traverse these *Outside Lands,* as they were called. This meant a bumpy, uncomfortable ride over the sand dunes. When the city purchased the tract to make a park, it was laughingly referred to as a *white elephant* and *The Great Sand Bank.* But far-sighted city fathers, in their zeal to make San Francisco the *Paris of the West,* recognized the need for a public park which would be the *lungs* of the city.

Frederick Law Olmsted, the designer of Central Park in New York City, paid a visit to San Francisco in 1866 at the request of the Board of Supervisors, and his ideas moved the city to reserve 1,000 acres of the so-called outside lands for a major park. To many it seemed foolish to grow trees and grass on the shifting sand. Ten years later, the need for the park was more clearly recognized, and **John McLaren,** a young Scottish landscape gardener, was put in charge and began the battle for *his* park. From 1890 and for 53 years until his death at the age of 96, *Uncle John* was park superintendent. His love and uncanny understanding of nature coupled with his stubborness and imperiousness made the dream a reality. McLaren personally carried out the planting. He imported varieties of trees and plants from the world over. In his time he planted over one million trees in the park, including redwoods, eucalyptus, conifer and acacia groves. There was morning after morning when he woke to find thousands of young trees covered with sand. But each time he patiently dug them out and coaxed them back to life. In these early days, needing fertilizer, he asked for and was given the horse sweepings from the streets. He was quite peeved when, many years later, the automobile replaced the horse, depriving him of this easy source. Still superintendent of the park at age 90, he was asked what he wanted as a birthday gift. With no hesitation he replied, *10,000 yards of good manure!* Until the end of his life, McLaren kept shaping *his* park as his dreams dictated. People laughed when he planted redwood seeds at age 80. Today, these trees are over 30 feet tall. To create a country-like retreat in the midst of the city, to be used and enjoyed by the people, he forbade keep off the grass signs. He also tried to prevent the park from becoming cluttered with pompous-looking statues. The statues that did land in the park were stuck away in corners and nearly hidden from view by rapidly growing shrubs. Even a statue of McLaren stands in the park, marking the entrance to the **Rhododendron Dell. Strawberry Hill** was used as a reservoir to store the water for the park's use.

25 **The Panhandle.** The trees here are the oldest in the park. Beginning with barley, then sand grass, then blue gum and live oak trees, park engineer **William Hammond Hall** gradually worked up the botanical chain, as the hardier plants took root and more diversified shrubs could be planted.

The park today is a man-made countryside of flower beds, meadows, lakes, gardens, waterfalls, rolling hills and forests. You could spend days in it and be unaware of the surrounding metropolis. It offers something for everyone. Park recreation facilities include those for baseball, soccer, bowling, horseshoe pitching, flycasting, golf, horseback riding, tennis, polo and picnicking.

The park has a huge network of walking paths and bicycle tracks, more than 6,000 varieties of flowers, dozens of species of trees, several lakes, bowling greens, boccie courts, a football field, checker pavilions, and a bandstand.

In 1906 the park was a refuge for over 40,000 homeless victims of the earthquake and fire.

The great calamity...left no one with the impression that it amounted to an irrecoverable loss. This afternoon everyone is talking about it but no one is in the slightest downcast...Nowhere is there any doubt but that San Francisco will rise again, bigger, better and after the very briefest of intervals. **HG Wells,** English writer (1866-1946) in *The Future in America; a Search after Realities*

---

26 **McLaren Lodge.** The home of John McLaren throughout his term as superintendent of the park. The Richardsonian Romanesque pile of sandstone is now the headquarters of San Francisco's Recreation and Parks Department. Information and maps are available here. *Fell and Stanyan Sts. 558-3706*

27 **Children's Playground.** Golden Gate Park's Children's Playground has reclaimed its glorious past by bringing back the carousel housed in a turn-of-the-century Greek Temple. The animals and turning platform were made in New York by the **Herschell-Spillman Co.** around 1912, and came to San Francisco sometime after the 1939 World's Fair on Treasure Island. The wooden menagerie consists of 62 animals, 2 chariots, one turning tub and one rocker. The 6 year restoration project involved cutting away rot and mildew, filling pitted surfaces and sanding and applying brilliantly colored lacquers. You'll find a spirited zebra, dancing horses, a fierce stork, lion, rooster, pig, goat and hound dog, among others, all racing to various show tunes, polkas and mazurkas coming from the 50-year-old organ. Definitely a good time and well worth the 25-cent ride. *141 Golden Gate Park.*

28 **Tennis Courts.** *Just north of the Children's Playground. 566-4800*

29 **The Conservatory of Flowers.** The oldest existing building in the park, it was modeled after the Palm House at Kew Gardens in London and erected by **Lord** and **Burnham** (1878) for eccentric millionaire **James Lick.** It was shipped from Dublin around Cape Horn and has survived the 1906 earthquake and a major fire. The conservatory's permanent displays of tropical plants and flowers are enriched by seasonal flower shows. Tours given by prior arrangement. *Open daily 10AM-5PM. Admission free. 558-3973*

30 **Rhododendron Dell.** This is a memorial to McLaren, honoring him with his favorite flower. There are over 3,000 plants and 500 species. *Between JFK Dr., Middle Dr. and Academy of Sciences.*

31 **Skating.** JFK Drive is closed to auto traffic from Kezar Drive to Transverse Drive on Sundays. The road is open to roller skaters and joggers who sail past, many of them rolling to private rhythms emanating from their headphones. There are skate rental facilities nearby.

32 **Shakespeare Garden.** Flowers and plants mentioned in Shakespeare's sonnets and plays. *South of the Academy of Sciences on South Dr. Stow Lake.*

33 **Baseball Diamonds.** Big Rec Playfield near 7th Avenue and Lincoln Way.

34 **Thrills on Wheels.** Rent skates and bicycles. *Open daily 10AM-6PM.*

I'd go out into the country and walk along a stream until I came to a bonnie brook. Then I'd come back to the park and I'd reproduce what Nature had done... **John McLaren**

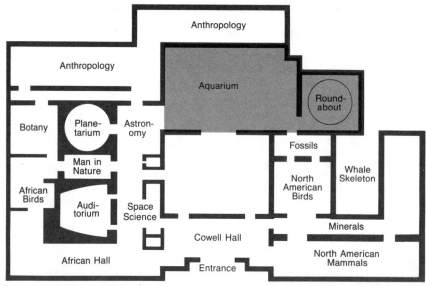

35 **California Academy of Sciences.** Situated on the south side of the Museum Concourse facing the De Young Museum. Three museums in one, there are several halls of **Natural History,** the **Steinhart Aquarium** and the **Morrison Planetarium.** The entrance, **Cowell Hall,** contains a large geophysical globe and a 27-foot-long skeleton of a 130 million-year-old dinosaur. The natural history and science halls flank the courtyard just past the entrance. The **Wattis Hall of Man** exhibits life-size replicas of man in different cultures and ages. Dioramas of animals and birds are on view in the **Simson African Hall** and **North American Hall.** The North American Hall, the oldest part of the museum, which opened in 1916, is filled with exhibits of botany, mammals, fossils, birds, minerals, insects, a whale skeleton, clocks, a scale model of the moon and more. **The Discovery Room** is designed for children, who are allowed to handle and touch the nature exhibits. Swinging continually as the earth rotates, the **Foucault Pendulum,** in the entrance to the **Astronomy Hall,** is a favorite attraction.

Within the Academy are:

Morrison Planetarium. A continuous series of shows about the universe under the 65-foot dome. Multi-media laser light shows, such as *Lights Fantastic* and *Rock Fantasy,* are special attractions. (There is an additional admission charge to these.) *Phone for information about these special shows, 387-6300*

Steinhart Aquarium. Here some 14,500 specimens of aquatic life float, swim or crawl in 190 tanks. Coral reefs, kelp beds, sharks, an infinite variety of fish, plus seals and dolphins live here. The dolphins and seals are fed every 2 hours, beginning at 10:30AM—a popular attraction! Upon entering the aquarium, you may wonder what so many people are staring at, clustered around a railing. This is **The Swamp,** a simulated native habitat for a collection of alligators, lizards, tortoises and other reptiles. Laconic, slow-moving, seemingly harmless, they never fail to amuse. The newest, most exciting display is the **Fish Roundabout.** Built in 1977, it is unique in the U.S. The Roundabout crowns the top of a spiralling ramp which takes you past a California tidepool and a mural display of marine life. Fast-swimming open ocean fish careen through 100 gallons of water around a doughnut-shaped tank, 204-feet in circumference. The viewing area is in the center of the ring of water. You feel as if you are underwater, with fish swimming all around you. There is a large cafeteria downstairs. **The Nature Store** is a marvelous book and gift shop, located in the entrance hall. *Open daily 10AM-5PM. Admission charge. Children under 6 free. First W of each month is free. Free parking available in front of the museum. 221-4214*

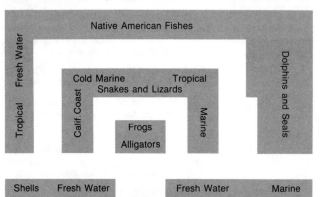

36 **M.H. de Young Memorial Museum.** Part of the **Fine Arts Museums of San Francisco,** along with the **California Palace of Fine Arts.** The nucleus of the museum evolved from the California Midwinter International Exposition of 1894, held in Golden Gate Park. Civic leader and newspaper publisher **Michael de Young** initiated a building program to expand the museum's size and collections. Its cornerstone was laid in 1917. This is the city's most diversified museum. Its permanent collections detail the history of western civilization from ancient Egypt, Greece and Rome, through medieval and Renaissance times to the 20th century. Painting, sculpture, stained glass and decorative arts, including period rooms, are laid out in a series of galleries surrounding a central courtyard. Significant collections include the **Samuel H. Kress Collection** of **Rubens, Van Dyck** and their contemporaries, and the **Roscoe and Margaret Oakes Collection** of 17th and 18th century Italian paintings. There is a gallery devoted to the traditional arts of Africa, Oceania and the Americas. The **American Wing** has one of the West's most comprehensive collections of American art, including more than 100 paintings bequeathed by **John D. Rockefeller III.** The **Archives of American Art,** a branch of the Smithsonian Institution, is housed here. (Open by appointment, 556-2530.) There is also a **library**. Free docent tours are available. Lectures and concerts are regular features. The well-stocked **bookstore** sells small artifacts and museum replicas, plus books, posters, cards and slides. *Admission charge. Open W-Su 10AM-5PM. First W of each month is free. 558-2887*

36 **Cafe de Young.** ★ $/$$ You can reach the cafe through galleries 21-25 of the de Young Memorial Museum. This cafeteria puts together some really nice lunches at reasonable prices. Any salad, or any of the fish dishes, is bound to be good. It's a pleasant place to take people when you're showing them Golden Gate Park. You may take your repast outside in the adjacent, delightful pocket-size garden, with its trellises and clipped hedges, and pretend you're in France. *American. Open M, Tu, Th-Su 10AM-4PM; W 10AM-7:30PM. Ground level of the de Young Museum. 752-0116*

1	The Ancient World
2	Tribal Weavings
3	El Greco and the Spanish Baroque
4	Medieval and Renaissance Spanish Art
5	The Renaissance in the North
6	Eighteenth-Century North Italian Room
7-11	The Renaissance in Italy
8	Eighteenth-Century German Room
12,13	The Age of Rembrandt
15	Sixteenth-and Seventeenth-Century Flemish Art
16	Rubens, Van Dyck, and Their Contemporaries
17	Gainsborough, Reynolds, and Eighteenth-Century British Art
18	Neoclassic English Dining Room
19	Eighteenth-and Nineteenth-Century British Art
20	Tudor Room
21	Late Eighteenth-and Nineteenth-Century British Art
22	*Changing Exhibitions*
23	Eighteenth-Century French Room
25	The Franz W. Sichel Glass Collection
27-32,39-40	The American Galleries: American Painting and Decorative Arts, Seventeenth-Early Twentieth Centuries
33-34	Seventeenth-and Eighteenth-Century Italian Art
35	Nineteenth-Century European Painting
36	Mural from Mexico: Experiencing the Art of Teotihuacan
41,44	The Director's Choice: *Changing Exhibitions*
42	Art of Africa, Oceania, and the Americas
43	Africa, Oceania, and the Americas
48	American Glass

37 **Asian Art Museum.** The museum opened in 1966 after **Avery Brundage** donated his world-famous collection of Asian art to San Francisco. The collection is located in the west wing of the de Young Museum. It contains nearly 10,000 paintings, sculptures, ceramics, decorative objects, bronzes, architectural elements, jades and textiles gathered from all over Asia. The exhibitions are rotated periodically, since only a portion of the extensive collection can be displayed at one time. The 1st floor shows objects from China. The **Jade Room** displays pieces dating as far back as 3,500 years. The 2nd floor is devoted to the arts from the rest of Asia. Of special interest is the **Leventritt Collection** of Chinese blue-and-white porcelains. There is also a 12,000-volume library. *Open W-Sa 10AM-5PM. 558-2887*

BESTS

Rand Castile
Director
Asian Art Museum of San Francisco

Seated Buddha. (Gilt bronze; China; dated 338 A.D.) The world's oldest dated Chinese Buddha sculpture—as beautiful as it is venerable.

A King Of Hell *Scroll Painting.* (Korea; Choson period; 15th-16th century) A very important recent acquisition; a rare old Buddhist painting to add to our growing collection of Korean art.

Dog (Earthenware Burial Pottery). (China; Western Han period, ca. 1st c. B.C.;) My favorite piece in the collection; he has an alertness that makes me smile.

Siva and Devi. (Sandstone scultpures; Khmer; late 11th c. A.D.) The understated royal elegance of Khmer (Cambodia) civilization at its best; the most elegant stone in the collection.

Rhinoceros *tsun.* (Ceremonial wine vessel; China; late Shang dynasty, 11th c. B.C.)

This rhino has attained world celebrity for its ample and unique form.

Umbrella-bearer. (Schist stone sculpture; India; Gandhara, ca. 3rd c. A.D.) The sensuous curve of the umbrella as it envelops the figure is wonderful.

Nyoirin-Kannon. (Wood/dry lacquer sculpture; Japan; Heian period, 900-950 A.D.) Radiates a calm, cool assurance and inner peace.

Vessel in the Shape of a Stag. (Earthenware; Iran; ca. 10th c. B.C.) In its elegant simplicity, this piece is timeless in design.

Summer Mountains Misty Rain *Handscroll* by **Wang Hui.** (China; dated 1668) It was a coup to recently find what I think is the best painting by the most innovative Orthodox School artist of the 17th century; works like this rarely appear.

Seated Ganesha, Elephant-Headed God. (Stone sculpture; India [Hoysala]; 12th-13th c. A.D.) A particularly appealing image of the rotund, humorous god that more children worship than any other god in the world.

Two Birds on a Blossoming Branch. (Anonymous artist; China; Southern Song dynasty, 12th-13th c. A.D.) The courtly grace of the paired birds painted in the delicated, exquisite brushwork of the best Southern Song artists.

Tiger. (Nephrite [jade]; tan with brown markings; China; late Eastern Zhou, 4th-3rd c. B.C.) Among the most refined of objects, this jade is unusual for its color and form; it has often been reproduced in books and articles.

Lacquer Box with Gardenia Decoration. (Carved cinnabar red lacquer; China; inscribed *Made by Zhang Cheng,* who was a famous Yuan dynasty lacquer artist) We have one of the finest collections of Chinese 10th-14th century lacquers; this piece is exceptional for its elegant, deeply carved design.

38 **Strybing Arboretum.** A quiet sylvan retreat. There are many walks among the 3,000 varieties of trees and shrubs, native and exotic. Be sure to visit the **Garden of Fragrance** for the blind. Labels are in braille, and the plants are chosen for their taste, touch and smell, watched over by a statue of St. Francis of Assisi. *No admission charge. Open M-F 8AM-4:30PM, Sa & Su, holidays 10AM-5PM. Tours daily at 1:30PM. Map available at the information booth. 9th Av. and Lincoln Way. 661-0822*

39 **Music Concourse.** Free Sunday afternoon concerts at 1PM, weather permitting.

40 **Hana.** ★ $/$$ One of the most delightful, delicious and, unfortunately, crowded of San Francisco's many neighborhood Japanese restaurants. There's a distinct talent here for making everything light, flavor-

ful and succulent, brightening a cuisine that can be dull unless prepared with care. A tiny, noisy room, and you'll have to wait. Once you get in, and it's worth it, try the fried oysters, chicken teriyaki and tempura. *Japanese. Open M-Sa 11:30AM-2PM, 5-9PM. 408 Irving St. 665-3952*

41 **Milano Pizza and Italian Restaurant.** $/$$ Lots of pizzas to choose from; ask for extra cheese and extra tomato sauce when you order. Also heaping platters of Italian food, not the best but filling and inexpensive. *Italian. Open M-Th & Su 3PM-midnight, F & Sa 3PM-1AM. 1330 9th Av. 665-3773*

Restaurants/Nightlife red
Hotels blue
Shops/Galleries purple

42 **Japanese Tea Garden.** Built for the California Midwinter Exposition of 1894, along with the **Music Concourse**, these are the only structures which McLaren did not tear down after the fair ended. In 1895 the tea garden became the charge of the **Hagiwara** family, who tended it with loving devotion. **Makato Hagiwara** is credited with inventing the fortune cookie here. Ironically, the cookies have come to be called Chinese fortune cookies. They are now a favorite item of the tourist trade in Chinatown. The Hagiwara family maintained the park until World War II, when they, along with 110,000 other Japanese-Americans, were sent to internment camps. The tea garden is the jewel of the park. It is so artfully designed that even hordes of visitors cannot mar the experience of tranquility.

Architecture, landscape and man blend subtly and beautifully in a harmonious pattern of bridges, footpaths, pools, flowers, maple, cherry and bonsai trees, statuary, shrines and gateways. If you visit in April when the cherry trees are in blossom, you are lucky. The **Bronze Buddha,** donated by the **Gump** brothers in 1949, was cast in Japan in 1790. The **Shinto Pagoda** is a 5-tiered wooden shrine. The **Moon Bridge,** also called the **Wishing Bridge,** casts its semi-circular reflection in the pool below, making a full circle. There is also a gift shop and a **Tea House**, serving tea and fortune cookies. *Open daily 8AM-6PM. Admission charged between 9AM and 5PM. Free first W each month and national holidays. Brochure and map are available at the ticket booth. Music Concourse area.*

43 **Ruins.** The piles of old stones lying in a clearing behind the Japanese Tea Garden are the disassembled remains of a medieval Cistercian monastery from Spain. In 1932 **William Randolph Hearst** bought the monastery, had it dismantled and shipped over here, and later donated it to the **de Young Museum**. Except for the reconstruction of the chapel portal, which still stands in the de Young's central court, and the unobtrusive incorporation of some of the ruins in retaining walls and rockeries around the park, the stones have never been reassembled, due largely to lack of funds.

44 **Rose Garden.** Fifty-three beds of roses in great variety. *Between JFK Dr. and Fulton St., at the south end of Presidio Pkwy.*

45 **Stow Lake.** The largest lake in the park and the only place to rent row boats, pedal boats and motor boats. Picnicking is also fun, either by the lakeside or in the middle of the lake on the tiny island named *Strawberry Hill*. Small snack bar lakeside. *Open Tu-Su 9AM-4PM. Boat rental fees. 752-0347*

46 **Strawberry Hill.** Located in the middle of Stow Lake is this 428-foot-high, man-made island which once stored water for the park. Footbridges connect the shore with the hill and a winding road leads to its top. Nice views of the city.

47 **Japanese Cherry Orchard.** During the first week of April, the grove is in its peak, with bright blossoms and perfume filling the senses.

48 **Sunset Bookstore.** Loads of comics and the owners have set up a special corner for kids. You can take the books off the shelves and read them here. *Open M 9AM-8PM, Tu-Sa 9AM-9PM, Su 9AM-7PM. 2161 Irving St. 664-3644*

49 **Columns.** These 2 survivors of the 1906 quake once graced the porch of a Nob Hill home. Now they're a favorite site of city weddings.

50 **Spreckels Lake.** For operating sail and motor-powered model boats. It is also a way station for migratory birds. *Near 35th Av. and Fulton St.*

51 **Buffalo Paddock.** A dozen buffalo roam this 35-acre paddock. There have been as many as one hundred buffalo, all descendants from 2 cows and a bull. *West end of JFK Dr. at 38th Av.*

52 **Horseback Riding.** *Rent horses daily 10:30AM-4PM. Closed Mondays in the winter. Guided rides are available. Golden Gate Park Stables. JFK Dr. and 34th Av. 668-7360*

53 **Golden Gate Golf Course.** Nine holes. *Near 47th Av. and Fulton St. For information call 751-8987*

54 **Murphy Windmill.** (1905) Built to take advantage of the strong winds blowing from the ocean and to pump fresh water from underground to irrigate the newly established park, this was, at its time, the largest windmill in the world. The sails spread 114-feet from tip to tip. Dutch Windmill is nearby at the northwest corner of the park. Recently restored. *JFK Dr. at the Great Hwy.*

55 **Ocean Beach.** Near the celebrated **Cliff House** on the Great Highway and close to **Golden Gate Park**. This beach is easily accessible. Wading, jogging, stone collecting and picnicking are popular, but **swimming is not safe** due to a strong undertow.

Scenic Vistas

Golden Gate Bridge Vista Point. From the south end of the bridge at the toll plaza you can see the islands in the Bay, the bridge and the north waterfront.

Telegraph Hill. Look down on the Bay, the bridges and Fisherman's Wharf.

Twin Peaks. From the top of Market Street you can see the best of the Bay Area in every direction— the city, the Bay and its islands, the bridges and the mountains to the north and south.

Strawberry Point. Catch a glimpse of San Francisco's skyline from the point just off of Highway 101 at the end of Seminary Drive.

Mt. Tamalpais. On a blue sky day, the views from the summit extend out to the Farallon Islands and on to the city, east to Mt. Diablo and the East Bay and sometimes as far as the Sierra Nevadas 200 miles away.

Parks/Outdoor spaces green
Museums/Architecture/Narrative black

The **Richmond** district and **Presidio Heights** are bounded on all 3 sides by some of the best open spaces and resources for recreation in a metropolitan area in the country. Near the little known lake where **Juan Bautista de Anza** camped with his soldiers in 1776 (now **Mountain Lake Park** at **8th Avenue** and **Lake Street**) are beaches with seals on the rocks, impressive homes and the endless rows of stucco dwellings and a large park with **Rodin's** *Thinker* in the museum atrium.

Appropriately known as the *dunes* in the old days, it once took all day to reach **Seal Rocks** by railroad and horse drawn carriage. Before 1900 most of the San Franciscans in windy, foggy Richmond were deceased inhabitants of the **Municipal Cemetery** or the **Chinese Cemetery.** After a road was cut through in 1863, a few roadhouses opened up and the first of a series of **Cliff Houses** was built by **Sam Brannan.** It soon burned down.

Then along came **Adolph Sutro**, an engineer who made his fortune in the Comstock Lode, became mayor of the city and set about to open the area for development. He created a Victorian fantasy of a castle on the cliff's edge to replace the Cliff House that had burned. Then he erected a fabulous group of glass-enclosed swimming pools on the ocean called the **Sutro Baths,** planted **Sutro Forest** and built his own house and elaborate gardens which he opened to the public. After providing such incentive for people to visit the area, he built a steam railroad on **California Street** to make sure they could get there more easily. No wonder they called him the *Father of the Richmond.*

Now only a ruin marks the place where the once spectacular baths were situated and a few marble statues are all that remain of the mansion. But Sutro's projects succeeded in their purpose—to attract potential residents to the Richmond district, and thousands of houses were built here between 1910 and 1930. The area contains more residential land than any other and that's how the residents want it to stay: the Richmond district remains staunchly middle class and married.

There are a few more ambitious blocks at one end of the district—**Presidio Terrace,** a one-street neighborhood entered from **Arguello Boulevard** near the **Presidio Wall.** Near the other end lies **Sea Cliff,** perched on the edge of a sheer rock face and sporting large, pink Mediterranean houses, winding streets and the sound of fog horns most mornings.

After World War I, Russians and East European Jews moved into the Richmond district. Their religious centers still form the major landmarks: **Temple Emanu-El** on Arguello at Lake, and the gold-domed **Cathedral of the Holy Virgin** on Geary at 26th Avenue, definitely the place to go for a Russian Orthodox Easter celebration. Russian restaurants and businesses still thrive side by side with the enterprises of the Jews and Japanese who moved in after World War II.

More Japanese live here than in any other area of the city. And so many Chinese bought houses along Clement Street that the stretch between 1st and 11th Avenues is called *New Chinatown*. They have become the largest minority group in the area. Today 56 percent of Richmond residents are foreign-born. The area has superseded Chinatown as San Francisco's center for Asian cuisine. Discouraged by Chinatown's overcrowding and high rents, entrepreneurs are opening restaurants in the Richmond district. Not only Chinese, but also Vietnamese, Thai, Korean, Laotian and Cambodian restaurants abound.

Clement Street in particular reflects the marvelous ethnic diversity of the Richmond neighborhood, mingling the traditions of the Orient and Europe. It's a profusion of Chinese restaurants, Italian pizzerias, Irish bars and an Irish bookstore, Russian bakeries, Japanese markets, Middle Eastern and German delis, Austrians, Armenians, Hungarians, Ukranians, Czechs, and Caucasian refugees from Shanghai and Singapore—and Clement Street unites them all into a warm-hearted community.

The Presidio is a district apart. This federal property is governed by the U.S. Army and National Park Service. In addition to verdant scenery and a variety of views, it has 2 great beaches, **Fort Point** and **Winfield Scott**, old-time fortifications, a golf course, lake, historic sites and picnic sites everywhere. It's well worth a drive through, even if time is short.

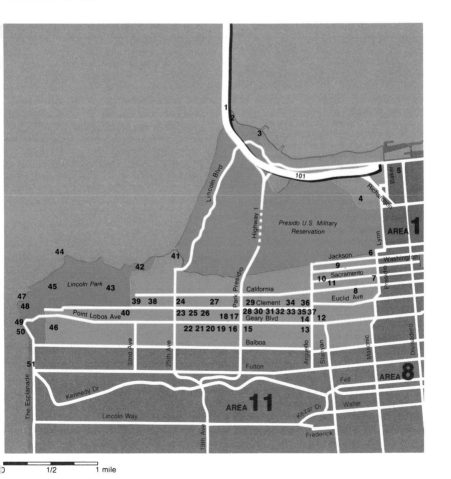

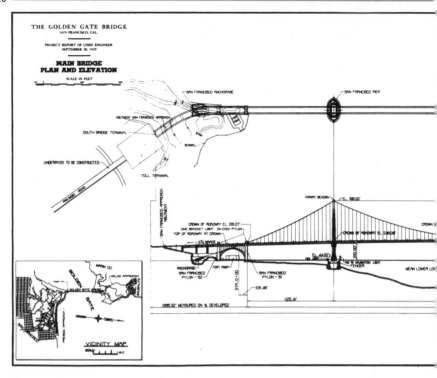

1 **Golden Gate Bridge.** (1937, Joseph Strauss) Undoubtedly one of the most beautiful bridges in the world, on account of its spectacular location, graceful lines, Moderne detailing and not the least, its emblematic color. The clear span of over 4,200-feet was until 1959 the longest in the world. **Joseph Strauss** was the chief engineer of the bridge, which took 4½ years to build. At mid-span, the roadway is 260-feet above the water, a height requested by the Navy to allow their battleships to pass beneath. One of the piers is located in the water and the other is on the Marin shore. The main cables are 36½ inches in diameter. The bridge was designed to be able to withstand winds of over 100-miles-per hour and to be able to swing at mid-span as much as 27 feet. The best views are from Vista Point on the Marin side and from Fort Point below on the San Francisco side.

The Golden Gate celebrated its 50th birthday in May 1987. Hard as it is to believe, it was more than a half century ago that **President Roosevelt** punched a telegraph key in the White House giving the cue 3,000 miles away for a clamor of bells, sirens, foghorns, squadrons of Navy planes and the most enormous peacetime concentration of Naval strength ever (and never repeated again after Pearl Harbor attack). After surviving 200,000 pedestrians swarming over the structure the day before, and the endless parade vehicles of politicos the day after, the bridge was finally and offically opened.

On 24 May 1987, more than 200,000 pedestrians took over again. Winners in a silly and hard-fought battle with local bureaucracies, they took advantage of the closure of the bridge for a few hours and walked across, their weight flattening the center span, causing the bridge to drop 10 feet.

The celebration included marching bands, poster contests, steelworkers from Pottstown, PA, where the bridge steel was made, brilliant fireworks displays, more politicos, and the *piece de résistance*—the inauguration of the lighting of the 746-foot towers.

Although the bridge was built for the automobile age, its designers wisely included sidewalks, doubtlessly recognizing the fact that it must be crossed on foot to be properly appreciated. The walk, round trip, takes about an hour—it is 1.2 miles across. Pedestrians use the walk on the east side daily from 5AM-9PM. To bicycle, use the path on the west side at the same hours. And don't forget an extra sweater—there's wind. You'll find a convenient parking area east of the **Toll Plaza** and nearby, a glass roundhouse containing a new **Visitor's Center.** One of the 2 surrounding gardens is a memorial to the bridgeworkers; the other is a friendship garden in tribute to the nations of the Pacific Rim.

Since its opening, the Golden Gate Bridge has become as symbolic of San Francisco as the Eiffel Tower is of Paris. Both structures have an unenviable record for suicides. Few people survive the 260-foot fall.

But the bridge itself is in good health and has aged well. With an additional network of girders to strengthen the roadway and new suspender ropes, she is stronger than ever and just as beautiful—the most photographed man-made structure in the world. Happy Birthday. dear bridge! *Toll Hwy. 101.*

2 **Fort Point.** The fort lies under the southern end of Golden Gate Bridge and was originally built between 1853 and

Courtesy Golden Gate Bridge Highway and Transportation District

1861 to guard San Francisco from sea attack. It houses a museum filled with old swords, guns, cannons, uniforms and photos of earlier days. With reservations, there are guided tours anytime. *Open daily 10AM-5PM. Weekend tours are usually conducted every hour on the hour. Civil War cannon loading and firing demonstrations at 12:30 & 2:30PM. Take Lincoln Blvd. to Long Av. 561-3837, 556-1693*

3 **Golden Gate Promenade.** It extends from Fort Point underneath the Golden Gate Bridge to Aquatic Park and provides 3½ miles of spectacular Bay views. It's also popular for biking and fishing.

4 **Presidio.** Located at the entrance to the Golden Gate on the northernmost point of the San Francisco peninsula, the Presidio has been a military outpost for over 200 years. In 1776, while the American colonies on the east coast were writing the Declaration of Independence, the Spanish rulers of Mexico were establishing a series of missions and military posts. The farthest north of these posts was the Presidio of San Francisco. The original Presidio was a walled camp 100 yards square surrounded by a palisade-type wall. When the Mexicans gained their independence in 1822, they took over the Presidio, and it remained this way until it was forcibly possessed by the United States in 1846. Originally, the 1,400-acre Presidio consisted of bare hills and rocks. In the 1880's, it was planted with pine and eucalyptus trees so that today it forms one of the most beautiful wooded areas in the city. The Presidio was used for training Union regiments during the Civil War. After the 1906 earthquake and fire, it became a vast refuge camp for the homeless and injured.

During World War II, it was the Headquarters of the Fourth Army and Western Defense Command.

Places to visit include the beaches at **Baker Beach** off Lincoln Boulevard and the gun emplacements **Battery Chamberlain, Battery Crosby** and **Batteries Cranston, Marcus Miller** and **Boutelle** near the **Golden Gate Bridge.** These latter areas including Baker Beach are all under the jurisdiction of the **Golden Gate National Recreation Area.** There is also an Historical Trail Guide produced by the National Park Service which was intended primarily for use by youth organizations. It features the many historic and scenic points of interest to be seen while hiking or driving through the preserve. *Additional information is available from the Presidio Community Relations Office. Group tours can be arranged. Main entrances located at Lombard and Lyons Sts., Presidio Blvd. and Broadway, Arguello Blvd. and Jackson St., Lincoln Blvd. at 25th Av., and the Golden Gate Bridge Toll Plaza. 561-3870*

Within the Presidio are:

Presidio Army Museum. The former **Old Station Hospital,** built in 1857, this is the oldest surviving building in the Presidio. On view are army uniforms, weapons, photographs and other memorabilia pertaining to the army's history in San Francisco. *Admission free. Open Tu-Su 10AM-4PM. Lincoln Blvd. and Funston Av. 561-4115*

Officers' Mansions and Barracks. (1895-1909) The Presidio was originally established in 1776 by **Juan Bautista de Anza** and his Spanish settlers to guard the Golden Gate. The barracks—built much later—are fine brick buildings with wooden loggias and porches. *Lincoln Blvd.*

5 **Palace of Fine Arts.** (1915, Bernard Maybeck) Originally built for the Panama-Pacific Exposition, it now houses the **Exploratorium**, a museum of inventions for kids. The building was the *pièce de résistance* of Maybeck's career as well as of the Exposition. It has a great stage set consisting of a classical Roman rotunda with 2 curved colonnades, behind which is the curved exhibition shed. The setting is in the midst of a small park, complete with an artificial lake. The Palace became so popular that, after the Exposition ended, the buildings were retained and completely rebuilt in 1962. *Baker St. between Bay and Marina Blvds.*

Exploratorium. Opened in 1969, this hands-on science museum has been called the best science museum in the world. Conceived on the premise that one learns by doing, the more than 500 exhibits require visitor participation. You can pull, push and manipulate various objects to demonstrate principles of prisms, sound, electricity, lasers, mathematics, animal and plant behavior, and more. The special **Tactile Gallery** has an admission charge and requires reservations. The store sells books, games and intriguing objects. *Open Tu, Th 1-5PM, W 1-9PM, Sa, Su 10AM-5PM. Admission charge for persons over 18. Free each W. 3601 Lyon St. 563-7337*

6 **3200 Block of Pacific Avenue.** One of the most unusual groups of houses in the city, located on a wedge-shaped lot that steps downhill. The entire block is clad in brown shingles and contains some of the best domestic architecture of the turn-of-the-century. Each house retains its own special identity with distinct windows or doorway detailing while maintaining the unity of the entire block. 3203 and 3277 by **Willis Polk;** 3233 by **Bernard Maybeck;** 3232 and 3234 by **Ernest Coxhead.** 3232 is of particular interest for its fine doorways and bizarre balcony above. *Private residences. 3200 Pacific Av. between Walnut and Presidio.*

7 **Le Castel.** ★ ★ ★ $$$ From the day it opened in 1981, Le Castel immediately established itself as one of San Francisco's finest fancy French restaurants. Located in a restored old house, it is a delightful place to eat. They have a wonderful touch with fish, particularly the scallops baked in puff pastry, a superb squab-on-sauerkraut main course inspired by Alsace, and an incredibly good steak topped with marrow in a red wine sauce. One of the best French meals you'll ever eat, and less expensive than the famous downtown and Nob Hill French restaurants. *Open M-Sa 6-10:30PM. 3235 Sacramento St. 921-7115*

8 **La Rocca's Oyster Bar.** ★ $$ Another of the delightful, authentic San Francisco Italian seafood restaurants, serving only the freshest fish. The specialties here are those fish native to the Bay Area like rex and petrale sole, sand dabs, Dungeness crab and salmon. Always fresh and always good. *American. Open M-Sa 8AM-8PM. 3519 California St. 387-4100*

9 **Roos House.** (1909 & 1926, Bernard Maybeck) A highly personalized example of English Tudor with typical Maybeck window and eaves detailing. *Private residence. 3500 Jackson St.*

Restaurants/Nightlife red
Hotels blue
Shops/Galleries purple
Parks/Outdoor spaces green
Museums/Architecture/Narrative black

9 **House.** (1952, Eric Mendelsohn) A mixture of Bay Region and International styles. Early Mendelsohn details such as the rounded corner bay and the porthole windows. *Private residence. 3778 Washington St. at Maple.*

10 **Lem House.** (1986, Daniel Solomon and Associates) A stucco clad rowhouse with an imposing Palladian window and rusticated base. *Cherry St. between Sacramento and Clay Sts.*

11 **Sacramento Street.** Restrained and exclusive. More than a whiff of affluence wafts across these few blocks of expensive specialty shops and antique stores. Many of them are open by appointment only or keep socialite hours, opening around noon. The street has more childrens' stores than any other in San Francisco. Highlights include:

Dottie Doolittle. Fine kid's clothes, mainly European imports. *Open M-Sa 10AM-5:30PM. 3680 Sacramento St. 563-3244*

Land of Counterpane. A children's bookstore with a display of award-winning books. *Open M-Sa 10:30AM-6PM. 3654 Sacramento St. 921-5961*

Gingerbread. Childrens' shoes and socks. *Open M-Sa 10AM-5:30PM. 3610 Sacramento St. 931-0861*

The Littlest Mouse. Fine toys, such as rocking horses, dollhouses and educational playthings as well as clothing. *Open M-Sa 10AM-5PM. 3480 Sacramento St. 922-8866*

Marilyn Brooks. Original women's fashions by this Toronto designer. *Open M-F 10:30AM-6PM; Sa 10:30AM-6PM. 3376 Sacramento St. 931-3376*

Goldberry. Custom-made capes for that night at the opera or that visit to grandmother's house in the woods. By appointment. *3516 Sacramento St. 921-4389*

Subrosa. Couture lingerie. (Its store at 318 Miller Av. in Mill Valley is friendlier.) *Open Tu-Sa 10AM-6PM. 3375 Sacramento St. 921-7955*

Forrest Jones. Culinary ware, stocks lots of exotic-looking baskets. (If you're in the Financial District, stop at its branch in the Golden Gateway, 151 Jackson St. Closed Su. 982-1577. There's also a store in Marin County at 1016 C St., San Rafael. 453-9444) *Open M-Sa 10AM-6PM, Su 11AM-5PM. 3274 Sacramento St. 567-2483*

12 **Sorento.** $$ Sorento serves well prepared Persian food, with an emphasis on highly spiced kebabs, presented in a contemporary pink and gray dining room. *3750 Geary. 751-4350*

12 **Pat O'Shea's Mad Hatter.** ★ ★ $$ As well as being a friendly, well-run neighborhood bar, Pat O'Shea's boasts a marvelous kitchen, which produces delicious and unusual specials at low prices, offering such delights as perfectly grilled veal sweetbreads and angler fish with mussels. *Restaurant open M-Sa 11:30AM-9PM, Su 11AM-3PM; bar until late. 3848 Geary. 752-3148*

The coldest winter I ever spent was summer in San Francisco. **Mark Twain**

13 **Cafe Riggio.** $$ An interesting Italian place that uses local California products to the best advantage. The appetizers and seafood entrees are the best things here; avoid the pastas and desserts. The dining room is so filled with the odor of garlic it nearly ruins the taste of the food. *Open daily 5-11PM. 4112 Geary Blvd. 221-2114*

14 **Golden Turtle.** ★ ★ $/$$ The proliferation of Vietnamese restaurants in the Bay Area has brought us a real winner in Golden Turtle, the literal translation of the name of the chef, **Kim Quy.** The food in this small, family-run restaurant is a subtle blend of contrasting flavors and colors, looking as good as it tastes. Two Vietnamese staples, crispy Imperial rolls and a juicy, aromatic 5 spice chicken, are outstanding here. But also try some of the more unusual dishes, like lot leaf beef and sour fish soup. *Open Tu-F 5-10:30PM; Sa & Su 11AM-11PM. 308 5th Av. 221-5285*

15 **Mike's Chinese Cuisine.** $/$$ A favorite Cantonese restaurant known for its poultry, fish dishes and excellent spring rolls. *Open Su & M, W-Sa 4:30-10PM. 5145 Geary Blvd. 752-0120*

16 **The Acropolis.** $/$$ A pleasant neighborhood restaurant and bakery serving traditional Russian favorites, such as spinach soup, *varenki* and beef stroganoff. Their hearty beef and chicken cutlets are a bargain, served with soup, salad and delicious, nutty flavored *kasha*. Also not to be missed is their *pelemini*, a kind of Russian ravioli in chicken stock, served with sour cream and dill. *Open daily 8AM-9PM. Geary Blvd. 751-9661*

16 **Russian Rennaissance.** ★ $$$ This dark, atmospheric restaurant features dark paneling, icons and live Russian music. The full bar creates complex and powerful drinks. Though the food is good, the real attraction here is the ambience, which brings to mind a cozy inn in Czarist Russia. *Open daily 5:30-10:30PM. 5241 Geary Blvd. 752-8558*

16 **Joe's.** The best ice cream out on the Avenues, particularly the *Its* (their version of the famous *its it*), a vanilla ice cream sandwich on oatmeal cookies dipped in chocolate, if you can believe that. *Open Su-F 11AM-11PM, Sa 11AM-11:30PM. 5351 Geary Blvd. 751-1950*

17 **Kabuto.** $$ **Sachio,** the premier chef at a downtown sushi bar called **Kinokawa,** has opened his own restaurant. He provides his customers with fresh, inventive sushi and entertainment; his sushi and personality draw a crowd of followers. *Open Tu-Su until 3AM. 5166 Geary Blvd. 752-5652*

18 **Shenson's Delicatessen.** $ This kosher deli makes hearty, homey salads, cold cuts and soups. Their smoked whitefish is to die for, as is their rich, flavorful borscht! *Open Tu-Sa 8AM-5:45PM. 5120 Geary Blvd. 751-4699*

19 **5665 Geary Boulevard.** (1982, Daniel Solomon and Associates) Another example of this firm's reinterpretation of traditional San Franciscan urban elements—bay windows, entrance portal, in this case also incorporating passive solariums. *Private residences.*

20 Cambodia House. $ As inexpensive as any of the nearby Chinese restaurants, Cambodia House offers a delicious and rather elegant alternative, featuring tablecloths and attentive service. The food is light, delicate and greaseless. *Open daily 11AM-3PM, 5-10:30. 5625 Geary Blvd. 669-5888*

21 Khan Toke Thai House. ★ ★ ★ $$ The best and most elegant of San Francisco's growing crop of Thai restaurants. Even though some of the dishes are hot, there's a beautiful contrast of textures and flavors; you can always taste far more than the chili peppers. The pork balls and squid as appetizers are superb; so are the stews with curry and coconut milk, the noodles, and the fish. You can sit on the floor at low tables if you want. Prices are surprisingly reasonable considering how pleasant and good this restaurant is. *Open daily 5-11PM. 5937 Geary Blvd. 668-6654*

22 Ton Kiang. ★ ★ $/$$ A strikingly different kind of Cantonese cuisine called *Hakka,* which originates in Southern China, is served here. Hakka dishes are popular in China, but virtually unheard of in the West. Not to be missed are the *yu yuhn,* Chinese fish balls similar to French *quenelles.* Hakka cuisine emphasizes beautifully fresh fish, meat and vegetables, with simple, skillfully prepared sauces. *Open daily 11AM-10PM. 5827 Geary. 387-8273*

23 Bill's Place. ★ $ The place for hamburgers, in the view of the crowds who jam into Bill's all day. Coleslaw and old-fashioned milk shakes the way they're supposed to be made. Greasy french fries are the only disappointment. Eat on the back patio in good weather. *Open daily 11AM-9PM. 2315 Clement St. 221-5262*

23 Shimo. ★ $$ Shimo-san expertly carves fish and seafood that is so fresh, it's nearly alive. Try the *ama ebi* (raw prawns), *saba* (mackerel) or *mirugai* (briny clams). Tempura treats have the lightest touch of sesame oil. This authentic sushi bar has a small *tatami* room in back. *Open M, Tu, Th-Su 5:30-11PM, sushi bar until midnight. 2339 Clement St. 752-4422*

24 Seacliff Cafe. $$ This cafe offers stick-to-your-ribs, homey, midwestern cuisine. A sign on the wall proclaims that *Meat and potatoes are spoken here.* The decor is straightforward and simple, with colonial designed tables and chairs and gingham tablecloths. For those who are bored with nouvelle cuisine, Seacliff Cafe offers delectable stews, sandwiches and stuffed potatoes. No midwestern meal is complete without dessert, and the desserts here are worth destroying your diet, like the chocolate fudge cake, Shaker sugar pie and scones with cream and homemade jam. The prices are reasonable and the service is excellent. *Open Tu-Su 11-9PM. 2450 Clement St. 386-6266*

25 Hahn's Hibachi. $$ Interesting and inexpensive Korean food, with good stews. *Open M, W-Su 11:30AM-9:30PM. 2121 Clement St. 221-4246*

26 Kum Moon. ★ $/$$ An outstanding Cantonese restaurant, spartan and jammed with people. Surprisingly, it's not that easy to dine well on Cantonese food in San Francisco, but this is an exception. Good fish, shellfish and vegetables. *Open daily 11AM-9:30PM. 2109 Clement St. 221-5656*

27 Alejandro's Sociedad Gastronomica. ★ ★ ★ $$ An absolute madhouse, with huge portions of sensational Spanish food. The *paella* is the kind you always want from a restaurant but so rarely get: it's loaded with shellfish, sausage, chicken, pork, fresh vegetables and saffron-coated rice. Try the rabbit and the boned trout too. Another highlight is *tapas* (Spanish hors d'oeuvres), which have replaced nouvelle cuisine as the latest trendy nibble. Here they are done to perfection. It's possible to make a meal of the tapas alone. Don't miss the *Conchitas* (scallions with butter, wine and grated cheese, eggs and jalepenos). There's also a whole menu page of Mexican entrees that are as good as the best in the Mission district. Be sure to reserve; even then you'll have to wait. *Spanish. Open M-Sa 5-11PM, Su 4-11PM. 1840 Clement St. 668-1184*

28 Red Crane. $/$$ Specializes in seafood and vegetarian dishes. Their Szechuan clams and prawns in lobster sauce are particularly impressive. Red Crane also creates meatless *meat* dishes such as almond pressed *duck* made from bean curd, and *chicken curry* made from gluten. These dishes could fool the eye and the palate of the most die-hard carnivore. *Open daily 5-11PM. 1115 Clement. 751-7266*

29 Clement Street Bar And Grill. $$ This restaurant offers excellent service, good food and reasonable prices. The cuisine is nouvelle California, with an emphasis on grilled meats and exquisitely fresh vegetables. The dark wood paneling, plants and linen tablecloths contribute to the elegant yet relaxed ambience. *Open Tu-F 11:30AM-3PM, Sa-Su 5-10:30PM. 700 Clement. 386-2200*

30 King of China. $ This huge second floor restaurant presents such dim sum delicacies as quail egg *sui mai,* shrimp *har gow,* rice noodles stuffed with peanuts, pork and black mushrooms and Cantonese roast duck. Some of their better dinners are exquisitely prepared rock fish with ginger, coriander and scallions and spinach sauteed with ginger. Though diners may be daunted by the noise and bustle of this cavernous space, the excellent and remarkably reasonable food more than compensates. *Open daily 9AM-10PM. 939 Clement St. 668-2618*

31 Ocean. ★ ★ $/$$ This is Cantonese food as good as it can be done. The Cantonese specialize in seafood, and here the salt and pepper prawns (which can be eaten shell and all) and the other fish dishes are remarkable, never served in the gloppy corn-starched sauces that characterize bad Cantonese cooking. The problem with Ocean is that the wait can be long at peak hours and the service, rude. *Open daily 11AM-9:30PM. 726 Clement St. 221-3351*

31 **The Caspian.** Described as *the sort of bar you take your grandmother to,* assuming Grandma likes plush decor, pricey drinks and unlimited free caviar (which is really black lumpfish). Nevertheless, the Caspian provides an elegant, low key alternative for those seeking a quieter night on the town. *517 Clement St. 387-0603*

32 **Firehouse Station No. 1 Barbecue.** One of the classiest of San Francisco's barbecue joints, serving good, smoky beef ribs. *Open daily. 501 Clement St. 221-7427*

32 **Taiwan Restaurant.** ★$ An airy, contemporary deco restaurant serving Taiwanese food, not often seen in San Francisco. Taiwanese rejects the fire of Hunan and Szechuan in favor of subtle, sweet/salty and garlicky flavors. Not to be missed are the spareribs and the Taiwan Country Favorite Chicken. *Open M-F 11:30AM-midnight, Sa & Su 1:30PM-midnight. 445 Clement. 387-1789*

33 **Toy Boat.** This delightful little cafe, in addition to selling windup toys, makes delicious coffees, Italian sodas and desserts. This is a perfect place to go after music or comedy at the Holy City Zoo or Last Day Saloon. *Open M-F 7:30PM to midnight, Sa & Su 9:30PM-midnight. 401 Clement.*

34 **Holy City Zoo.** San Francisco's oldest comedy club, where **Robin Williams** got his start and occasionally drops in for a surprise visit. *The club features 2 shows nightly at 9 and 11PM. 407 Clement St. 386-4242*

34 **Last Day Saloon.** Last Day features good, danceable local bands, more classic rock than new wave. They occasionally feature blues and comedy. *406 Clement St. 387-6343*

35 **Java Restaurant.** $/$$ Indonesian food, good but not great, in a pleasant setting at moderate prices. *Open W-M 11:30AM-11:30PM. 417 Clement St. 752-1541*

36 **Le San Tropez.** $$$ This neighborhood restaurant serves elegant, imaginative and expensive nouvelle French cuisine in an old world setting. *Open M-Sa 5:30-10PM. 126 Clement. 387-0408*

37 **Mai Viet-Nam.** ★★$/$$ There are things on the menu here not to be missed by any Asian food gourmet. *La lot* beef, ground beef seasoned with exotic spice, wrapped in a leaf resembling a grape leaf, and charcoal-grilled, is spectacular. Also try the imperial rolls, the Vietnamese rolls and the chicken salad. *Vietnamese. Open daily 11:30AM-11PM. 316 Clement St. 752-1541*

38 **Tsing Tao.** ★★ $/$$ A plain Chinese restaurant distinguished by truly great food at remarkably low prices. The chili pepper prawns are not to be missed. Consider also the hot braised chicken legs, the hot and sour soup, shredded pork with garlic and eggplant in Szechuan sauce. The waiters are as helpful as can be, so don't hesitate to question them about dishes that sound good. *Open M-F 11:30AM-11PM, Sa & Su 11:30AM-10PM. 3107 Clement St. 387-2344*

39 **Lincoln Park.** 270 verdant acres on the Pt. Lobos Headlands. Striking views of the Bay and Golden Gate Bridge. Its 2 main attractions are the **golf course** and the **California Palace of the Legion of Honor.** *Main entrance, Clement St. and 34th Av.*

Lincoln Park Municipal Golf Course. 18 holes. *34th Av. and Clement St. Phone for information, 221-9911*

40 **El Mansour.** ★$$ The big attraction here is the belly dancer who flutters and spins each night around 8PM. But the good Moroccan food shouldn't be overlooked. The fixed price meal includes lentil soup, salad and entrees of lamb, seafood, chicken or rabbit. This is finger food at its best. *Open daily 5-10PM. 3123 Clement. 751-2312*

41 **Baker Beach.** A mile-long stretch of sandy shore. Swimming is dangerous, but the fishing is fine, especially for striped bass. Picnic and barbecue facilites are provided, as are drinking water and restrooms. No camping; dogs allowed on leash. *Main entrance at the southwest corner of Gibson Rd. For information call 751-2519*

Baker Beach Bunkers. Concrete bunkers built to defend the Golden Gate Bridge from aerial attack during World War II. The guns have been removed, but the clear, functional shapes are still visible. *25th Av.*

42 **Phelan Beach.** This small beach nuzzled into a cove is one of the few San Francisco beaches where swimming is permitted. Lifeguards are on duty from April to October. Formerly called China Beach after Chinese fishermen who used to camp here. No dogs allowed. Restrooms. *Open daily 7AM-dusk. At the end of Seacliff Av. Lifeguard station: 221-5756*

The **Golden Gate National Recreation Area** is a huge public wilderness in the midst of a great metropolitan area. Established in 1972, it encompasses 34,000 acres and is 1.5 times larger in area than San Francisco. The park covers more than 68-square-miles of land and water, including 28 miles of the Pacific Ocean, Tomales Bay in Marin and the San Francisco coastline. Its diverse natural environment offers sandy beaches, rugged headlands, grasslands, forests, lakes, marshes and streams. The area is administered by the **National Park Service** of the **U.S. Department of the Interior**. Commercial and recreational development is rigorously monitored and kept to a minimum. The most built-up area of the GGNRA is concentrated at Fort Mason in San Francisco. The rest of the expansive preserve is maintained as closely as possible in its natural state, as intended by Congress: *...In carrying out the provisions of this Act, the Secretary [of the Interior] shall preserve the recreation area, as far as possible, in its natural setting, and protect it from development and uses which would destroy the scenic beauty and natural character of the area.* Public Law 92-589

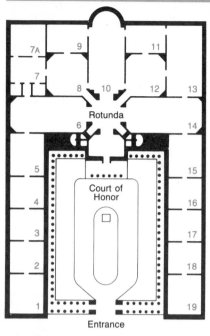

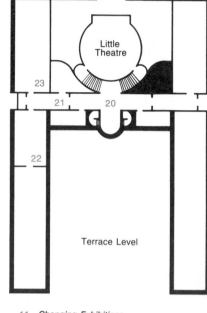

1-3 Medieval and Early Renaissance Art
4 The school of Fontainebleau
5 Baroque Art in France
6 The Age of Louis XV
7 Rococo Art in France
7A Louis XVI French Room
8,10,12 Rodin and His Contemporaries
9 Eighteen-Century French Decorative Arts

11 *Changing Exhibitions*
13 Neoclassical Art
14 The Nineteenth Century in France
15-19 *Changing Exhibitions*
20-22 Recent Acquisitions
23 Italian Maiolica from the Arthur M. Sackler Collections

43 **The California Palace of the Legion of Honor.** The museum commands a spectacular view of the city and the Bay from its hilltop site in Lincoln Park. It was designed by architect **George Applegarth,** based on the Palace of the Legion d'Honneur in Paris, and was given to the city in 1924 by **Mr. and Mrs. Adolph Spreckels** in memory of California's dead in World War I. The museum is unique in America for its extensive collection of French art. One of the 5 original bronze casts of *The Thinker* by **Auguste Rodin** graces the entrance. Twenty of the museum's galleries house its permanent collections of French painting, sculpture and decorative arts. There are tapestries, period rooms, 18th century paintings, works by the Impressionists, such as **Monet, Renoir** and **Degas** and many Rodin sculptures. The art of **Picasso, Turner, Constable, Velazquez** and **El Greco** are also represented here. Special exhibitions are held regularly. The museum has a theater, a small bookstore and a cafe. Free tours. *Open W-Su 10AM-5PM. First W each month is free. Lincoln Park. 221-4811*
Within the Palace is:
The Achenbach Foundation for Graphic Arts. This is the most comprehensive collection of works of art on paper in the western U.S. Only a portion of the 100,000 prints and drawings can be displayed at a time.

44 **Lands End.** Wonderful views from this promontory. Steep trails that contour along the cliffs are only for the skilled hiker.

45 **VA Hospital.** Moderne buildings on a spectacular hilltop site overlooking the ocean. *Lincoln Park.*

45 **West Fort Miley's Gun Batteries.** Fun to explore. Picnic and barbecue facilities, water and restrooms. *Ranger station, 556-8371*

46 **Sutro Heights Park.** Its bluff-top site overlooking the Cliff House and ocean beyond makes it an ideal spot for watching the sunset. It was formerly the home and grounds of **Adolph Sutro,** a mining engineer and one of the city's great benefactors. He bought up much of the seafront property in the city and planted a forest of ecalyptus on Mt. Sutro. The park has a haunting charm, with fragments of statuary lying half-hidden among the groves of fir, Monterey cypress and Norfolk Island pine. *Point Lobos and 48th Av.*

47 **Point Lobos.** The westernmost tip of San Francisco. Named by the Spanish *Punta de los Lobos Marinos* after the sea lions, whom they called lobos marinos, sea wolves.

48 **Sutro Baths.** Opened in 1896 by **Adolph Sutro,** the 3-acre spa resembled the baths of Imperial Rome in scale and splendor. Six salt water swimming pools heated to different temperatures sparkled beneath a colored glass roof. The building was destroyed in a spectacular fire in 1966. Today the remains look like classical ruins. An algae-covered puddle is all that is left of the baths.

49 **Cliff House.** Originally built in 1863, San Francisco families would day trip from the big city to sun at this resort spot. Later the house became associated with the local powerbrokers, crime bosses and their molls. When the schooner *Parallel* crashed on the rocks below the house with its load of dynamite, one whole wing of the building was lost in the explosion. Seven years later, on Christmas Day, the original Cliff House burned to the ground.

Adolph Sutro built the second Cliff House in 1895, and this one also burned within the year. The present building opened in 1909 and is the 5th on the spot. It houses the popular **Cliff House Restaurant** which is a good place for drinks and a view.

Within the Cliff House is:

Musee Mecanique. A tribute to the days of the Penny Arcade. This large collection of antique mechanical amusement machines claims to be the world's largest collection of coin-operated automatic musical instruments. (Another Musee Mecanique, located at Fisherman's Wharf, also has electronic games to play.) *Open M-Th 10:30AM-6PM, F-Su 10AM-7PM. Admission free. 109 Point Lobos Av. 386-1170*

50 **Seal Rocks.** 400-feet offshore and below the Cliff House, the rocks swarm with sea lions and various sea birds. Watching them loll on the rocks is a favorite Sunday pastime.

51 **Ocean Beach.** When San Franciscans say the beach, they are referring to this one. It's fun for jogging, hiking or frisby-tossing. The undertow is extremely dangerous; swimming is prohibited. Wading is inadvisable.

BESTS

Sylvia Chase
News Anchor, KRON-TV

My earliest memories of the Bay Area are about light. Sunny or foggy or—best of all—in between, there is brilliance to this place. It comes from acres of water which shower reflections on geographically young mountains and constantly changing clouds. I like to see it on my feet.

Urban Walk: I'm a walker and San Francisco's **waterfront** is ideal for me. There are a few colorful miles of almost completely flat terrain which begin at the **Ferry Building** and pass the piers along the way to **Pier 39.** (For a good view of **Alcatraz, Mt. Tamalpais** and the **Golden Gate Bridge,** make a loop around the outside of the Pier.) Next come **Fisherman's Wharf** and **Ghirardelli Square.** Then it's up the hill at **Fort Mason** and straight through **Marina Green** into **St. Francis Yacht Club.** From here, it's just a couple more miles to the **Golden Gate Bridge.**

Country Walk: With **Mt. Tamalpais** less than a half hour away, who needs Switzerland? I like spring here because of the wild flowers. My personal favorite is called *Blue-Eyed Grass,* although the Douglas Iris is pretty special too. If I have no more than an hour, I'll take the **Cataract Trail** to **Laurel Dell** and back. There are beautiful woods and rushing water in the wet season. At Laurel Dell there are restrooms, water and picnic tables. For a spectacular afternoon walk, I choose the **Matt Davis Trail.** The city appears distant and futuristic as you wind your way down to the beach. The Ocean is vast. Gigantic ships appear to crawl toward the horizon. In spring, the hills look firm and green and are awash with poppies. The trip down takes maybe 2 comfortable hours, and there are buses back to the top in the afternoon. The Mt. Tam rangers couldn't be more hospitable, so before I hike, I usually check in to see what they're recommending.

Aside from walking, my passion is people watching over **breakfast** or **lunch.** There's nothing finer than morning errands around **Union Square** and then stopping by the **Campton Place Hotel** for an expensive, elegant, delicious breakfast or lunch.

But if it's *hanging out* I'm after, it's **North Beach.** This is where you'll see a kind of Olympics of hanging out, but it must be by day to avoid the honky-tonk. There are remnants of the *beatnik* era here (**City Lights Books**) and the city's vital Italian immigrant tradition. I stroll right down to **Enrico's,** where Mr. Banducci himself is likely to be tending the kitchen. Here's where San Francisco's politicos table hop on weekend mornings. And Enrico, resplendent in his beret, entertains the likes of Bill Cosby, who—in his early career—played Enrico's other North Beach establishments. After breakfast, a gang has usually assembled and we wander over to **Columbus Avenue** for latte, capuccino or espresso at the **Puccini** (you'll have to *find* it; they've no phone) or the **Roma** across the street. The shops on **Grant Avenue** are worth a look as you trudge up to **Coit Tower** for the view on a sunny day. Then I walk down the **Filbert Steps,** stopping to admire the gardens and make my way back home to Russian Hill.

It's worth going over the **Bay Bridge** for breakfast too. There are many better known places on the *Berkeley Food Community* map. But it's breakfast I like, and the **Bridge Creek** serves wonderful pancakes (*Heavenly Hots*), and you'll never have a better down-home breakfast than **Bette's Ocean View** on 4th Street. And while you're waiting for a table (and you will wait for a table, with no view of the ocean to divert you), you can lounge about in the chairs, read the newspapers and watch the Berkeleyites at play.

San Francisco's fireworks blast celebrating the Golden Gate Bridge's 50th birthday cost nearly half a million dollars.

The **Sunset** district encompasses a large area with row after row of single family, pastel-colored look-alike houses, thought by some to be the best place in San Francisco to rear children. **Golden Gate Park** is to the north; **Stern Grove,** the **Zoo** and **Lake Merced** are to the south; and the wide open ocean lies to the west. The area incorporates a hodgepodge of other districts as well.

Sunset emerged as a residential neighborhood during the 20s and 30s with most of the houses financed by the FHA. **Henry Doelger** built 2 houses a day throughout the depression, selling them for $5,000 each. Many of the San Franciscans who first settled here shortly after the sand dunes were paved over are now retired. But while the general image of the district is conservative, white, middle-class family, an international air is gradually being added. There are a number of Asians, a young Irish colony and enough patrons to justify the existence of some good French bistros. The so-called *Inner Sunset* around **Irving Street** has restaurants and shops with an international flavor and you can find different kinds of ethnic dancing and entertainment in the cafes and clubs. It is also home to the **San Francisco Conservatory of Music,** the **Shriners Hospital, Lake Merced** and **San Francisco State University.**

Lake Merced was originally named *Lake of Our Lady of Mercy* and was part of a surrounding ranchero granted by **Jose Castro** to **Jose Antonio Galino** in 1835. Today it is a standby reservoir for the city as well as its *backyard fishin' hole.*

Stern Grove comes alive on Sundays during the summer, when thousands of picnickers come for the free jazz and classical music concerts. **Ingleside District** was the site of one of San Francisco's early race tracks and is now a large-scale residential neighborhood. Beautiful **St. Francis Woods** is a more expensive development of large houses with gates and fountains designed by Beaux Arts architect **John Galen Howard.** Nearby is sedate, middle-class **West Portal,** with diagonal and curving streets that make it look somewhat like a Swiss village because of its appearance and location. It lies at the foot of 3 hills: **Mt. Davison, Forest** and **Edgehill Heights. Outer Mission** is an area of relatively uncrowded single family homes and gardens, many of which are strikingly well manicured. Land here was originally part of the Spanish land grant *Rancho Canada de Guadalupe de la Visitacion y Rodeao Viejo.* In the **Excelsior** area, there are still many of its original farm houses next door to 1930s-style homes. **Bayview-Hunters Point** to the east of Highway 101 became an area of shabby temporary housing after WWII, when the largest shipyard on the West Coast took over Hunter's Point. But the scenery is looking up, and now it looks as if there is a brighter future in store. **Candlestick Park,** home of the San Francisco Giants and 49ers, is nearby. Designed by **John S. Bolles,** it is the first major league baseball stadium to be built entirely of reinforced concrete.

Twin Peaks, the second and third highest hills in the city, offers wonderful 360-degree panoramas of the Bay Area.

Even view-crazy San Franciscans left the area alone until World War II. (**Daniel Burnham** did brave the heavy fog and chilling winds when he lived up there long enough to draw up a new plan for the city in 1905). But today it has become a very popular neighborhood, with spectacular houses the size of great villas and many apartment complexes. On the south side, single family homes face the San Bruno mountains and the ocean. **Noe Valley** nestles below the protective eastern slopes of Twin Peaks, between 21st and 30th Streets, Grand View and Dolores, and maintains a low profile as a friendly family neighborhood. Also with the transferral of some of Bohemia across town from Telegraph Hill, it has been called San Francisco's residential *Greenwich Village*.

Above Noe Valley on the eastern edge of the area is the **Castro** district, a quaint neighborhood of Victorian storefronts and homes which was taken over by the city's gay population in the 1970s. On Sunday afternoons, Castro Street is as alive as a Mexican Plaza.

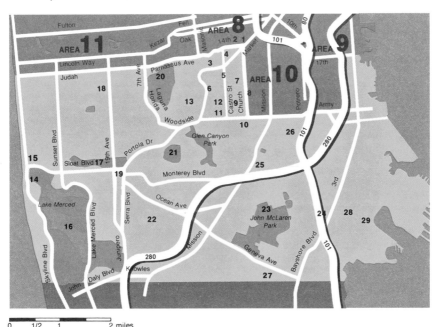

0   1/2   1   2 miles

1 **Le Piano Zinc.** ★ ★ ★ $$$ This restaurant successfully carries off its claim to *a renaissance of classic French cuisine*. Dinners ordered *a la carte* or from a daily *prix fixe* four-course menu don't skimp on quality or flavor, and the ambience is distinctly Parisian. An ivory baby grand dominates and Limoges china helps present sensitive renditions of medallions of fresh salmon, *magret* of duck with fresh peaches, rabbit and venison. Jazz dinner music accompanies the stylish and memorable meals. *Reservations. Open Tu-Su 6PM-midnight. 708 14th St. (Market and Church Sts.) 431-5266*

2 **The Willows.** *Moderate.* A quiet, 12-room bed and breakfast on a sunny corner of Market, Church and 14th Streets, central to Castro, Mission and Downtown and with easy connections for BART and MUNI. The graceful California Gypsy Willow furniture was designed specifically for each room. Together with the muted colors and potted plants, they create a beautiful and tranquil environment for relaxing after a day of city touring. There is a telephone, wash basin and Kimono in each room, and continental breakfast is served in your room along with a morning paper. Complimentary wine is offered in the late afternoon. *Shared baths. 710 14th St. 431-4770*

3 **Josephine D. Randall Junior Museum.** The emphasis at this museum is on participation, with live animals and a petting corral, dinosaur and mineral exhibits, ceramics room, woodworking shop, seismograph, chemistry and biology labs. There are many special workshops and events, especially during the summer. *199 Museum Way (off Roosevelt Way). 863-1399*

Restaurants/Nightlife red
Hotels blue
Shops/Galleries purple
Parks/Outdoor spaces green
Museums/Architecture/Narrative black

4 Inn on Castro. *Moderate.* One of the smaller guest houses in the city (5 rooms with private baths), but the intimate surroundings make it truly a home away from home. Although located in a Victorian flat, the interiors are contemporary: white walls, track lighting, classic furniture, brilliant flowers and the original art of one of the owners, interior designer and painter **Joel Roman.** The owners live upstairs where breakfast is served every morning on an extensive and everchanging collection of imported china and stoneware dishes. *321 Castro St. 861-0321*

5 Castro Street. This center of San Francisco's gay social life is a crowded collection of unique shops, bars and restaurants. Highlights on and around Castro include:

Does Your Mother Know? Unusual, outrageous and funny cards. *4079 18th St.*

Double Rainbow. Yet another parlor claiming to serve San Francisco's best ice cream. Rich, and on the *chewy* side. Their *ultra chocolate* is, well, ultra. *407 Castro St. 621-2350*

Castro Theatre. San Francisco officialdom dubbed the Castro Theatre *the finest example of a 1930s movie palace in San Francisco.* The 1,600-seat theater has earned its reputation because of its remarkable Spanish Colonial design. The auditorium ceiling is probably the most noteworthy architectural feature, an extraordinary affair cast in plaster to resemble a giant cloth canopy tent complete with swags, ropes and tassels. And in what better setting could you enjoy an everchanging series of movies from Hollywood's heyday? Located in the middle of the gay Castro district, the movie house attracts patrons who sometimes carry their enthusiasm too far. But anybody who swoons over *Camille* or drools over the exquisite timing in *Bringing up Baby* will want to take in a flick at this classic theater. *429 Castro St. 621-6120*

Castro Village. Wine from excellent local wineries and daily wine tasting. *4121 19th St.*

Castro Photo. Quality—and uncensored—photo finishing and supplies. *4115 19th St.*

Headlines. Card, accessories, clothing and ticket outlet. *557 Castro St.*

Walt Whitman Bookstore. A gay literary place for men and women featuring local art exhibits, Sunday evening readings and book signings. *2319 Market St.*

Adela's Yarn. A wide variety of yarns, patterns and instructions. *421 Castro St.*

All That Jazz. For crystal, tabletop accessories and (around the corner at 4109 19th St.) a wild range of greeting cards and gifts. *506 Castro St.*

6 Nobby Clarke's Folly. An eclectic pile built in 1892 by **Alfred Clarke,** alleged to have cost $100,000—a fortune in those days. *250 Douglass St.*

7 Noe Valley. This area set at the foot of Twin Peaks has been called the *Greenwhich Village of San Francisco* because of the eclectic mix of families and Bohemians from Telegraph Hill. Historically, the area is part of the 4,000-plus acre land grant given to the last Mexican mayor of San Francisco, **Jose de Jesus Noe,** by California Govenor **Pio Pico** in the 1840s. Noe's ranch house was one of the first buildings in the district and stood at the corner of 22nd and Eureka Street. After the ranching days were over, the residents were mostly working class Germans, Scandinavians and Irish. Today, it is a relaxed urban village where residents raise chickens and sometimes spot raccoons in their backyards, gather for an annual picnic and a local history day at the library and spend the weekends fixing up their old houses. The mix of ages, income levels and occupations makes it a favored place to live. 24th Street is one of the best shopping areas in town, with supermarkets, repair and antique shops, coffee houses and ethnic delis where you can buy a burrito, a knish and a quiche within 2 blocks. To preserve the small town quality where people shop and chat together, one residential group is promoting a hard line on establishments selling liquor.

While it is technically part of the greater Mission District, residents have always insisted they live in Noe Valley. Said a former president of a neighborhood organization, *We have a lot of care about the neighborhood... there's a feeling that neighbors here will get together to get something done...*

In Upper Noe Valley, there is a somewhat older population enjoying an edge on the quality of life. Here there are steep streets and hills which create truly spectacular housing sites. (Bound by Randall, Laidley, Douglass and 30th Sts.)

8 Ramis Caffe. ★ $$ This predominantly neighborhood diner dispatches with relish the fresh fish, pork, chicken, pasta and vegetables owner **Ramy Sternfeld** describes as *California cuisine with an Israeli and Middle Eastern touch.* Recently, patrons from farther afield have also discovered this Noe Valley cafe as a relaxing and gracious spot for dinner or brunch with friends. A changing collection of work by local artists adorns the walls. The characteristic Mediterranean mix of hot and cool, salty and sweet and aromatic and mild typifies the food here. California and European wines and domestic and imported beers compliment the food. *Open M & W-F 5:30-10PM, Sa 5:30-10:30PM, Su 10AM-3PM, 5:30-10:30PM. 1361 Church St. 641-0678*

17th Street

New York City Deli
Eureka Valley Market
Pier 1 Imports
German Oak *Bavarian*
Scandinavian Deli
Sweet Inspirations
Midtown Stationers
Leticia's *restaurant*
Gladwin's Mesquite
Record Factory
Stereo Plus

Sanchez

Noe

Market

Bank of America
Tony Leonarda Hair Design
Margarita's Hairstyling
barber **Marcello's**
Rossi's Deli
clothing **Bio**
deli **Norse Cove**
Cafe Orient
bar **Cheer**
Federal Bank/Big Empire
Bay Area Furniture
Muni/Bart station **Castro Station**
restaurant **Without Reservation**
Welcome Home Restaurant
Mueller's Deli
Valley Pride Market
bar **Phoenix**
Castro Cafe
Walgreens

Market

CASTRO STREET

Twin Peaks *grocery store*
Double Rainbow *ice cream*
The March Hair *hairdresser*
The Castro Bean *coffeebeans*
The Bead Store *jewelry*
Adela's Yarn
The Castro Cheesery
The Castro Theater
Eureka *bank*
Baker's of Paris
Mrs. Field's Cookies
The All American Boy *clothing*
Cliff's Variety Store
Obelisk *gifts*
The Cut Up *hairdresser*
The Village Deli
24 Hour Donuts
1 Hour Photo

18th Street

---

restaurant **The Elephant Walk**
Haagen Dazs Ice Cream
crystal & gifts **All That Jazz**
Main Line Gifts
Crown Books
Canton Restaurant
cards **Browser's Nook**
Books etc.
Luisa's Garden Restaurant
Attainable Treasures
Castro Place
fitness **Always Tan and Trim**
eye doctor **For Your Eyes Only**
Paragon Printing
Castro Hotel
bar **JV Bones**
Tommy's Plants
drugstore **Brand X**
Liquor Express
Western Union
Golden Fleece Hairstyling

Collingwood

CASTRO STREET

Hibernia Bank
Founder's Title Company
The Sausage Factory *Italian*
Vallys *restaurant*
Patio Cafe *restaurant*
Jerusalem Shop *clothing*
Sid's Pipe Dreams *tobacco*
Skin Zone *cosmetics*
Rolo *clothing*
Castro Video
GW Finley *men's clothing*
Headlines *club*
Prima Facie *facial salon*
Anchor Oyster Bar
Le Roy on Castro *hairdresser*
Hiro's Gifts
China Court

Hartford

Noe

19th Street

Cock-A-Doodle-Do *restaurant*
The Pendulum *bar*
Metro Video
Dino's Liquors

bar **Francines**
clothing **David Andrew**
South China Cafe
Unique Custom Frames
Hartford Properties
Passport to Leisure
Castellana Bakery
crystal & gifts **All that Jazz**

CASTRO STREET

Presto Prints
Duo *restaurant*
The Wash Tub *laundry*
The Village *bar*
Lupanni's Cafe
Mai Wah *restaurant*

18th Street

Hibernia Bank
Butch Wax Records
Does Your Mother Know?
ice-cream **Latest Scoop**
clothing **New York Man**
The Neon Chicken
flowers **Floratex**
Superstar Video
Castro Cleaners
bar **Moby Dick**
cookies **Hot 'N Hunky**
florist **Hidden Garden**
Rosie's Cantina

Hartford

9 **Little Italy.** $$ A bustling, happy place to eat dinner. Good food, too, if you stick with the fish dishes (particularly those baked in tomato-based sauces) and the interesting appetizers, like fried mozzarella. *Italian. Open daily 6-11PM. 4109 24th St. 821-1515*

10 **Speckmann's.** $$ Through the bakery and deli on the corner you will find hearty German food—and lots of it. The upstairs dining room and more formal room downstairs feature *konigsberger klopse*, meatballs with a caper sauce, *weiner schnitzel* and a fine Hungarian goulash. *Open M-Th 11AM-9PM, F & Sa 11AM-10PM. 1500 Church St. 282-6850*

11 **Bud's.** ★ $ A tiny store with long lines for take-out ice cream. Perhaps the most famous San Francisco ice cream emporium. *Open daily. 1300 Castro St. 647-2573*

12 **Diamond Street Restaurant.** $$ A little neighborhood restaurant baking its own breads and using the freshest available ingredients. Good salads, fish and casseroles and a friendly, informal atmosphere.

Open daily 5:30-10:30PM. 737 Diamond St. 285-6988

13 **Twin Peaks.** The Costanoan Indians believed that the peaks—the 2nd and 3rd highest hills in San Francisco—were created when a married couple quarreled so loudly that the Great Spirit separated them with a clap of thunder in order to have peace. Spanish explorers named them *Breasts of the Indian Girl*. But unimaginative Americans changed the name to Twin Peaks. The steep, grassy slopes are a wonderful, if windy, lookout, providing a 360-degree view of the entire Bay—the best available view of San Francisco. At night, Twin Peaks is surrounded by a twinkling sea of lights spreading in every direction, and by day, you can get a good overview of the city. Sometimes the view isn't all that pretty—when hazy smog mars it or if you're perceptive enough to see how the hills have been carved up and nearly obliterated by stacks of housing developments. Take a sweater, the winds here are chilly even in summer. It was from this vista that **Daniel Burnham** conceived the city plan in 1905.

Gay Scene

From the boom days of the Gold Rush, statistics have favored San Francisco's ultimate claim to the title of *Gay Capital of the World*. The mass influx of '49ers put the ratio of men to women at around 50 to 1 and well before the town picked up the monicker *Baghdad by the Bay*, ministers in the midwestern hinterlands were calling the town *Sodom by the Sea*, a nickname which only became more apt as years rolled on. Most historians date the genesis of the city's large gay community to World War II when the military drummed out thousands of homosexuals from the Pacific Theater, sending them back to their point of debarkation, San Francisco. Rather than return home in disgrace, many settled in the city's rolling hills, forming some of the nation's first gay organizations and creating a lively gay night life.

San Francisco as Gay Mecca became a self-fulfilling prophecy during the 1970s when gays' active politicization drew national attention to local gays, their neighborhoods and their leaders, all of which drew more gay immigrants. An estimated 100,000 gays now live in San Francisco, not much compared to New York or Los Angeles, but a huge chunk of a city that has only some 660,000 people. Lesbians and gay men are ingrained in every facet of the city's mainstream, holding all levels of public office from the city's Board of Supervisors to the Police Commission and even a judicial slot in the Municipal Court. They are also responsible for one of the most massive jobs of private urban renewal in the country, giving face-lifts to entire neighborhoods of the city's valuable Victorian houses.

Cast aside stereotypes for your trip to San Francisco. Fathers now worry if a son's hair is too short, if his dress is too macho or his muscles too well-developed, since these are the trademarks of the new breed of San Francisco gay men. San Franciscans have learned to roll with the punches of the sexual revolution and just about any cab driver or native will have no second thoughts about directing a needy tourist to Castro Street, usually with recommendations about the currently fashionable bars. Visitors may want to keep a few specific dates in mind for a gay tour of the city. The last Sunday of June is the high point of the gay calendar, of course, for the annual **Gay Freedom Day Parade.** The event is supposed to be political, but rhetoric usually takes a back seat to fun when the crowds swell to their usual quarter-million level. Bars have specials, the city's major halls come alive with parties and gay cultural events continue through the week. The 1st Sunday in October is the next major annual event for gays—the **Castro Street Fair.** It is usually accompanied by perfect weather. Some of the city's finest entertainers regularly take to the stage to belt out songs for dancing in the closed-off streets while street performers and craftspeople lure patrons. The air gets chillier on Halloween, but both Castro and Polk Streets come alive with revelry those nights, when you will see the most outrageous costumes this side of Mardi Gras. Every May 22, nighttime parties on Castro Street celebrate the birthday of San Francisco's first openly gay public official, the late **Supervisor Harvey Milk.** On a more solemn note, the day Milk and **Mayor**

George **Moscone** were assassinated, **November 27,** is observed each year with a candlelight march from Castro Street to City Hall, the site of the murders. Though the march is sobering, it is emblematic of an aspect of the gay community which is sometimes masked by the cornucopia of gay bars and lusty night life. Gays have gained both bars and martyrs in their drive for acceptance here.

Castro Street

Any tour of gay San Francisco must start on Castro Street, the quaint neighborhood of 1880s Victorian storefronts and homes which was taken over in the city's *gay invasion* in the 1970s. This is no mere gay enclave like Greenwich Village, but something of an insular small town where denizens can shop, work, live and party without ever coming in contact with a heterosexual. Boutiques abound for every taste and expense account, but the most popular recreation is just soaking up the ambience, not to mention the scenery which is adorned every weekend by thousands of young men from all corners of the globe. Sunny Sunday afternoons are particularly frolicsome and a good time to visit the local watering holes. Imbibe at such genial pubs as **The Elephant Walk** *(18th and Castro),* the **Midnight Sun** (video bar), **The Cafe San Marcos** *(Market and Castro)* or the laid-back **Cafe Fiora** *(Noe and Market).* For a cruisier afternoon, check out the **Badlands** *(4121 18th),* **Moby Dick's** *(18th and Hartford)* or the favorite spot of the neighborhood's Naugahyde set, **Castro Station** *(456 Castro).*

For eats, take in the mellowed-out (and reasonably priced) restaurants like **Welcome Home** *(464 Castro),* the **Norse Cove,** a few doors up or the **Patio Cafe** or **Castro Gardens** on the next block. Though you might want to drift a few blocks away from the neighborhood to **Le Domino** *(2742 17th)* for a classy dinner, you could also check out the dinner menus of the **Neon Chicken** *(4063 18th).*

Polk Street

Though Castro Street is the most internationally famous gay strip in town, Polk Street has been gentrified decades longer and offers some of the trendiest clothing boutiques in the city as well as a nice assortment of gay bars and restaurants. The mood is less macho and brash here than on Castro with the bars focused more on good times than cruising. For a quiet ambience, try the **Q.T.** *(1312 Polk)* or **Kimo's** *(1351 Polk).* Younger crowds can be found in **The Giraffe** *(1131 Polk),* the get-down **Polk Gulch Saloon** *(at Polk),* the country western **Cinch** *(1723 Polk)* or at the local disco **The N Touch** *(1548 Polk).*

Restaurants are Polk Street's forte, however, so the strip is a popular gay dining area. Good Italian food can be found at **La Piazza** *(1247 Polk)* and **Peppino's** *(1247 Polk),* while the less formal **Grubstake** *(1525 Pine)* can be counted on to consistently put out the best burger in San Francisco. Try **Red's** *(1475 Polk)* for Chinese food.

Folsom Street

Every night is Halloween on Folsom Street, a hyper-macho strip where grown men can be seen wandering around in the clothing of straight-off-the-range cowboys, grizzled construction workers and rough-and-ready motorcyle riders. The costumes' bark however, is much sterner than any bites meted out on the street.

Those who prefer this genre of gay life should check out **The Eagle** *(12th at Harrison),* **Power House** *(1337 Folsom),* **Folsom New World** *(1225 Folsom)* and **Watering Hole** *(1145 Folsom).* No, these are not the bars you want to take your mom to.

Where to Stay

San Francisco has some 20 hotels catering primarily to gay tourists. The most popular Castro area bed and breakfast spot is **The Inn on Castro** *(321 Castro, 861-0321).* Two others in the area are the **Willows** *(710 14th St., 431-4770)* and **24 Henry** *(710 14th St., 864-5686).* Most of the larger hotels are near the Polk Street area located between downtown and the other gay enclaves. Among the most popular hotels here are the **Atherton Hotel** *(685 Ellis, 474-5720),* **The Essex Hotel** *(Ellis and Larkin, 474-4664),* **The York Hotel** *(940 Sutter, 885-6800)* and **The Brothel Hotel** *(Sutter and Gough, 775-6969),* which is one of the city's best-appointed gay hotels (despite the sleazy-sounding name). For Folsom fans, there are the **Folsom Street Hotel** *(1082 Folsom, 552-3390),* **Brown's Hotel** *(1188 Folsom, 864-9141)* and the **Hotel El Dorado** *(150 Ninth St., 552-3100).*

The Lesbian Scene

Many lesbians have gravitated to the East Bay, leaving the San Francisco gay scene overwhelmingly male. One of the most popular northern California lesbian bars, for example, is in Oakland at **Ollie's** *(4130 Telegraph).* In San Francisco, the most popular women's bars are devoted to dance: **Different Strokes** *(Polk and California),* **Amelia's** *(647 Valencia)* and **A Little More** *(15th and Portrero).* For those less inclined to disco, there are 2 classic lesbian bars for talk and pool-playing: **Maud's** *(Cole and Karl)* and **Peg's Place** *(4737 Geary).*

Courtesy San Francisco Zoo

14 **San Francisco Zoo.** Millions of dollars spent on innovative exhibitions have transformed this century old institution into a world-class zoo. Iron cages are out and incredible natural habitats are in, with nearly 1,000 exotic animals hanging from treetops, roaming through fields and lounging on foggy islands. Zoo Director **Saul Kitchner** says the settings enable visitors to see the animals behave naturally, which leads to a better understanding of them. The **Thelma and Henry Doelger Primate Discovery Center,** completed in 1985, highlights this philosophy. Here, from multi-level walkways, you can watch 16 species of monkeys leap from tree to tree in a rain forest and sprint across a wild meadow. A highlight of the exhibit is the **Phoebe Hearst Discovery Hall,** which has 23 interactive exhibits, including computer terminals where you can play *Construct a Primate.* The zoo is only one of 3 in the country that has koala bears (San Diego and Los Angeles are the others). The cuddly, eucalyptus-eating Brisbane, Australia natives live on a grassy knoll in **Koala Crossing.** When the weather is bad, they move to an indoor thicket of eucalyptus boughs. Its always black tie on **Tuxedo Junction Island,**

where a colony of about 50 Magellanic penguins with names like Anne Arctica, Popsicle and Oreo nestle in specially landscaped burrows. The **Lion House** is home to African Lions, Siberian and Bengal tigers (including Prince Charles, a rare white tiger) and snow leopards. A crowd always shows up at 2PM (except Mondays) to watch the feeding of the big cats. The **Children's Zoo** features a **Barnyard** where you can pet and feed the assorted menagerie of domestic animals. The **Zebra Zephyr Train** takes you on an informative 20-minute safari tour of the zoo, daily during the spring, summer and fall and on weekends in the winter.

The Zoo got its start in 1889 with a grizzly named Monarch, who was donated by the *San Francisco Examiner.* It moved to the present site in 1929, and now takes up 65 of the 125 acres of land. The rest of the park is scheduled to be developed in the coming decade under the Zoo 2000 Plan. *Admission charge. Open daily 10AM-5PM. Children's Zoo open daily 11AM-4PM. Informal walking tour on weekends leaves from the Koala Crossing at 12:30 and 2:30PM. Sloat Blvd. at the Great Hwy. 661-4844 or 661-2023*

15 **Leon's Bar-BQ.** ★ ★ $/$$ This is the classic of all San Francisco barbecue joints. It looks like a roadside diner, is jammed at peak hours and dishes out some of the best ribs, chicken and sausage you'll ever eat. Try the sampler plate, which gives you a huge portion of everything. Great homemade desserts like pecan pie. *Open daily 11AM-10PM. 2800 Sloat Blvd. 681-3071*

16 **Lake Merced.** This large fresh water lake was once part of a ranchero and is now a standby reservoir for the city and a good trout fishing hole in season. The **Recreation and Parks Department** has built a boathouse where small sailboats may be rented. There is a special children's pier below. Nearby is a bar and restaurant, and across the road are a barbecue area and model race car track. Row boats are for rent every day; sailboats on weekends. The boathouse is *open during fishing season, 21 Apr to 31 Dec, daily 6AM-7:30PM. Off Harding Way, adjacent to the Zoo. Phone for rates and availability, 566-0300*

17 **Sigmund Stern Memorial Grove.** A 63-acre grove of eucalyptus, redwood and fir trees that shelters a sunken natural amphitheater. This is a favorite spot among city dwellers for the free Sunday afternoon concerts. A variety of programs from opera to jazz are presented. Concerts are given in the summer, June through August, starting at 2PM. There are picnic and barbecue facilities too. There is a yellow gingerbread house in the grove that was once **Trocadero Inn,** a gambling house and hide-out for **Abe Rueff,** political shyster. It has been renovated since by **Bernard Maybeck,** who left the 2 bullet holes in the door as souvenirs of the shoot-out that led to Rueff's capture. *Sloat Blvd. at 19th Av. For program information call 398-6551*

18 **Tien Fu.** ★ $/$$ A popular Northern Chinese place, with some innovative dishes like cold smoked fish and green onion pancakes. Also lots of Hunan and Szechuan entrees. *Open daily. 1395 Noriega St. 665-1064*

Restaurants/Nightlife red
Hotels blue
Shops/Galleries purple
Parks/Outdoor spaces green
Museums/Architecture/Narrative black

19 **St. Francis Woods.** A beautifully landscaped, expensive development of large houses with gates and a fountain designed by **John Galen Howard,** a noted *Beaux Arts* era architect.

19 **Commodore Sloat School.** (1975) A renovation of an existing school together with a new extension by **Marquis Associates** that has been designed as a series of courtyards. It is faced in stucco and given a nautical look with the large portholes that have become a feature of the school's design. *Sloat Blvd. at Ocean Av.*

20 **Sutro TV Tower.** (1968) Located on top of Mount Sutro, this tower supports television antennae for several of San Francisco's stations. Once a controversial design because of its tripods form and size, it is now an accepted part of the landscape.

21 **Mt. Davidson.** The highest spot in San Francisco, 938 feet up. A great white concrete-and-steel cross rises 103-feet above the summit. This was part of **Adolph Sutro's** 12,000-acre estate. **George Davidson,** surveyor for the U.S. Coast and Geodetic Survey, originally surveyed the mountain in 1852 and named it Blue Mountain. It was later renamed in his honor. Easter sunrise services have been held at the base of the cross since 1923.

22 **Ingleside.** One of the city's earliest racetracks opened here to a crowd of 8,000 people on Thanskgiving Day, 1885. The loop of track is now Urbano Drive. Twenty years later the track was closed and **Ingleside Terrace** built in its place. Development was slow until the **Twin Peaks Tunnel** was completed in 1917 and large scale residential neighborhood building began.

23 **John McLaren Park.** The large neighborhood park was named to commemorate McLaren for his outstanding work in creating Golden Gate Park. Several residential districts make use of the rugged, wooded tract: Bayshore, Portola Valley, Bayview and the Outer Mission. There are good views of Visitacion Valley and the San Bruno Mountains from the park's steep slopes.

24 **Eaton/Shoen Gallery.** Changing exhibits, mainly of new artists. They also have a large selection of artist-made books, one of a kind and limited editions. Viewing of the books is by appointment. *Open Tu-Su 10AM-5PM. 500 Paul Av. Southbound on 101 take the Paul Av. exit; northbound on 101 take the 3rd St. exit. Parking available. 788-3476*

25 **Club Elegante.** Club with Latin and disco music and International shows on Sundays. Dancing. *Open W-Su 9PM-2AM. 3395 Mission. 282-6116*

26 **170-80 Manchester Street.** (1986, William Stout) Built on the slopes of Bernal Heights, these modern stucco-clad houses capture the spirit of the white architecture of the Modern Movement. *Private residences.*

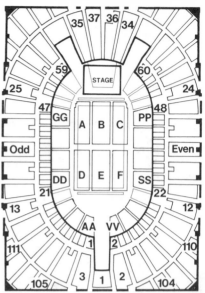

27 **Cow Palace.** Everything from livestock shows to the Beatles in their first live appearance in the U.S. have shown up at the inelegantly named Cow Palace. With a seating capacity from 10,300 to 14,300, the Palace offers an ever-changing series of events. *Geneva Av. and Santos St., Daly City. 469-6000*

28 **Bayview-Hunter's Point.** This area to the east of Highway 101 is 66 percent black, representing the largest concentration of blacks in the city. The residents are primarily skilled laborers who are struggling with unemployment. During the 1860s, **William Ralston** built a million dollar granite drydock which was in use until 1916. But in spite of other efforts by various businessmen, nothing seemed to take hold in this area besides shipping and cattle slaughtering. People never really moved here until World War II when Hunter's Point became the biggest shipyard on the West Coast. The 18,500 employees moved into temporary housing and by the time the freeway opened up in 1952, it had become a neighborhood of shabby temporary houses. These buildings are constantly in the process of being replaced by public housing. But now, at last, it looks as if there is a brighter future in store for the neighborhood. The old **Victorian Bayview Opera House** is worth seeing—it has been renovated and is run by the Neighborhood Arts Program. *47045 3rd St.*

Distances From SF		
	Miles	**By Car**
Berkeley	12	**25 min.**
Los Angeles	390	**8 hours**
Napa/Sonoma	44	**1 hour**
Oakland	10	**20 min.**
Palo Alto	33	**1 hour**
Sacramento	88	**1 hour**
SF Int'l.		
Airport	14	**25 min.**
Sausalito	8	**20 min.**
Yosemite	200	**4 hours**

Shops/Galleries purple
Parks/Outdoor spaces green
Museums/Architecture/Narrative black

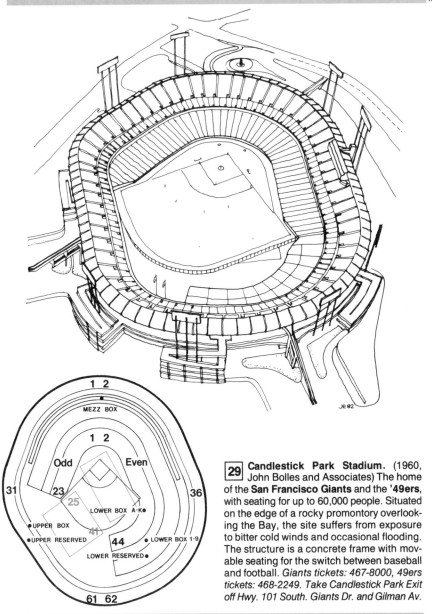

JE 82

29 **Candlestick Park Stadium.** (1960, John Bolles and Associates) The home of the **San Francisco Giants** and the **'49ers**, with seating for up to 60,000 people. Situated on the edge of a rocky promontory overlooking the Bay, the site suffers from exposure to bitter cold winds and occasional flooding. The structure is a concrete frame with movable seating for the switch between baseball and football. *Giants tickets: 467-8000, 49ers tickets: 468-2249. Take Candlestick Park Exit off Hwy. 101 South. Giants Dr. and Gilman Av.*

Things for Kids to Do

Exploratorium. Take a bus to the Exploratorium Bring bread crumbs to feed the swans at the Palace of Fine Arts.

Fort Point National Historic Site. See the Golden Gate Bridge from underneath. Visit the museum in the fortress where they keep souvenirs from Civil War days.

San Francisco Zoo. Don't miss the Gorilla Works and Insect Zoo and the new bone cart exhibit where you can handle animal skulls, porcupine quills, bones, beaks, and teeth. There's a special petting zoo also.

Japanese Tea Garden in Golden Gate Park. Wander over this exquisitely pretty miniature gardens with bridges and statues and take tea and cookies overlooking a waterfall.

Walk the Golden Gate Bridge. It's about 1.2 miles and takes about an hour, but bring a warm sweater. Or, you could bicycle over and back; it's allowed on the west side path.

Discover the Ferry to Sausalito. This ride from Ferry Building is even better than the regular sightseeing boats.

Children's Playground and Carousel in Golden Gate Park. Slide down a slide that is the fastest on the West coast, and other curly-Q slides and state-of-the-art playground equipment.

The Victorian Conservatory. Walk through a fairy-tale glass palace filled with fabulous flowers including orchids in bloom.

Cliff House. Watch for the seals on Seal Rock, and take a walk on the beach. There are telescopes, operated by coins, to help you seal watch.

Ghirardelli Chocolate Manufactory. Watch them stir vats of gooey chocolate while you wait for your own super sundae.

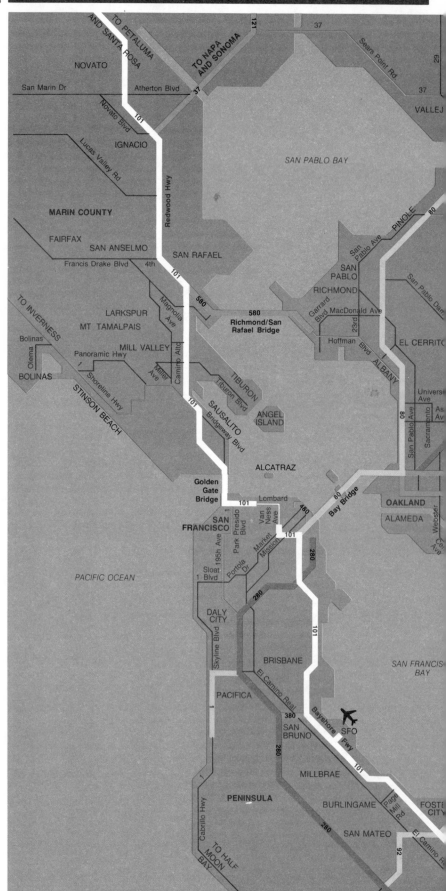

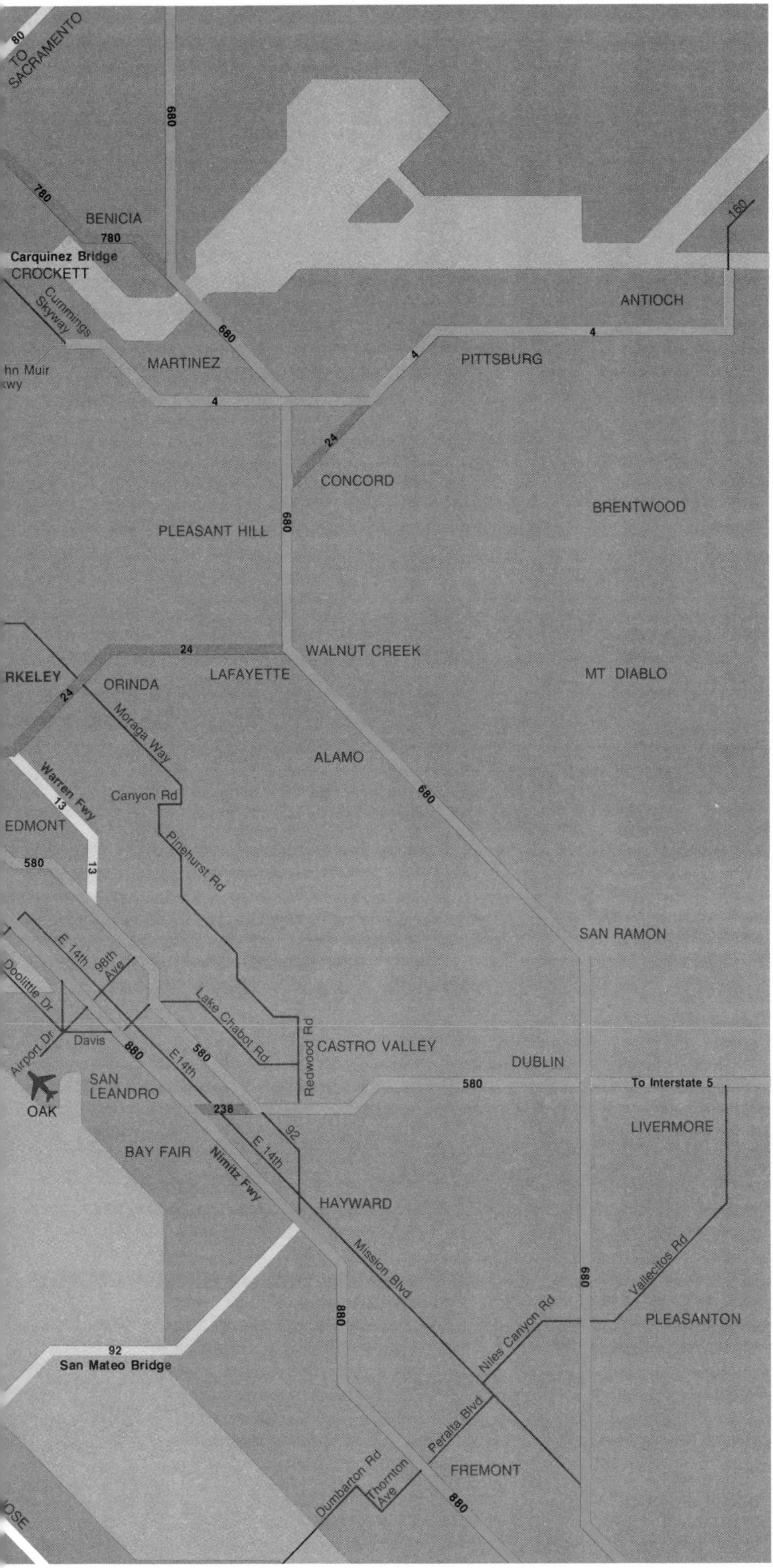

80
TO SACRAMENTO

680

780

BENICIA

Carquinez Bridge
CROCKETT

Cummings Skyway

680

hn Muir
kwy

MARTINEZ

4

ANTIOCH

4

PITTSBURG

4

24

CONCORD

BRENTWOOD

680

PLEASANT HILL

24

WALNUT CREEK

RKELEY

ORINDA

LAFAYETTE

MT DIABLO

24

Moraga Way

ALAMO

Warren Fwy

13

Canyon Rd

680

EDMONT

580

13

Pinehurst Rd

SAN RAMON

E 14th

96th Ave

Doolittle Dr.

Lake Chabot Rd

Redwood Rd

CASTRO VALLEY

DUBLIN

Airport Dr.

Davis

880

580

E 14th

580

To Interstate 5

OAK

SAN LEANDRO

238

92

LIVERMORE

BAY FAIR

Nimitz Fwy

E 14th

680

HAYWARD

Vallecitos Rd

Mission Blvd

Niles Canyon Rd

PLEASANTON

92

880

San Mateo Bridge

Peralta Blvd

OSE

Dumbarton Rd

Thornton Ave

880

FREMONT

Oakland

Oakland was named for the extensive groves of live oak trees that grew in the sandy loam of the Peralta land grant where Oakland was chartered in 1852. Thirty years before, **Don Luis Mario Peralta** was granted more than 44,000 acres of land as reward for his 40 years of soldiering for the Spanish crown. He named it *El Rancho de San Antonio*. Peralta never made a home on the land, but after all 4 of his sons were established there, he divided the property equally among them. Each rancho was like a separate village. Other land grants brought neighbors, and trails began to connect the homesteads. The land teemed with wild game, fish and huge trees. So contented were the people that there were no plans for any settlements. The founding of a town had to await arrival of the Americans. By the time the Yankees arrived, Don Luis was tired—he was almost 92 and had lived under 4 flags. The years that followed were violent ones, involving land leases obtained by force from the peace loving Peralta family who were not prepared to deal with the ruthless group of squatters who were overrunning their land. Led by **Horace W. Carpentier,** who later became the first mayor of Oakland, the subdividing of the rancho had begun. A year later, old Don Luis was dead.

*Oakland? There is no there, there...*said **Gertrude Stein.** In spite of Ms. Stein's opinion, while San Francisco has been fighting and faltering over an aging waterfront, Oakland has been expanding its port for the past 20 years, using its large share of prime waterfront to install efficient containerized cargo handling equipment. With its convenient rail and highway connections, Oakland has prospered in the competition for Pacific Basin trade and far surpassed San Francisco as the Bay Area's busiest port. In fact, it now ranks as the second largest port on the West Coast (first is Long Beach). The new prosperity is revitalizing the downtown area as well. A massive redevelopment program which includes a convention center complex, an international trade center and countless renovations of Victorian houses into shops and restaurants is now underway. The population slide (from 370,000 to 340,000 in the last 2 decades) has halted and the numbers have begun to climb again. There is renewed pride among the natives, and neighborhood organizations are growing stronger. Surrounding Oakland in the hills reminiscent of the Tuscany region in Italy are some of the loveliest homes and estates in the Bay Area. Many of these were originally built as summer homes by fog-weary San Franciscans: **Piedmont, Kensington, El Cerrito,** and a bit further out, **Lafayette, Moraga, Orinda, Concord** and **Walnut Creek.**

---

1 **Metropolitan Oakland International Airport.** Located 5 miles from downtown Oakland, the airport is convenient to Napa, Sonoma, Marin, Alameda and Contra Costa counties. It is served by many local and national airlines, including American, TWA and PSA. Parking is never a problem and there is also local bus service, BART and the SFO Airporter for gettting to and from the airport. Oakland Airport Hotels include: **Oakland Airport Hilton,** *1 Hegenberger Rd.* 635-5000; **Edgewater Hyatt House,** *455* *Hegenberger Rd.* 562-6100; **Holiday Inn of Oakland,** *500 Hegenberger Rd.* 562-5311

2 **Knowland Park and Zoo.** A petting zoo for young children and a small amusement park. *Admission free, fare for rides. Open M-F 10AM-4PM, Sa-Su 10AM-4:30PM. Take Hwy. 580 to Golf Links Rd. exit. Watch for sign.* 569-8819

Hotels blue
Shops/Galleries purple
Parks/Outdoor spaces green

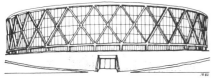

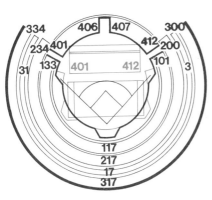

Mills College. There are 2 art galleries on campus:

Antonio Prieto Memorial Gallery stands next to the Student Center, it exhibits ceramic works, largely by local artists or from its permanent collection. Meetings are sometimes held in the gallery, so it's best to call ahead if you're making a special trip. *Open during the school year, Tu-Su 10AM-4PM. Admission free. 430-2164*

Mills Art Gallery was constructed in 1925 by **Walter Ratcliff** and originally used also as a ballroom. The building itself is worth a visit, with its wrought-iron gates, Spanish-tiled steps and ornate ceilings inside. The gallery's permanent collection includes works of art on paper dating from the 16th century; 19th and 20th century American and European painting; textiles, notably Asian and Central American; and ceramics, especially Chinese, Japanese and American. Traveling and performance shows also take place. *Open during the school year, Tu-Su 10AM-4PM. Admission free. 5000 MacArthur Blvd. 430-2164*

5 **Taqueria Morelia.** ★$ The burritos here are mouth-watering, particularly those with sausage or pork. Located in an interesting Mexican-American neighborhood. *Mexican. Open daily 10AM-11PM. 4481 East 14th St. 261-6360*

Restaurants/Nightlife red
Museums/Architecture/Narrative black

3 **Oakland-Alameda County Coliseum Complex.** The complex consists of one outdoor and 2 indoor facilities. The Arena, where you can see the **NBA Warriors, Ringling Bros. Circus**, concerts and major indoor events, seats up to 14,200 people. The 54,500-seat stadium has been the home of the Oakland (now LA) Raiders and the Oakland A's. The Exhibit hall boasts 50,000 square feet of exhibition space. There's a 10,000-space parking lot and easy access by BART. *Nimitz Fwy. and Hegenberger Rd. 569-2121*

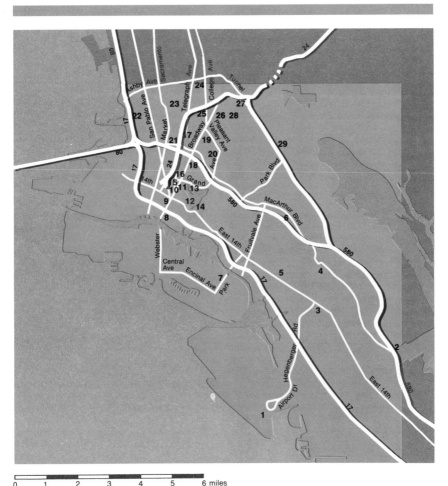

0   1   2   3   4   5   6 miles

6 **Mormon Temple.** (1963, Arthur Price) Because of its unusual profile and nighttime floodlighting, this has become one of Oakland's most noticeable landmarks. In form, it consists of a large white granite-clad block with a pinnacled tower surrounded by 4 smaller towers. In front is a long reflecting pool. *Lincoln Av. and the Warren Fwy. Hwy. 13.*

7 **Acapulco** (Alameda). $$ One of the East Bay's most popular Mexican restaurants; a big place but still often jammed. Huge portions. A fairly standard Mexican menu. *Open M-Th 11:30AM-9PM, F & Sa 11:30AM-10PM, Su 1-9PM. 2104 Lincoln Av. 523-4935*

8 **Jack London Square.** This area, which includes the adjacent **Jack London Village,** is Oakland's Fisherman's Wharf. Souvenir shops, boutiques, convention facilities and TV and radio stations are situated here along the Oakland estuary. There are 2 historical attractions: **The First and Last Chance Saloon,** where adventure writer Jack London, in his youth, hung out; and a dilapidated log cabin in which London supposedly sheltered during a gold-mining junket in the Klondike. The area is blighted with enormous parking lots. (For those interested in Jack London, a trip to his estate at **Glen Ellen** in **Sonoma County** is more worthwhile. The drive there is lovely, and it's warmer.) *Broadway, Webster and 1st Sts.*

8 **Best Western Boatel.** *Moderate.* Jack London Square is located at the water's edge and is accessible by both land and sea—with complete boating facilities and private dock. Rooms on the Bay side enjoy a view of ships sailing to and from the Pacific. Free continental breakfast served in lobby or in rooms. *21 Jack London Square. 836-3800; 800-528-1234*

8 **Jack London Inn.** *Moderate.* Really a businessmen's hotel and busy from Sunday to Thursday. However, it *is* on the Square, clean, modern, no frills but close to BART and the shuttle downtown. *444 Embarcadero West. 444-2032*

8 **London Lodge.** *Moderate.* Especially suited to families as some of the rooms are unusually spacious and have kitchenettes. *7th & Broadway. 451-6316*

9 **Gulf Coast Oyster Bar & Specialty Co.** ★ ★ $$ In downtown Oakland, you can enjoy genuine Louisiana Gulf produce and cooking at this restaurant. Gulf Coast offers a wide variety of clams and oysters, and the wine list is extensive. Beer, aperitifs and espresso are also available. Located 2 blocks from the Oakland Convention Center, the Gulf Coast is only a convenient walk away. Parking on the street. *Lunch and dinner reservations strongly suggested. Open Tu-F 11:30 AM-2:30PM, 5:30-10PM; Sa 5:30-10PM. 736 Washington St. 839-6950*

9 **Jade Villa.** ★ ★ ★ $ Renowned for its dim sum, Jade Villa offers an incredible variety, ranging from crisp, greaseless egg rolls and aromatic curry beef turnovers to items you may never have tasted or seen before. Dim sum is available for lunch only and take-out. At night, Jade Villa becomes a conventional Cantonese restaurant. It is considered one of the best Chinese restaurants in the Bay Area. Service is attentive and personable. *Reservations accepted on weekends. Open M-F 10AM-9:30PM. 800 Broadway. 839-1688*

9 **Hyatt Regency Hotel and Oakland Convention Center.** (1984, ELS Design Group) The hotel is a diagonally organized slab that responds to the rotated grid of the nearby Clorox Building, whereas the low-rise convention center occupies the remainder of the two block site. Post modern styling. *Broadway between 10th and 11th Sts.*

10 **Rattos.** ★ $/$$ An international delicatessen which has to be seen to be believed—every spice you ever thought existed and then some, canned goods from all over the world, a fine selection of cheeses and lots more. Next door is their cafeteria-line restaurant, one of the most popular eating spots in Oakland, with emphasis on Italian food. *Open M-Sa 8AM-5PM. 821 Washington St. 832-6503*

11 **St. Mary's Housing.** (1979 Peters, Claybourne and Caulfield) This public housing complex for the elderly is excellently designed and detailed. Low-rise in scale, it relates to its neighborhood and gives identity to each block. *Market and 12th Sts.*

11 **Oakland City Hall.** (1911-14, Palmer and Hornboster) A New York-based firm was the winner of an architectural competition for the new City Hall. It is a *Beaux Arts* style building with a *wedding cake* cupola on top. An imposing staircase inside the entrance hall leads to the council chamber on the 2nd level. *Washington, San Pablo Av. and 14th Sts.*

1890–Downtown traffic in Oakland was so congested that horse-drawn vehicles were restricted to a 5 mile per hour speed limit.

1906–after the earthquake, a wave of refugees moved their homes and businesses to Oakland, little damaged in comparison to San Francisco.

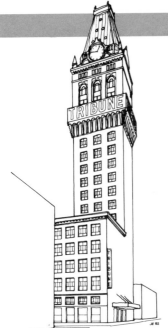

11 **Oakland Tribune Building.** (1923, Edward Foulkes) Oakland's landmark—it is noteworthy for its emblematic tower with large lettering on the projecting balcony and deck which have dominated the Oakland skyline for decades. Originally the tower contained a radio station and in 1976 the building was designated as an official city historical landmark. *13th and Franklin Sts.*

11 **Broadway Building.** (1907, Llewellyn B. Dutton) A fine flatiron building with a strong base and elaborate clock on the corner. *Broadway, San Pablo & 14th Sts.*

11 **Victorian Row.** Two city blocks of 1870s buildings restored by **Storek and Storek** in 1983. Remarkably, most of the buildings had remained pretty much unaltered and were merely run down. *8th to 10th, Broadway to Washington Sts.*

11 **Alameda County Court House.** (1936 Corlett, Plachek, Werner, Morton and Shirmer) This streamlined *Moderne* WPA building is one of the best examples of its kind, with some heroic marble mosaics in the lobby depicting the early history of Alameda. *12th and 13th, Oak and Fallon Sts.*

11 **Hotel Oakland.** (1912) Filling an entire city block and built around a U-shaped courtyard, this used to be one of the most important hotels in the Bay Area. Originally by **Bliss and Faville**, during World War II it became a VA Hospital and, in 1979, it was converted into a senior citizens' apartment building by **Ratcliff Architects** of Berkeley. *13th and 14th, Harrison and Alice Sts.*

11 **Oakland City Square.** (1987, IDG Architects and Cesar Pelli) A new retail and office development that will be the heart of the proposed City Center Redevelopment Project. Organized about the 13th Street mall, it is the latest in a long series of proposals that have been designed to replace the downtown blight. Crucial to the project is the re-opening of 12th Street, which was closed when the previous suburban style scheme was being planned.*13th St. between Clay and Broadway.*

11 **Houden Building.** An exquisitely detailed terra cotta clad 3-story office building, built to advertise the wonderful richness of the material—it is probably one of the finest examples of its kind in the country. *17th and Webster Sts.*

11 **Caribe Dance Center.** DJ and live reggae and calypso music. *Open W & F-Su 9PM-2AM. 2424 Webster. 835-4006*

11 **Flint's.** ★ ★ $ A barbeque tradition in the East Bay with 3 different locations in Oakland neighborhoods. The places are not immaculate, but the food is excellent—there's even barbequed turkey. The brick-oven barbeque smell overwhelms you within a block of the restaurant, and the ribs are an experience. Prices are inexpensive and all locations are open until early morning. Cash and take out only. *Open Su-Th 11AM-3AM, F-Sa 11AM-5AM. Shattuck Av. 653-0593. (Also 6672 E. 14th St., 569-1312 and 3314 San Pablo Av., 658-9912)*

11 **Holmes Book Co.** The Bay's bibliophile headquarters. Founded in 1894, it was salvaged from the great earthquake and moved to safety in Oakland. Browse through 3 stories of new, out-of-print and antiquarian books and first editions. *Open M-W 9:30AM-6:30PM, Sa 9:30AM-5:30PM, Su 11AM-5PM. 274 14th St. 893-6860*

12 **Hunan.** ★ $/$$ The best Chinese restaurant in Oakland's Chinatown. Beautifully crispy whole fish, hot eggplant and spinach sauteed in garlic. Chili peppers and garlic is their specialty. *Northern Chinese/ Hunanese. Open daily 11:30AM-10PM. 366 8th St. 444-1155*

12 **Peking.** $/$$ Delicious hot and sour soup, whole fish, sauteed bean curd with ground pork. *810 Franklin St. 452-2160*

12 **Sorabol.** ★ ★ $$ Even with all the good Asian restaurants in the Bay Area, this is worth a trip to the shores of Lake Merritt. Korean food features barbecued meats and spicy stews, and it's different enough from other Asian foods to make it well worth trying. You'll want to extend dinner into the whole evening. *Korean. Open daily 11:30AM-9:30PM. 372 Grand Av. 839-2288*

13 **Children's Fairyland, Lakeside Park** (Lake Merritt). More than 7 acres of land devoted to everyone's fantasies. There are walks into scenes of favorite fairy tales and nursery rhymes come to life. Also, a baby zoo with sea lions, farm animals and wallabies for viewing. *3:30PM is feeding time. Open weekends and school holidays during the school year, W-Su during summer. Call 832-3609 to verify schedule. Grand Av. and Park View Terrace.*

14 **Bellevue Staten Apartments.** (1929, A.C. Bauman) This 15-story brick and stone-clad Spanish Baroque-style apartment tower overlooking Lake Merritt has a fine entrance lobby and elaborate skyline.

Restaurants/Nightlife red
Hotels blue
Shops/Galleries purple
Parks/Outdoor spaces green
Museums/Architecture/Narrative black

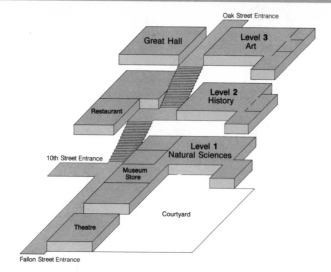

Oak Street Entrance
Great Hall
Level 3 Art
Level 2 History
Restaurant
Level 1 Natural Sciences
10th Street Entrance
Museum Store
Courtyard
Theatre
Fallon Street Entrance

14 **Oakland Museum.** The **Museum of California** is an oasis in the midst of stark urban surroundings. The award-winning concrete building, designed by **Kevin Roche** and **John Dinkeloo,** was constructed in 1969. This is a unique, marvelous environment and museum. Don't miss it! Three museums in one are set out on 3 levels: **Natural Sciences:** Hall of California Ecology, level 1; **History:** The Cowell Hall of California History, level 2; **Art:** Gallery of California Art, level 3. The **Great Hall,** level 3, is the major space for temporary exhibitions. A Collector's Gallery, on level 1, sells and rents works by California artists. The museum store offers an excellent selection of books, posters, cards and slides on art and natural sciences. The spacious restaurant and snack bar/dining room looks out to the gardens and serves good soups and salads and specialties that frequently change. An interesting place to have lunch in a beautiful museum that's not often seen by tourists. *No admission charge. Museum open W-Sa 10AM-5PM, Su noon-7PM. Docent tours are given daily at 2PM. Parking is available underneath the museum—the 200-car garage is open M-F 8AM-6PM; Sa 10AM-5PM, Su noon-7PM. Entrances on Oak and 12th Sts. Reasonable rates. 1000 Oak St., near Lake Merritt. 273-3401*

BESTS

Dr. Julian Euell
Director, Oakland Museum

We are a regional museum that focuses on California's ecology, history and art and the connections between them. The **Hall of Ecology** is arranged as a walk across California. Through exhibits, specimens, photographs and sounds, you can travel through eight biotic zones. In one area the bird calls come from five speakers. Acorn wood peckers seem to fly from tree to tree, chasing scrub jays or feeding their young, with Cooper hawks flying overhead.

One of my favorite cases contains, simply, a **decaying log from the forest floor,** which is habitat for many plants, animals and fungi.

The **Hall of California History** is arranged as a journey from prehistory to contemporary times. Floating above the exhibitions are mounted quotations, the words of people who have lived in California. The path through the gallery can be direct, but I like to detour into the side galleries. There is the **Assay Office** where the first Comstock Lode silver was assayed in 1860. There is a **pioneer family's kitchen** and a **California custom car.** There is **Lois Anderson's** strange and wonderful psychodelic **dressing table** from the 1960s, **Country Joe MacDonald's guitar** and personal objects from the **Brotherhood of Sleeping Car Porters'** west coast headquarters in Oakland.

The **Art Gallery** has many photographs and paintings that reveal the changing face of California. There is a **panorama** of San Francisco in 1877 by **Eadweard Muybridge,** the pioneering photographer, and a painting of **Gold Rush San Francisco** by **George Henry Burgess.** In contrast, there is a **Wayne Thiebaud** painting of San Francisco in the late 1970s.

Our **1930s Gallery** has fine paintings of the era by artists such as **Maynard Dixon, Lucien Labaudt** and **John Langley Howard,** and I particularly like the strong collection of **figurative paintings** from the 1960s by **Natan Oliveira** and **David Park,** among others.

We have many significant pieces from the **Arts and Crafts Movements** in California from the late 19th century to the present and also small-scale photography by **Dorothea Lange, Imogen Cunningham, Roger Sturtevant** and **Edward Weston.**

Being a regional museum, we are able to delve deeply into this diverse and geographical area. Far from being limited, California presents infinite possibilites.

15 **Mama's Royal Cafe.** $$ A nice neighborhood place for brunch, with a long list of omelettes, some of them fairly unusual. If you like hot sauce, get the Spanish omelette. Informal and pleasant for hanging around and drinking coffee. *Open daily 7AM-3PM. 4012 Broadway. 547-7600*

15 **Cathedral Building.** (1914, Benjamin E. MacDougal) Another flatiron building (similar to the Broadway Building), only this one is Gothic. The ground floor is marred by the 1950s-style cafe with its zigzag roof. *Broadway and Telegraph St.*

15 **I. Magnin Department Store.** Another green terra cotta clad *Moderne* building from the 1930s, carefully maintained. *2000 Broadway.*

15 **Bruener Building.** (1931, Albert F. Roller) A green terra cotta clad *Moderne* building built as headquarters of the Bay Area Home Furnishing Company. Now occupied by a clothing store. *21st and Broadway.*

15 **Oakland Title Insurance and Guarantee Building.** (1921, Maury I. Diggs) A handsome 3-story Italian renaissance-style office building clad in terra cotta. *15th and Franklin Sts.*

16 **Oakland Floral Depot.** (1930s) A blue tile-clad row of shops in *Moderne* style. Notice the beautiful silver colored decoration contrasting with the dark blue tiling. *19th and Telegraph Av.*

16 **Fox Oakland Theatre.** (1928, Maury Diggs) When built, it was the largest theater west of Chicago, with 3,200 seats. The terra cotta facade is based on the Brahman temples of Northern India. There is a colored tile dome and 2 towers. *19th St. and Telegraph Av.*

16 **Original Kaspar's.** $ If you like hot dogs, this is one of the leading candidates for *Best in the Bay Area. Open M-Sa 11AM-7:30PM. 4521 Telegraph Av. 655-3215*

17 **Blue Nile.** $ Exotic and delicious Ethiopian food, eaten with your fingers from big platters. You get long sheets of a moist, flat bread called *injera,* tear off pieces and use it to scoop up the various dishes you order. The vegetarian entrees are particularly good. Tent-like decor, friendly and inexpensive. *Open daily 11:30AM-10PM. 3109 Telegraph Av. 540-6777*

18 **Oakland Ballet.** When people think about Bay Area dance, the Oakland Ballet is rarely the first company that comes to mind. And that's a shame because this 20-year-old troupe is enjoying a string of successes. Since 1973, the company has earned a reputation for reviving famous but long unseen classic ballets. At the same time, they've also premiered important new works. Because the troupe lacks a permanent home, they're based either at the **Paramount Theatre,** *465-6400* or **Zellerbach Auditorium,** *642-9988*. Their schedule in Oakland centers around a popular Fall Season of Dance.

Restaurants/Nightlife red
Shops/Galleries purple
Museums/Architecture/Narrative black

18 **Paramount Theatre.** If you love Art Deco, you have to visit the Paramount. Painstakingly restored in 1973, the theater is quite simply a sublime presentation of the Art Deco form. It was originally designed by **Timothy Pflueger** in 1931 and is considered his masterpiece. The 3,000-seat facility is a stopping point for touring shows, ballet, modern dance, jazz, recitals and rock. *Admission charge. Tours are conducted the 1st and 3rd Sa of each month. Cameras welcome. 2025 Broadway. 465-6400*

18 **Highways 24 and 580 Interchange/ MacArthur BART Station.** Built at the same time, the BART tracks and station are above grade in the median strip of the Highway 24 freeway. The station itself is an interesting example of late 60s structural expressionism built out of rusted *corten* exposed steel trusses with references to Mies van der Rohe and Kevin Roche. The freeway interchange is one of the most spectacular anywhere on the West Coast with 80-foot high curved concrete ramps sweeping over each other. LA, eat your heart out! For the best view, leave 580 East and take Highway 24 towards the Orinda Tunnel. *Hwy. 580 and Hwy. 24.*

19 Fenton's Creamery. ★★$ This is where you go when you want to really indulge—the ice cream portions are so incredibly huge that 4 people can be satisfied with one banana split. This is an old-fashioned ice cream parlor, circa 1922, and all the standard ice cream specialties are available: ice cream sodas, shakes, malts, sundaes, parfaits, floats cones, etc. All the ice cream is made fresh on the premises. The menu also offers salads and sandwiches; their crab sandwich is very popular. The service is friendly and relaxed. Sometimes crowded on weekends. *Open M-Sa 11AM-midnight, Su 12PM-midnight. 4226 Peidmont Av. 658-4949*

19 I.C.I. A Woman's Place Bookstore. Books by, for and about women. One of the most comprehensive collections of women's literature in the world, it has national and international feminist books, newspapers and journals. There is also a lending library, children's area and an information bulletin board. I.C.I. stands for Information Center Inc. *Open Su & M, Th-Sa 10AM-6PM; W 10AM-9PM. 4015 Broadway. (There's a parking lot at 40th St.) 547-9920*

20 The Oakland Rose Garden. Organized and funded by a group of East Bay women, the place is a floral extravaganza. There are one hundred varieties of roses flourishing on the 3 acres. A fabulous background for a wedding, which they will allow for a small fee. *Open daylight hours from Mother's Day to October. 700 Jean St. 273-3187*

21 ELI's Mile High Club. Live blues music. *Open W-Su 8PM-2AM. 3629 Martin Luther King Jr. Way. 655-6661*

22 Town House. Club with 50's and 60's rock and country music. *Open M-Th 9PM-1AM, F-Sa 9:30PM-1:30AM. 5862 Doyle, (Emeryville). 652-5336*

23 Lois the Pie Queen. ★$/$$ The place to go in Oakland for soul food breakfasts popular with professional athletes. Also hearty lunches and Louisiana-style dinners on Fridays and Saturdays. *American. Open W-F 8AM-2PM, Sa & Su 8AM-3PM. 851 60th St. 658-5616*

24 Yoshi's. $$ What started out as a tiny place run by journalism students is now one of Berkeley's busiest and largest restaurants. A sushi bar for fish freaks, a couple of dining rooms, and still generally a wait for tables. Excellent *yakitori*, a sort of Japanese shish-kabob. The jazz club upstairs is one of the best in the Bay Area. *Open M-F 11:30AM-2PM, 5:30-9PM; Sa & Su 5:30-10PM. Sushi bar open until midnight. 6030 Claremont Blvd. 652-9200*

25 Bertola's. $/$$ Italian family-style dining. Huge portions; low-priced drinks. Bustling and friendly. *Open 11:30AM-9:45PM. 4659 Telegraph Av. 547-9301*

25 Edible Complex. $ This casual, active place is perfect for a light meal, reading, relaxing and just hanging out. All the local newspapers are piled on the window sill for your convenience. The atmosphere is busy but friendly and comfortable. Bagels, sandwiches, salads, soups and a varied selection of desserts, including ice cream, are all offered on the menu. Espresso, beer and wine are also available. Counter service only. *Open M 10:30AM-midnight, Tu-Th 7:30AM-midnight, F & Sa 8:30AM-1AM, Su 8:30AM-midnight. 5600 College Av. 658-2172*

25 Rockridge Cafe. ★$ This cafe has a large assortment of items to choose from: hamburgers, top sirloin, pasta, fish, omelettes, soups, salads and sandwiches. The hamburgers are out of this world. The desserts are fresh and available whole and uncut for special orders. Espresso, drinks, beer and wine are available. *Open M-Sa 7AM-10:30PM, Su 8AM-10:30PM. 5492 College Av. 653-1567*

26 Juan's Place. $ Informal, tucked in an industrial area. Heaping portions and reasonable prices. *Mexican. Open daily 11:30AM-10PM. 941 Carlton. 845-6904*

27 Lake Temescal. Boats for rent, fishing, sandy beach and swimming during the summer. *Lifeguard. Picnic facilities. Admission free. Follow Hwy. 580 to Hwy 24. Exit at Warren Fwy. and follow signs to lake. 6500 Broadway. 531-9300*

28 Broadway Terrace Cafe. ★★★★ $$/$$$ Owner and chef **Albert Katz** has created one of the most outstanding and still largely undiscovered restaurants in the Bay Area and definitely Oakland's best traditional restaurant. Nestled in the Oakland Hills near the Berkeley border, Katz prepares exceptionally inventive California cuisine which gets better every year. There are remarkable soups and grilled fish (don't miss soft shell crab with beurre blanc in season), homemade sherbets and great cheesecake. Three dining rooms with just 38 seats offer a quiet and relaxed ambience with friendly and knowlegeable service. Small core menu with large list of specials. *Reservations required. Open Tu-Sa 5:30-10PM, Su 5-9:30PM. 5891 Broadway Terrace. 652-4442*

29 The Equinox. $$ American cuisine—steaks, seafood, homemade soups—is the specialty. The decor of the large restaurant and bar combines natural surroundings, rattan furniture, plants and fireplace with contemporary style. Entertainment and dancing are available Friday and Saturday nights. Close to the freeway with parking on the street. *Reservations suggested. Open M-Sa 11:30AM-2PM, 5:30-10PM; Su 5:30-9PM. 2062 Mountain Blvd. (Antioch). 339-8472*

Newspapers. San Francisco has 2 daily newspapers: the *San Francisco Chronicle* comes out every morning and the *San Francisco Examiner* hits the newstands in the evening. They join forces on the weekends to produce the *San Francisco Examiner-Chronicle.*

Berkeley

Berkeley, restless, challenging and experimental, is the vanguard of any campus movement, whether political, artistic or philosophical. The dazzling diversity found here can be overpowering in the range of experiences, blending scholarly dedication with the political avant garde and mixing interests in Zen and haute cuisine, punk rock and Bach. Berkeley the town and Berkeley the school are almost one and the same—it is hard to tell where one leaves off and the other begins. After **Jose**, the son to whom **Don Luis Peralta** gave the northernmost part of the **Rancho San Antonio**, had yielded to the pressures of the squatters who were claiming his lands and joined his brothers in selling their inheritance, the site of Berkeley was transferred into Yankee hands. Meanwhile, the **Reverend Henry Durant** had arrived in Oakland in 1853 from New England intent on starting a college. Circumstances dictated that he make a more modest beginning with a preparatory school which he set up in a fandango house on Broadway at 5th Street. His **Contra Costa Academy** prospered so quickly that the ambitious Durant was soon able to move the school to more suitable quarters and also to incorporate a **College of California.** By 1869, 8 freshmen were admitted to his college classes.

The school enrolled 50 pupils and gained a state charter. This growth encouraged the trustees to look for a campus away from the distractions of a rapidly growing Oakland. They settled on a site 3 miles north. A short time later the state offered to merge its still unorganized university with the College of California.

After considerable debate concerning the use of public funds for what had begun as a religiously oriented school and argument on the relative roles of liberal arts and scientific disciplines, a compromise was reached and the merger accomplished.

But another debate on what to name the new town followed. Eventually a name was chosen to honor **George Berkeley,** an 18th century poet, philosopher and bishop who once had traveled to the West Indies to start a college. **Frederick Law Olmsted,** the first landscape architect of the U.S., was hired to design both the 160-acre campus and part of the community around it. (Tragically, developers used almost nothing of his master plan. Amateurs laid out the adjoining streets for the convenience of homesteaders.) The town was incorporated in 1878, planning a government for 2,000 people. Partially due to the fire and earthquake of 1906, which caused many San Franciscans to move to the East Bay, the population rose to over 40,000 by 1910. It was 109,000 by 1980. Today the campus has grown to 720 acres, has nurtured more Nobel Prize winners than any other university, and is recognized as one of the world's foremost educational, scientific and cultural institutions.

By now, half the world knows about the explosion in numbers of trendy restaurants in Berkeley, an area that at times seems suffocated with mesquite grills, veggie fads and offset with menus full of honest-to-God gooey, super-satisfying desserts. But the fact is, *Gourmet Gulch* (as local journalist Margot Patterson Doss calls it) should most emphatically not be missed. This proliferation seems to have originated with **Chez Panisse** on Shattuck Avenue and quickly spread along University Avenue, Walnut, Cedar and lesser streets, along with some unusual and relatively inexpensive shopping oportunities from teddy bears and travel gimmicks to offbeat fashion and books and more books.

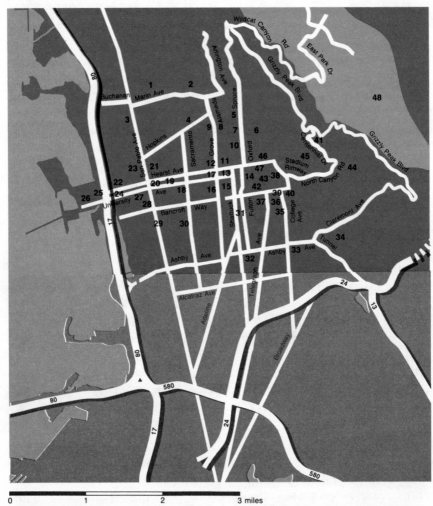

1 **Chin Szchawn.** ★ ★ $$/$$$ San Pablo Avenue, running through Berkeley and Albany, is home to many Chinese restaurants. Chin Szchawn, a long established restaurant, has one of the most interesting menus, with dishes you won't see anywhere else. The food tends to be spicy. *Open M-Sa for dinner. 1166 Solano Av., Albany. 525-0909*

2 **Shin-Shin.** $ For great and authentic Chinese feasting, this family-owned and operated restaurant goes to the top of the list. Don't miss the crispy chicken and garlic spinach. Wine and beer only. *Open Su-Th 11:30AM-9:30PM; F & Sa 11AM-10PM. 1715 Solano Av. 526-4970*

2 **McCallum's.** $ For many people, this is the best ice cream in the Bay Area. Anything with fudge or nuts is outrageously good. Sandwiches too, but don't bother. *Open daily. 1825 Solano Av. 525-3510*

2 **Tsing Tao.** ★ $$ A Northern Chinese restaurant that will satisfy the desires of any garlic freak. Their chicken and pork dishes in garlic sauce will leave you reeking for days. The whole fish is wonderful here, particularly if you order it sauteed with ginger and green onions. Good vegetables, like sauteed spinach with garlic and Szechuan-style eggplant. Not fancy, but friendly and good. *Open M-Th 11:30AM-9:30PM, F & Sa 11:30AM-10PM. 1767 Solano Av. 526-6223*

3 **Oisho/So Too.** ★ $ This restaurant offers sushi and other Japanese cuisine in an elegant and imaginative atmosphere set away in a quiet corner of Berkeley. The dining area is small but comfortable and relaxed. All kinds of sushi are available for moderate prices and for take-out. Sake, beer and wine. *Open M-Sa 11:30AM-2PM, 5-10PM. 1019 Camelia St. 552-9443*

4 **Monterey Market.** With everything from quail eggs to New Zealand goose berries and 5 varieties of apples, this gourmet produce market will have all the fresh vegetables and fruits, both in and out of season, that you can possibly imagine. Organically grown produce, Chinese vegetables, fresh herbs, dried fruits, bulk grains and a small packaged goods section all co-exist with an adjacent outdoor produce section. The quality of the food is good and the prices range from cheap to semi-expensive. Be prepared to be patient; it's crowded and lines can be long. *Open M-Sa 9AM-6PM. 1515 Hopkins St. (cross street California). 526-6042*

5 **Easy Going.** True to its name, *The One-Stop Travel Shop,* this complete travel store sells everything from travel books and maps to water purification kits and portable smoke alarms. They also take instant passport photos while you wait. *Open M-Sa 10AM-6PM, Su 12-5PM. 1400 Shattuck Av. 843-3533 (also 1617 Locust, Walnut Creek, 947-6660)*

5 **Berkeley Fish Market.** The individual portions of pre-prepared sushi are much better than you'd think. Buy the freshest fish for your dinner, then go next door to the Cheese Board for soft bread and some sharp cheese. *Open M-Sa 9AM-6:340PM. 1504 Shattuck Av. 845-7166*

5 **Bridge Creek.** ★ ★ ★ $$/$$$ Nostalgia has taken over the menu here in a positive way. Owner-chef **John Hudspeth** started out to serve a collection of breakfast dishes, carefully re-created from memories of his Oregon and California childhood. Next he expanded to lunch and weekend dinners, bringing back the most memorable recipes of the 30's, 40's and 50's with truly outstanding results: biscuits and gravy, roast chicken, hamburgers and bread pudding are gourmet quality. *Reservations essential. Open W-F 8AM-2:20PM, 6PM-9PM; Sa & Su 8:30AM-3PM, 6-9PM. 1549 Shattuck Av. 548-1774*

5 **Saul's Delicatessen.** ★ ★ ★$ Hailed as one of the best Jewish delis in Northern California, Saul's will satisfy your craving for corned beef, potato knishes, pastrami, chicken soup, kugel, latke, chopped liver and much more. Saul's is open for breakfast, lunch and dinner with table service plus a take-out counter. This deli has to be the most authentic Jewish deli you'll find outside of New York, so expect a short wait for tables on the weekends. Breakfast served all day. Beer, wine espresso available. *Open M-Th 11AM-9PM, F 11AM-10PM, Sa 9AM-10PM, Su 9AM-9PM. 1475 Shattuck Av. 848-DELI*

5 **The Cheese Board.** This worker-owned and operated store offers over 300 cheeses and fresh bread baked on the premises. Busy and friendly, this store carries reasonably priced goods, including spices, eggs and yogurt. When you walk in, take a number and then pick out any of a dozen of the freshest breads around and your favorite cheese from their outstanding collection. Buy a bottle of wine, and you are set for lunch. *Open Tu-Sa 10AM-6PM. 1512 Shattuck Av. 549-3183*

6 **Rose Walk.** (1913, 1925-36) **Bernard Maybeck** designed the walk which extends along the entire curving block to create a perfectly planned environment. After the 1923 fire, **Henry Gutterson** (with Maybeck's advice) built a series of dwellings along the landscaped path. *Rose Walk from Euclid to Buena Vista.*

6 **Walnut Square.** A 2-story, informal jumble of woodsy shops. It is located about half a mile north of University Avenue and includes: **Green Grocery**, plant shop; **By Hand**, a woman's boutique featuring handmade clothes; **Peet's Coffee and Tea**; and **Cocolat**, a chocolate lover's paradise.

7 **French Hotel.** *Expensive.* Full of surprises! The building began life as a French laundry and now houses a small but elegant hotel with a cafe and wine bar in its lobby. Each room is well done in contemporary taste with exposed brick walls, muted colors and an aura of sophisticated luxury—a welcome relief from the over-abundance of matching chintz you often finds in bed and breakfast establishments. Fourteen of the rooms have their own patio or deck, and many have views of San Francisco or the Berkeley hills. *1538 Shattuck Av. 548-9930*

7 **French Hotel Cafe.** $ This small cafe next to the French Hotel has a definite European air to it, with small tables placed outside on the sidewalk for people watching. It is usually crowed throughout the day, expecially in the morning with commuters getting their coffee and muffins to go. *Open M-Sa 7AM-midnight, Su 8AM-midnight. 1540 Shattuck Av. 843-8958*

7 **Chez Panisse.** ★ ★ ★ ★$$$$ Perhaps the best French restaurant in the Bay Area. Chez Panisse is the *mother* of much of the California cuisine and the training school for many Bay Area chefs. It is located in the ground floor of a renovated old house and offers a fixed-price dinner that changes every night. The menu for the next week comes out on Saturdays, but weekends are often fully reserved long before then. **Alice Waters** creates elegant and earthy *California nouvelle cuisine,* using the freshest ingredients available to create simple but elegant dishes. No heavy sauces or elaborate concoctions that many people associate with French restaurants here. The fish dishes are especially good, always with the freshest fish perfectly poached or grilled and usually with a light sauce that enhances the fish rather than masks it. Although they take their food very seriously, the atmosphere is informal, and you can dress however you like. If you have just one meal in the Bay Area, this should be it. *Reservations. Open Tu-Sa 6-9:15PM. 1517 Shattuck Av. 548-5525*

7 **Cafe at Chez Panisse.** ★ ★ ★.★ $$ The French restaurant, renowned through out the U.S., is downstairs; this bustling cafe is on the 2nd floor. There's is a long wait and no reservations, but it's worth it! The *calzone,* fold-over pizza stuffed with mozzarella, goat cheese and prosciutto, is so good that it was featured in the *N.Y. Times Magazine.* It might be the best pizza you'll ever eat. There's always a choice of several interesting salads, a couple of innovative pastas and a meat and fish entree. The homemade pastas with their interesting sauces are always worth trying, as are the excellent fruit tarts and homemade ice creams and sherberts for dessert. There's a reasonably priced and well-chosen wine list as well. The perfect place to spend several hours talking with friends in a delightful cafe atmosphere. *French/Italian. Open M-Sa 11AM-midnight. 1517 Shattuck Av. 548-5555*

8 **Fat Apple's.** ★ ★ $ Nothing on the menu but hamburger and steak, but it's always jammed out the door. The reason: the hamburgers are among the best in the Bay Area. Outrageously good desserts, including apple pie, and excellent breakfasts, with homemade croissants and muffins. *American. Open M-F 6AM-11PM, Sa & Su 7AM-11PM. 1346 Grove St. 526-2260*

9 **Mr. Mopp's.** One of the last of the old fashioned toy stores. It has an enormous variety and range of toys. Party favors, joke items, educational toys, marionettes, kites, scientific games and costumes are a portion of the stock. The book department is also excellent. *Open M-Sa 9AM-5:30PM. 1405 Grove St. 525-9633*

10 **Cha Am.** $ A Thai restaurant that uses authentic Thai herbs. There is a small deck for outside eating, weather permitting. The service is helpful and friendly, the portions good-sized and the atmosphere warm and informal. Wine and beer served during lunch and dinner. *Open M-Th 11:30AM-4PM, 5-9:30PM; F 11:30AM-4PM, 5-10PM; Sa 12-4PM, 5-10PM; Su 5-10PM. 1543 Shattuck Av. 848-9664*

11 **Warszawa.** ★ ★ $$/$$$ The Polish food is so filling that it's too bad this restaurant can't be at a ski resort. If you're in the mood for a big, gutsy Eastern European meal, you can't do better than here. The pleasant decor is incongruously Early American, but the food is authentically Polish. The pea soup with chunks of ham is splendid, particularly if eaten with their crusty black bread. Try the succulent roast duck half, served with little dumplings and done in a rich sauce with prunes and apples, or the heartiest of Polish stews. *Polish. Open M-Th 5:30-10PM, F & Sa 5:30-11PM. 1730 Shattuck Av. 841-5539*

11 **Venezia Caffe.** ★ ★ $ A small and busy Italian favorite in the East Bay, offering a variety of fresh pasta dishes and other Italian delicacies for reasonable prices. The decor is tasteful and interesting with murals covering the walls that depict the canals of Venice. Across the street from the more expensive Ristorante Venezia, the Caffe is a nice alternative when the budget for a night out is small and you want a more casual evening. It can be crowded but it is very friendly. It has an excellent but small wine list. *Open M-F 7-10:30AM, 11:30AM-2:30PM, 5-10PM; Sa & Su 5-10PM. 1903 University Av. 849-4681*

12 **Au Coquelet Cafe.** $ A late night spot featuring a dessert assortment of fresh fruit tarts, pastries and cakes. They are also open for breakfast and lunch. Beer, wine, aperitifs and an espresso bar are available. On the weekends, a champagne brunch is offered from 9AM to 3PM. *Open M-F 6AM-2AM, Sa 8AM-2AM, Su 8AM-1AM. 2000 University Av. at Milvia. 845-0433*

Restaurants/Nightlife red
Hotels blue
Shops/Galleries purple
Museums/Architecture/Narrative black

13 **Ristorante Venezia.** ★ ★ ★ $$ One of the East Bay's best secrets. Open for dinner only, this *ristorante* offers a varied selection of inventive Italian food such as mussels stuffed with rice, pine nuts and currants. Full bar service is available and the wine list is extensive. In the spring and summer, the patio is open in the back. The atmosphere is cheerful and informal and on Tuesday evenings, live opera creates an added touch of Venetian romance. The desserts are all homemade. This ristorante won the *Best Italian Restaurant Award* from *San Francisco Focus* in 1986. *Open Tu-Th 5:30-9:30PM, F & Sa 5:30-10:30PM, Su 5-9PM. 1902 University Av. 644-3093*

13 **Sheltered Housing.** (1982, Hershen, Trumbo, Gambill in association with Mui Ho) Housing for the elderly designed in a vernacular style. *Martin Luther King Jr. Way at Hearst.*

14 **Cafe Pastoral.** ★ ★ $$ This cafe has an airy, artistic feeling, with a large glass front and second floor balcony that serves as a painting studio for the owner's partner, wife and restaurant chef. The menu features continental cuisine with subtle traces of the chef's Korean heritage. All of the appetizers include a mass of colorful, finely sliced vegetables; several dishes have sauces with *shoyu* and fresh ginger. Typical entrees are albacore with mustard-lemon *beurre blanc* and fettucine with prawns, red bell peppers, leeks and cream. Service is attentive but relaxed. Beer, wine and espresso are served. *Open Tu-Th 11:30AM-2:30PM, 5:30-10PM; F & Sa 5:30-10PM; Su 5:30-9:30PM. 2160 University Av. 540-7514*

15 **Gertie's Chesapeake Bay Cafe.** ★ ★ $$ A wonderful seafood restaurant and oyster bar which specializes in dishes of Maryland and Louisiana, with different specials every night. Especially good is their Eastern Blue Crab, flown in live daily. The chef, **John Shields**, also does beautiful soups and salads. Highly recommended for those who miss delicacies from the East Coast. *Open M-Th 10:30AM-2:30PM, 5:30-9:30PM; F 10:30AM-2:30PM, 5:30-11PM; Sa 11:30AM-2:30PM, 5:30-11PM; Su 4:30-9:30PM. 1919 Addison St. 841-2722*

15 **2300 Shattuck Avenue.** (1926) This block-long mixed-use building with apartments and offices above shops was originally designed by **William Plachek**. It was remodeled in 1980 by **Research Planning Design Associates**. The corner of Shattuck and Bancroft has been remodeled to form offices and showrooms for the Continuing Education at the Bar and has exposed ducts and task/ambient lighting through-out. *Shattuck between Bancroft and Durant.*

15 **Berkeley Public Library.** (1930) A Zigzag *Moderne*-style hall by **William Plachek**. *Shattuck Av. and Kittridge St.*

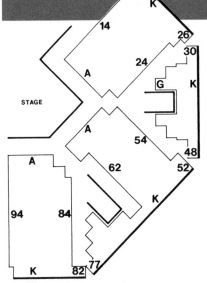

Berkeley Repertory Theatre. The Berkeley Rep., founded in 1968, is the East Bay's only professional resident theater. With an ensemble of resident actors, it presents a broad range of classical and contemporary dramas in an intimate performance space. With its 401 seats comfortably wrapping around 3 sides of the thrust stage, you're ensured of excellent sightlines from every vantage point. *Reserved seating. 2025 Addison St. Box office, 845-4700*

Berkeley Post Office. An exquisite early Renaissance Italianate building—homage to Brunelleschi. Finely detailed interior with original counters, hardware, etc. *Milvia and Kittridge.*

Vivoli's. ★ $ Famous across the Bay for their sinfully rich Italian-style ice cream, with long lines to get their famous espresso, amaretto, vanilla and fresh fruit flavors. Some people are never able to go back to regular ice cream again. *Open Su-Th 12-11PM, F & Sa 12PM-midnight. 2115 Allston Way. 845-6458*

Taiwan. ★ $$ The island of Taiwan has its own variety of Chinese food, and this is one of the few restaurants that serves it, as well as more standard Northern and Hunan dishes. Try the squid, eel and turnip cakes from the Taiwanese part of the menu, then go on to some of their excellent fish and vegetable dishes. Their Northern-style Chinese brunch on weekends is unusual and interesting, featuring such delicacies as long, non-sweet *Chinese donuts* that you wrap in sesame pastry and dip in a bowl of soybean milk soup. *Taiwanese. Open M-F 11:30AM-9:30PM, Sa-Su 10:30AM-9:30PM. 2071 University Av. 845-1456*

Sushi California. ★ $ Situated in the basement of a building with windows looking out onto the sidewalk, this small sushi restaurant has a neighborhood feel. The decor is minimal with an artistic *new age* flair. The sushi comes in the usual varieties and is inexpensive. An excellent place to visit frequently with a few friends and an equally comfortable place to dine alone. Sake, beer and wine. *Open M-F 11:45AM-2PM, 5:30-10PM; Sa 5:30-10PM. 2033 Martin Luther King Jr. Way. 548-0737*

Poppy. This bright, airy store carries an extensive variety of domestic and imported fabrics. It is very popular. *Open M 10AM-9:30PM; Tu, Sa 10AM-5:30PM; Th, F 10AM-9PM; Su noon-5PM. 2072 Addison St., off of Shattuck Av. 841-2100*

Dakota Bar And Grill. ★ ★ $$ This restaurant serves an exciting mixture of American, Southwest and Mexican cuisine, 3 meals per day. Entrees contain unusual ingredients such as *Anejo* cheese, *calabacitos* and *chile guajillo* sauce. Imaginative food in elegant surroundings make this dining experience worthwhile. Desserts are just as creative: bananas and toasted coconut stuffed into taco shells made from graham crackers, for example. Service is attentive and parking accessible on the street or in a paid garage near by. *Open M 7-10AM, 11:30AM-2:30PM; Tu-F 7-10AM, 11:30AM-2:30PM, 5:30-10:30PM; Sa & Su 5:30-10:30PM. 2086 Allston Way. 841-3848*

Restaurant Metropole. ★ ★ ★ $$/$$$ A rustic French country inn serving classic cuisine (albeit tempered with an innovative California approach), reasonably priced and situated in the middle of Berkeley. It's an unusual combination of virtues, but chef/owner **Serge Bled** seems determined to offer an ambience both friendly and elegant, with romantic touches of fresh flowers at all times, live music by way of classical piano, and a menu that re-creates many of the dishes that were childhood favorites as he was growing up in France. After working as a chef for 22 years, including a stint at the ever popular **Le Central** in San Francisco, Serge still at times participates in the sauce preparation in his kitchen, but mostly concentrates on providing attentive service that isn't too pretentious and planning menus that offer specialties such as wild game, fresh fish from everywhere—East and West Coasts, Mexico, Europe—and fantastically delicious desserts. There's a fine wine list and full bar. It's no wonder that 60 percent of his customers return regularly. *Open M-F 11AM-10PM, Sa 11AM-10:30PM, Su brunch. 2271 Shattuck Av. 848-3080*

Downstairs at the Metropole is:

Cafe Bistro. Here you will find a mixed crowd of college students and their professors mingling with jazz fans from all over the Bay Area. Live jazz may be heard from 9PM to midnight and until 1AM Fridays and Saturdays. There is food service in this cozy room from 11AM to 10PM, and the ambience is collegial and casual. From the same kitchen as the Metropole, the menu includes sandwiches, steamed clams, great soups, an oyster bar in season and many different coffees. *2271 Shattuck Av. 848-3080*

Inn Season. ★ ★ $$/$$$ A beautiful French restaurant with high ceilings, wood walls, intimate dining, classical guitar on Saturdays—all for considerably less than you'd pay for such atmosphere in San Francisco. Good food too; well-prepared but not as innovative as some other Berkeley French restaurants. Terrific desserts. *1921 Martin Luther King Jr. Way. 548-0350*

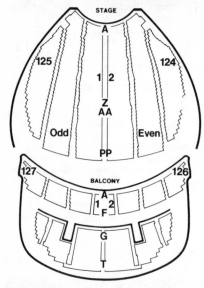

16 **Berkeley Community Theatre.** This 3,491-seat theater is one of the largest on the West Coast. Part of the **Berkeley High School** complex, the theater presents the full gamut of entertainment: rock shows, symphony, ballet and community concerts. *1930 Allston Way. Box office. 845-2308*

17 **Ay Caramba.** $ Stand in line for heaps of filling, well-prepared Mexican food. A college hangout for a good, cheap meal. *Open daily 11:30AM-9PM. 1901 University Av. 843-1298*

18 **University/Sacramento Housing.** (1982, Lyndon and Buchanan) High density student family housing arranged around a series of courts and alleyways. The architects have carefully integrated some of the adjacent buildings into the overall design. *University Av. at Sacramento.*

19 **Santa Fe Bar & Grill.** ★ ★ ★ $$ **Jeremiah Tower,** the talented chef who first cooked at Chez Panisse, turned this renovated railroad station into one of the most interesting examples of *new California cuisine.* Tower is no longer the chef, but the food is still the same. The fish comes in many varieties, from *ceviche* (Latin American marinated raw fish) to much more French-style sautés. The black bean soup is one of the most heavenly dishes ever created, and the squab and poultry are wonderful. The menu changes frequently. They take reservations, but you might have to wait anyway and put up with indifferent service. But the food is worth it, and prices are reasonable. *American/French. Open M-Th 11:30AM-2:30PM, 5:30-10:30PM; F & Sa 11:30AM-2:30PM, 5:30-11PM; Su 10:30AM-2:30PM, 5:30-10PM. 1310 University Av. 841-4740*

20 **Siam Cuisine.** ★ ★ ★ $/$$ It looks like an American cocktail lounge, which is exactly what it used to be. But the food is authentically Thai; don't order the hot dishes unless you really like your palate to be set on fire. The food is made of the freshest ingredients, beautifully prepared, cooked and served by members of the same family. All of the calamari dishes, particularly the cold salad served as an appetizer, present squid

as good as you'll ever get. The pork and chicken dishes in red and green curry sauces are almost like stews, with the bouquets of a host of interesting spices enlivening every bite. The *paht Thai* (soft noodles cooked with dried shrimp and ground peanuts) and the stuffed boneless chicken wings are perfect mild foils to the roaring hot chili peppers in many of the other dishes. Try *Singha Thai* beer with your meal. *Open Su-Th 11AM-3PM, 5-11PM; F & Sa 11AM-3PM, 5PM-midnight. 1181 University Av. 548-3278*

21 **Freight and Salvage.** Club with folk, bluegrass, Greek, Yiddish and blues music. *Show Tu-F at 7:30PM, Sa & Su 8PM-1AM. 1827 San Pablo Av. 548-1761*

22 **Bette's Diner and Bakeshop.** ★ ★ $ Everything you could possibly want for your own Sunday brunch at home—fresh OJ, coffee, tea, baked goods, meat, fish, cheeses, dairy, bread and such delicacies as blintzes and corned beef hash. The diner is styled after an old-fashioned diner and is as busy and noisy as you would expect, but this place is a real find! Beer, wine and espresso bar. *Open Su 8AM-3PM, M 6:30AM-2:30PM, Tu-Sa 6:30AM-4PM. 1807 4th St. 548-9494*

23 **Acme Bread Company.** There are 2 ways to get this wonderful bread; wait in line at the bakery or go next door to Fanney's where they use it for their sandwiches. The bread is known to be the best in the East Bay and you must get to the bakery before noon for any selection. It's worth it. *Open Tu-Su 10AM-4PM (or whenever they sell out). 1601 San Pablo Av. (near Cedar). 524-1327*

24 **Fourth Street Grill.** ★ ★ ★ $$ Each week a different menu of international specialties is presented here, from East Indian to African to Italian, as well as delicious offerings in the California cuisine style. **Kermit Lynch,** wine merchant, offers a wide variety of wine suggestions for the international menus. The fixed lunch and dinner menus offer fresh salads, sandwiches and mesquite-grilled meats. The full bar stays open throughout the day, even between the lunch and dinner hours, and also offers hors d'oeuvres. The dining area is intimate but slightly noisy. *Reservations suggested. Open M-F 11:30AM-2:30PM, 5:30-10PM; F 11:30AM-2:30PM, 5-10PM; Sa & Su 5-10PM. 1820 4th St. 849-0526*

24 **Spenger's Fish Grotto.** ★ ★ $ An old family owned business and an ideal family restaurant for fresh seafood from the area. The menu is also supplemented by seafoods from all parts of the world delivered fresh every day. It is the largest Bay Area seafood restaurant in terms of pounds of fish prepared. The maritime setting is authentic, and all of the decorations in the dining area are ancient relics taken from old and famous vessels. Adjacent to the restaurant is a fish market with food-to-go (anything from the menu) and a banquet room. The **Diamond Bar**—a new addition—features fresh Eastern Blue Point oysters and claims to be the only East Bay oyster bar to do so daily. *Open daily 8AM-midnight. Market open 9AM-10:30PM. 1919 4th St. 845-7771*

24 **China Station.** $$ A good late-night spot when most of Berkeley is locked up tight. It has a delightful atmosphere and is in an abandoned, renovated railroad station. The clams and other shellfish dishes are excellent, the rest of the menu more spotty. *Cantonese. Open daily 11:30AM-1AM. 700 University Av. 548-7880*

25 **Adventure Playground.** A fun place for kids as well as parents, this unusual play area supplies tools and scrap wood for the children to build forts, clubhouses, etc. There's always one staff person on site for supervision, although it is recommended for parents with children under age 6 to help supervise their children's play. A traditional play area is also available. *Open weekends and school holidays Sept-June; weekends, weekdays and school holidays July-August. Foot of University Av., across from the Berkeley Marina Sports Center at 225 University Av. 644-6530*

26 **Skates by the Bay.** $$ Fish, poultry, pasta, meat, fresh catch of the day, oysters and sushi are all just part of the California cuisine offered at Skates by the Bay. The decor in this large restaurant mixes elegant, old-fashioned charm with a few modern touches—track lighting and large windows with a clear view of the city. *Open M-Sa 11:15AM-3PM, 5-10PM; Su 4-10PM. 100 Seawall Dr. 549-1900*

27 **Balabosta.** ★ $$/$$$ The specialty here is smoked meats and fish, as well as live Maine lobster. Pleasant, relaxed atmosphere. Also take-out next door. *French/Continental. Open daily for dinner. University Av. and 6th St. 548-0300*

28 **Edokko.** ★ $ An inexpensive, informal Japanese restaurant well off the beaten path, filled with students and neighborhood regulars. First-rate sushi and excellent chicken and beef teriyaki. The service is slapdash and there might be a little kid watching TV at one of the tables, but you'll love the food. *Open daily 11AM-2PM, 5-9PM. 2215 San Pablo Av. 841-9505*

29 **KC Bar B-Q.** ★ $ Some like it hot, and the hot sauce on KC's ribs will set you on fire. Milder varieties are also available, all spooned over smokey, moist, tender ribs that aren't the least bit fatty. *Open Tu-Th 11:30AM-9PM, F-Sa noon-2AM. 2613 San Pablo Av. 548-1140*

30 **A La Carte.** ★ ★ $$/$$$ A tiny, unpretentious neighborhood French restaurant with some of the best classic French cuisine in the Bay Area. The menu changes nightly and features one fish dish, one meat dish and several appetizers. The fish is always superb, and the sauces are a marvel. Great chocolate desserts and fruit tarts. The neighborhood isn't the best, but the food is so good it's definitely worth the drive. *Open daily 6-9:30PM, Su brunch 10:30AM-2PM. 1453 Dwight Way. 548-2322*

31 **Giovanni's.** ★ ★ $$ One of the better Italian restaurants in the East Bay, where Italian food tends to be far inferior to the best places in San Francisco. An amazingly good and inexpensive wine list; it's worth coming here just to drink. *Open M-F 11:30AM-11PM, Sa & Su 5-11PM. 2420 Shattuck Av. 843-6678*

32 **Omnivore.** $$/$$$ One of those unpretentious neighborhood Berkeley French restaurants with young people whipping up decent food in an informal atmosphere. *Open M-F 5:30-9:30PM, Sa & Su 5:30-10PM. 3015 Shattuck Av. 848-4346*

33 **Judah L. Magnes Memorial Museum.** A repository for art, artifacts, documents and photographs of Jewish life, history and religion from ancient times to the present and from countries around the world. Changing exhibitions on Jewish themes. There are 2 libraries: one is general and includes antiquarian books; the other contains archives on Jews living on the West Coast. Records of bar mitzvahs, marriages, etc. are kept in the library of West American Jewry. There is also a bookshop. Located in a spacious old Berkeley house. *Open Su-F 10AM-4PM. 2911 Russell St., above College Av. near Ashby Av. 849-2710*

34 **Claremont Resort Hotel.** *Deluxe.* **Frank Lloyd Wright** called the Claremont *one of the few hotels in the world with warmth, character and charm...*It encompasses 22 acres in the Oakland/Berkeley hills, 20 minutes from San Francisco. Here, you can play tennis day and night, swim in an Olympic-size pool, stroll through 20 acres of palm trees and exquisite gardens (the roses are spectacular), and relax with personal service reminiscent of the good old days. The hotel does have an unusual history dating back to the Gold Rush days. One Kansas farmer struck it rich and, wishing to humor his wife, bought 13,000 acres from the old Peralta land grant. On this land he built her an English castle. After their daughter married a British Lord and his wife had died, he sold the spread to a family who enjoyed it for a short time before the castle burned to the ground. (The stables were saved and later became the locker room of the Pool and Tennis Club.) Subsequently, the property finally ended up in the hands of one **Frank Haven** who won it by virtue of a game of checkers. He began to build *his* dream hotel in 1906 but construction halted with the earthquake. In 1910 he allied himself with **Erick Lindblom** and the building was completed in time for the Panama-Pacific Exposition in 1915.

The grounds, natural setting and magnificent views have always given the structure a romantic, picturesque ambience. With all the refurbishing of the past few years, it still has the presence of a glistening white palace high in the hills, and although many of its patrons are business travelers during the week when it serves as a site for conferences and corporate meetings, management is making a special effort on weekends to encourage its use as a total resort for tourists and Bay Area residents as well. *Seasonal and weekend rates. Su brunch 10AM-2PM. All recreation facilities included. Ashby and Domingo Avs., east of Berkeley. 843-3000*

35 **Julia Morgan Center for the Arts.** Formerly a Presbyterian Church, it's designer has in recent years achieved recognition as one of the finest architects of this century. To truly enjoy this architectural masterpiece, you should know that Morgan chose to build the former church out of redwood and Douglas fir, an economy move at the time, reflecting her sense of harmony with the surrounding land, just as the magnificent structure's low profile reflected her concern for harmony with the surrounding architecture. Today, the Center's 450-seat theater showcases local and out-of-town theatrical, musical and dance events. The acoustics of the lush, dark wood hall are extremely lively and resonant, making it especially suited for chamber music. *2640 College Av. 548-7234*

36 **Hotel Durant.** *Moderate.* This 1928 hotel became a habit with its clientele and a landmark as well, yet grew shabbier while no one noticed. Now, with new ownership, a tasteful restoration has kept the best of the old and provided the conveniences today's travelers expect. There are 140 rooms (some connected for family accommodations), meeting rooms and a new restaurant, **Henry's Publick House and Grille.** The welcoming atmosphere is still there. The Durant is the only full service hotel within steps of the university. *Complimentary brunch M-Sa 7-9:30AM. 2600 Durant Av. 845-8981*

36 **Larry Blake's.** *Live bands M & Th-Sa 9:30PM-2AM, R&B Tu, big-screen movies and music videos W. Dancing 9:30PM-2AM. 2367 Telegraph Av. 848-0886*

36 **College Avenue.** A parade of shops near the **U.C. Berkeley** campus including **Sweet Dreams and Candy Store; Sweet Dreams Toy Store; Trading Post,** which sells art and crafts; and **Caravansary,** a coffee, tea and cookware store.

36 **Telegraph Avenue at South Campus.** Telegraph Avenue leading south from the Berkeley campus is a crowded street of interesting shops and eateries, and it's bookworm's paradise! Bookstore highlights include **Shakespeare & Co., Cody's, Comics and Comix, Shambhala Booksellers, Moe's** and **Logos Bookstore.**

Also in the South Campus area:

Caffe Mediterranean. $$ Called *the Mediterranean,* it is one of the establishments that has weathered the fads and upheavals of Telegraph Avenue. Espresso, Italian and Greek food and pastries. European atmosphere. *Open M-F 7AM-midnight, Sa-Su 7:30AM-midnight. 2475 Telegraph Av. 841-5634*

Augusta's. ★★ $$/$$$ Another of those limited-menu, informal neighborhood French restaurants that have popped up all over Berkeley. *2955 Telegraph Av. 548-3140*

Berkeley Repertory Children's Theater. Stages musicals, fairy tales and audience participation performances every *Sa 10AM. 2980 College Av. For information, 845-4700*

Unitarian Church. (1898, AC Schweinfurth) An old wooden church with low eaves and a fine circular fan window. *Dana and Bancroft.*

37 **Gramma's Bed and Breakfast Inn.** *Moderate.* A beautifully restored Tudor mansion, incongruously manicured in this quiet neighborhood gone a bit downhill. However, Gramma's is an experience from the moment you approach on the walk lined with incredible rose bushes to the warmest of welcomes given by any one of the attractive, hardworking staff. Each room has its own antique furnishings, including a handmade quilt; most have private decks, fireplaces and access to the English country garden. In the morning there is a complimentary breakfast of baked breads, but the outstanding plus is the *we will pamper you* attitude. *2740 Telegraph Av. 549-2145*

37 **Christian Science Church.** (1910, Bernard Maybeck) One of Maybeck's finest buildings—a combination of Romanesque, Gothic and Japanese eclectic construction using materials as diverse as heavy timber and asbestos cement panels, poured-in-place concrete and steel. Of particular interest is the layered facade and, inside, the huge wooden trusses. National Historical Register. *Open Su. Dwight Way and Bowditch.*

37 **Casa de Eva.** ★ $/$$ This unpretentious and inexpensive Mexican restaurant is a favorite with Berkeley college students and actually one of the best Mexican restaurants in the Bay Area. There are a number of unusual dishes, like *chalupas* (cornmeal pastries with spicy sausages inside) and *flautas* (crispy tortillas filled with shredded beef). You can sample lots of things in their extensive list of combinations. *Open daily 11AM-9:45PM. 2826 Telegraph Av. 540-9092*

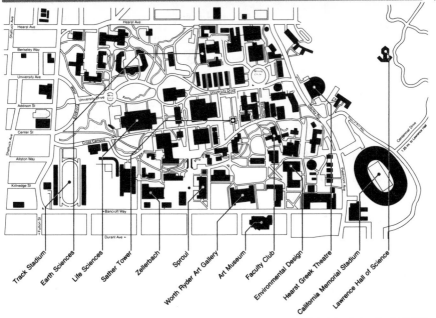

Track Stadium · Earth Sciences · Life Sciences · Sather Tower · Zellerbach · Sproul · Worth Ryder Art Gallery · Art Museum · Faculty Club · Environmental Design · Hearst Greek Theatre · California Memorial Stadium · Lawrence Hall of Science

38 **University of California at Berkeley.** Founded in 1868, U.C. Berkeley has grown to 1,200 acres. Here, nearly 31,000 undergraduate and graduate students study subjects ranging from social welfare to chemistry, education to law and microbiology to women's studies. Berkeley enjoys an outstanding academic reputation. Its faculty includes 10 Nobel Prize winners and 82 members of the National Academy of Sciences. The U.C. Berkeley campus features several interesting buildings and exhibits.

38 **Hearst Memorial Gymnasium for Women.** (1927, Bernard Maybeck and Julia Morgan) One of the favorite student buildings on campus. Notice the small courtyards off the main corridor. Also the emblematic urns on the front facade. *U.C. campus on Bancroft Way.*

38 **Earth Sciences Building.** Includes the Paleontology Museum, rock and map collections.

38 **California Memorial Stadium.** Completed in 1923, it seats 76,000.

38 **Student Union.** Arts and crafts displays, shops, restaurants and recreation center.

38 **Bancroft Library.** Art of Gold Rush California, rare book and manuscript exhibitions.

38 **Hearst Greek Theatre.** 8,500-seat amphitheater built in 1903 was designed after the original at Epidaurus, Greece.

38 **Wurster Hall, College of Environmental Design.** The original building constructed in the early 1960's under the design direction of **Joseph Esherick** is a powerful example of Brutalist architecture. Its poured-in-place concrete framework, sun shades and emphatic structure, together with the exposed ducts and internal services, were part of the current architectural ideology. Recently, it has had 2 additions, both of which have adhered to the original intentions of the design. The internally located auditorium was designed by **Stanley Saitowitz** (1986)

and at the entrance is a renovation of **Ramona's Cafe** by **Fernau and Harman.** The latter has a new outdoor seating area, with custom designed umbrellas. *U.C. campus at College Av.*

38 **U.C. Press Building.** (Remodeled in 1983 by ELS Design Group) The original unassuming concrete warehouse has been remodeled into offices for the U.C. Press. Gray and white paint striping on the outside and a formal main staircase inside have transformed the building into a showpiece of intelligent interior design. *Berkeley Way near Shattuck Av.*

39 **University Art Museum.** A low, reinforced concrete block designed by **Mario Ciampi.** Seven galleries on 5 levels fan out from the central space. The late abstract expressionist artist **Hans Hoffman** was instrumental in the museum's creation. His generous contribution helped finance the museum's construction, and he donated over 40 of his paintings, which form the nucleus of the permanent collection. One of the museum's most popular assets is the **Pacific Film Archive,** headquartered downstairs. It contains research facilities, several screening rooms and a film collection spanning the history of cinema. Two screenings per night are usually scheduled.

Within the museum is:

The Swallow. $/$$ Elegant quiches, salads and French desserts from a cafeteria line. A place to sip espresso and read poetry. *Continental. Open W-Sa 11AM-8PM, Su 11AM-5PM. 2626 Bancroft Way. 841-2409*

40 **Lowie Museum of Anthropology.** Located in **Kroeber Hall** on campus. Founded in 1901, it has the largest anthropological collection in the West with changing exhibits drawn from its own permanent archive and borrowed from other museums' traveling shows. *Admission charge; Th free. Open M-Tu, Th-F 10AM-4:30PM, Sa & Su noon-4:30PM. Bancroft Way and College Av. 642-3681*

41 **U.C. Campanile/Sather Tower.** (1914, John Galen Howard) The U.C. landmark, it can be seen from all over the Bay Area and is on an axis with University Avenue and the Golden Gate. *U.C. campus Campanile Way (Telegraph Av. continued) at University.*

41 **Lawrence Hall of Science.** (1968, Anshen and Allen) Established in 1958 to commemorate physicist **Ernest Orlando Lawrence,** who developed the cyclotron and was U.C.'s first Nobel Laureate. This popular science center is dedicated to promoting scientific knowledge and improvement of science education. It offers imaginative programs, hands-on science exhibits, special events and classes to the general public and to students. It also serves as a teacher training facility and education research unit of the University. The Hall's specialties include one of the largest computer facilities in the U.S., a **Wizard's Lab** where visitors may perform physics experiments and a biology lab with living animals. The **Holt Planetarium** is also very popular. Films for children are scheduled on weekends and holidays. Activities and exhibits are geared to the schedules of public schools in the area. Many exhibits only operate on weekends, holidays and daily during summer vacation. It's best to call for information. *Open daily 10AM-4:30PM, Th until 9PM. Admission charge. Children under 7 free. Th after 4PM free. Centennial Dr., above the Lawrence Radiation Laboratory. 642-5132. Galaxy Sandwich Shop open M-F 10AM-4PM, Sa-Su 10AM-4:30PM. Library open F-M noon-5PM, Th 5-9PM.*

42 **Intermural Sports Center/Harmon Gymnasium.** (1983, ELS Design Group) A large extension to the original *Moderne* Harmon Gym, this new building contains a variety of sports facilities, from a squash court to a gymnasium, indoor running track and multi-purpose rooms. They are arranged around a 4-story gallery with stairs, bridges and balconies. The somewhat overwhelming scale on Bancroft Way is softened by the pastel colors. *UC Campus on Bancroft Way.*

43 **Sproul Plaza Student Union Complex, Zellerbach Auditorium.** (1965, De Mars and Reay/Hardison) A series of modern university buildings arranged around an open plaza. The 2,000-seat house brings a wide array of touring productions to the Berkeley campus. A fine theater with excellent sound and sightlines. *Dwight Way and Telegraph Av. 642-9988*

43 **University of California Visitor Center.** Situated in the main lobby of the Student Union Building. 1½ hour guided walking tour covers main points of interest. *Tours M-F 1PM. 642-5215*

44 **University of California Botanical Garden.** More than 50,000 plants and 7,500 species grow in the garden. There is a large section devoted to native California plants; the **Mather Redwood Grove** (named after U.C. alumnus **Stephen Mather** who was the first director of the National Park Service); and many exotic cacti and succulents brought from the South American Andes. The **Rhododendron Dell** is spectacular in April and May. The multi-colored display of *alstroemeria*—Peruvian lilies, the native flower of Chile—is a sight to behold. They're in full bloom late May and early June. Free garden tours are given Sa and Su at 1:30PM. The **Information Center,** open on weekends, sells maps, books, floral posters, seeds and plants. *Admission free. Open every day except Christmas, 9AM-4:45PM. Strawberry Canyon. 642-3343*

45 **Mining and Metallurgy Building.** (1907, John Galen Howard) What is interesting about this building is that it combines a classical Roman design with what was then the most modern materials—steel trusses and columns. The entrance lobby, a vaulted basilica-type space, is one of the great interiors of the Bay Area. *U.C. campus east of the Campanile.*

46 **Graduate Theological Union Library.** (1981, Louis Kahn, followed by Peters Clayborne Caulfield in association with Esherick, Homsey, Dodge and Davis) **Kahn** did the schematic layout just before he died in 1974. It consisted of a pyramidal form with a centrally lit library reading room and stacks below. After almost a decade of negotiation and re-design, the first phase is now complete. It does not yet have the master's touch in either plan or detailing. *Euclid at Le Conte.*

47 **Seeley Mudd Building.** (1980, Charles Stickney) A teaching building built out of poured-in-place concrete. It is one of the best Brutalist buildings in the Bay Area contrasting extremely well with the contemporary GTU library opposite, both in design and detailing. *Scenic at Le Conte.*

48 **Charles Lee Tilden Regional Park.** Part of the East Bay Regional Park District. The 2,065-acre forested preserve in the Berkeley hills is a nature and recreation area for East Bay residents. The park includes chaparral-covered hills, eucalyptus, pine, madrone, bay and live oak woods, lakes and meadows.

The **Peninsula** is a relatively small land mass stretching from San Francisco to San Jose and encompassing an incredible range of scenic gems and cultural artifacts, all held together by the remains of the **El Camino Real,** the highway of the Spanish king.

Posh bedroom communities built on the sites of the turn-of-the-century summer estates of San Francisco's wealthiest dot the Peninsula, as do bridle trails for the area's horsey Woodside set, produce ranches, the seaside hamlet of **Half Moon Bay**, a major university (**Stanford**), a skyline drive through a redwood forest, hot sunny weather, and at the southern end, the fastest growing metropolis in California (**San Jose**).

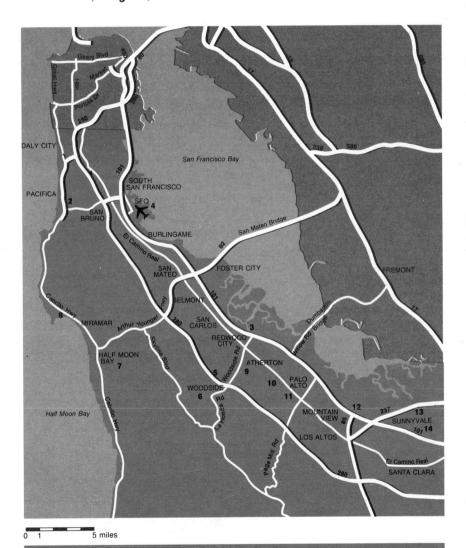

0 1   5 miles

1 **Rod McLellan Company.** The largest orchid and foliage plant nursery in the world. Daily tours begin with a walk through thousands of flowering plants, then go behind the scenes to the foliage plant growing range, scientific laboratories and the cut flower department. *One hour tours start at 10:30AM and 1:30PM. Special arrangements required for groups. 1450 El Camino Real, South San Francisco. 871-5655*

2 **Sanchez Adobe.** This historic adobe is one of the Mexican period buildings on the Peninsula that is open to the public. A small museum displaying artifacts of the period adjoins the adobe. *Open Tu-Th 10AM-4PM, Sa-Su 1-5PM. Linda Mar Blvd., Pacifica (1 mile east of Hwy. 1). 359-1462, 574-6441*

3 **Marine Ecological Institute.** Discovery voyages aboard an 85-foot research vessel offer an introduction to the ecology of the San Francisco Bay. Studies are conducted on marine life and geological formation of the area. *1200 Chesapeake Dr., Redwood City. 364-2760*

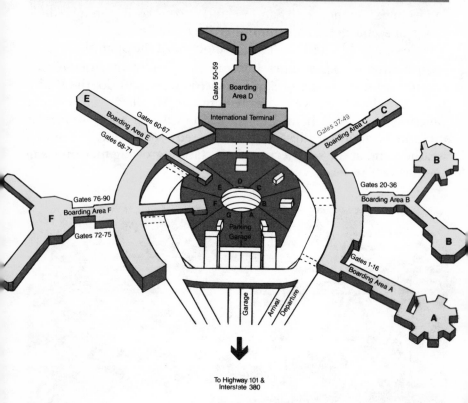

To Highway 101 &
Interstate 380

NORTH TERMINAL	INTERNATIONAL (CENTRAL) TERMINAL		SOUTH TERMINAL
Air Cal	Air France	Lufthansa	Alaska Airlines
Air Canada	British Airways	Mexicana	Braniff
American	CAAC	Northwest Int'l	Continental
American Eagle	Canadian Pacific	Pan Am	Delta
Eastern	Cathay Pacific	Philippine Airlines	Northwest Domestic
Piedmont	China Airlines	Qantas	PSA
United Domestic Flights	Hawaiian	Singapore	SFO Helicopter
United Express	Japan	TACA Int'l	Southwest
	LTU Int'l	United Int'l	TWA
		UTA	US Air

4 **San Francisco International Airport.**
SFO is 14 miles south of San Francisco down Highway 101, and it is served by nearly 40 major national and international airlines. During heavy morning and afternoon commute hours, expect travel time of at least 35 minutes, and 25 minutes at other times. SFO is the eighth busiest airport in the world, with approximately 35,500 flights a month and 1,180 a day. A $400 million renovation program is still underway. The **North Terminal** has computerized information systems that give you details on ground transportation to hundreds of destinations within San Francisco and the Bay Area.

How to get to and from SFO:

Airporter Bus. Departures from the airport to the Downtown San Francisco Terminal at Taylor and Ellis Streets every 15 minutes from 6:15AM to midnight and every 30 to 45 minutes from midnight to 3:30AM. Service from the Downtown Terminal every 15 minutes from 6:15AM to 10PM and every 30 to 45 minutes from 10PM to 2:45AM. Door-to-door service to major hotels every 30 minutes from 6AM to 9:45PM. *Downtown information, 673-2433, 495-8404, 800-222-4740. Marin Airporter, 461-4222*

Super Shuttle. 24-hour door-to-door van service with 3 hours advance notice. *700 16th St. 558-8500; in US 800-554-5543; in CA 800-553-8585*

Samtrans. Bus service from San Fransisco to SFO. *Transbay Terminal, 1st and Mission Sts. 761-7000*

Taxis. Cabs are easy to find at the airport, but the ride into the city will cost up to 4 times as much as the Airporter Bus or Super Shuttle.

Woodside

5 **Woodside Store.** The first store in the area, it was built in 1854 and still contains the original equipment and furnishings. *Open M-W & Su 12-5PM. Group tours can be arranged 1 week in advance. Tripp Rd. and Kings Mountain Rd. Woodside. 851-7615, 574-6441*

6 **Filoli Estate Tours, Woodside.** This is the Carrington family seat—the *Dynasty* Carrington's, that is, where exterior shots of the *Denver* mansion are shot for the weekly television series. The fabulous 654-acre estate was most recently owned by the **Roth Shipping (Matson Lines)** family and is now under the protection of the National Trust for Historic Preservation. The 43 room mansion was designed by **Willis Polk,** and the formal gardens are beyond description. *Tours from mid-Feb to late Nov. Woodside. 364-2880*

Half Moon Bay

7 **Half Moon Bay.** This seaside hamlet 30 miles south of San Francisco is the secret site of weekend brunches and picnics for locals, but not well-known to tourists. The coast is home to the annual *Fog Fest* and *Pumpkin Festival,* as well as a public golf course with a restaurant in a clubhouse designed by **Willis Polk.**

7 **San Benito House.** *Moderate.* Behind an unpretentious facade is a charming 12-room country inn. Furnishings were brought from France, and in the kitchen, **Carol Regan** (trained by **Roger Verge** near Nice) prepares the country French and Northern Italian dishes that are becoming famous. Lunch is served in the garden, and often on Sunday evenings, a whole lamb or pig will be roasted on the barbeque. Continental breakfast included in the rates. *356 Main St., Half Moon Bay. 726-3425*

7 **Old Thyme Inn.** *Moderate.* The name is derived from the adjoining herb garden with more than 50 varieties of herbs. Rooms are furnished with antiques, some have fireplaces and all but 2 have private baths. *Reduced rates on weekdays. 779 Main St., Half Moon Bay. 726-1616*

7 **Half Moon Bay Lodge.** *Moderate/expensive.* A new and attractive Best Western resort motel with a sweeping view of the ocean. The hacienda-style building also overlooks an 18-hole golf course and features a sauna, swimming pool and fireplaces in the bedrooms. *Hwy. 1, Half Moon Bay. 800-528-1234, 800-368-2468*

7 **The Princeton Inn.** $$ A former speakeasy, it is now a popular country-style restaurant offering fresh seafood and American cuisine. Dancing Friday and Saturday nights. *Capistrano Rd., Half Moon Bay. 728-7311*

7 **Mill Rose Inn.** *Expensive.* A lovely retreat set in a garden with more than 200 blooming rose bushes. The richly decorated rooms have private baths, canopy beds, wood-burning fireplaces and a complimentary champagne breakfast. *615 Mill St., Half Moon Bay. 726-9794*

Princeton-by-the-Sea

8 **Princeton-by-the-Sea.** Here you'll find a remarkable resemblance to Cape Cod in both architecture and terrain. There are excellent inns and bed and breakfast establishments.

8 **Pillar Point Inn.** *Moderate.* A Cape Cod-style bed and breakfast inn with 11 lovely rooms overlooking the water. The owner points out that his inn is the kind of place that attracts homesick Easterners. Every room has a private bath, fireplace, feather bed, TV set with video player, refrigerator and telephone. *380 Capistrano Rd., Princeton-by-the-Sea. 728-7377*

8 **Shorebird Restaurant.** $$ This looks more like the home of a prosperous New Englander than a West Coast seafood restaurant. Near the entrance is a rusty anchor, recovered from an old square rigger found in the rocks off Pillar Point. *390 Capistrano Rd., Princeton-by-the-Sea. 728-5541*

Menlo Park

9 **Sunset Magazine.** Exquisitely landscaped adobe buildings house the offices, test kitchens and crafts workshops of the magazine in a lush garden setting. *Tours M-F. Middlefield Rd. and Willow Rd., Menlo Park. 321-3600*

9 **Stanford Park Hotel.** *Expensive.* A new luxury hotel near the Stanford campus. Although bordering on the heavily trafficked El Camino, the rooms are sound-protected, spacious and well done in a quiet way. The hotel has a physical fitness room, sauna, swimming pool and whirlpool spa. The **Palm Cafe and Bar** features California cuisine. *100 El Camino Real, Menlo Park. 322-1234. Best Western, 800-528-1234. Western Lodging, 368-2468*

9 **Late for the Train.** ★★$$ This restaurant takes pride in serving only the freshest fruits and vegetables, grown in small local farms and gardens. They also serve only fresh fish and poultry and offer a different special every afternoon and evening, which usually includes a vegetable dish, fresh pasta and the daily fresh fish. A list of omelettes, hot dishes, sandwiches and salads is also available. This place is different, but absolutely delicious! *Open Tu-F 7AM-3PM, 5:30-10PM; Sa-Su 8:30AM-2:30PM, 5:30-10PM. 150 Middlefield Rd., Menlo Park. 321-6124*

Palo Alto

10 **Stanford University.** After the death of their only son in 1885, Mr. and Mrs. **Leland Stanford** gathered the finest talents of the day to create a university in memory of their child. This modest, hard-working couple had come to California at the middle of the 19th century and built a fortune from the transcontinental railroad. Much of their wealth went into Stanford University, adding lands and buildings while the couple lived and creating a trust that would guarantee the institution's quality after their death. **Frederick Law Olmsted,** noted landscape architect, laid out the original plan for the campus around the Quadrangle, and the Boston firm of **Shepley, Rutan and Coolidge** supervised early building. Many of these original structures were toppled by the 1906 earthquake but were soon rebuilt. In 1916 the school's academic structure underwent renovation; 26 departments within 7 schools were created. Little growth occurred during the next 3 decades, except the initiation of **Hoover Institute on War, Revolution and Peace.** Other independent institutes within the universtiy include the **Center for Research in International Studies,** the **Hansen Laboratory of Physics,** and the **Stanford Linear Accelerator Center.**

Today Stanford is home to a superb faculty and is ranked among the top schools in the nation by other college educators. On staff are 8 Nobel, 11 National Medal of Science and 4 Pulitzer prize winners. Enrollment, far below the number of applications, is approximately 12,000 students, comprised of about 7,000 undergraduate and 5,000 graduate students. The school is considered third nationally in overall scholastic standards; it has graduated 45 Rhodes scholars in the last 30 years. On the Stanford campus are:

Kresge Auditorium, School of Law (1975, Skidmore, Owings and Merrill).
Dinkelspiel Auditorium, Music Building (1957, Milton T. Plfueger; Spencer and Ambrose).
Tresidder Memorial Union. (1962, Spencer, Lee and Busse).
Hoover Tower, (1941, Bakewell and Brown).
Green Library, (1919, Bakewell and Brown; 1980, Helmuth, Obata, Kassabaum).
Annenberg Auditorium, (1969, John Carl Warnecke and Associates).
Art Gallery, (1917, Bakewell and Brown).
Cubberly Auditorium, School of Education, (1937, Bakewell and Brown).
Memorial Church, (1903, rebuilt after 1906 earthquake, 1913, Charles Allerton Coolidge, C.E. Hodges).
White Memorial Plaza, (1964, Thomas D. Church).
Skilling Auditorium, (1969, Spencer, Lee and Busse).
Terman Engineering Center, (1977, Harry Weese and Associates).
Medical Center, Stanford University Hospital, (1959, Edward Durrell Stone).
Medical Plaza, (1959, Wurster, Bernard and Emmons; Lawrence Halprin, landscape architect).
Museum, (1892, Shepley, Rutan and Coolidge).
Stanford Linear Accelerator, (1968, Aetron, Blume and Atkinson, Charles Luckman and Associates).
Quadrangle, (1891, Shepley, Rutan and Coolidge; Frank Law Olmsted, landscape architect).
House, 737 Frenchman's Road, (1937, Frank Lloyd Wright).

Stanford University Museum of Art. The museum is distinguished in its permanent collection of antique and Asian art, 18th and 19th century painting and graphics, and more than 100 sculptures by **Auguste Rodin.** The museum's changing exhibits are also on view in the university art gallery. A small museum shop offers books, postcards and catalogs. *General Collection Tours Tu 12:15PM & Su 2PM; Rodin Collection Tours W 12:15PM & Sa 2PM; Print Collection Tours Th 12:15PM.*

Stanford University Art Gallery. Exhibitions of contemporary art, mainly by students and California artists. *Open Tu-F 10AM-5PM; Sa Su 1-5PM. 497-2842*

11 Sundance, the Restaurant. ★ $$/$$$ A rather traditional restaurant serving steak, chicken and a variety of fresh fish. Their blackened red rockfish and cajun chicken are excellent and they also offer a selection of delicious samplers, happy hour

tasters, soups and salads as well. The quality here is superior. The Sundance claims to specialize in birthday and anniversary celebrations. *Open daily 11:30AM-2PM, 5-10PM. 1921 El Camino Real, Palo Alto. 321-6798*

11 **Stanford Shopping Center.** Bordered by El Camino, Arboretum and Palm, this popular, state-of-the-art shopping center is situated amidst a landscape of flowers, fountains, pleasant walkways, a frog pond and clock tower plaza. The center's major stores include **Emporium Capwell, I. Magnin, Macy's, Neiman Marcus, Nordstrom** and **Saks Fifth Avenue.** *Palo Alto.*

12 **NASA/Ames Research Center, Moffett Field.** Sponsors a fascinating tour of a wind tunnel, centrifuge and research aircrafts. Also, there are tours in Aeronautics, Astronomy and Life Sciences. Advance reservations are necessary. *Tours daily through summer months. Open M-F 9:30AM-2:45PM. Closed weekends and holidays. 965-6497*

13 **Marriott's Great America.** Northern California's response to Disneyland, Marriott's Great America is a family entertainment center containing, among other attractions, monster rollercoasters, theaters, carousels, boating, old railroads and the chance to meet Bugs Bunny and other Looney Tunes characters. The park is divided into different sections, each with its own theme. The most famous roller coaster is the **Demon,** a corkscrew loop affair. On its 1½ minute journey, it will turn you upside down 4 times, twice in loops, twice in corkscrews, race you through gorges and tunnels complete with flashing lights and demonic laughter, barrel you under crimson waterfalls and finally back to safety. Restaurants and cafes are sprinkled throughout the park along with tourist shops and facilities for lost parents. *Admission charge. Open daily during the summer and school holidays, closed Oct-March. Phone for exact hours. Located 40 miles south of San Francisco off Hwy. 101 at the Great American Pkwy. exit, Santa Clara. 408-988-1776*

14 **Santa Clara Marriott Hotel.** *Expensive.* An oasis just of Highway 101, 4 miles from the San Jose Airport and adjacent to their famous theme park. The hotel itself has a relaxed Mediterranean theme carried throughout, and all rooms have private balconies, free access to the tennis courts, indoor/outdoor swimming pool, hydrotherapy pool and complimentary limousine service to and from the airport. *Great America Pkwy., Santa Clara. 408-988-1500*

15 **Santa Cruz Mountain Wineries.** This premium winegrowing district spreads over parts of Santa Cruz, Santa Clara and San Mateo counties. Some of finest Cabernets and red wines are produced in the area. Highlights include: **Sunrise Winery** *(13100 Montebello Rd., Cupertino, 408-741-1310);* **Santa Cruz Mountain Vineyard** *(2300 Jarvis Rd., Santa Cruz, 408-426-6209);* **Mount Eden Vineyards** *(22020 Mount Eden Rd., Saratoga, 408867-5832);* **Martin Ray Vineyards** *(Saratoga, 408-978-9463); and* **David Bruce Winery** *(21439 Bear Creek Rd., Los Gatos, 408-354-4214).*

Marin County

Marin County enjoys a heritage as a haven for artists, writers and bohemians. It's a marvelous amalgamation of seaport, tourist attraction, yachting center, farm village, artist colony, bedroom community, public land and prison. Since the early 19th century, those who came to Marin have been looking for something different from what those who settled on the Peninsula or the East Bay wanted. One proof is in the kind of houses they built (and are still building), with high regard for the environment, usually with taste, clearing no forests, leveling no mountains. Yet, it was the exploitation of natural resources that built the first extensive railroad system enabling commuters to enjoy this area. Efforts to transport redwood lumber by rail instead of water did not really work out, but meanwhile towns sprung up all along the line until finally, in 1941, the **Golden Gate Bridge** and the automobile managed to do the railroads in. It is interesting to note that in recent years the pendulum has swung back again—ferries are becoming a favored way of commuting to avoid the heavy traffic on the bridge.

Sausalito is a popular year-round retreat for San Francisco working people, artists, writers and sailors. Some of the first homes in **Belvedere** and **Tiburon** were *arks*—houseboats used by boatmen as permanent dwellings or by yachtsmen as weekend moorings. Like Sausalito, this area grew into a summer colony at the turn of the century and these arks became more elaborate in style as they were supplied with water and fresh groceries by local merchants who rowed out to offer their wares. By 1910, many were beached where they are still being rented today. On one side of **Belvedere Island,** cod from the Alaska waters was processed in large buildings. But when fishing fell on hard times, these were converted to studios and apartments for artists. On the thickly wooded slopes of the island, there are stunning villas with storybook gardens. Belvedere is joined to the mainland by a causeway with a group of contemporary homes on the bordering lagoon. Sailboats rock at their moorings in front of most of these. The **Tiburon Peninsula** was once the southernmost extension of the **Reed Rancho** until **Dr. Benjamin Lyford**, Reed's son-in-law, tried to develop it into a model community called *Hygeia,* devoted to health and virtue. His *Garden of Eden* did not prosper, possibly because of an edict against kissing on the property!

Legend tells of an Indian chief who refused to yield to the Spanish and withdrew to an island off San Rafael. Eventually captured and baptized, he still rejected the menial labor at the Mission and, utilizing his native know-how of the Bay's winds and tides, built a boat to ferry paying passengers across the Golden Gate. He was called **El Marinero** (the sailor). The name was also applied to his island, and later to the peninsula north of the Gate. Sometime along the way it was shortened to **Marin.**

Hotels blue
Shops/Galleries purple
Parks/Outdoor spaces green
Museums/Architecture/Narrative black

1 **Point Bonita.** Marking the northern entrance to the **Golden Gate,** this light house rises 124-feet above the water. It was built in 1855 and reconstructed in 1877. No longer in use and *not open to the public.*

2 **Vista Point.** Located at the north end of the **Golden Gate Bridge.** A turn-off allows you to park and admire the view of Bay and city beyond, and to watch the freighters glide in and out of the Golden Gate. A favorite place for taking pictures. *Accessible only from the northbound lane of the bridge.*

3 **Marin Headlands.** First inhabited by the **Coast Miwok Indians,** then in 1817 by the Spanish. In 1838 most of it—20,000 acres—was granted to an English seaman, **William A. Richardson,** and named **Rancho Saucelito** (*Little Grove of Willows Ranch*).

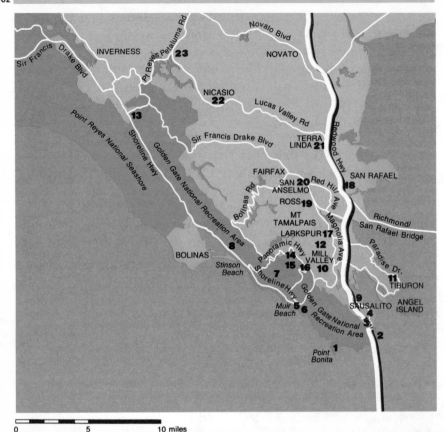

0   5   10 miles

After the Civil War, it became the property of the Federal government, which established military posts for defending the entrance to the bay: **Fort Baker, Fort Barry** and **Fort Cronkhite**. These emplacements and bunkers remain as macabre playground structures to clamber over and explore. The Headlands' location is unique: an enormous undeveloped wilderness within view of a big city. Beaches, woods, windswept rocky ridges and protected valleys are crisscrossed with trails that were old ranch or army roads. Most of the military buildings are abandoned now. Free ranger-guided walks take place on **Rodeo Beach** on weekends. Check schedules at the Ranger Station. **Note that swimming off the Headlands is very dangerous.** Water, restrooms, phone, but no food provided here. *For information on camping, trail maps and regulations in the Headlands, stop at the Ranger Station at Building 1050. 561-7612*

3 **Waldo Tunnel.** The northbound tunnel on Highway 101 has rainbows painted around the entrance and exit announcing your arrival in Marin County. Usually, even if San Francisco and the bridge are enshrouded in fog, the weather clears, magically it seems, when you pass through the tunnel.

Restaurants/Nightlife red
Hotels blue
Shops/Galleries purple
Parks/Outdoor spaces green
Museums/Architecture/Narrative black

Sausalito

4 **Sausalito.** This town of 7,000, whose name is Spanish for *little grove of willows,* is a popular get-away spot for the city-dwellers across the Bay. Since the **San Francisco Yacht Club** moved here, Sausalito has become a major recreational boating center. The village sprawls up the hillside, reminiscent of the French Riviera.

4 **Sushi-Ran.** ★ $$ As good as some of the best San Francisco sushi bars, but much easier for the first-timer to handle. The bite-size preparations of raw fish and rice are listed on a menu in English, and the helpful staff speaks fluent English. *Japanese. Open daily 5-10:30PM. 107 Caledonia St., Sausalito. 332-3620*

4 **Gatsby's.** $$ A popular Sausalito hangout featuring Chicago-style deep-dish pizza. The thick crust is excellent, but the toppings lack flavor. Also hamburgers. *American. Open Su-Th 11:30AM-11:45PM, F & Sa 11:30AM-1AM. 39 Caledonia St., Sausalito 332-4500*

4 **Scoma's.** $$ The best of the Bay Area Scoma's fish restaurant chain. Right on the water in Sausalito for a great view. Best choices include the fresh catches. *American. Open daily M-Sa 11:30AM-3PM, 5:30-10PM; Su 11:30AM-3PM, 5:30-9:30PM. 558 Bridgeway, Sausalito. 332-9551*

4 **Alta Mira Hotel.** *Moderate.* The place every Bay Area visitor seems to remember, usually because of the view from the terrace, which is high on the hillside looking at Belvedere Island and the San Francisco skyline. Reservations well in advance are a must. The rooms are decorated in a somewhat indifferent style, perhaps relying on the fact that it's the view from the window that interests the occupant. *125 Bulkley Av., Sausalito. 332-1350*

4 **Handcraft from Europe.** The original store is situated next to **Zack's** restaurant on the waterfront and run by the **Weiners.** It sells thousands of different sorts of imported trimmings: braids, laces, ribbons. There is also an extraordinary choice of buttons. Selecting here is difficult. You'll want everything. *Open M-Sa 10AM-5:30PM, Su noon-5PM. 1210 Bridgeway, Sausalito. 332-1633*

4 **Casa Madrona Hotel.** *Expensive.* Just a bit up the street from the Alta Mira but hidden amongst the trees and flowers overlooking the yacht harbor is the former home of a lumber baron resplendent with marble fireplaces, stained glass windows, wrought iron grillwork and stunning views. It's a comfortable and inviting reminder of the life that was lived during the late 19th century. A multi-level 16-room addition, dubbed *New Casa Madrona*, spills over the hills and extends down to Bridgeway. Each room is done with a different theme and showcases 16 top Bay Area designers, including **Alberto Pinto, Christa Hertzka, Wayne Ruga,** and **Lyn Bellati.** Many of the rooms have fireplaces, decks and superb views. Everywhere there is the ambience of warmth and privacy so typical of the best of the European-style country inns. Chef **Steve Simmons** creates fresh and imaginative California cuisine in the restaurant. *801 Bridgeway, Sausalito. 332-0502*

4 **Angelino's.** ★★ $$/$$$ Roman cuisine with specialties of mussels, veal, steamed clams and tortellini. Extensive wine list of Napa Valley wines and Italian imports. Some water-view tables. *Open daily 11AM-11PM. 621 Bridgeway, Sausalito. 331-5225*

4 **Caffe Trieste.** $ This sister of SF'S **Trieste** offers espresso, pastries, antipasti and salads, sandwiches, beer and wine. Specialties include various luscious flavors of gelato and *granita*, a sweet frozen espresso drink. *Open M-Th 7AM-11:30PM, F & Sa 7AM-midnight, Su 7AM-11PM. 1000 Bridgeway, Sausalito. 332-7770*

For one of the best views of the Bay Area—1,000 feet high in the sky—take the **Slice Blimp,** which cruises at 40 mph.

Muir Beach

5 **Muir Beach State Park.** A quiet, undeveloped beach. Hike the lookout hill above for the exercise and the view. *Parking. Chemical closets. Admission free. Open daily 9AM-1 hour after sunset. Hwy. 1.*

6 **The Pelican Inn.** *Moderate/expensive.* A theatrical and romantic getaway that would make a marvelous movie set for a cloak and dagger drama. This inn, built in the early 1970s, completely captures the spirit of a 16th century English roadhouse of the West Country. And indeed it is a copy of just such an establishment, adroitly built with old (and some imported) timbers, fireplaces, a priest's hole and Tudor pub. Host **Charles Felix** comes from a lengthy line of English innkeepers and has assembled an English staff as well. Situated at Muir Beach a short drive from the Golden Gate Bridge, the Pelican waits for its visitors amidst an old-fashioned garden, with easy access to Muir Beach and the redwood groves of Muir Woods. There are miles of hiking and riding trails. The 6 cozy bedrooms are furnished with antiques of the Tudor era. Authentic pub fare and a traditionally hearty English breakfast are available. There is often entertainment, such as Shakespearean readings by visiting professional actors. *For weekend reservations, it is important to apply well in advance. Rooms are more likely to be available during the week. Restaurant open Tu-F 6-9PM, Sa & Su 5:30-9PM. Muir Beach. 383-6000*

7 **Tennessee Valley.** A narrow, isolated valley with a gentle 2-mile trail leading to a small beach at Tennessee Cove. *Ranger station, 383-7717*

Stinson Beach

8 **Stinson Beach State Park.** When lifeguards are on duty from June to September, swimming is permitted. This smooth expanse of sandy beach is very popular on warm days with city residents as well as Marinites. Dogs are not allowed. There are picnic and barbecue facilities and showers and restrooms. Snack bars and grocery stores in the town are within walking distance of the beach. Fog can linger over the beach even when it is clear on the other side of the hills—for weather information call 868-1922. *Admission free. Open daily 9AM-1 hour after sunset. Hwy. 1. For information, call 868-0942*

8 **Claudia Chapline Gallery.** Contemporary art in all media—painting, sculpture and drawings. California artists are featured with special shows by other artists. *Open Sa & Su 1-5PM and by appointment. 3445 Shoreline Hwy., Stinson Beach. 868-2308*

8 **Stinson Beach Hillside House.** (1963) **Edward (Ted) Cullinan,** an English architect, built this house for a friend while studying architecture at Berkeley. Like many of his houses in England, it consists of a simple diagram of servant and served spaces arranged in a linear fashion. The materials consist of concrete blocks for the service wall—

bedrooms, kitchen, bathrooms and storage—and wood-frame and plate glass for the living/dining/sitting rooms. A precursor of the neo-primitivist houses being built now. *Private residence. Off Panoramic Hwy. above Stinson Beach.*

8 **Audubon Canyon Ranch.** Three miles north of Stinson Beach on Highway 1, this 1,000-acre bird sanctuary rises off **Bolinas Lagoon.** It is a rookery for great blue herons and American egrets. In 1968, the ranch became a Registered National Landmark. Over 150 species of birds, many of which nest in the tops of the redwood trees and feed in the lagoon below, can be seen here. Mounted telescopes on a nearby hill are provided for close-up viewing. An old white-painted ranch house built in 1875 is the park's headquarters. A nature book shop and exhibition area are located in an old milking barn. *Trails open to the public during nesting season, March 1 through July 4, Sa, Su, holidays. 4900 Shoreline Hwy. For information and to arrange special group tours, phone M-F 9AM-5PM, 383-1644*

9 **The Bay Model.** Completed in 1957, the Bay/Delta Hydraulic Model was built by the U.S. Army Corps of Engineers (San Francisco District) and it *is* worth a visit! It serves as a laboratory where engineers study and experiment with the effects of man and nature on the San Francisco Bay and the Sacramento/San Joaquin Delta. The model operates on 250,000 gallons of water to reproduce in scale the rise and fall of tides, currents, and mixing of salt and fresh water. The Model is located in a **Visitor Center,** a remodeled barrel-vaulted World War II-era warehouse that formerly housed parts for Liberty ships. Elaborate multi-media displays on the subject of water and the Model are connected by a series of ramps. *Open Tu-Sa 9AM-4PM. Admission free. 2100 Bridgeway, Sausalito. Watch for a sign on the right going north. Drive down a side road. Parking is signposted. The Visitor Center is situated along the wharf. 332-3870*

9 **Heath Ceramics.** Stoneware tile and pottery are made on the premises. The *seconds* shop (the imperfections are usually imperceptible) sells smooth, classic California ceramics. Casseroles, dishes, bowls and tiles: all make nice gifts to take back home. *Open daily 10AM-5PM. 400 Gate 5 Rd. 332-3732*

Mill Valley

10 **Giramonti.** ★ $$$ A popular family-run Italian restaurant in Mill Valley, where **Adriana,** the chef, puts her stamp on everything. Excellent fresh fish served in various forms, particularly interesting on pasta. The veal is tender; the sauces run under-seasoned. *Italian. 655 Redwood Hwy., Mill Valley. 383-3000. (Also try **Adriana's** in San Rafael, run by the same owner: 454-5000)*

10 **Susan Cummings Gallery.** You will discover wonderful and varied specimens of art, glass and ceramics in this friendly gallery in downtown Mill Valley. *Open M-Sa 10AM-6PM, Su noon-5PM. 32 Miller Av., Mill Valley. 383-1512*

10 **Sweetwater.** This is where some of the pretty people of Marin mellow out. The club's music is safe jazz or rock. *Shows M-Sa 9:30PM, Su 7, 11PM. Cover charge. Two drink minimum. No one under 21 admitted. 153 Throckmorton Av., Mill Valley. 388-2820*

10 **Mill Valley Library.** By **Wurster, Bernardi** and **Emmons.** A great barn-like space built out of redwoods set in a redwood forest. *Throckmorton Av., Mill Valley.*

10 **Marin Outdoor Art Center.** (1905, Bernard Maybeck) This simple wood building has trusses projecting through the roof expressing the structure both externally and internally. *Buena Vista and Blithedale, Mill Valley.*

10 **Ristorante Lucca.** ★ $$ An outstanding Italian menu and an excellent wine list. Delicious dishes feature generous portions of Tuscan cooking, served in what was once a delightful private residence. Lots of seafood and homemade pasta. *Italian. Open daily 5-10:30PM. Reservations essential. 24 Sunnyside, Mill Valley. 388-4467*

10 **Hilarita Reed Lyford Residence.** (1874) A romantic gingerbread-style house that has been beautifully restored. Now occupied by the Audubon Society. *376 Tiburon Blvd. off Hwy. 101, Mill Valley.*

10 **Perry's.** ★ ★ $$ Chef **Heidi Krahling** proves that Perry's formula works anywhere. This bistro has a view of sorts, but what's most important is the service and food (a few old Perry's San Francisco favorites plus other innovations). Grilled meats are juicy and satisfying, the omelettes about the best anywhere, and don't miss the cottage fried potatoes—superb thin, crunchy wafers. The upstairs dining suite, **Butler's,** serves top notch grilled meats and fish, light pastas and homemade breads. *Open M-F 11:30AM-2:30PM, 5:30-10PM; Sa 5:30-10PM. 625 Redwood Hwy., Mill Valley. 383-1900*

11 **Sam's Anchor Cafe.** $$ The place to come for hamburgers and drinks—right on the water with a great view of the sailboats on San Francisco Bay. A long-time institution among San Franciscans. *American. Open daily. 27 Main St., Tiburon. 435-4527*

Corte Madera

12 **Corte Madera Town Center.** The original shopping center, dating from the early 1950s, had been completely transformed by **Field and Gruzen Architects** into a Post Modern stage set—Universal Studios come to Marin! Rather more down market than **The Village** across the freeway, the center contains the usual array of shops including a very high tech **Wherehouse** record and video store. Generally the designs are quite skillful, with classical moldings added to the original boxy stores and sequences of urban streets and squares creating the illusion of an urban fabric. *Corte Madera at the Tamalpais Dr. exit.*

12 **The Village Shopping Center.** (1986, Jerde Partnership) One of Marin's newest shopping centers, built on what was previously marshland, this is intended for the upscale market of Marin County. Architecturally, it is planned as a ¼ mile long street linking 2 anchor department stores, **Macy's** and **Nordstrom.** At the center of the complex is a lookout tower that offers views out over the salt marshes to the Bay and San Quentin Prison. Several of the stores are by local architects, including **Arlequin,** a children's store designed by **Toby Levy.** *Paradise Dr. exit, Corte Madera.*

---

13 **Olema Valley.** This marks the northern boundary of the **Golden Gate National Recreation Area.** Old farm buildings, grassy hills and wooded canyons offer a variety of undeveloped scenery and hiking trails. Trails are fairly long and steep. Restrooms and picnic tables. *663-1092*

14 **Mt. Tamalpais State Park.** Mt. Tamalpais is to Marin County what the Golden Gate Bridge is to San Francisco: symbol and pride. Its undulating profile seen from the Bay side portrays the legendary *Sleeping Maiden.* The state park was established in 1928 and includes more than 900 acres. *Mt. Tam* has 3 peaks: West Peak, 2,560 feet; East Peak, 2,571 feet; and Middle Peak, 2,470 feet. The views from the summit are dramatic. They extend out to the **Farallon Islands** on the ocean's horizon, across to San Francisco glittering in the sun, east to Mt. Diablo and the East Bay cities, and on clear days, beyond the Sacramento Valley to the snow-capped peaks of the Sierra Nevada Mountains 200 miles away. From 1896 to 1930, the **Mill Valley and Mt. Tamalpais Railway,** known as the *Crookedest Railroad in the World,* carried tourists along an 8-mile track that had 281 curves. In one place the slope was so steep the track made 5 parallel double-knots, traveling 2,000 feet to rise 100 feet. The area contains several macro-environments—grassland, chaparral, oak savannah, laurel groves, windswept ridges, secluded valleys and trails. Dogs are not allowed on trails in the park. Park Headquarters is located at **Pan Toll.** Information, trail maps and guides are available there. There is also a campsite. Picnic areas are located at **Bootjack** and **East Peak.** During the dry summer months, the fire hazard on Mt. Tam is extreme, so it's important to heed the fire regulations posted in the park. **Mountain Theatre,** a natural amphitheater terraced with seats of serpentine rock, is set in a pine grove 2,000 feet overlooking hills and water, a magnificent setting for the annual **Mountain Play** presented each May. *The Park opens half an hour before sunrise and closes half an hour after sunset. 810 Panoramic Hwy. Park Headquarters, 388-2070*

15 **Muir Woods National Monument.** A world-famous stand of virgin coastal redwoods. In 1907, the ravine came close to being flooded and used as a reservoir, but was saved when **William Kent** bought the canyon, named it after the Scots naturalist, **John Muir,** and deeded it to the American people. The trees, centuries old, soar more than 200 feet. Unusual redwood formations, burls and albino shoots, as well as ferns, wildflowers and other trees make this a fascinating environment. The tallest tree, a 273-foot Douglas fir, was named the *William Kent Memorial Tree.* Self-guiding maps lead you through the loop trail. Picnicking is not allowed. The Visitors' Center has a snack bar and gift shop. The parking lot in front fills up quickly. *Open daily 8AM-sunset. Admission charge. 388-2595*

16 **Dipsea Trail.** The second oldest footrace in the U.S. In 1904, a couple of fellows from the San Francisco Olympic Club decided to run from Mill Valley over the southern ridge of Mt. Tam to Stinson Beach for a swim. Since then, a race along this trail has been held each June. Only the fittest survive the arduous 7-mile route, climbing up and down hills which have been given such daunting names as *Suicide, Dynamite, Cardiac, Insult, The Stairs, Windy Gap,* and *Steep Ravine. Larkspur.*

Larkspur

17 **Larkspur Ferry Terminal.** (1973, Braccia, Der Brer and Heglund) This triangular steel space frame creates a light, airy and symbolic gateway to the San Francisco ferries. Two sides are for ferries, the third is for buses and dropoff for vehicles. *Sir Francis Drake Blvd. East off Hwy. 101, Larkspur.*

17 **Lark Creek Inn.** ★ ★ $$/$$$ In 1888, a charming house was erected on the banks of Lark Creek. In the 1920s, the house was abandoned and rumor had it that a pair of lonely ghosts drifted through the dusty rooms. In the early 70s the gracious yellow and white house by Lark Creek became a restaurant. Nestled in a shady cluster of trees off of Magnolia Avenue, the restaurant is now owned by **Roland Gotti** (co-owner of **Ernie's** in San Francisco) and is well established as one of the top 100 restaurants of Northern California. Chef **Alga Samana,** trained at the Hyatt in Tahiti and the Sheraton in Maui, features local produce with grilled seafood and meats. House specialties such as roast duckling with strawberry or orange sauce and herbed fettucine with porcini mushrooms are not only beautifully prepared but exquisite to look at. The bar area is vintage 1930, with old photographs and memorabilia from San Francisco's **Land's End** and **Playland at the Beach.** The **Lillian Russell Room** is upstairs, reserved for more intimate dinner parties. A small garden area beside the creek shaded by enormous redwoods is a lovely spot for warm weather dining, afternoon or evening. *Open Tu-Th 11:30AM-2:30PM, 5:30-9:30PM; F 11:30AM-2:30PM, 5-10:30PM; Sa 5-10:30PM. 234 Magnolia Av., Larkspur. 924-7766*

17 **Larkspur Landing.** A cluster of some 60 white-trimmed, gray clapboard shops and restaurants. This Cape Cod-style development occupies the site of a former rock quarry. (You can see the old wood cladding of the demolished rock-crushing building re-used in the **Pelican Inn,** an English pub at Muir Beach.)

The best thing about Larkspur Landing is getting there. And the best way is to take the ferry boat from the **San Francisco Ferry Building** to the **Larkspur Ferry Terminal,** located on the other side of the pedestrian footbridge from the Landing. *By car, take Hwy. 101 to the Richmond Bridge exit. Most of the stores are open M-Th & Sa 10AM-6PM, F 10AM-9PM, Su noon-5PM. Some are open later, including the restaurants. Plenty of free parking. Ferry service information and schedules, from San Francisco and southern Marin, 332-6600; from northern Marin, 453-2100*

San Rafael

18 **Marin County Civic Center.** (1957-72) One of **Frank Lloyd Wright's** last works, it rests like a spaceship between the gently curving Marin foothills next to the freeway. Its curved blue roof, golden spire and pale pink walls contrast with the high foliage of the hillsides. You enter from below, driving under the archway beneath the buildings, catching a glimpse of its airy interior. Escalators take you to the long, open galleries that lead to the various county offices or to the circular library that acts as a pivot between the 2 wings. Walk up to the lookout point next to the library to see over the roof of the county courthouse and the ornamental gardens below. *Hwy. 101 at North San Pablo Rd., just north of San Rafael.*

18 **Commerce Clearing House Building.** (1968, Marquis and Stoller) In contrast to the Frank Lloyd Wright Civic Center across the valley, this building is square and angular, sitting atop its hill. Made out of poured-in-place concrete, it incorporates parking within its form on the lower level with offices above. *Northgate off Manuel Freitas Pkwy., San Rafael.*

18 **Rice Table.** ★ ★ \$\$ Indonesian food is rare in the Bay Area, and this is one of the best. The 12-dish *rijstaffel* (rice table) gives you a sampling of many of the great Indonesian specialties. Moderate prices considering the amount of food. *Indonesian. Open Th-Sa 5:30-10PM, Su 5-9PM. 1617 4th St., San Rafael. 456-1808*

18 **Maurice et Charles.** ★ ★ \$\$\$/\$\$\$\$ An outstanding French restaurant. Nothing *nouvelle* about their heavy sauces, rich with butter and cream, but they're made perfectly. The lovely dining room presided over by

Maurice, who runs from table to kitchen to table, never missing a thing. If you're lucky, they'll have game on the menu—wild boar here is a specialty. The wine list is expensive and disappointing. *French. Open Tu-Sa 6:30-9PM. 901 Lincoln Av. 456-2010*

18 **Cafe Tango.** ★ ★ \$\$ An alluring cafe offering exotic Spanish *tapas* (hors d'oeuvres), such as *empanadas* (Argentine pastries filled with choice of beef, chicken or cheese), *Butifarra amb Mongetes al Allioli* (grilled sausage with white beans and allioli), and *Gambas al Ajillo* (grilled prawns in garlic sauce). The Tango offers varieties of *paella*, but, Chef **Antonio Buendia** prepares a different 4-course Spanish dinner each night. The white-washed adobe walls adorned with colorful shawls are the entrancing backdrop for Tango dancing every Tuesday evening. The international wine bar boasts the largest selection of Spanish wine, sherry and champagne on the West Coast. Cafe Tango also offers classes in Spanish and Argentinian food and wine. *Open daily 11AM-11PM. 1230 4th St., San Rafael. 459-2721*

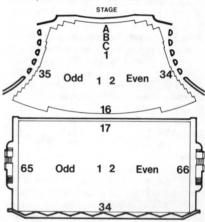

18 **Marin Veteran's Memorial Auditorium.** The auditorium is home for the Marin Symphony and Opera Companies. In addition, the Marin Ballet plays here in July and around the Christmas season. You'll also find headliners like **Joel Grey** popping up when they're in the Bay Area. Broadway touring shows also use the 2,089-seat house. An added plus: the auditorium is part of the **Marin Civic Center**, beautifully designed by none other than **Frank Lloyd Wright.** *Civic Center Dr., San Rafael. 472-3500*

18 **Adriana's.** ★ ★ \$\$\$ **Adriana Giramonti's** namesake and newest success is a pleasing family restaurant with excellent seafood, melt-in-your-mouth pasta, great cold dishes and healthy portions. The *Insalata di Mare,* a chilled salad with a splendid array of poached fish, is especially recommended. The spacious dining room with floor to ceiling windows is contemporary and colorful, with rose-colored walls and splashy floral paintings. The dining area is large with many tables so that it can be noisy. *Reservations recommended. Open M-F 11:30AM-2PM, 5-9PM; Sa 11:30AM-2PM, 5-11PM. From San Francisco, take Francisco Blvd. Exit, turn right on Bellam Rd. and then left at the 1st traffic light. 999 Anderson, San Rafael. 454-8000*

18 Richmond-San Rafael Bridge. (1957) Caltrans. A rollercoaster of a bridge, 4½ miles long between Marin and Contra Costa Counties, it rises to its maximum height over the 2 shipping lanes and dips in between. In addition, the bridge curves at the Marin end.

18 Daniel's. ★ $$$ An unpretentious family-style French restaurant run by Chef **Claude Colombe,** a veteran of **Ernie's** and **Maurice et Charles** restaurants. The deep blue dining room with copper accents lit by candle lanterns create a cool and restful atmosphere in which to enjoy these splendid regional delicacies of France. Dishes such as duck sauteed with cherry brandy sauce and *veal medallions Normande* are superb, served with flair and generous portions. *Reservations recommended. Open M 11:30AM-2:30PM; Tu-F 11:30AM-2:30PM, 5:30-10PM; Sa & Su 5:30-10PM. Plenty of parking in the rear of the building. 1131 4th St., San Rafael. 457-5288*

19 Le Coquelicot. ★ $$/$$$ One of the Bay Area's most interesting French restaurants, serving *nouvelle cuisine* with a South Pacific touch. A real bargain for their elaborate fixed-price dinner, and a reasonable wine list to boot. If you go there when they're having squid stuffed with fish mousse, count yourself lucky. Only the desserts, which look great, taste disappointing. A pretty, relaxed place. *French. Open Tu-Sa 11:30AM-2PM, 6-10PM. 18 Poplar Av., Ross. 707-833-6326*

20 San Francisco Theological Seminary. A Richardsonian set of buildings built out of stone and situated like a castle on top of a hill overlooking the valley. *Mariposa off Bolinas Rd., San Anselmo.*

21 Lo Coco's. ★ ★ $/$$ Shopping center pizzeria serving nothing less than the Bay Area's best pizza made by 3 Sicilian brothers. Soft, pillowy cheese, a crust that stays perfectly crisp and a choice of lots of different toppings. *Italian. Open Tu-Th 4-10PM, F & Sa 4-10:30PM, Su 4-9:30PM. 631 Del Granado Rd. off Freitas Pkwy., Terra Linda. 472-3323*

Whale Watching. The whales can be seen swimming past the San Francisco coastline on their southern migratory journey to breed in Baja, California, from late December through April and on their return trip to their summer feeding ground in the Bering Sea. It's a fascinating sight. If you whale-watch from land, the best place is from **Point Reyes in Marin County.** Bring binoculars for a good look at them. Boat tours are also available.

22 Nicasio School House. (1871) A little red school house—literally so—this cruciform planned framed school house is painted bright red with white trim. *Private residence. Take Lucas Valley Rd. from Hwy. 101 to Nicasio on your way to the Cheese Factory.*

Point Reyes

23 Station House Cafe. $$ A good place to stop after hiking at nearby Point Reyes. Excellent homemade soups, salads and desserts and marvelous fresh-baked breads. A real honest community restaurant where lots of locals come to eat. *American. Open M, W-Su 8AM-9PM. Main St., Point Reyes. 663-1515*

23 Marin French Cheese Company. Known as *The Cheese Factory.* The grounds make an idyllic spot to have a picnic. This pastoral setting in the midst of Marin's lovely rolling hills is reminiscent of the French countryside. The factory has been operated by a single family for 4 generations. They sell their own cheese under the *Rouge et Noir* label, (Camembert, Schloss and Brie) and other snacks as well. Picnic tables dot their lawn which spreads along a duck pond and borders a winding creek. About 1¼ hours' drive from San Francisco and well worth the trip. *Tours daily every hour between 10AM-4PM. Open daily 9AM-5PM. 7500 Redhill Rd. (also called the Petaluma Point Reyes Rd.) 707-762-6001*

BESTS

Stephen Simmons
Chef, Casa Madrona

Late-night sushi at **Kabuto** on Geary for cold sakki, uni and halibut fin.

Oysters and Champagne at **Stars** before the opera and hot soufflés afterwords.

Cafe Pranzo in San Rafael for quesadillas, tattomari and oven pizzas.

Sunday afternoon at **Domain Chandon** in Napa Valley, under the tutelage of Jerry Comfort, for Champagne, chocolate bag, sweetbreads and truffle juice and lobster lasagne.

Tadich Grill in San Francisco for Beck's light, deep-fried scallops and blanched french fries.

E Street Cafe in San Rafael for the tapas sampler plate and old East Indian sherry.

Muffins and Saturday brunch at **Joanne's** in South San Francisco.

Top of the Mark restaurant at the **Mark Hopkins Hotel** for *veuve cliquot* and cayenne peanuts.

Sam's Anchor Cafe in Tiburon for Sunday brunch. There is a 2 hour wait, but the view makes it worth it.

The best—and most expensive—breakfast in town at **Campton Place Hotel:** homemade breads, hot chocolate and exquisite pancakes.

The valleys of the northern **Wine Country** stretch from the Pacific coast to the Sierra Nevadas, carpeting the sea-to-mountain area with more than 60,000 acres of grape vineyards.

Fabled **Napa & Sonoma** counties are just an hour north of San Francisco. They are dotted with nearly 200 wineries producing such premium wines as Chardonnay, Cabernet Sauvignon, Zinfandel and Pinot Noir, as well as charming bed and breakfast inns and excellent restaurants. A few days of wine tasting, bike riding and even hot air ballooning in the Wine Country should top the day trip list of any visit to the Bay Area. September and October are the height of the grape harvest and the aroma of fermenting wine is everywhere. (This is also the most crowded time for touring, and advance reservations are a must.) Most wineries offer tours through the storage casks, some underground in the limestone caves carved out long ago by Chinese coolie laborers. Many farmers and craftsmen in the area will sell their products directly to the consumer at bargain prices. Heading home from a wine country weekend, you will see signs for apple cider, jams, nuts, fresh vegetables and fruits, pumpkins and Christmas trees.

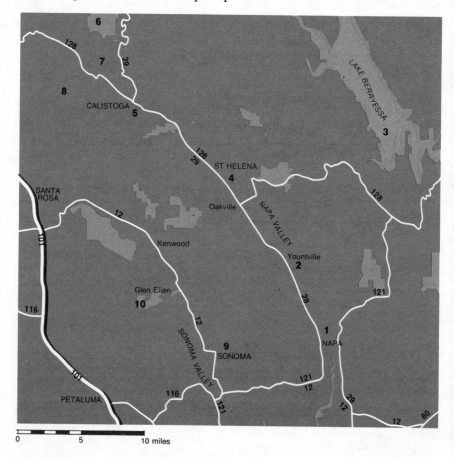

Wine Country Information

Wine Institute. Information on wines and tours. *415-986-0878*

CA Wine Tours Inc. *707-963-5205*

Concierge. A guest service providing professional help on everything from accommodations to gourmet picnics. *707-944-1250*

Bed & Breakfast Exchange. *707-942-5900*

Bed & Breakfast Referral. *707-257-1051*

Napa Valley, 35 miles in length, was once inhabited by 6 Indian tribes who were not able to converse with one another in a shared language, although separated by just a few *stones throws*. They lived in huts of wild swamp grass and tree boughs called *wickups* and named their valley *Napa,* meaning fish.

When Spanish explorers arrived, the valley was divided into 9 ranchos, each one becoming famous in its own right for its own special brand of hospitality. The Europeans introduced the fig, olive and grapevines and the golden mustard that still cover the valley floor in spring. The soil was rich and the climate superior, encouraging an increasing variety of crops as well as grazing livestock.

Today, many of these crops—like the prune and walnut—have given way to the vineyards climbing up the hills on both sides of the narrow valley. Grape acres now total 29,000. It is no wonder. The yearly adult per capita consumption of table wines in the U.S. has doubled in the past 10 years. In 1980, over 400 million gallons were consumed. From less than 30 bonded wineries in 1971, Napa County now has 155. And although the wine industry employs relatively few workers, it is still the county's biggest source of income. The State of California produces more than 90 percent of all U.S. wines and Napa County has a major stake in that production.

1 **Napa Chamber of Commerce.** Represents both Napa County and Napa Valley and delights in making information available to visitors. *P.O. Box 636, Napa 94557. 707-226-7455*

1 **Beazley House.** *Moderate.* In the heart of a fine old neighborhood with tree-lined streets and surrounded by other dignified homes, this house has had few owners since it was built in 1902, therefore maintaining its original character and half-acre grounds. There are 6 oversized guest rooms with high ceilings, comfortable period furnishings, interesting decor and quantities of handmade quilts. The master bedroom has a fireplace and a half bath; every 2 rooms generally share a bath. Breakfast of fresh fruits, home baked muffins. A 2 night stay is required on weekends. *1910 1st St., Napa. 707-257-1649*

1 **Napa Fairgrounds. Spring Fair** in April features a fiddling contest, 4-H animal exhibits, highland dancers, a high school rodeo, a horse show, Renaissance games for children, a demolition derby and a children's circus. **County Fair** in August ranks among the best in the country. *575 3rd St. off Silverado Trail in Napa.*

SILVERADO

1 **Silverado Country Club.** *Deluxe.* A luxury resort complex, handily located for touring the vineyards, has been built on the original 1,200-acre estate of Civil War General **John Miller.** His mansion, newly expanded, serves as clubhouse, with a commanding view of huge oak trees, palms and a panorama of hills and mountains beyond. There are clusters of studios and apartments designed to put a premium on privacy with patios and balconies, grouped around 8 swimming pools, 2 championship golf courses and 20 tennis courts. The **Silverado Dining Room** is famous for Sunday brunch and elegant continental cuisine. Overlooking the gardens is the **Royal Oak** restaurant, which features prime beef, live Maine lobster and other seafood in a medieval setting of antlers, dark oak, copper and tapestries. The **Silverado Bar and Grill** has informal service

at breakfast and lunch. *1600 Atlas Peak Rd., Napa. 707-255-2970, 800-227-1117*

1 **Coombe's Residence.** *Moderate.* Built in 1852, this house on the edge of downtown Napa is one of the oldest surviving residences in the area. Antique furnishings are balanced nicely with comfortable chairs and sofas, while the bedrooms are distinguished by exceptionally fine hand-pressed linens, lace-trimmed pillows and white duvets on the brass beds. Four rooms share 2½ baths. Continental breakfast, swimming pool and jacuzzi. *720 Seminary, Napa. 707-257-0789*

1 **Gallery Osgood.** *Moderate.* Drawing on recipes from a cookbook collection of over 400 volumes, artist and innkeeper **Joan Osgood Moehrke** serves her guests the most lavish gourmet breakfasts in the valley, and since she has so many returnees, she keeps notes so that they can count on savoring a different menu with each visit. There is original art throughout this charming 1898 redwood Queen Anne and fresh flowers from the garden everywhere. A recent addition to the garden is a gazebo in a setting of camellia trees, bound to be a popular background for the outdoor weddings Joan caters. Three delightful rooms and a shared bath. *2230 First St., Napa. 707-224-0100*

1 **La Boucane.** ★ $$$ Here is a small country inn serving classic French haute cuisine. Specialities range from prawns *provencale* and escargot to *souffle glacé praliné.* The setting is understated but pleasant. *French. Open M-Sa 6-10PM. Closed Jan. 1778 2nd St., Napa. 707-253-1177*

BESTS

Deirdre De Corsia
Concierge
Meadowood Resort and Country Club

When in the Napa Valley, don't miss:

Oakville Grocery, Oakville.

Vanderbilts in St. Helena for shopping.

Meadowood Resort in St. Helena.

Calistoga Spa for mud, mud, mud.

Chateau Montelena in Calistoga for wine, wine, wine.

1 Joseph Mathews Winery Complex. The foundation for this winery building was laid in 1880, becoming the seventh winery in the valley. Joseph Mathews himself completed the structure 2 years later, cutting the stone by hand to build his walls 2-feet thick. His wines became highly regarded, especially a prize-winning sherry which was made in the section of the winery now housing the **Sherry Oven Restaurant.** There is now a tasting room where the various Mathews award-winning wines may be sampled and purchased (these are for sale only at the complex), as well as a selection of other mementos of the wine country. *1727 Main St., Napa. 707-226-3777*

Within the complex are:

Sherry Oven Restaurant and Seafood Bar. ★ ★$$ On the main level of this historic building, you will find an excellent seafood restaurant featuring fresh oysters, clams, shrimp and other seasonal specialties, a full bar and an outdoor dining patio. On the upper level, the dining room is more formal, and you can view the working winery from windows cut into one of the walls. The cuisine is American, with a hint of French, and concentrates on what is available in fresh seafood, poultry and fowl, game and beef that is dry aged 18 days before preparation. *Open M-Th 11:30AM-2:30PM, 5:30-10PM; F & Sa 11:30AM-2:30PM, 5:30-11PM. 707-226-3777*

Hennessey House Bed and Breakfast. *Expensive.* Formerly the residence of a Napa County physician, this Queen Anne Victorian has 9 rooms each with private bath, Queen-sized beds with old-world featherbeds and quilts, antique furniture of the period and many other details of Victorian elegance. The carriage house rooms have whirlpool tubs and 2 have fireplaces. An old-fashioned country breakfast is included, served in the large dining room with a rare, hand-painted tin ceiling. *141 1727 Main St., Napa. 707-226-3774*

1 Wild Horse Valley Ranch. The most extensive horse riding facility in northern California. It includes race track, polo field, cross country jumping course and 50 miles of trails. Riding school for beginners to advanced. *5 miles east of Napa. 707-224-0727*

Yountville

2 Yountville. Although almost half way into the valley as you drive from San Francisco, emotionally this is where the wine country begins. This is where **George Yount** came in search of new frontiers, and where he settled to become a close compatriot of **General Vallejo.** Yount was the first U.S. citizen to be ceded a Mexican land grant— the 12,000 acres comprising the heart of Napa Valley called **Caymus Rancho.**

2 Napa Valley Lodge. *Expensive.* This is no mere motel. All 55 rooms in this Best Western hostelry are spacious, sound-proofed and have balconies with spectacular views of the surrounding vineyards and hills. There is tasteful use of brilliant Mediterranean tile. There are 2-room suites for families, an extra large swimming pool, hot whirlpool spa and bicycle rentals. The staff is unusually helpful. *Hwy. 29, Yountville. 707-944-2468*

2 Domaine Chandon. ★ ★$$$ One of the most beautiful restaurant settings in the Bay Area. You can dine outdoors surrounded by vineyards of the famous Moet et Chandon champagnery when the weather is warm. The restaurant is so pretty it's worth visiting for lunch. If you do, try the *l'eouf moscovite*, a nouvelle version of Eggs Benedict, with salmon and caviar. *French. Open Tu-Su 11AM-9PM. California Dr. off Hwy. 29, Yountville. 707-944-8848*

2 The Diner. $/$$ The old-fashioned American breakfasts here are spectacular, particularly the cornmeal pancakes. It is also open for sandwiches at lunch and Mexican dinners on weekends. A nice, informal *home cooking* restaurant. *American/Mexican. Open Tu-Su 8AM-3PM. 6476 Washington St., Yountville. 707-944-2626*

Courtesy Napa Valley Art Studio and Gallery

2 Magnolia Hotel. *Moderate/expensive.* A cozy old stone building operating as a hotel since 1873. All of the rooms are furnished with antiques (king and queen-sized beds are available) and have private baths. Innkeeper **Bruce Lochen** is the former manager of the **Clift Hotel** in San Francisco. There is a large swimming pool and a jacuzzi spa for hotel guests. No children under 16, and no pets or smoking please. Breakfast included. *6529 Yount St., Yountville. 707-944-2056*

2 Vintage 1870. Graceful conversion of **Gottlieb Groezinger's** original winery building, circa 1870, into a shopping gallery featuring art, antiques, boutiques, specialty shops, restaurants, gifts, etc. Over 35 shops. *6526 Washington St., Yountville. 707-944-2451*

2 Burgundy House. *Moderate/expensive.* This special inn is close to those you might find on a winding road in the hills of southern France. The original builder, a Frenchman, wrestled fieldstone from the countryside to lay up 22-inch thick walls around hand hewn posts and beams, then settled down to a life of distilling brandy. The result of his careful building is an inn that is cool in summer and snug around the huge hearth when the days turn crisp. The 6 rooms with shared baths are each unique and tastefully appointed with French country antiques collected by the proprietor. There is also exceptional art on the walls by local artists and a good library of reading materials in the common room. *6711 Washington St., Yountville. 707-944-2855*

2 **Bordeaux House.** *Moderate/expensive.* This unique red brick structure was built in the 1970s, designed by owner architect **Robert Keenan** with interiors by **Richard Tam.** It may be the only inn in this area built from the beginning to serve this function. Bordeaux House resembles a modern day chateau in miniature, with tower and outside staircase. The 6 air-conditioned, spacious rooms are named after local vintages, decorated in soft shades of camel and wine, and each has its own fireplace and private bath. Breakfast is included. *6600 Washington St., Yountville. 707-944-2855*

2 **Mama Nina's.** ★★$$ A casual and romantic atmosphere and good prices. The pasta, soups and desserts made on the premises are the trademarks here. Try the minestrone soup and Tortellini Nina as well as the grilled scampi, Sonoma baby lamb chops, veal piccata and marvelous *Torta de Sabbia* for dessert. The attractive staff gives informal but caring service. Extensive wine list. *Italian. Open M,Tu,Th-Su 11:30AM-3PM, 5-9:30PM; W 5-9:30PM. 6772 Washington St. Yountville. 707-944-2112*

2 **Vintage Inn.** *Moderate/expensive.* Newly built on an old winery estate, this luxury country inn has 80 rooms and suites. Each room has a fireplace, wine bar and refrigerator, TV concealed in an armoire, whirlpool bath, over-sized beds with hand-painted fabrics in grape tones and original art on the walls. A complimentary champagne breakfast is served every morning. The complex was created by California artist **Kipp Stewart,** who also designed **Ventana** in Big Sur. It incorporates a pool and spa, an Alhambrain waterway with fountains and vineyards. *6541 Washington St., Yountville. In CA 800-351-1133, in US 800-982-5539*

2 **French Laundry.** ★★$$$ A beautiful restaurant in an historic old building, with classic French food and a huge California wine list. The fixed-price dinner is served in leisurely fashion, so plan on spending an entire evening. Also plan on reserving far in advance, since it's small and popular. *French. Open W-Su 6-9PM. Reservations required. Washington at Creek St., Yountville. 707-944-2380*

2 **Oakville Grocery.** The granddaddy of all gourmet food stores in the Bay Area. The best of breads, cheeses, pâtés, imported canned goods and a prime selection of wines. The place to stop if you want to eat a picnic lunch during your tour of Napa Valley. *Open daily 10AM-6PM. Hwy. 29, Yountville. 707-944-8802*

2 **Auberge du Soleil.** ★★★★$$$ A glorious restaurant jutting out on a hillside overlooking the Napa Valley. In terms of both aesthetics and food, this is a 3-star French country restaurant transported to California. Every dish is beautiful to look at; swirls of color in the sauces and in the bouquets of vegetables make you almost sorry you have to eat it. The fish and desserts are particularly good. Weekends are often booked a couple of months in advance. *French. Open daily 11:30AM-2PM, 6-9PM. 180 Rutherford Hill Rd., Yountville. 707-963-1211*

2 **The Webber Place.** *Moderate.* A cheerful red farmhouse built in the 1850s by pioneer farmers and painstakingly restored to its present charm. All of the rooms are furnished authentically with lovely quilts on antique beds. Accommodations consist of 3 rooms and a suite. The setting here is especially genuine—it is inevitable one feels several steps back in time. Rooms have both private and shared baths. Ask for the **East Room** for the private bath. Continental breakfast and wine included. *6610 Webber St., Yountville. 707-944-8384*

3 **Lake Berryessa.** From Rutherford, take Hwy. 128E for 25 miles to the turn-off. There are 7 resorts offering boating, camping, fishing, water skiing and houseboat rentals. *707-966-2111*

Rutherford

4 **Rancho Caymus Inn.** *Expensive.* **Mary Tilden Morton,** a highly respected sculptress (and member of the pioneer **Morton Salt** family), has created a 26-unit complex where each room is planned as a separate work of art: beautifully carved beds, hand-thrown basins, tooled leather and wrought iron accessories, unusually shaped fireplaces, hand-woven rugs and spreads by the Ecuadorean Indians. There are 4 master suites with Jacuzzi tubs, full kitchens and large balconies—ideal for longer stays. The building is situated on land that was part of the original land grant, **Caymus Rancho,** which **General Vallejo** gave to **George Yount.** Within the interior is a courtyard and lovely garden where a gentle fountain reflects the serenity of the area. *Wine and continental breakfast included. Just off Hwy. 29, Rutherford. 707-963-1777*

St. Helena

4 **St. Helena.** This friendly small town in the heart of the vineyards has come alive in the past few years with some exceptional restaurants and inns. And yet, it's like taking a momentary step back in time when entering Main Street—easy to imagine long white dresses and parasols emerging from the arched doorways of stone buildings.

4 **Meadowood Resort.** *Expensive/deluxe.* A jewel of a resort in its own miniature natural valley setting. Rebuilt after a devastating fire, the 70 hotel-style units and cottages still maintain the intimate feeling of an old-fashioned resort. There are spacious porches, well-stocked refrigerators, a challenging 9-hole golf course, 6 championship tennis courts, a swimming pool, a school offering courses in wine appreciation and international-quality croquet lawns with a Australian pro to provide instruction in America's fastest growing participatory sport. Highly recommended. *900 Meadowood Ln., St. Helena. 707-963-3646; within CA 800-458-8080*

Within the hotel is:

Starmont. ★ ★ ★ $$/$$$ This first-class restaurant is presided over by chef **Hale Lake,** formerly of **Domaine Chandon** and **Silverado,** who believes in preparing the freshest possible ingredients in a simple but imaginative manner and brings fresh seafood from his native Hawaii 6 days each week. The fresh salmon cured in mint and gin and the charred *carpaccio* with capers, almond and chutney are outstanding first courses. Loin of red deer venison and the domestic quail are not to be missed. Dinner is served on the wide terraces under the stars whenever weather permits. *707-963-3646*

4 **Villa St. Helena.** *Expensive.* The site of the filming of party scenes in the television series *Falcon Crest,* this palatial 13,000-square-foot home high on the hill overlooking the Valley offers hundreds of orchids and fantastic views plus a spacious courtyard and magnificent pool, 3 luxury suites and spectacular furnishings. To add to the glamour, there is a history of political power and Hollywood personalities. Owners **Ralph** and **Caroline Cotton** are wonderful hosts, weekends and weekdays. *2727 Sulphur Springs Av., St. Helena. 707-963-2514*

4 **Wine Library.** For anyone interested in wine lore, the collection of eclectic literature is worth a visit. Browsers and borrowers are made to feel welcome. *Open M-W 10AM-9PM, Th-F 10AM-6PM, Sa 10AM-2PM. 1492 Library Ln., St. Helena. 707-963-5244*

4 **Sutter Home.** *Moderate/expensive.* This delightful bed and breakfast began life as the home of winemaker **John Thoman** in 1884. Many years later it was opened to the public as an antique shop, with the spacious upstairs rooms refurbished for the enjoyment of overnight guests. Soon, a replica of the old tank tower was completed, adding 4 guest rooms each with private bath, air-conditioning and fireplaces. All of the rooms here are a long step back into the past with lace curtains, handmade quilts on ornate beds, quaint wallpapers and claw footed tubs. Breakfast features freshly baked muffins and homemade jams. *225 St. Helena Way, St. Helena 707-963-4423*

4 **Wine Country Inn.** *Expensive.* This small country hotel was designed in the tradition of the inns of New England and is located off the highway in the midst of a quiet meadow. Each of its 25 rooms is oriented to rural views, some have patios, others have balconies, many have fireplaces. Mellow country antiques are balanced with fresh colors and fabric designs reflecting the seasonal moods of the Valley. Each room has a private bath. *1152 Lodi Ln., St. Helena. 707-963-7077*

4 **Bale Mill Inn.** *Moderate.* This cozy hideaway lies just north of the town, with 5 rooms (2 shared baths) over an antique shop of the same name. The theme of each room is based on a legendary person who is characterized by its furnishings and accessories, a challenge well met by the clever decorator. There is a sitting room for guests to sip their wine and a garden terrace and deck to enjoy breakfast pastries the innkeeper bakes himself. *3431 N. St. Helena Hwy. 707-963-4545*

4 **Silverado Museum.** Eight thousand items related to the life and work of **Robert Louis Stevenson.** *Open Tu-Su 12-4PM. 1490 Library Ln., St. Helena. 707-963-3757*

4 **St. Helena Hotel.** *Moderate/expensive.* This once shabby inn has celebrated its first 100 years with a total facelift and a dramatic return to elegance. The rooms are decorated with unusual papers, fabrics and authentic accessories, and every effort is made to anticipate the needs and whims of guests. There are generous-sized baths for the rooms that share a bath, as well as some rooms with private baths. Breakfast included. *1309 Main St., St. Helena. 707-963-4388*

4 **Miramonte.** ★ ★ ★ $$$ The Swiss-born chef **Udo Nechutny** turns out some of the most innovative *new wave* French cooking in the Bay Area. Moreover, you eat it in pleasant surroundings, such as an outdoor courtyard in warm weather, with all the beautiful contrasts of colors and textures of California-style *nouvelle* cuisine, but more substance. It is one of the best Wine Country dining experiences for food and service. Reserve well in advance for weekends. *French. Open W-Su 6-9PM. 1327 Railroad Av., St. Helena. 707-963-3970*

4 **La Belle Helene.** ★ ★ $$/$$$ Classic French cooking at reasonable prices in a beautiful castle-like building. Outdoor dining is possible in warm weather. The food is acceptable, but it won't be nearly as good as nearby Miramonte. *French. Open Th-M 6-9PM. 1345 Railroad Av., St. Helena. 707-963-1234*

4 **Old Bale Mill.** This site may look familiar as it was used by Walt Disney in filming *Polyanna.* It was designed and built by **Dr. Bale** in 1840 and was recently restored as a working grist mill. *3369 St. Helena Hwy.*

4 **Sterling Tramway.** The Sterling Winery is approached by way of a tramway. The ride in suspended cars is breathtaking. And the self-guided tour set up in the handsome cluster of winery buildings is worthwhile for any age group. *Fee for those over 16. 1111 Dunaweal Ln., St. Helena. 707-942-5151*

4 **Ambrose Bierce House.** *Moderate/expensive.* Superbly restored and decorated, a modest exterior hides a hospitable, fastidiously run guesthouse—a mini-museum crammed with memorabilia of **Ambrose Bierce** and friends (the likes of **Lillie Langtry**, **Edward Muybridge** and **Lillie Coit**). Bierce lived here for 13 years plotting ghost stories before his own mysterious disappearance. The inn has 4 spacious rooms, 2 with private bath. There are complimentary bicycles, and an extraordinary Continental breakfast featuring fresh fruit in grapefruit shell and *sfogliatelle*, Italian pastry stuffed with ricotta cheese. *1515 Main St., St. Helena. 707-963-3003*

4 **Le Rhone Restaurant.** ★ $$$$ Specializing in the cuisine of the Rhone Valley, the French owners offer unusually authentic dishes ending with a fantastic array of irresistible desserts. The atmosphere is welcoming (enter from Hunt Street around the corner through a courtyard) and the wine list is excellent. *Reservations required. Open M-Sa 12-3PM, 6-10PM. Closed Jan. 1234 Main St., St. Helena. 707-963-0240*

4 **Mustard's Grill.** ★ ★ $$ Although this pleasant place with a view of the valley is open every day, the customers crowd in on weekends, so reservations are a good idea. Entrees are reasonably priced and range from fresh Sonoma duck and rabbit with garlic and thyme to always fresh fish dishes. The restaurant is a cousin to the popular **Fog City Diner** in San Francisco. *Open M-F 11:30AM-3PM, 5:30-9PM; Sa & Su 5-10PM. 7399 St. Helena Hwy., St. Helena 707-944-2424*

4 **Creekwood.** *Moderate.* An enchanting cottage situated on the flower-covered banks of a winding stream near the fabled **Silverado Trail**—surely this is a hideaway made-to-order for any couple valuing beauty and seclusion. The suite includes a canopied bed, cozy wood-burning stove, kitchenette, bath and a private deck overlooking the creek, a footbridge and the woods beyond. A full breakfast is served in the cottage. *850 Conn Valley Rd., St. Helena. 707-963-3580*

4 **Chestelson House.** *Moderate.* Located just a short walk from St. Helena's unique shops and restaurants, Chestelson has the relaxing ambience of a comfortable family home, and a stop in **Jackie Sweet's** kitchen confirms your welcome. Breakfast is an event here, with Mrs. Sweet drawing on her success as a caterer and cooking teacher to plan mouth-watering, creative, family-style breakfasts. The attractive bedrooms are authentically old-fashioned, with queen-sized beds, private or semi-private baths, carefully chosen reading materials, and wine served in front of a fire each evening. *1417 Kearney St., St. Helena. 707-963-2238*

Calistoga

5 **Calistoga.** With its geysers, hot springs and lava deposits, the area is a clear-cut reminder of the tempestuous geological beginnings of the valley. Some of the eruptions formed the gray stone with which the Italian and Chinese workers built bridges and wineries, such as the Christian Brothers Greystone Cellars. The first spa at Calistoga was built by **Sam Brannan**, California's first millionaire. He designed a spectacular hotel to attract the newly wealthy San Franciscans, now known as *Pacheteau's Spring Grounds.* Brannan also brought the first railroad to the valley, and donated a costly engine to the first fire department. Sam Brannan coined the name Calistoga by hybridizing *California and Saratoga* (the famous New York resort). Set in the middle of the wine country, this small old country town, with its western-style main street still intact, is known for its mineral water and mud baths. Almost every motel or inn is equipped with at least a jacuzzi. Contact the Calistoga Chamber of Commerce for a list of spas. *1139 Lincoln Av., Calistoga. 707-942-6333*

5 **Calistoga Inn.** *Moderate.* On Calistoga's main street, this building houses one of the most highly recommended restaurants in the valley. The rooms are old-fashioned, simply furnished in a country inn manner, and immaculate. 17 rooms with shared baths. Continental breakfast is included. *1250 Lincoln Av., Calistoga. 707-942-4101*

Within the inn is:

Calistoga Inn Restaurant. ★★ $$$ A favorite eating place for Napa Valley winemakers. The wine list goes on for pages and pages; you'd be hard-pressed to think of a single wine the Napa Valley produces that's not on this list. Seafood is their specialty, much of it cooked French-style. Don't miss artichoke with prawn and scallop sauce or their asparagus vinaigrette with pimento, breast of duck with black currant sauce and pate of snow peas. *Continental. Open daily for lunch and dinner. 707-942-4101*

5 **Calistoga Soaring Center.** The valley's warm, up-currents of air, called *lifts*, are perfect for gliding. Rides over the Napa Valley last about 20 minutes. *Reasonable rates. Open every day 9AM-sunset. 1546 Lincoln Av., Calistoga. 707-942-5592*

Mount View Hotel. *Moderate/expensive.* A complete change of pace from bed and breakfast or motel type accommodations, this 100-year-old hotel has undergone complete renovation and it is now a showplace dedicated to the Art Deco days of the 20s and 30s. Suites and rooms are furnished with real flair. The elegant *Coit Suite* has $27,000 worth of antique furnishings, the *Tom Mix Suite* is accented with bull and steer horns, the individual rooms are large, with private baths. There is a large heated pool, jacuzzi, evening maid service and a most accommodating staff. A Continental breakfast is provided. *1457 Lincoln Av., Calistoga. 707-942-6877*

Within the hotel is:

Mount View Hotel Restaurant. ★ ★ ★ $$ No longer focusing only on French cuisine, the quality of the food has become top of the line. Once a month there is a special dinner planned with a local winery, and during summer, mesquite barbecues by the pool. Very much worth a stop. *Open daily 8AM-2PM, 6-9:30PM; Sa & Su brunch from 9AM. 707-942-6877*

Calistoga Spa. For those who enjoy natural mineral bathing, mud baths and massage, this family-run facility offers full value in clean attractive surroundings. All rooms are equipped for light housekeeping with color TV and air conditioning. Included is the unlimited use of 2 hot mineral water pools and the giant-size Roman Olympic Pool. Families are welcome. *Reasonable rates. 1006 Washington St., Calistoga. 707-942-6269*

The Sharpsteen Museum. Pioneer history comes alive in 3-dimensional form with a scale model diorama of the Calistoga of 1865 covering one wall. Three dimensional shadow boxes re-create areas like the old China Camp, Toll House and downtown buildings. *Open weekends 12-4PM. 1311 Washington St., Calistoga. 707-942-5911*

Larkmead Country Inn. *Moderate.* Here, in a home set down amongst the grapevines, guests share almost all of the living area of this delightful house, where attention to detail includes warming the sheets in advance of a guest's arrival! There are lovely flower arrangements, many books, Persian carpets, fine old paintings and views from the verandas. Four guest rooms with shared baths. *1103 Larkmead Ln., Calistoga. 707-942-5360*

Boskos. $ Seven kinds of pasta made on the premises. This is a brick, beamed and sawdust-on-the-floor kind of place where the whole family will be happy with the food and prices. Homemade desserts, espresso bar, wine and beer. *Open daily 11AM-10PM. 1403 Lincoln Av., Calistoga. 707-942-9088*

Wine Way Inn. *Moderate.* This inn, built as a family home in 1915, adjoins one of the oldest vineyards in Calistoga. On the remains of the hillside terraces, a mountain forest of pine, redwood and maple trees protects the spacious deck at the rear. There are 3 rooms with private baths, 2 with shared baths and a secluded guest cottage with private bath offering a view of the mountains. Rooms are furnished with 19th century American and English antiques, and there are fresh flowers and a decanter of wine for each guest. *Closed Dec and Jan. 1019 Foothill Blvd., Calistoga. 707-942-0680*

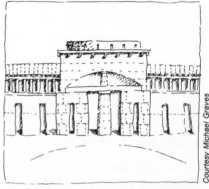

Courtesy Michael Graves

Clos Pegase Winery and House. (1986, Michael Graves) This set of buildings was the result of a major design competition sponsored by the client and the San Francisco Museum of Modern Art. It was won by **Michael Graves** and **Edward Schmidt,** the artist. Located on a small, tree-covered hill just south of Calistoga, the house looks out across the valley and down to the winery below. Graves' design, which was the most informal and convincing of all the competition entries, consists of a picturesque arrangement of buildings and art works organized about a sequential route starting at the entry court. One of the showpieces of the design is the cylindrical room containing frescoes depicting allegorical scenes about wine making painted by Schmidt. *Highway 29 at Calistoga.*

Foothill House. *Moderate.* Finally, the ultimate bed and breakfast. The hosts, **Susan** and **Michael Clow,** took a small, turn-of-the-century farmhouse nestled in the foothills and turned it into a romantic, comfortable, tastefully decorated and soothing hideaway, where one would prefer to spend far longer than is usually on the schedule. Their secret is superb attention to detail and service which is offered with total respect for a guest's privacy—a combination not easy to achieve. There are 3 guest suites, each taking its color cues from an elaborate handmade quilt on the antique bed. Each room has a refrigerator, wood burning fireplace and wine and homemade treats from the hostess. Breakfast features home-baked goodies too. *3037 Foothill Blvd., Calistoga. 707-942-6933*

Restaurants/Nightlife red
Hotels blue
Museums/Architecture/Narrative black

6 **Robert Louis Stevenson Park.** Located at the northern end of the valley, this largely undeveloped area contains an abandoned silver mine at the end of the winding road that was once menaced by highwaymen in search of mine payrolls and shipments of silver. Stevenson spent some time here and later wrote about the area in *Silverado Squatters*. He also patterned *Spyglass Hill* in *Treasure Island* after Mount St. Helena.

7 **Old Faithful Geyser.** Located 2 miles to the north of town, this is one of 3 regularly erupting geysers in the world. Boiling water and vapor come roaring out at 350-degrees more than 60 feet into the air. *Picnic facilities nearby on Tubbs Ln. Admission fee.*

8 **Petrified Forest.** Six miles from Calistoga are gigantic redwoods turned to stone, 6 million years old. *Picnic facilities nearby. Route well marked from town.*

SONOMA

Sonoma Valley lies 46 easy miles from the metropolitan Bay Area. This is where a resident named **Jack London** borrowed a legend from the Suisun Indians and created a romantic image so effective that today the whole world seems to know about the Valley of the Moon. And indeed, this valley does its name full justice. To anyone watching from the valley floor, separated as they are from the adjoining Napa Valley by the *Mayacamus Range*, the moon seems to rise not once but many times as it shows itself between the succeeding peaks. Mellow in climate, rich in agriculture, this miniature jewel of a valley extends just 17 miles before it runs out into the hills. From its earliest days, Sonoma County history was made under 7 different banners: Spain, England, Russia, Mexican Empire, Mexican Republic, California Republic (born in Sonoma with the raising of the Bear flag), and finally our own Stars and Stripes. It might well have been called *Valley of the Flags*. In the tiny pueblo that was Sonoma in 1823, Franciscan fathers founded their most northerly mission, *San Francisco Solano*—the 21st and last in the chain of missions linked together along the old *El Camino Real*. Here the first grapes were planted by the padres so that wines for sacramental purposes would be available. In 1834, the popular Mexican commander, **General Mariano Vallejo** (who successfully bridged the gap between the Mexican and American governments) planted other varieties of grapes here for table wines. And here also, America's first big experimental vineyard was established by an enterprising Hungarian nobleman at Buena Vista. **Count Agoston Haraszthy** imported 100,000 grape cuttings—140 varieties of European vintage—to plant and later distribute throughout the entire state. Thus, this farsighted man, working with his energetic neighbor, **General Vallejo,** almost single-handedly provided the roots which were to become the multimillion dollar wine industry that flourishes in California today. The **Chamber of Commerce** on the Sonoma Plaza in the park is a friendly, helpful source of local lore and good maps. Maps of the wineries of both Sonoma and Napa Valleys are available in many of the restaurants, hotels and bookstores—a necessity for suc-cessful touring in this area. There are also interesting route guides for bicycling. A *Sonoma Walking Tour* brochure of historic buildings, public and private, is available at the headquarters of the **Sonoma League for Historic Preservation (Vasquez House)** and at various shops around the Plaza at a nominal price.

9 **Train Town.** Sited on a 10-acre park with several lakes and a miniature town of 9 tiny buildings, Train Town offers scenic rides on a little steam train, departing every 20 minutes. *Open daily during summer; weekends and holidays the rest of the year. 20264 Broadway, Sonoma.*

9 **Cafe Pilou.** $$ Basque food with a French accent, owned by a member of the Sonoma Bakery family. *Basque. Open for dinner Th-Su; breakfast and lunch Tu-Sa; Su brunch. Place de Pyrenees, Sonoma. 707-996-2757*

9 **Sonoma French Bakery.** Some claim that the baguettes here are the best in the Bay Area. The croissants are faultless, too. Also try the sourdough bread. Bring some home for your freezer. *Open W-Su. 468 1st St. E., Sonoma. 707-996-2691*

9 **Sonoma Depot Museum.** Housed in a rebuilt train depot, the museum features a room for railroad buffs with all the paraphernalia of by-gone railroading, another room devoted to western artifacts such as a stagecoach, antique firearms, early leather goods, and stage settings with manikins depicting various historical events of the area. *Modest charge; children with parents free. 285 1st St., Sonoma.*

9 **Depot Hotel 1870.** $$ American and Continental food in a pleasant and beautifully restored old hotel. *Open W-Su. 241 1st St. W., Sonoma. 707-938-2980*

9 **Mariani's.** $$ One of those *surf 'n' turf* type restaurants, specializing in good, juicy steaks and seafood. *American. Open Tu-Su. 8 Spain St., Sonoma. 707-996-6866*

9 **Thistle Dew Inn.** *Moderate/expensive.* A pristine bed and breakfast inn consisting of 2 separate houses, simply decorated and landscaped. The house at the rear of the property sleeps 6, including on a pair of bunk beds, has its own sun deck and would be ideal for a family outing. Continental breakfast provided. *Opens Easter week. 171 W. Spain St., Sonoma. 707-938-2909*

9 **Sonoma Hotel.** *Moderate.* This now historic building on one corner of the **Sonoma Plaza** was originally constructed as a 2-story adobe, probably in the late 1860s. Recently restored, the old hotel's 17 rooms were refurbished with authentic items from the days of the *wild, wild West:* brass beds, armoires, original chandeliers and other memorabilia. No 2 rooms are alike. Five have a private bath complete with claw-footed tub and water closet. Continental breakfast. *110 W. Spain St., Sonoma. 707-996-2996*

Within the hotel is:

Sonoma Hotel Restaurant and Saloon. ★ $$ This is an old-time saloon with a 100-year-old bar to lean on and funky accessories which lend authenticity. Meals are served in the justly-popular dining room, which extends into a garden patio in the summer months. The dinner menu changes twice each month and utilizes fresh produce and herbs from the hotel garden and local sausages, cheeses and baked good from a wonderful bakery nearby. Lunch and Sunday brunch are also served. *Open daily 11:30AM-2:30PM, Th-Tu 5:45-9:30PM, Su brunch 10:30AM-3PM. 707-996-2996*

9 **Lachryma Montis (General Mariano Vallejo's home).** The terraces above this picturesque Victorian mansion are furnished with picnic tables and there are wooded trails to explore the hillside. *Sonoma.*

9 **Sonoma Cheese Factory.** A combination of factory and store, this one is crammed with every kind of wonderful picnic fare imaginable. Kids can watch the cheese being made in giant vats and sample the different varieties originating here, like Sonoma Jack. *2 Spain St. in the Sonoma Town Plaza.*

9 **Old City Pottery.** Located in a former bakery, the oven is now a pottery kiln. Kids are encouraged with signs that read *please come in, ice cream won't hurt our floors* and *touch, feel and enjoy.* If the schedule is agreeable, kids can watch molding or firing process. *Walk through entrance to El Paseo de Sonoma from E. Spain St.*

9 **El Dorado Inn.** *Moderate.* Among the first adobe buildings erected in Sonoma. The inn was first used as a home, then converted to a hotel during the Gold Rush. Now, after extensive restoration, the El Dorado offers 30 rooms decorated with great charm in country antiques. The large and handsome dining room and garden patio serve breakfast, lunch and dinner daily, featuring international cuisine, with chicken and veal specialties and a lavish weekend brunch. *405 1st St. W., Sonoma. 707-996-3030*

9 **Sonoma Mission Inn and Spa.** *Expensive.* On the site of what is believed to be an ancient Indian healing ground and later a mid-19th century spa, the present inn was built in the 1920s. It has been totally renovated by the present owners. The result is a luxury retreat of 100 guest rooms, each with original ceiling fan, plantation shutters and half canopied bed in contemporary decor. There are tennis courts, an Olympic-sized pool, and a full spa. The Inn is set in 7 lush, secluded acres with a spring-fed stream, source of the Inn's private label bottled sparkling water. Continental breakfast is included. *In Boyes Hot Springs, north of Sonoma. 707-996-1041; in CA 800-862-4945*

Within the Sonoma Mission Inn is:

Provencal Grill. ★ ★ $$ This dining room and poolside terrace provides an imaginative menu of California cuisine cooked over a mesquite grill. Executive Chef **Gary Arthur** creates dishes that are delicious and presented with flair, especially the appealing diet menus. *Open daily 8AM-10PM, F-Su bar until 2AM. Reservations requested. 707-938-4953*

9 **Trojan Horse Inn.** *Moderate.* The 8 room inn features such antiques as wonderful old bedsteads converted for queen size mattresses. The owner's collection of handmade porcelain dolls and a carousel horse accent the decor. Visit the delightful gardens and patio by Sonoma Creek and enjoy breakfast served in the dining room. No children under 16. *19455 Sonoma Hwy. 12, Sonoma. 707-996-2430*

10 **Jack London State Historic Park.** Paths lead throughout this park to various buildings and landscapes associated with this well known author. **The House of Happy Walls,** built by the author's widow, is now a museum containing many of London's mementos. There are breathtaking views throughout the park and ideal settings for picnics, hiking and horseback riding. *Entrance fee per car. Glen Ellen on Hwy. 12, 10 minutes from Sonoma.*

10 **Beltane Ranch.** *Moderate.* A beautifully remodelled 1892 bunkhouse on a ranch originally owned by the notorious **Mammy Pleasant,** this gracious inn overlooks the vineyards and hills beyond. There are 3 living/bedroom suites with private baths. Breakfast (included) is served on a porch overlooking the view, and horseback riding is available at nearby **Jack London State Park.**

Adapted from a poster designed by James Cross
and Susan Holzhauer for Wine Country Tours

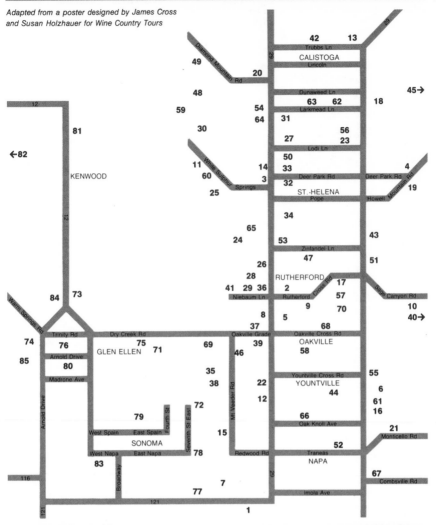

WINERIES: NAPA

1 **Acacia Winery.** *2636 Las Amigas Rd., Napa. 707-833-4666 or 226-9991*

2 **Beaulieu Vineyard.** Turn-of-century winery with museum/visitors' center. *Open daily 10AM-4PM. 1960 St. Helena Hwy., Rutherford. 707-963-2411*

3 **Beringer Vineyards.** Visitors' center in **Rhine House,** 17-room mansion. *2000 Main St., St. Helena. 707-963-7115*

4 **Burgess Cellars.** *1108 Deer Park Rd., St. Helena. 707-963-4766*

5 **Cakebread Cellars.** *8300 St. Helena Hwy., Rutherford. Open daily 10AM-4PM. 707-963-5221*

6 **Calafia Wines.** *6150 Silverado Trail, Napa. 707-944-2666*

7 **Carneros Creek Winery.** *1285 Dealy Ln., Napa. 707-226-3479*

8 **Cassayre-Forni Cellars.** *1271 Manley Ln., Rutherford. Open Apr-Oct. 707-944-2165*

9 **Caymus Vineyards.** *8700 Conn Creek Rd., Rutherford. Open daily 10AM-4PM. 707-963-4204*

10 **Chappellet Vineyard.** *1581 Sage Canyon Rd., St. Helena. 707-963-7136*

11 **Chateau Chevalier Winery.** *3101 Spring Mountain Rd., St. Helena. 707-963-2342*

12 **Chateau Chevere Winery.** *2040 Hoffman Ln., Yountville. 707-944-2184*

13 **Chateau Montelena Winery.** European-style castle with oriental appointments. *Tasting/sales daily 10AM-noon, 1-4PM. 1429 Tubbs Ln., Calistoga. 707-942-5105*

14 **Christian Brothers Mount St. Helena.** Historic building houses aging, sparkling wine production. *Open daily 10:30AM-4:30PM. 2555 Main St., St. Helena. 707-963-2719*

15 **Christian Brothers Mt. La Salle Vineyards.** County landmark where the company's wine production is housed. *Open daily 10:30AM-4:30PM. 4411 Redwood Rd., Napa. 707-963-4480*

16 **Clos Du Val Wine Co., Ltd.** *Open daily 10AM-4PM. 5330 Silverado Trail, Napa. 707-252-6711*

17 **Conn Creek Winery.** *8711 Silverado Trail, St. Helena. 707-963-9100*

18 **Cuivaison Winery.** *Tasting W-Su 10AM-4PM, sales daily 10AM-4PM. 4550 Silverado Trail, Calistoga. 707-942-6266*

19 **Deer Park Winery.** *Sales daily. 1000 Deer Park Rd., Deer Park. 707-963-5411*

20 **Diamond Creek Vineyards.** *1500 Diamond Mountain Rd., Calistoga. 707-942-6929*

21 **Diamond Oaks Vineyard/Maniar Cellars.** *1055 Atlas Peak Rd., Napa. Open Apr-Oct. 707-224-2022*

22 **Domaine Chandon.** One of Napa's premier *champagne* houses. *California Dr., Yountville. 707-944-2280*

23 **Duckhorn Vineyards.** *3027 Silverado Trail, St. Helena. Open Apr-Oct. 707-963-7108*

24 **Flora Spring Wine Co.** *1978 W. Zinfandel Ln., St. Helena. 707-963-5711*

25 **Forman Winery.** *2555 Mandrona, St. Helena. 707-963-4613*

26 **Franciscan Vineyards.** Guide your own tour, then taste in the garden atrium. *Open daily 10AM-5PM. 1178 Galleron Rd., Rutherford. 707-963-7111*

27 **Freemark Abbey Winery.** *Sales daily 10AM-4:30PM. 3022 St. Helena Hwy., St. Helena. 707-963-9694*

28 **Grgich Hills Cellar.** *Sales daily 10AM-4PM. 1829 St. Helena Hwy., Rutherford. 707-963-2784*

29 **Inglenook Vineyard Co.** Storybook winery with European atmosphere. *Open daily 10AM-4:45PM (tours on the hour until 4PM). 1991 St. Helena Hwy. So., Rutherford. 707-963-2616; 963-7184*

30 **Robert Keenan Winery.** *3660 Spring Mountain Rd., St. Helena. 707-963-9177*

31 **Hanns Kornell Champagne Cellars.** Sparkling wines created by traditional German methods. *1091 Larkmead Ln., St. Helena. 707-963-2334*

32 **Charles Krug Winery.** Stone buildings circa 1860 still house operations. Concert series during summer. *Open daily 10AM-4PM. 2800 Main St., St. Helena 707-963-2761*

33 **Markham Winery.** *2812 St. Helena Hwy. No., St. Helena. 707-963-5292*

34 **Louis M. Martini Winery.** Instructive tour through post-prohibition facilities. *Open daily 10AM-4:30PM. 254 St. Helena Hwy. So., St. Helena. 707-963-2736*

35 **Mayacamas Vineyards.** *1155 Lokoya Rd., Napa. 707-224-4030*

36 **F. Justin Miller.** *8329 St. Helena Hwy., Napa. 707-963-4252*

37 **Robert Mondavi Winery.** One of the best places for newcomers to start, great tour! Summer jazz concerts. *Open daily 10AM-5PM. 7801 St. Helena Hwy., Oakville. 707-963-9611*

38 **Mt. Veeder Winery & Vineyards.** *1999 Mt. Veeder Rd., Napa. 707-224-4039*

39 **Napa Wine Cellars.** *Open daily 10:30AM-5:30PM. 7481 St. Helena Hwy., Oakville. 707-944-2565*

40 **Nichelini Vineyard.** *2349 Lower Chiles Rd., St. Helena. 707-963-3357*

41 **Niebaum-Copola Estate.** *1460 Niebaum Ln., Rutherford. 707-963-9435*

42 **Robert Pecota Winery.** *3299 Bennett Ln., Calistoga. 707-942-6625*

43 **Joseph Phelps Vineyard.** *200 Taplin Rd., St. Helena. 707-963-2745*

44 **Pine Ridge.** *Open W-Su 11AM-3:30PM. Picnic areas. 5901 Silverado Trail, Napa. 707-253-7500*

45 **Pope Valley Winery.** Built in 1909 with timbers from an old quicksilver mine, refurbished in 1972. *Open Sa-Su 10AM-5PM. 6613 Pope Valley Rd., Pope Valley. 707-965-2192*

46 **Quail Ridge.** *3230 Mt. Veeder Rd., Napa. 707-944-8128*

47 **Raymond Vineyard Cellars.** *Tours 11AM daily. Sales daily 10AM-4PM. 849 Zinfandel Ln., St. Helena. 707-963-3141*

48 **Ritchie Creek Vineyards.** *4024 Spring Mountain Rd., Calistoga. 707-963-4661*

49 **Roddis Cellar.** *1510 Diamond Mountain Rd., Calistoga. 707-942-5868*

50 **Round Hill Cellars.** *1097 Lodi Ln., St. Helena. 707-963-5251*

51 **Rutherford Hill Winery.** *Tours/tasting 11AM daily, sales 10AM-4:30PM. 1673 St. Helena Hwy. So., Rutherford. 707-963-4117*

52 **St. Andrew's Winery, Inc.** *2921 Silverado Trail, Napa. 707-252-6748*

53 **V. Sattui Winery.** Deli and large picnic area. *Tasting daily 9:30AM-6PM. White Ln. at Hwy. 29 So., St. Helena. 707-963-7774*

54 **Schramsberg Vineyards.** *St. Helena Hwy. No., Calistoga. 707-942-4558*

55 **Shafer Vineyards.** *6154 Silverado Trail, Napa. 707-944-8642*

56 **Charles & Shaw Vineyard & Winery.** *1010 Big Tree Rd., St. Helena. 707-963-5459*

57 **Shown & Sons Vineyards.** *Open W-Sa 10AM-4PM. Picnic area. 8643 Silverado Trail, Rutherford. 707-963-9004*

58 **Silver Oak Cellars.** *PO Box 414, Oakville. 707-944-8866*

59 **Smith-Madrone Vineyard.** Great view of Napa Valley! *Retail sales daily. 4022 Spring Mountain Rd., St. Helena. 707-963-2283*

60 **Spring Mountain Vineyards.** *Tours M-F 2:30PM. 2805 Spring Mountain Rd., St. Helena. 707-963-5233*

61 **Stag's Leap Wine Cellars.** *5766 Silverado Trail, Napa. 707-944-2020*

62 **Sterling Vineyards.** Ride the skyway to this gothic hilltop winery *(small fee). Open daily 10:30AM-4:30PM (closed M-Tu 1 Nov- 30 April). 1111 Dunaweal Ln., Calistoga. 707-942-5151*

63 **Stonegate Winery.** *1183 Dunaweal Ln., Calistoga. 707-942-6500*

64 **Stony Hill Vineyard.** *PO Box 308, St. Helena. 707-963-2636*

65 **Sutter Home Winery.** *Open daily 9AM-5PM. 277 St. Helena Hwy. So., St. Helena. 707-963-3104*

66 **Trefethen Vineyards.** *1160 Oak Knoll Av., Napa. 707-255-7700*

67 **Tulocay Winery.** *1426 Coombsville Rd., Napa. 707-255-4699*

68 **Villa Mt. Eden.** *Oakville Crossroads, Oakville. 707-944-8431*

69 **Vose Vineyards.** *4035 Mt. Veeder Rd., Napa. 707-944-2254*

70 **Z/D Wines.** *8383 Silverado Trail, Napa. 707-963-5188*

WINERIES: SONOMA

71 **Adler Fels.** *5325 Corrick Rd., Santa Rosa. 707-539-3123*

72 **Buena Vista Winery.** Classic mid-1800s wine estate with original buildings, picnic area. *Open daily 10AM-5PM. Reservations suggested. 18000 Old Winery Rd., Sonoma. 707-938-1266*

73 **Chateau St. Jean.** Romantic French country chateau houses tasting facility. *Open daily 10AM-4:30PM. 8555 Sonoma Hwy., Kenwood. 707-833-1434*

74 **H. Coturri & Sons, Ltd.** *6725 Enterprise Rd., Glen Ellen. 707-996-6247*

75 **Fisher Vineyards.** *6200 St. Helena, Santa Rosa. 707-539-7511*

76 **Grand Cru Vineyards.** Gothic atmosphere. *1 Vintage Ln., Glen Ellen. 707-996-8100*

77 **Gundlach-Bundschu Winery.** On site of winery closed after 1906 earthquake. *Open daily noon-4:30PM. 3775 Thornberry Rd., Sonoma. 707-938-5277*

78 **Hacienda Wine Cellars.** Primo Spanish Colonial setting. *Tasting/sales daily 10AM-5PM. 1000 Vineyard Ln., Sonoma. 707-938-3220*

79 **Hanzell Vineyards.** *18596 Lomita Av., Sonoma. 707-996-3860*

80 **J.J. Haraszthy.** Winery founded by *The Father of California's Wine Commerce. 14301 Arnold Dr., Glen Ellen. 707-996-3040*

81 Kenwood Vineyards. State-of-the-art wine production on display. *Open daily 10AM-4:30PM for tasting/sales. 9592 Sonoma Hwy., Kenwood.* 707-833-5891

82 Matanzas Creek Winery. *6097 Bennett Valley Rd., Santa Rosa.* 707-542-8242

83 Sebastiani Vineyards. Birdseye tour is excellent introduction to winemaking. *Open daily 10AM-5PM. 389 4th St. E., Sonoma.* 707-938-5532

84 St. Francis Vineyards. *Open daily 10AM-4:30PM. 8450 Sonoma Hwy., Kenwood.* 707-833-4666

85 Valley of the Moon Winery. *Open 10AM-4PM except Th. 777 Madrone Rd., Glen Ellen.* 707-996-6941

Wine Tasting:
The Davis 20-Point System

Whether you are only an occasional wine drinker or plan to become a connoisseur, a simple judging system will help you quickly learn to recognize and enjoy wines. Scoring here works equally well with inexpensive and rare vintages. Remember, it is a personal test, a rating of your own reaction to a particular bottle.

Factor	*Max. Points*
Appearance:	
Brilliant = 2	
Clear = 1	
Cloudy = 0	2
Color:	
Perfect = 2	
Slightly off = 1	
Off = 0	2
Aroma/Bouquet:	
Distinct = 4	
Slightly recognizable = 3	
Indistinct = 2, 1.	
Subtract 1, 2 for maladors.	4
Acescence/Volatile Acidity:	
Vinegary:	
None = 2	
Slight = 1	
Obvious = 0	2

Total Acid:	
Right = 2	
Slightly off = 1	
Obviously off = 0	2
Sugar/Acid Balance:	
Good = 1	
Off = 0	1
Body:	
Right for type = 1	
Too light or heavy = 0	1
Flavor:	
Good for type = 2	
Slightly off = 1	
Off = 0	2
Astringency/Bitterness:	
Normal = 2	
Slightly noticable = 1	
Offensive = 0	2
General Impression:	
High = 2	
Average = 1	
Low = 0	2

Total Points Max.	*20 Total Points Max.*

Evaluation:
17-20 = Outstanding
13-16 = Good
9-12 = Acceptable
8 or less = Unacceptable

Smelling
(Judge these characteristics before tasting)

Appearance—Absence of sediment or haze, brilliance of clarity.

Color—Appropriateness of color: Rose should be pink with a hint of orange. Whites should be a rich yellow gold or wheat-color, but not too amber or too watery. Reds are acceptable with violet or amber tints, but not with brown tints or washed-out red.

Aroma/Bouquet—Aroma is the fruit smell; bouquet is the odor produced by the fermentation and aging process. Aroma should be fresh, fruity and distinctly recognizable as the wine's grape of origin, i.e. *varietal*. Score high if distinct type is identifiable, score lower for indistinct and general wine odor. Judge bouquet similarly (from pleasant and distinct to unpleasant and vague.) Subtract points for musty, moldy, woody or other unpleasant odors.

Acescence/Volatile Acidity—Vinegar odors.

Tasting
(You can take a sip now!)

Total Acidity—Balance is important: too much causes a sour, sharp taste while too little makes the wine flat or *flabby*.

Sugar—Evaluate the balance between sweetness and acidity.

Body—Feel by swishing the wine around in your mouth. Judge for appropriateness to style.

Flavor—Is the flavor right for the wine style, and does it complement the scent?

Astringency/Bitterness—A trace of bitterness (it makes your mouth pucker) is all right in old red wines, but should be absent from other wines.

General Quality—Overall impression, based on your personal reaction to the wine. Wines should only be judged against like wines.

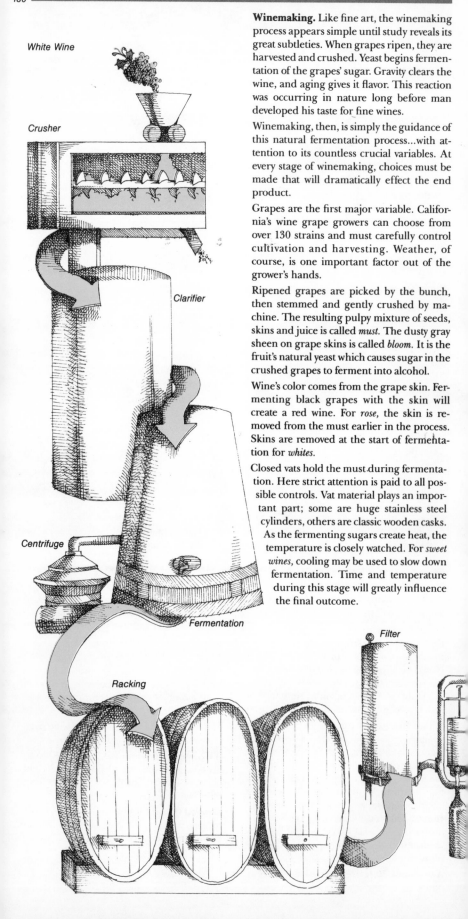

White Wine

Crusher

Clarifier

Centrifuge

Fermentation

Racking

Filter

Winemaking. Like fine art, the winemaking process appears simple until study reveals its great subtleties. When grapes ripen, they are harvested and crushed. Yeast begins fermentation of the grapes' sugar. Gravity clears the wine, and aging gives it flavor. This reaction was occurring in nature long before man developed his taste for fine wines.

Winemaking, then, is simply the guidance of this natural fermentation process...with attention to its countless crucial variables. At every stage of winemaking, choices must be made that will dramatically effect the end product.

Grapes are the first major variable. California's wine grape growers can choose from over 130 strains and must carefully control cultivation and harvesting. Weather, of course, is one important factor out of the grower's hands.

Ripened grapes are picked by the bunch, then stemmed and gently crushed by machine. The resulting pulpy mixture of seeds, skins and juice is called *must*. The dusty gray sheen on grape skins is called *bloom*. It is the fruit's natural yeast which causes sugar in the crushed grapes to ferment into alcohol.

Wine's color comes from the grape skin. Fermenting black grapes with the skin will create a red wine. For *rose*, the skin is removed from the must earlier in the process. Skins are removed at the start of fermentation for *whites*.

Closed vats hold the must during fermentation. Here strict attention is paid to all possible controls. Vat material plays an important part; some are huge stainless steel cylinders, others are classic wooden casks. As the fermenting sugars create heat, the temperature is closely watched. For *sweet wines*, cooling may be used to slow down fermentation. Time and temperature during this stage will greatly influence the final outcome.

Fermentaton will stop naturally when all sugar is converted, resulting in a dry wine with 10-14 percent alcohol. If it is stopped earlier (using sulphur dioxide or pasteurization), leaving unconverted sugar, a sweeter wine will result. Brandy is often used to stop the process in dessert wines.

The fermented wine is then placed in large casks or tanks for settling—where gravity helps clear the wine by pulling out leftover grape and yeast particles.

While maturing, the wine is often pumped from one vat to another, called *racking*, to expedite the settling process or to expose the wine to different types of cask wood for flavor. Natural substances such as *bentonite* (fine clay) or *albumen* (egg white) may be added at this stage to speed clarification, and inert nitrogen will be pumped into the tanks to fill air pockets and prevent air (oxygen) from affecting the sensitive wine.

After maturing, wines may be blended to combine desirable characteristics of different grapes.

Then, before bottling, wines are usually filtered or centrifuged for even further, or *brilliant,* clarity.

In the large wineries, bottling is accomplished by ultramodern assembly lines that process up to 8,500 bottles an hour—each one being vacuum-filled to keep out oxygen, filled with wine, capped or corked, fitted with a plastic or foil cap cover, and finally labeled.

Red wines age in the bottle for 1 to 6 years, while white wines are considered best when young. During bottle aging today, bottles are usually stored upside down on their corks to keep the corks moist and swollen, thus preventing air from leaking in.

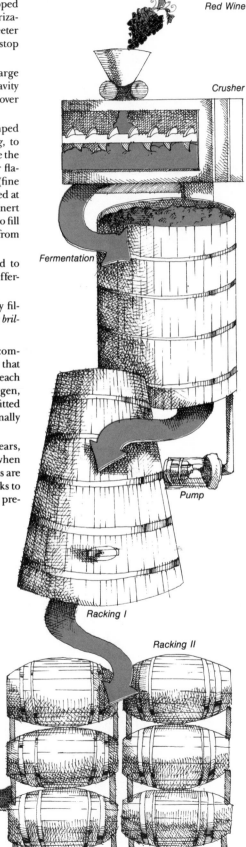

Red Wine

Crusher

Fermentation

Pump

Filter

Bottling

Racking I

Racking II

Paula Kornell
VP, Hanns Kornell Champagne Cellars

I love to take people on their first balloon ride over the Valley—there couldn't be a better way to get a feel of the Valley. **Once in a Lifetime Balloon Rides** takes off from our winery in St. Helena.

Meadowood Resort seems to be my home away from home. Not only is the ambiance marvelous, but there is always something going on.

I am a movie freak and St. Helena has been blessed with **Liberty Theater** which shows a terrific blend of current, old and esoteric films.

When I was little my grandmother took me as a special treat to the **Olive Oil Factory** in St. Helena. You feel like you are somewhere in Northern Italy. When you're going on a picnic, it's a must stop—they have everything you'll need.

If you want plain, simple, good food, go to the **Triple S Ranch.** Their fried chicken, onion rings and steaks are the best! Say hello to Tex the barman for me.

It's nice to have a special place like the **Mt. View Hotel** nearby. There's always something like a jazz combo or a comedian to spice up their beautiful art deco bar.

My favorite gift for people is an enzyme bath at the **International Spa** or an herbal mud wrap at **Lincoln Avenue Spa.**

Napa Valley is full of history. Everyone should take the time to see the **Robert Louis Stevenson Museum** or the **Wine Library.** The paths of many interesting historical characters have crossed here.

REGIONAL TRANSPORTATION

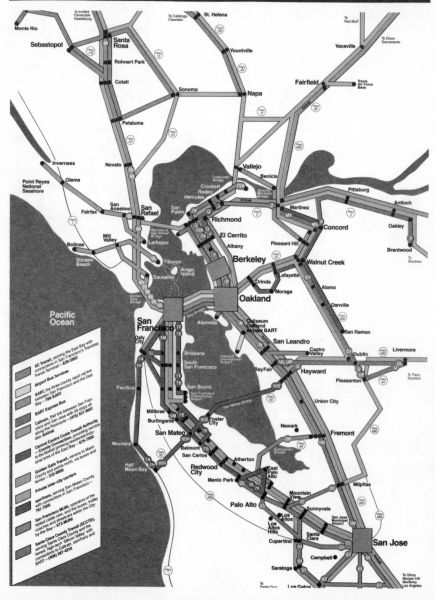

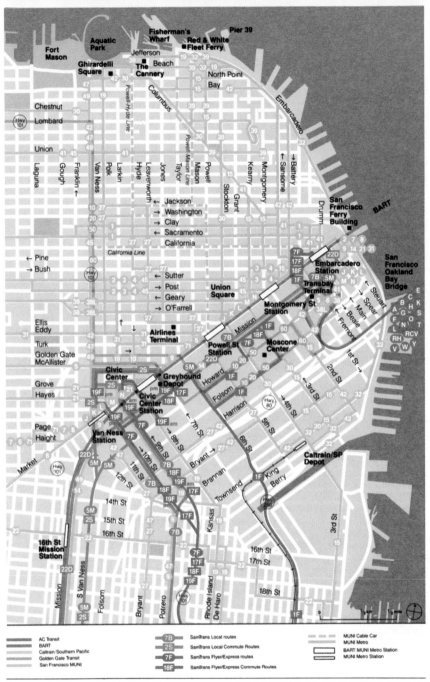

▬▬▬ AC Transit	
▬▬▬ BART	
▬▬▬ Caltrain/Southern Pacific	
▬▬▬ Golden Gate Transit	
▬▬▬ San Francisco MUNI	

7B	SamTrans Local routes
2S	SamTrans Local Commute Routes
7F	SamTrans Flyer/Express routes
18F	SamTrans Flyer/Express Commute Routes

▬ ▬ ▬ MUNI Cable Car
▬▬▬▬ MUNI Metro
▭ BART/MUNI Metro Station
▭ MUNI Metro Station

Parking in Downtown San Francisco

Finding a parking space in the downtown area can be an aggravating experience, with many private garages charging exorbitant hourly fees. But if you know where to look, you can find bargains, some of which are listed below:

Civic Center

—Sutter-Stockton Garage
—Union Square Garage
—1650 Jackson St.
—1234 Pine St.
—750 California St.
—1101 Sutter St.
—Civic Center Garage

North Beach/Fisherman's Wharf

—Vallejo Street Garage
—2850 Taylor St.
—2550 Powell St.
—Ghirardelli Square
—2490 Mason St.

Financial District

—Portsmouth Square Garage
  743 Kearny St.
—Golden Gateway Garage, 250 Clay St.
—Embarcadero Center One through Four

South of Market

—50 11th St.
—1140 Mission St.
—5th and Mission Garage

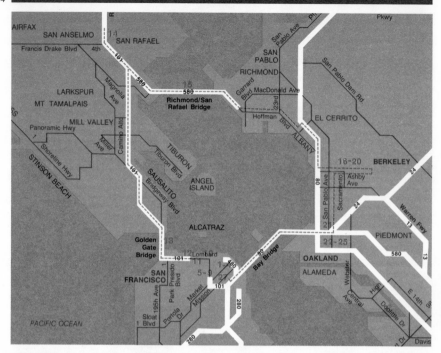

Bay Area Architectural Blitz. A lightning tour of the Bay Area.

Start at the **Ferry Building (1)** at the foot of Market Street. Drive along Market past the **Hyatt Regency Hotel (2)**, **101 California** tower (1982) by Johnson and Burgee **(3)**, and the **Shaklee Terraces** tower (1981) by SOM **(4)** at Market and Front. Continue on Market to McAllister Street and bear right to the **Civic Center (5)**. There you will see **City Hall** (1915) by Arthur Brown, the new **Louise M. Davies Symphony Hall** (1981) by SOM, and the identical edifices of the **Opera House** and **Veterans Building** also by Brown. Turn right on Franklin and left on Geary until you reach the modern **St. Mary's Cathedral (6)** at Gough Street. Turn back on Franklin to California Street. Turn right on California and continue across Van Ness and up Nob Hill to Jones Street, where you can see the city's illustrious hotels, the **Mark Hopkins** and the **Fairmont (7)**. Continue downhill on California to the Financial District. At Kearny Street view the **Bank of America World Headquarters Building (8)** by SOM . Turn left on Sansome and right on Washington past the **Transamerica Pyramid** (1973) by William Pereira and Associates **(9)**. Take Columbus Avenue towards North Beach until you reach Northpoint. En route notice **Coit Tower (10)** on top of Telegraph Hill. Turn left on Northpoint until you reach **Ghirardelli Square (11)**, the converted chocolate factory that is now a complex of boutiques and restaurants. Turn left on Van Ness, right on Bay, and head westward through the Marina District to Marina Boulevard. At Lyon and Baker Streets you'll see Maybeck's **Palace of Fine Arts (12)**, a remnant of the Panama-Pacific Exhibition of 1915. The next step is to head north on Hwy. 101, across the **Golden Gate Bridge (13)** into Marin County. Continue north 15 miles, past San Rafael,

to take a look at the **Marin County Civic Center** (1957) designed by Frank Lloyd Wright **(14)**. Reach it via the North San Pedro Road exit. Drive under the arches and walk up to the viewing deck next to the library. Then return south on Hwy. 101 through San Rafael and take the Hwy. 17 exit. Drive across the **Richmond-San Rafael Bridge (15)**. Follow the signs for Oakland through the industrial area along Cutting and Hoffman Boulevards, and join Hwy. 80 at Albany. Exit at University Avenue and travel 1½ miles east until you reach the **University of California (16)** campus at Oxford Street. Turn right on Oxford and then left on Durant and continue up to Bowditch. Turn right on Bowditch to see Maybeck's famous **First Church of Christ Scientist (17)** (1910). Also see the **Sigma Phi Fraternity (18)** house by Greene & Greene (1908) at Durant and Piedmont. On campus see the **Campanile (19)** and the **Mining and Metallurgy Building** (1907) by John Galen Howard **(20)**. Continue back down Bancroft to Shattuck, turn left towards Oakland and follow the Adeline and Grove Street route until it joins Hwy. 24 at MacArthur. Marvel at the heroic scale of the **Freeway Interchange (21)** between 580 and 24 as you head towards downtown Oakland. Take the 12th Street exit and aim for Broadway. Notice the new **Hyatt Regency Hotel and Convention Center** (1982) by ELS **(22)**, the emblematic **Tribune Tower (23)**, and the **Clorox Building (24)** by Cesar Pelli. Continue along 12th Street to Oak and you will come across the half buried **Oakland Museum** (1964) by Kevin Roche/John Dinkeloo and Associates **(25)**. Return to San Francisco via Hwy. 17 across the **Bay Bridge (26)**. Take the Downtown 5th Street exit and go past the recently completed **Moscone Convention Center** (1981) by Hellmuth Obata Kassabaum (HOK) on Howard Street **(27)**, which contains the largest vaulted space in the West.

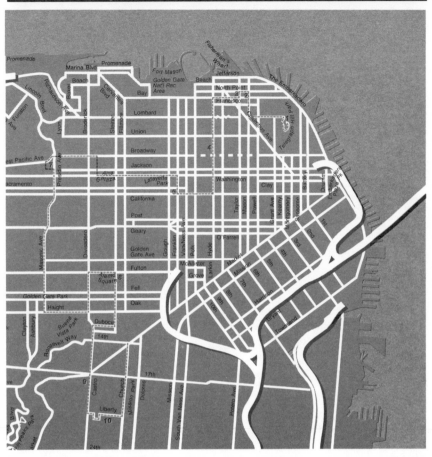

House Tour. A tour of some of San Francisco's domestic architecture.

Starting at the top of **Telegraph Hill (1)**, walk down **Filbert Steps (1)** on the east side of the hill. Here you will see some of the earliest houses in San Francisco perched precariously on the steep slopes. Access is only by footpath and steps through the lush foliage that has grown all around. Notice the Carpenter Gothic style of many of the houses. Return to the top and drive down Lombard Street towards Columbus, observing the typical bay windowed false-front houses. There is a particularly fine row on the west side of **Powell St. (2)** between Lombard and Francisco. Turn left on **Vandewater Street (2)**, a short alley between Powell and Mason Streets, half a block south of Bay. Note the condominiums by Dan Solomon, #55 (1981); Donald MacDonald, #33 (1981); and Esherick Homsey Dodge and Davis, #22 (1977). At the end of the alley is the **Northpoint** public housing scheme recently repainted in pastel colors **(3)**. Turn left on Mason, right on Francisco, and continue across Columbus up Russian Hill to Leavenworth Street. Turn left here and cross Union to **Green Street (4)** where you can see one of the best examples of the 1930s-style apartment towers. Russian Hill has many such buildings. The location of these buildings on the top of the hill tends to exaggerate their silhouettes when seen from afar, and also affords everyone on the slopes an unimpeded view. Turn right on California Street, following the cable car

tracks and cross Van Ness until you reach Franklin and you will find the superb **Haas-Lilienthal House (5)** at 2007, a romantic Queen Anne-style mansion. Tours available. This is part of **Pacific Heights (5)**, one of the most affluent parts of the city, with many substantial dwellings on its slopes. Turn left on Broadway and you will pass a whole series of apartment towers and mansions as you approach the Presidio. There are also many fine Victorian houses on the surrounding streets. Of particular interest is a row of false fronted Italianate houses on **Clay Street (6)** between Fillmore and Divisadero opposite Alta Plaza. Turn right on Divisadero to the summit of the hill and left at Pacific until you reach the famous **3200 Pacific (7)** block between Walnut and Presidio, with houses by Maybeck, Coxhead, Polk and others. Head south on Presidio across the Panhandle of Golden Gate Park to Fulton Street. Notice the ornate late Victorian houses in this, the **Haight-Ashbury** district. Continue on Fulton to **Alamo Square (8)**, where you can see the well-known group of identical houses on the east side. Turn right on Steiner and head south to Duboce Street where you turn left towards Market and turn right on Castro Street. Cross Market and continue on Castro Street for 6½ blocks. At Market and Castro is **Castro Commons (9)** by Dan Solomon and Associates (1982). At **Liberty Street (10)** you can see a good cross section of older San Franciscan dwellings of various styles. From here you can easily return to downtown via Church Street to Market Street.

INDEX

INDEX

INDEX

RESTAURANT INDEX